# INTRODUCTION
# TO
# CORPORATE LAW

By

## The Institute for Paralegal Training

Michael J. Kline, Volume Editor
Caroline S. Laden, Institute Series Editor

---

**PARALEGAL SERIES**
William P. Statsky, Editor
David Matz, Editor

ST. PAUL, MINN.
WEST PUBLISHING CO.
1978

Inst.Par.Train.–Corp.Law

**2nd Reprint—1987**

∞

**To Tammy and our beloved Jessica.**

*

# PREFACE

This book is an outgrowth of materials written and published for students in the corporate law section of the general practice course at The Institute for Paralegal Training in Philadelphia, Pennsylvania. It is designed to challenge and educate students who have had little or no prior exposure to corporations and corporate law.

Hundreds of problems and questions have been added to the materials which will hopefully challenge and motivate the student. Many of the questions have intentionally not been directly answered in the book in order to promote class discussion and independent thought by the student. In addition, many of the questions raised may not have one answer, and the instructor can properly provide guidance as to these gray areas. Some questions are repeated elsewhere in the text where it is believed appropriate to tie together different concepts.

The primary purpose of the book is to be a teaching tool rather than a reference book or treatise. However, the forms and checklists should prove useful to paralegals in their careers. As a teaching tool, the book has attempted to emphasize and isolate those areas in which paralegals can be particularly useful in assisting lawyers. My experience in teaching the corporate course at the Institute for several years and in the supervision of paralegals has led me to believe that certain areas of corporate practice are most conducive to the use of paralegals. It is these areas on which the book concentrates.

Although many tasks of paralegals may be relatively simple, the text was written on the theory that competence can only be based on understanding, not rote. The learning of concepts in a vacuum is relatively useless; the comprehension of the "why", even on an elementary level, is critical.

To go through the entire volume in depth may require more hours than would customarily be allotted to a basic college or junior college course. The book includes an adequate number of topics for instructors to select those which should be included in a basic course in the available time. For schools that may have more time available for the course, there is ample material to be covered.

I wish to thank Caroline S. Laden, Esquire, of the Institute for her encouragement and counselling, as well as the able assistance provided by the Institute.

MICHAEL J. KLINE, ESQ.
Member, Cohen, Shapiro,
Polisher, Shiekman and
Cohen

Philadelphia, Pennsylvania
November, 1977

# ACKNOWLEDGMENTS

This book is intended to be utilized as a course text for students studying Corporate Law. It is primarily designed for the education of legal assistants but it will be useful for anyone concerned with the structure of corporations and the manner in which corporations operate as fictitious persons. The book does not concern itself with the intricacies of securities regulation or acquisitions and mergers, topics which are usually covered in more advanced Corporate Law classes.

The author of the book is The Institute for Paralegal Training in Philadelphia, Pennsylvania, a unique educational institution established in 1970 to train para-professionals for careers as lawyer's assistants. More than 2500 people have successfully completed programs at the Institute. Of course, an institution cannot write a book—but so many people connected with it have contributed their efforts that the Institute itself gets the credit for making this book possible. This book is the outgrowth of the General Practice–Corporate Law course materials first written, assembled, edited and taught by Daniel Promislo, Esquire and Richard Braemer, Esquire of the Pennsylvania Bar and founders of The Institute for Paralegal Training. Over the years several authors and editors have revised the materials. This volume owes its life to the painstaking work of Michael J. Kline, Esquire of the Pennsylvania and New Jersey Bars who has taught in the Corporate Law and General Practice courses at the Institute for four years.

Special thanks are due to William P. Statsky, Professor of Law at Antioch School of Law and David E. Matz of Boston University whose comments and critiques helped to guide the project. Our thanks too, to Irwin A. Shein, Anne F. Finley and Ruth Scott of the Institute staff for their tireless work in preparing this manuscript.

CAROLINE S. LADEN, ESQUIRE
THE INSTITUTE FOR PARALEGAL TRAINING

Philadelphia, Pennsylvania
November, 1977

\*

# SUMMARY OF CONTENTS

## SUMMARY OF CONTENTS

### CHAPTER FIVE. CLOSE CORPORATIONS

### CHAPTER SIX. FICTITIOUS CORPORATE NAMES

### CHAPTER SEVEN. SHAREHOLDERS' AND DIRECTORS' MEETINGS

### CHAPTER EIGHT. CORPORATE EQUITY AND DEBT SECURITIES

### CHAPTER NINE. EMPLOYMENT AGREEMENTS

### CHAPTER TEN. SHAREHOLDERS' AGREEMENTS

# SUMMARY OF CONTENTS

## CHAPTER ELEVEN.  CORPORATE DISTRIBUTIONS

*

# TABLE OF CONTENTS

## TABLE OF CONTENTS

# TABLE OF CONTENTS

## CHAPTER THREE.  QUALIFICATION OF CORPORATIONS IN FOREIGN JURISDICTIONS

# TABLE OF CONTENTS

## CHAPTER FOUR. AMENDMENT OF ARTICLES OF INCORPORATION AND BY-LAWS

# TABLE OF CONTENTS

## CHAPTER FIVE. CLOSE CORPORATIONS

## CHAPTER SIX. FICTITIOUS CORPORATE NAMES

## CHAPTER SEVEN. SHAREHOLDERS' AND DIRECTORS' MEETINGS

# TABLE OF CONTENTS

# TABLE OF CONTENTS

## Forms Within Chapter Seven

## CHAPTER EIGHT.  CORPORATE EQUITY AND DEBT SECURITIES

# TABLE OF CONTENTS

## TABLE OF CONTENTS

### Forms Within Chapter Eight

## CHAPTER NINE. EMPLOYMENT AGREEMENTS

# TABLE OF CONTENTS

# TABLE OF CONTENTS

## Forms Within Chapter Nine

## CHAPTER TEN. SHAREHOLDERS' AGREEMENTS

# TABLE OF CONTENTS

# TABLE OF CONTENTS

## CHAPTER ELEVEN. CORPORATE DISTRIBUTIONS

# TABLE OF CONTENTS

## Forms Within Chapter Eleven

# INTRODUCTION
## TO
# CORPORATE LAW

---

Chapter One

## INTRODUCTION TO CORPORATIONS

**Introduction**

This book contains materials designed to teach students about various tasks undertaken by lawyers and their legal assistants in organizing and subsequently representing corporations. Before discussing specific activities of the lawyers and paralegals, this Chapter will provide students with a preliminary understanding of the nature of a corporation and how it is structured.

Chapter One is intended to provide the paralegal student with an initial exposure to "corporate law" which will prove useful throughout the balance of the course. Chapter One will require the student to begin working with the language and structure of state corporate laws, thereby providing a starting point for the development of skills necessary to deal with statutory materials.

## I. LEGAL FORMATS FOR CONDUCTING A BUSINESS

People usually think of a corporation as a business enterprise. Not all businesses, however, are carried on by corporations. It might be helpful to consider initially some other common forms of conducting a business.

A decision must be made by the person starting a business as to the nature of the entity which will operate the business. It may be operated by one individual, by a group of individuals or by a corporation. The choice is usually determined on the basis of several considerations: (a) the nature of the business; (b) the liabilities (obligations) to be incurred upon formation of the new business entity; (c) the complication involved in operating the entity in one form rather than another; (d) the income tax consequences of the entity; and (e) inheritance and estate tax implications. The decision as to the nature of the entity will be made by the lawyer and the client.

The first form of business available is a "sole proprietorship" conducted, as the name indicates, by one person. It is a form of busi-

1

ness in which there is one owner who receives all the income and has personal liability to pay all the debts of the business. Personal liability means that all assets of the individual, both those in the business and those that are personal, such as a savings account or a home, may be reached by business creditors for satisfaction of the obligations of the business. For example, a retail shoe store may be operated as a "sole proprietorship", in which the owning individual owns all of the assets and receives all of the income derived from the store, out of which the store's expenses must be paid. The owner is personally responsible for all of the debts of the business, not only to the extent of the assets dedicated to the business, such as bank accounts and inventory of shoes, but also all other assets of the individual, including furniture, home, and personal car. Since everything is owned by one person, that person also has full authority to make all decisions concerning the operation of the store. When the owner dies, so does the business entity.

Often a group of individuals about to start a business form a "partnership". A partnership is an arrangement between two or more persons to carry on a business together and to make contributions of cash, services and property to the business and to share profits and losses therefrom.

An interest in a partnership is the personal property of the partner. It is the partnership entity which holds title to the assets of the partnership, not the individual partners. The partners have no separate interest in any partnership assets. For example, real estate acquired with partnership funds becomes partnership property.

Although the law may differ from state to state, partnership actions may generally be taken on behalf of the partnership by any general partner. For example, a decision by one partner to buy a limousine for the partnership will bind the partner who arranged the purchase, the partnership and the other partners to pay for the automobile.

Partners have unlimited personal liability as individuals for the debts and obligations of the partnership just as a sole proprietor does. This means that if one or more partners of the partnership incurs debts or liabilities on behalf of the partnership which exceed the value of the property owned by the partnership, the assets of the individual partners will be subject to claims by creditors. A partner will be required to meet these claims out of personal assets without regard to the proportion of assets which the partner contributed to the partnership or whether the partner incurred any of the unpaid debts. Thus, each partner would be liable to the extent of all personal assets to pay for the limousine described in the preceding paragraph.

All partners have a legal right to take part in the management of the partnership. Partners can, however, give up this right or limit it in a partnership agreement signed by all the partners. For example, the right to vote on decisions of the partnership may be made to depend on the relative contribution of assets to the partnership by the partners.

When one of the partners dies or otherwise leaves the partnership, the partnership may dissolve and the assets, after provision for the payment of all business debts, will be distributed to the remaining partner or partners.

### PROBLEMS

1. If a partnership agreement between partners prohibits any one partner from buying an automobile for the partnership, can the agency selling the limousine to one partner for the partnership's benefit collect payment from all partners and the partnership if the agency did not know of the terms of the partnership agreement? *Yes, but indiv. partners could sue*

2. Assume that Smith is a sole proprietor of a shoe business. The business is worth $50,000 and in addition Smith owns a house worth $100,000. If Jones is injured in Smith's store, sues Smith and recovers a judgment against Smith, how much can Jones recover from Smith? From what sources? *$150,000 Store + home*

3. Assume that X and Y are partners in a shoe store. James slips in the store of X and Y. The partnership has assets of $100,000. X has a house worth $100,000 and Y has a house worth $110,000. If James gets a $200,000 judgment against the partnership, how much can James recover? From what sources? *$100,000 from each*

The business of the shoe store might also be conducted by a "corporation". A corporation is an entity separate and apart from its owners, thus different from a proprietorship or a partnership. A corporation is also a legal creation of the state where it is incorporated (i. e., formed). The principal differences between the corporate form of conducting the business, and the partnership or sole proprietorship forms are the following:

A. A sole proprietor and the partners in a partnership are personally liable for the debts incurred by the business they own to the full extent of both their business and personal assets. The debts of a corporation are paid out of the assets of the corporation and neither the shareholders, directors, nor officers of the corporation are personally liable for the debts of the business enterprise if the corporation is unable to satisfy all of them. This is referred to as "limited liability".

B. In the event of the death of the sole proprietor or one of the partners, the existence of the proprietorship or partnership terminates. In contrast, the death of a shareholder, director or officer of a corporation does not terminate the corporation as a separate entity. This is referred to as "perpetual existence".[1]

C. A sole proprietorship and, in most instances, a partnership are managed directly by the owners of the business. A corporation is managed by corporate officers and a board of directors who need not be shareholders. It may not be directly managed by the shareholders who are in fact the real owners of the corporation.[2]

D. Shareholders (sometimes called stockholders) in a corporation are issued stock certificates to evidence their ownership. In the absence of an agreement preventing transfer, the certificates are negotiable and freely transferable.[3]

E. Corporations are subject to state and federal tax treatment which is different from that imposed on sole proprietorships and partnerships.[4] A corporation is a separate entity for taxation purposes while partnerships and proprietorships are not. The corporate entity is not ignored for federal income tax purposes. The income, deductions and losses relating to the operation of the business are attributed to the corporate entity, and the corporation pays income tax at special corporate tax rates on its net income. If any net profits are distributed to the corporate shareholders as dividends, the individual shareholders pay income tax, at their respective tax rates, on the dividends they receive. Partnership and proprietorship income is taxed only directly to individual partners or proprietors.

A business is usually operated in corporate form to take advantage of one or all of these corporate characteristics. In order to achieve the purpose for incorporation, it is the obligation of the lawyer and paralegal to be certain to comply with all of the legal requirements and procedures in creating the corporation and in maintaining it.

## PROBLEMS

1. Assume that X corporation has assets of $100,000. Its two shareholders, A and B, each have assets of $50,000, consisting of personal residences. If Jones (our old friend) obtains a judgment against the corporation for $125,000, how much will Jones recover? From what sources?

2. Can a corporation with only one shareholder who is also the only officer and director, have a "perpetual existence"? Why or why not?

1. See Chapter Two for a discussion of the term of existence of a corporation.

2. See Section III of this Chapter.

3. See Chapter Two for a discussion and forms of stock certificates.

4. See Section V of this Chapter for a discussion of the tax treatment of corporations.

## II. BUSINESS CORPORATIONS

It is possible to look at a business from several vantage points. In business school, the study of corporations normally involves a study of the means by which the corporation buys raw materials and then manufactures and sells products. The focus of such studies is on the economic aspects of a business. From that point of view, it might well be irrelevant whether or not the business being considered was a corporation, as opposed to a partnership or a sole proprietorship. This is not, however, the focus of this book. You will find no mention of any specific products produced by a corporation nor how such products are produced. Rather, this book describes and defines the legal characteristics of a corporation and the legal interrelationships, requirements and agreements which are an everyday part of its affairs.

There are corporations other than business corporations. State laws provide for the creation of non-profit corporations such as charitable organizations, as well as municipal corporations, such as cities, townships, school districts and other subdivisions of states, which perform governmental functions. Moreover, corporations have been created under both state and federal law for special purposes, such as the Federal Deposit Insurance Corporation which guarantees bank deposits up to certain maximum amounts. Such corporations are not the subject of this book. This book focuses entirely upon "for profit" or "business" corporations.

### A. AUTHORITY TO ORGANIZE AND OPERATE CONTAINED IN STATE LAW

Perhaps the most important thing to know about a business corporation is that it is a distinct legal person or entity formed by the authority of state law and according to the procedures set forth in such laws. This means that a corporation created under the laws of Delaware will have different characteristics from a corporation created under the laws of New York or California.

### B. ORGANIZING THE CORPORATION

Sections 53 to 56 of the Model Business Corporation Act ("MBCA")[5] set forth the procedure for creating a corporation.

---

5. The Model Business Corporation Act is an attempt by the Committee on Corporate Laws of the Section of Corporation, Banking and Business Law of the American Bar Association to establish an "ideal" state corporation law. Most states which have in recent years significantly revised their corporations laws have used the MBCA as a guide. Reference is made to the MBCA throughout the materials as a useful guide to a "typical" modern corporation law. However, the MBCA is only a model. It contains many features that older corporate statutes do not and many features that new statutes have modified or rejected. Accordingly, the reader must not assume the MBCA to be the law for any specific state. The entire text of the MBCA is reproduced in this book as Appendix I.

Without the existence of a general authorizing corporate statute in each state, corporations could not be created except by a cumbersome procedure of a special legislative act granting authority to each proposed corporation.

State law also grants the corporations the capacity to conduct a trade or business.

## 1. Articles of Incorporation

A corporation is formed by filing "articles of incorporation" (in some states called a "certificate of incorporation" or "charter") with the designated state agency. While state law permits the formation of corporations, describes the mechanics of creating a corporation and establishes rules and regulations applicable to all corporations formed pursuant to its terms, each corporation is also governed by its own unique articles of incorporation. The articles normally contain at least the following minimum characteristics:

    a.  Name of the corporation.

    b.  Location of an office of the corporation.

    c.  Purpose of the corporation.

    d.  The number of shares and the special characteristics, if any, of the various classes of stock which the corporation is authorized to issue.[6]

Many other provisions may, at the option of the persons filing the articles be included.[7]

## 2. Bylaws

Every corporation has bylaws in addition to the articles of incorporation. The bylaws of a corporation normally contain provisions for the regulation and management of the affairs of the corporation which must not be inconsistent with either state law or the articles of incorporation. Bylaws go into much more depth as to the operation of the corporation than the articles. The bylaws, in effect, provide some of the particular rules by which the activities of the officers, directors and shareholders of the corporation are governed.[8]

## 3. Reasons for Articles of Incorporation and Bylaws in Addition to State Law

The fact that a corporation is governed by different sets of rules may first appear both confusing and cumbersome. At the very least, however, it is necessary that each corporation establish its own separate set of rules and regulations for its own operation within the broad guidelines of state law. State law, of course, must be broad enough to

---

**6.** Section III of Chapter Two contains a full discussion of articles of incorporation.

**7.** See Section III of Chapter Two.

**8.** Section VI of Chapter Two discusses the adoption and contents of bylaws. Note that some states spell the word as "by-laws".

accommodate a wide variety of corporate enterprises. Individual corporations are permitted under law to decide in certain aspects which rules and regulations are most appropriate for their own operation.

This does not answer the question of why there must be both articles of incorporation and bylaws, especially since it would be possible under most state laws to include within the articles of incorporation everything that is normally included in the bylaws. One reason is flexibility. The articles of incorporation of a corporation are, in effect, its constitution and a public document on file with an agency of the state. Anyone can inspect or obtain copies of the articles from the state agency. As you will see later, changes may be made in the articles of incorporation by specific filings with the state.[9] This involves expense and time for preparation and filing. In addition, and of most importance, changes in the articles of incorporation require approval by the shareholders of a corporation. This is sometimes, particularly in the case of a corporation with a large number of shareholders, a time-consuming and expensive process.[10] Bylaws, on the other hand, are not required to be filed with a state agency and may, if the bylaws (or articles of incorporation) permit, be changed by action of the board of directors alone. This makes the amendment of bylaws a more private and faster and less expensive process than amending the articles.

It is worth repeating that bylaws may never permit any conduct or action by a corporation which is inconsistent with the articles of incorporation or state law. Nor may the bylaws permit any action reserved by state law for inclusion in the articles of incorporation alone. In the same way, the articles of incorporation may never permit any action or conduct which is inconsistent with state law.

## PROBLEMS

1. If the state law requires a corporation to have at least three directors, can the bylaws provide for two directors of the corporation? If the bylaws cannot so provide, can the articles of incorporation do so? Can the bylaws provide for four directors? How about a provision allowing for between two to five directors as may be determined from time to time by the directors?

2. If the state law says that the bylaws may be amended by the directors only if the articles of incorporation so provide, would a provision only in the bylaws allowing the directors to amend the bylaws be effective? What if the articles of incorporation state that the bylaws could be amended by the directors but the bylaws contain no such provision?

3. If the articles of incorporation of a corporation call for one director, the bylaws call for two directors and the state law requires at least three directors, how many directors must the corporation have?

---

9. See Chapter Four.                    10. See Chapter Four.

4. A state law has no requirements as to the minimum number of directors of a corporation. If the articles of incorporation call for nine directors and the bylaws call for five directors how many directors must the corporation have? Is it generally a good idea to have provisions in the articles and bylaws which are inconsistent?

State law sanctions the use of both articles of incorporation and bylaws and to some extent governs what is included in each.[11] There are circumstances where state law (a) permits certain regulations to be in either the articles of incorporation or the bylaws, (b) requires the regulation to be in the articles of incorporation or (c) suggests that the regulation be in the bylaws.

## PROBLEM

Look at Sections 35, 36, 37, 40, 42 and 43 of the MBCA, and decide whether each falls into (a), (b) or (c) of the previous paragraph. Why?

## III. OWNERSHIP AND MANAGEMENT OF A CORPORATION

The three central classes of characters in corporate law are the shareholders, directors and officers. State law defines them and the relationship among them. What follows is a summary description of some of the more important characteristics, responsibilities and rights which state law establishes for these different classes of persons. It is important to note that state law does not prohibit the same person from being a shareholder, a director and an officer of the same corporation. As a matter of fact, in most corporations one or more individuals function in more than one role.

### A. SHAREHOLDERS

A shareholder is defined in rather simple and basic terms:

"Shareholder means one who is a holder of record of shares in a corporation."

Section 2(f), MBCA

The term "shares" is defined as "the units into which the proprietary interests in a corporation are divided.[12] Simply stated a "share" is an interest in the corporation.

### QUESTIONS

Is a share an interest in any specific asset of the corporation or the totality of assets? If a corporation has a total of 100 shares, what interest does a holder of 60 shares have?

The shareholders are the owners of a corporation. The nature of this "ownership" can only be appreciated, however, when some of the

11. See, for example, Section 54 of the MBCA.

12. Section 2(d) of the MBCA.

rights granted to a shareholder under state law are examined. Some of the more important rights granted under the MBCA and most corporate statutes are as follows:

### 1. Election of Directors

State law always provides that the business affairs of a business corporation shall be managed by a board of directors.[13] Directors are only elected by action of the shareholders other than in the case of filling vacancies.[14]

### 2. Amending the Articles of Incorporation

No changes may be made in the articles of incorporation of a corporation without the vote of the shareholders of a corporation.[15] This in effect means that the principal format established by a corporation, as embodied in the articles of incorporation, may not be changed without shareholder approval.

### 3. Dissolution

A corporation may not decide to voluntarily dissolve and wind up its affairs without shareholder approval.[16]

### 4. Sale of Substantially All of Assets

A corporation may not voluntarily decide to sell or exchange all or substantially all of its property and assets without shareholder approval.[17]

### 5. Removal of Directors

Shareholders may, with or without cause, remove directors of a corporation.[18]

### 6. Merger or Consolidation

Except for a merger with a subsidiary (see Section 75, MBCA), corporations may not merge or consolidate without shareholder approval.[19] A merger is not the same as a consolidation. A merger is a formal combination of two or more corporations where one corporation is absorbed by another, the latter of which is called the surviving corporation. In a consolidation, two or more corporations combine to create an entirely new corporation which is different from any of the absorbed corporations.

---

13. See, e.g., Section 35 of the MBCA.

14. See, e.g., Section 36 of the MBCA and the discussion of shareholders' meetings in Chapter Seven.

15. See Section 59 of the MBCA and Chapter Four.

16. See Sections 83 and 84 of the MBCA and Chapter Eleven.

17. See Section 79 of the MBCA.

18. See Section 39 of the MBCA.

19. See Section 73 of the MBCA.

## PROBLEMS

1. If X Corporation combines with Y Corporation and the result is Y Corporation, is the combination a merger or a consolidation?

2. If X Corporation combines with Y Corporation and the result is Z Corporation, what is the combination called? If X, Y and A result in Z corporation?

### 7. Limited Liability

Except for the obligation to pay the full consideration for the shares issued by a corporation, shareholders are not liable for the debts of the corporation. This restricted liability is called "limited liability".

## QUESTIONS

Does the liability of a shareholder differ from that of a sole proprietor or partner?[20] Does the corporation itself have limited liability?

### 8. Receipt of Dividends

The distributions out of income with respect to shares of stock are called "dividends". Since dividends are paid on the "shares" of a corporation, shareholders are entitled to all dividends.[21]

The foregoing is not an exhaustive list of all the corporate attributes and the rights and privileges of shareholders. It is only intended to suggest that the characteristics of a shareholder must be defined by reference to state corporation law. The MBCA is a convenient model which has been adopted to a large degree in many states. However, it is not the form which has been adopted in its entirety in any state. The paralegal must review the relevant state law in each case to ascertain its requirements.

## B. DIRECTORS

State law provides that a corporation is managed by the board of directors. The following MBCA model is an example:[22]

"The business and affairs of a corporation shall be managed by a board of directors, except as may be otherwise provided by the articles of incorporation."

Section 35, MBCA.

---

20. See Section I of this Chapter.

21. See Section 45 of the MBCA and Chapter Eleven.

22. Chapter Seven discusses generally the actions of directors.

Furthermore, state law tells us certain characteristics of a person who may be a director of a corporation:

> "Directors need not be residents of this state or shareholders of the corporation unless the articles of incorporation or bylaws so require."
>
> Section 35, MBCA.

The following is an outline of certain of the powers of the board of directors:

## 1. Election of Officers

The board of directors of a corporation elects its officers who are responsible for the day-to-day business operations.

> "The officers of a corporation shall consist of a president, one or more vice presidents as may be prescribed by the bylaws, a secretary and a treasurer, each of whom shall be elected by the board of directors at such time and in such manner as may be prescribed by the bylaws."
>
> Section 50, MBCA.

## 2. Issuance of Stock

The board of directors of a corporation has the power, subject to the restrictions provided by the articles of incorporation or the bylaws, to issue shares of stock and to determine the consideration (value) which must be paid for such shares of stock. It is interesting to note that this right is sometimes not spelled out directly in state law, but may be implied, as the following sample provision from the MBCA demonstrates:

> "Each corporation shall have power to create and issue the number of shares stated in its articles of incorporation."
>
> Section 15, MBCA.

## 3. Dividends

The board of directors of a corporation may, from time to time, and within the restrictions imposed by the articles of incorporation and state law, make distributions to shareholders (i. e., pay dividends) in cash or property on the outstanding shares of a corporation.[23]

## 4. Initiation of Certain Actions

While shareholder approval may be required in certain instances, the board of directors may initiate action under the MBCA in certain instances: (a) certain sales of a corporation's assets (see, e. g., Sec-

---

23. See Section 45 of the MBCA.

**QUESTION: Why would the directors have the power to pay dividends rather than the shareholders?**

tion 79, MBCA), (b) approval of the merger of a corporation (see, e. g., Section 71, MBCA) or (c) the voluntary dissolution of a corporation (see, e. g., Section 84, MBCA).

## C.  OFFICERS

State law recognizes the corporation's need to have officers who can manage its affairs on a daily basis.  Normally, state law makes reference to at least a president, secretary and treasurer.  Section 50 of the MBCA provides a model form of statement of the role of the officers of a corporation:

> "All officers and agents of the corporation, as between themselves and the corporation, shall have such authority and perform such duties in the management of the corporation as may be provided in the by-laws, or as may be determined by resolution of the board of directors not inconsistent with the by-laws."

While the state law specifies certain offices and outlines the role of officers in general, the bylaws and the board of directors define the actual day-to-day functions of the officers.  The board of directors sets forth the general direction of the corporation; the officers execute the individual tasks, such as hire employees, purchase inventory, sign checks, set prices of individual products, etc.  In a few areas, state law may designate a specific activity to be undertaken by a particular officer of a corporation.[24]

## IV.  FORMAL CORPORATE DECISIONS

### A.  METHOD USED BY SHAREHOLDERS AND DIRECTORS

In order for either shareholders or directors to take action, it is normally necessary for them to hold meetings to authorize the action. Both state law and the bylaws of a corporation set forth a corporation's specific requirements in connection with the meetings of directors and shareholders.[25]

The specific form of the decision taken by directors or shareholders is referred to as a "resolution".  A resolution is no more than a written statement of the specific authorization or approval which is agreed to by the shareholders or directors of a corporation.  Normally, these resolutions are contained within the record called "minutes" of proceedings at a directors' or shareholders' meeting or within the written consent if the action was taken by consent.[26]

---

24.  See, for example, Sections 23, 61 and 74 of the MBCA.

**QUESTION:  What tasks do these Sections impose on specific officers?**

25.  Chapter Seven discusses in detail meetings of shareholders and directors and alternatives thereto.

26.  See Section 44 of the MBCA for an example of a statute authorizing written consents.

## B. MANAGEMENT BY SHAREHOLDERS

In some states [27] it is possible to have the shareholders directly run the corporation. It is called a statutory "close corporation". A "close corporation" is permitted to have, in its articles of incorporation, a provision that its business and affairs will be managed by the shareholders rather than by the board of directors. If such a provision exists, the shareholders need not elect any directors, and the shareholders are deemed to be the directors of the corporation for all purposes. This right, in effect, removes one tier of the corporate hierarchy and permits the shareholders to act both as shareholders and directors. A "close corporation", however, must meet certain requirements.[28]

## V. TAXATION

### A. INCOME TAX

The federal government, nearly all state governments, and some municipal governments impose a separate tax on the income corporations earn. This is contrasted to the situation of sole proprietorships and partnerships where there is no separate entity and only the owners are taxed on income. The current federal tax rate is approximately 48%, and payment of the tax is an obligation of the corporation and not its shareholders, directors and officers. If a corporation pays a dividend to its shareholders, the dividend is paid out of the profits of the corporation after the payment of taxes (i. e., "after-tax profits") and such a dividend is taxable to the individual shareholder as income. This means that corporate earnings which are passed on to shareholders in the form of a dividend are subject to a second federal tax.[29] The fact that the corporate income was taxed and the distribution of income to shareholders remaining after such taxes was also taxed is commonly referred to as "double taxation".

### QUESTIONS

Does a partnership have "double taxation"? A sole proprietorship?

### B. "SUBCHAPTER S" CORPORATIONS

To avoid the double federal income tax described above, Subchapter S of the United States Internal Revenue Code ("IRC") allows corporations which meet certain requirements to be taxed as

27. For example, Section 382 of the Pennsylvania Business Corporation Law.

28. See Chapter Five for a description of close corporations.

29. The subject of corporate distributions is discussed in greater detail in Chapter Eleven.

"small business corporations". Corporations that take advantage of the benefits of this provision of the IRC are usually referred to as "Subchapter S corporations". In order to become a Subchapter S corporation for tax purposes, all of the following requirements must be met:

1. The corporation must have authorized and issued only one class of stock.[30]

2. The corporation must have no more than 10 stockholders, and each of these stockholders must be a natural person, not a corporation, trust, estate, etc.[31]

3. All stockholders must join in the election to be taxed under Subchapter S.

4. The Corporation must elect to be taxed as a Subchapter S corporation and notify the Internal Revenue Service within a specified period of time. (Note that the size of the corporation with respect to revenues, assets or earnings is wholly immaterial in determining whether it qualifies for taxation as a Subchapter S corporation.)

The major tax benefit of a Subchapter S corporation is that there is no federal income tax at the corporate level.

Corporate income is, therefore, except in certain limited situations, attributed directly to the stockholders in proportion to their "ownership" of the corporation and taxed as income to them only. Any losses which the corporation incurs in its operations are also attributed directly to the stockholders, who may use these losses to offset income from other sources. In effect, a Subchapter S corporation is treated with some variations, for tax purposes, in a manner substantially equivalent to a partnership.

An example of this situation is as follows. Assume that A and B are the shareholders in X Corporation. A owns 60 shares and B owns 40 shares. If X Corporation earns $100,000 and is not a "Subchapter S corporation", it will pay federal income taxes of about $48,000. If X Corporation declares a dividend of the remainder after taxes to A and B, A will receive cash of $31,200 and B will receive cash of $20,800. A and B will then each pay personal income taxes on these distributions. If A and B are each in the 50% tax bracket, A will be left with $15,600 and B with $10,400.

The situation is quite different if X Corporation has validly elected Subchapter S status. In such a case there will be no tax at the corporate level. Instead $60,000 of income will be attributed directly to A and $40,000 directly to B. Why? Even if A and B are in a 60% tax bracket (because of the higher income level) A will be left

---

30. See Chapter Eight for a discussion of different classes of shares of stock.

31. The Tax Reform Act of 1976 has modified this provision slightly in certain circumstances.

with $24,000 and B with $16,000. Thus a substantial tax saving is effected by means of the Subchapter S corporation.

## C. STATE INCOME TAXATION

States are generally permitted to tax corporations which do business within their borders. Where a corporation does business in several states, the state tax may be determined by an "allocation formula". Most allocation formulas in effect today weigh several factors such as sales, assets and employee payroll in determining what percentage of a corporation's net income is attributed to the particular state. The diversity of allocation formulas used, however, and the inclination of state governments to devise formulas most beneficial to themselves, results in payment by many multi-state corporations of state income taxes in excess of those taxes they would be required to pay if every state had an identical formula. The current squeeze of inflation has encouraged states to attempt to realize the highest tax revenue possible.

## D. "FRANCHISE" AND "CAPITAL STOCK" TAXES

In addition to income taxes, most states levy a special tax on domestic corporations, i. e., corporations incorporated under the laws of the state. These taxes, most commonly known as capital stock or franchise taxes, are frequently based on the number of shares which a corporation is authorized to issue, the authorized capital of these shares, or some similar factors, and may be a one-time tax payable upon incorporation or an annual franchise tax or both. Foreign corporations (corporations organized under another state law) which qualify to do business within the state are usually subjected to a similar charge, often termed a "license fee".

## VI. SECURITIES LAWS

The federal government and the states have elaborate legislation regulating the offering and sale of stock by corporations, as well as other securities, evidencing a share in a corporation or a debt owed by a corporation.[32] Although such legislative schemes cover virtually all types of transactions in securities, they have the greatest impact on corporations whose securities are "publicly-held", that is, owned by a large number of persons, such as Xerox, General Motors, IBM and many smaller corporations as well. Corporations become publicly-held by having a "public offering", a sale of securities to the general public in accordance with applicable federal and state laws.[33]

---

32. See Chapter Eight for a detailed discussion of some of the more common types of securities.

33. State securities laws are often called "blue sky laws". Each state statute differs from another, and the statute of the particular state must be consulted. A service such as the Commerce Clearing House's *Blue Sky Law Reporter* will be helpful in this regard.

The complex area of securities laws is beyond the scope of this book.[34] However, paralegals should be generally aware of their existence and their purpose of providing prospective investors with full information about a corporation which is offering securities to the public to raise capital and regulating a fair market for trading publicly-held securities.

The opposite of a "publicly-held" corporation is a "closely-held" corporation, which, as its name indicates, has only a few shareholders. This course will concentrate on closely-held corporations, although mention will be made of publicly-held corporations where appropriate.

**34.** Readers who are interested in a preliminary introduction to Federal securities laws and their objectives may find helpful an article by Carl W. Schneider, Esq., and Joseph M. Manko, Esq. entitled "Going Public—Practice, Procedure and Consequences", originally published in Villanova Law Review, Volume 15, No. 2, pp. 283–312 (Winter, 1970) and revised in September, 1971 and October, 1972. An older article providing an introduction to the Federal securities laws is "Guideposts for a First Public Offering" by Francis M. Wheat, Esq., and George A. Blackstone, Esq., originally published in the April, 1960 issue of *The Business Lawyer*. A book which provides a more detailed introduction to the process of going public is *When Corporations Go Public*, edited by Carlos L. Israels, Esq. and George M. Duff, Jr., Esq., published in 1962 by the Practicing Law Institute.

Chapter Two

# FORMATION OF CORPORATIONS

## I. INTRODUCTION

The impetus to form a corporation is found in the desire of one or more persons to conduct some business activity and the decision, generally after consultation with counsel, that the business activity can most advantageously be conducted in the corporate form. Chapter One outlines the basic differences between corporations and other forms of business entities. This Chapter will consider the initial procedures to be followed in forming the corporation ("incorporation"), including the various documents which must be prepared and filed with the state in which the entity is formed, some of the substantive factors which must be considered in the incorporation process, and other matters relating to the basic structure and operation of a corporation which must be considered at the very beginning of the corporation's existence. After the procedures relating to the incorporation and structure of corporations have been analyzed, there will be a discussion of the methods whereby the structure that has been created can be modified.

## II. PRE-INCORPORATION ACTIVITY

### A. PREPARATION OF WORKSHEET

Once a person has, in conjunction with the lawyer, determined that a corporation should be formed, it is essential that a worksheet be completed listing all of the information which must be known in order to follow through with the incorporation. The following example is of an information worksheet. Many of the items referred to in the worksheet will be more completely understood after the study of this Chapter.

**EXAMPLE—Information Needed for the Formation and Organization of a Corporation**

1. Is this to be a regular business corporation or a close corporation?

2. Corporate name:
   Please check and/or complete one of the following:

   (Name is available)

   (Check availability of name)

   (Check availability and reserve name in following states)

3. State of incorporation:

4. Registered office:

5. Registered agent (if required by state of incorporation): *Usually atty at first*

6. Mailing address for state tax purposes:

7. Term of existence: *forever*

8. Brief statement of the kind or kinds of business actually to be engaged in:

   *must be legal*

9. Purpose clause if other than general purpose clause:

10. Authorized capital (number of shares, class and par value) (Please also include designations and preferences if other than common stock or state whether Board of Directors is to have the power to fix, by resolution, designations and preferences):

11. Names and addresses of first directors:

12. Are directors to be named in articles or certificate of incorporation?

13. Names and addresses of officers:

14. Please circle provisions desired:

    (a) Pre-emptive rights for shareholders. If so, describe.

    (b) Cumulative voting for Directors.

    (c) Classification of Directors. If so, describe.

    (d) Shareholder action by less than unanimous consent in writing.

    (e) Restrictions on transfer of securities. If so, describe.

15. Number of shareholders and state of residence (for purposes of applicable state securities exemption):

16. Names of shareholders; number of shares and type and class of stock:

17. Do you want subscription agreements?　If so, for whom?

18. Type of minute and stock book:
    Please check one of the following:
    　　　　(Inexpensive)　　　　(Expensive)

19. State(s) in which to qualify corporation to do business:

20. Date of organization meeting:

21. Bank account and signatures:

22. How many signatories must sign each check?

23. Total consideration to be paid for stock to be issued:
    (If total is less than $500,000 disregard)

24. Fiscal year:

25. Annual meeting date: _____ of _____
    　　　　　　　　　　　　(day)　　　　　(month)
    　　　　　at _____ a. m./p. m.

(A nominal incorporator will be used unless advised to the contrary)

　　　　　　　　　　　　　　Lawyer: _____
　　　　　　　　　　　　　　Dated: 　_____

## B. NAME

### 1. Choice

Before a corporation can be formed, a name must be chosen. State law imposes certain restrictions on the names of corporations. The corporate name must generally contain the word "corporation", "company", or "incorporated", or an abbreviation thereof, e. g., General Motors Corporation, American Telephone and Telegraph Company and Aluminum Company of America. In addition, corporate names which imply a governmental activity or connection or the conduct of business which is specially regulated by statute (e. g., banks, insurance companies, public utilities, etc.) are prohibited unless special permission is obtained from the state regulatory agency directly responsible for the regulation of the particular business. Within these limitations, any name selected for the corporation is permissible; provided, however, that the name chosen may not be deceptively similar to the name of a company already incorporated or doing business within the state of incorporation. The prohibition against deceptively similar names is for the benefit of the government in avoiding confusion, not to protect the corporation's interest in its own name.

Throughout the course, reference will be made to corporate statutes to set forth examples of requirements for corporate compliance. In addition, references will be made to the Model Business Corporation Act (which will be called "MBCA"). The MBCA is not a real statute which has been adopted by any state but is a model for legislation and contains many common provisions which are common in corporate statutes. The student should always check the actual provision of the relevant state business corporation code in actual practice. The MBCA was written by the American Bar Association Committee on Corporate Laws in 1950. It was originally based on the corporate statute of Illinois but has been revised since that time. Many states have borrowed its concepts and provisions in modifying, revising or updating their corporate statutes. It is because of its wide applicability that this text will utilize MBCA provisions often. The complete text of the MBCA is set forth in Appendix I.

Section 8 of the MBCA provides, with respect to a corporation's name, as follows:

The corporate name:

"(a) Shall contain the word 'corporation', 'company', 'incorporated' or 'limited', or shall contain an abbreviation of one of such words.

"(b) Shall not contain any word or phrase which indicates or implies that it is organized for any purpose other than one or more of the purposes contained in its articles of incorporation.

"(c) Shall not be the same as, or deceptively similar to, the name of any domestic corporation existing under the laws of this State or any foreign corporation authorized to transact business in this State, or a name the exclusive right to which is, at the time, reserved in the manner provided in this Act   .   .   . "

What problems does this create?  Note that "limited" (implying limited liability) may be used in the name under the MBCA.  A "foreign" corporation is a corporation organized under the laws of a state other than the state in question.

## PROBLEMS

1.  Is XYZ Corporation deceptively similar to XYZ Company?  To XYZ Associates, Inc.?  To X and Y, Corp.?

2.  Can a corporation be formed with the following names?
   (a)  World Bank, Ltd.
   (b)  Universal Travel, Ltd.
   (c)  Limited Resources
   (d)  The World's Best Corporation
   (e)  United States Travel, Inc.

Note that abbreviations may be used in a name.  Always be certain that the name is precisely stated as the client desires it, e.g., whether "Corporation" or "Corp." or "Inc." is used in a name is a decision to be made by the client.

## 2.  Availability

In order to determine if the name chosen for the corporation is available, it is normal practice to contact the Secretary of the Department of State of the proposed state of incorporation, either by telephone or letter, and ascertain the availability of the name.  Many states require a written request.  Check with your own state.  A nominal charge is sometimes imposed for this service.

## C. NAME: RESERVATION

In those cases where a corporation will not be formed for some period of time, it may be desirable to "reserve" the proposed name in order to insure its availability. Many states permit the reservation of a name for a limited period (e. g., three or six months) upon the payment of a small charge.

A form for the reservation of corporate names which can be used in states which have a "reservation" procedure comparable to that set forth in the MBCA is included below.

**EXAMPLE—Application for Reservation of Corporate Name**

[*Date*]

FOR THE SECRETARY OF STATE
    OF THE STATE OF _____:

    Pursuant to the provisions of subparagraph (_____) of Section _____ of the _____ Business Corporation Act, the undersigned hereby applies for reservation of the following corporate name for a period of _____ days:

[*Corporate name*]

I am enclosing a fee in the amount of $_____ to reserve the name.

_____
Applicant
[*Capacity—e. g. incorporator*]

Typically, the reservation of a corporate name will be evidenced by a document or letter from the Department of State or the Secretary of State. Such a document or letter must normally accompany the articles of incorporation (which is the incorporating document) when they are filed so that the incorporator may establish that the name for the new corporation has been reserved by him.

Delaware is a state where many of the largest corporations have been formed because of its liberal tax statutes and corporate law. DuPont and General Motors are only two of these many corporations. Many new corporations are also formed there. No fee is required for reserving a name in Delaware, but reservation of a name should be in writing. When filing the articles of incorporation later, it is a good idea to include a copy of the confirming letter sent by the state previously.

## D. PRE–INCORPORATION SUBSCRIPTION

In some states it is required that the person or persons who will be the incorporator or incorporators (those who are forming the corporation) to sign pre-incorporation subscriptions for one share each before the filing of articles of incorporation. A subscription is an agreement to purchase some initial stock in a corporation. A sample of such a pre-incorporation subscription is set forth below.

**EXAMPLE—Simple Pre-Incorporation Subscription**

### XYZ CORPORATION
### PRE-INCORPORATION SUBSCRIPTION

The undersigned, intending to be legally bound hereby, subscribes for one share of the one dollar ($1.00) par value common stock of XYZ CORPORATION, a corporation to be incorporated under Pennsylvania law, at a cash price of $1.00.

Dated: _____

_____ [*Seal*]

The incorporator will most likely not be a shareholder of the proposed corporation. The reason for such a subscription is often to satisfy a state law requirement that the incorporator also be a "subscriber", or to have a subscriber in existence after the corporation is formed. A subscriber is defined in the MBCA at Section 2(e) as "one who subscribes for shares in a corporation, whether before or after incorporation." Once a corporation is formed, certain states specify that persons who subscribed for shares prior to incorporation are shareholders of the corporation.[1]

As will be seen below, persons who sign a nominal pre-incorporation subscription will assign it (simply meaning to transfer it) to a person who will in fact be a shareholder of the corporation after incorporation has become effective.

In certain cases, the incorporators desiring to form the corporation have decided what percentage of the corporation's stock ownership each will have, and the percentage will be reflected in the number of shares each incorporator will purchase. In this event, and in order to bind the incorporators to purchase stock, they will sign, prior to incorporation, a subscription agreement in which they agree to purchase a specified number of the corporation's shares of stock at a stated price. A sample form of such a pre-incorporation subscription agreement is set forth below.

**EXAMPLE—Pre-Incorporation Subscription**

I, _____, hereby subscribe for five hundred (500) shares of the common stock of XYZ Corporation, a corporation to be organized under the laws of the State of Delaware, with an authorized capital stock of Two Thousand ($2,000) Dollars, divided into two thousand shares of com-

---

1. See e. g., Pennsylvania Business Corporation Law at Section 207.

mon stock, par value $1.00 per share. I do hereby agree to pay for said stock the sum of Ten ($10) Dollars per share, or an aggregate sum of Five Thousand ($5,000) Dollars, in full, or in such installments and at such times as the Board of Directors may determine, on demand of the Board of Directors of the Corporation.

Dated: January 2, 19__.

/s/ John Doe
_____

Since the corporation will generally be formed in reliance upon this undertaking to purchase shares, most corporation statutes provide that, absent a specific provision in the subscription agreement to the contrary, the subscription is irrevocable for a limited period of time.[2]

Once the corporation is formed, and if the pre-incorporation subscriptions are still binding on the subscribers, the corporation will have the power to accept the subscriptions and demand that the agreed upon purchase price be paid.

## QUESTION

**What problems could arise if the formation of the corporation is later than the period of irrevocability?**

## E. CONSENT FROM INITIAL DIRECTORS

If initial directors are named in the articles of incorporation state law may imply that a written consent be obtained from the persons so named.[3] The form of such a consent is included below.

**EXAMPLE—Consent of Director**

I hereby consent to serve as a director of XYZ Corporation, a proposed Pennsylvania Corporation, and also consent to the use of my name in that capacity in the Articles of Incorporation which will be filed by an incorporator with the Commonwealth of Pennsylvania.

_____
[*Signature*]

Date: _____

Some state laws require directors to be named in the articles of incorporation.

## QUESTION

**Where would directors be named if not in the articles of incorporation?**

2. See, for example, Section 17 of the MBCA which provides for irrevocability for 6 months.

3. Section 204B of the Pennsylvania Business Corporation Law ("PBCL") suggests such consent may be required.

### III.  INCORPORATION

Many persons take part in the actual formation of a corporation, e. g., all the organizers, counsel to the proposed corporation, a paralegal, the office of the Secretary of State, etc.  An existing corporation may create a corporation.  This would ordinarily be called a "subsidiary", a corporation run and owned by another corporation which is called the "parent".  From a strictly legal standpoint the person (or entity) who forms the corporation is the "incorporator(s)" who sign the articles of incorporation [4] which are filed with the state.

### PROBLEM

**How many incorporators are required by your state's corporation law?**

See Section 53 of the MBCA for a model approach.

Usually one or more of the organizers of the corporation or the person preparing the articles of incorporation act as the incorporator(s).  As noted above, under the law of many states, the incorporator is required to be a subscriber for at least one share of the corporation's stock, and the information with respect to the subscription for this share is required to be set forth in the articles.  Generally, the only other qualification for serving as incorporator is that the incorporator, if a natural person, be of full age.

### QUESTION

**What is "full age" for this purpose?**

With respect to the qualifications of the incorporator, Section 101 of the Delaware General Corporation Law is typical:

> "Any person, partnership, association or corporation, singly or jointly with others, and without regard to his or their residence, domicile or state of incorporation, may incorporate or organize a corporation under this chapter by filing with the Secretary of State a certificate of incorporation which shall be executed,[5] acknowledged,[6] filed and recorded in accordance with Section 103 of this title."

## A.  HOW DOES THE CORPORATION BECOME INCORPORATED?

### 1.  Filing of Articles of Incorporation

A corporation is a creature of the state and only exists by virtue of state law.  Under most modern corporation statutes, a corporation

---

4.  The articles of incorporation may be called the certificate of incorporation or charter in some states.

5.  "Execution" is the act of formally signing a document.

6.  "Acknowledgment" is signing a paper under oath before a public official such as a notary public.

is formed and its independent existence begins either upon the filing of articles of incorporation, usually in duplicate, with the state agency designated in the statute, or upon the issuance of a certificate of incorporation by such state agency after receipt of the articles. Note that some states have both articles and a certificate of incorporation which are two separate documents. The articles are filed by the incorporator, and the state issues a certificate evidencing corporate existence.

For example, Section 106 of the Delaware General Corporation Law provides as follows:

"Upon the filing with the Secretary of State of the certificate of incorporation, executed and acknowledged in accordance with section 103, the incorporator or incorporators who signed the certificate, and his or their successors and assigns,[7] shall, from the date of such filing, be and constitute a body corporate, by the name set forth in the certificate, subject to the provisions of section 103(d) of this title and subject to dissolution or other termination of its existence as provided in this chapter."

Note that Delaware only has one document—the certificate of incorporation.

Section 56 of the MBCA typifies the statutes which provide for the commencement of corporate existence upon the issuance of a certificate of incorporation:

"Upon the issuance of the certificate of incorporation, the corporate existence shall begin, and such certificate of incorporation shall be conclusive evidence that all conditions precedent required to be performed by the incorporators have been complied with and that the corporation has been incorporated under this Act, except as against this State in a proceeding to cancel or revoke the certificate of incorporation or for involuntary dissolution of the corporation."

The commencement of the corporate existence means that certain legal liabilities and protections as to limited liability [8] are incurred.

### 2. Other Documents to Be Filed with Articles

A particular state's corporation law may require that other documents be submitted at the same time the articles of incorporation are filed. Section 206 of the Pennsylvania Business Corporation Law, for example, requires the submission, with the articles of incorporation, of a registry statement containing information about the officers and

---

7. Consider what are "assigns". See Section II.D.

8. See Chapter One for a discussion of limited liability.

other corporate matters, in triplicate, which is used by the Department of Revenue for taxing purposes.

An example of a Registry Statement is set forth below.

## EXAMPLE—Registry Statement

DSCB:BCL—206 (Rev. 8-72)

Filing Fee: None

Registry Statement—Domestic or
Foreign Business Corporation
(File in triplicate)

COMMONWEALTH OF PENNSYLVANIA
DEPARTMENT OF STATE
CORPORATION BUREAU

In compliance with the requirements of section 206 of the Business Corporation Law, act of May 5, 1933 (P. L. 364) (15 P. S. § 1206), the following information concerning the foreign business corporation or proposed domestic business corporation hereinafter named is hereby certified for registration:

1. Name of Corporation:_____

2. Address to which Corporation desires correspondence to be directed by Department of Revenue and other Commonwealth agencies:

_____
   (Number and Street)              (City)         (State)    (Zip Code)

* 3. Date of incorporation:_____

4. Act of Assembly or authority under which incorporated:

_____
(Give full citation of statute or statutes, including, in the case of a foreign business corporation,
the state or jurisdiction of incorporation)

5. Kind or kinds of business in which the Corporation intends to engage in this Commonwealth within one year of the execution of this registry statement:

_____

**BUSINESS ACTIVITY CODE**
| | | | | | †

6. Name and residence address of its Treasurer:

_____
   (Name)        (Number and Street)      (City)     (State)   (Zip Code)

* 7. The text of its purposes as stated in its Articles of Incorporation, Certificate of Incorporation or equivalent charter document is (attach rider if required):

Completion of Paragraphs 8 et seq. is optional. However, failure to supply such information will result in a subsequent request from the Department of Revenue for substantially the same information.

8. Place of business in Pennsylvania:

                                        Pennsylvania
_____
   (Number and Street)           (City)                  (Zip Code)

* 9. The Corporation has been doing business in Pennsylvania since:_____

*10. The location and post office address of its principal office is:

_____
   (Number and Street)           (City)         (State)    (Zip Code)

  * To be completed by foreign corporations only.

  † The Business Activity Code should be inserted in paragraph 5 if known. However, the furnishing of such number is not mandatory.

                                                              [B6688]

DSCB:BCL—206-2 (Rev. 8-72)-2

11. The Corporation's fiscal year ends: (See Note Below) _____

12. Amount of capital authorized:_____

13. Amount of capital paid in:_____ Date:_____

14. Names and addresses of its President and Secretary:

President:_____
          (Name)          (Number and Street)      (City)      (State)      (Zip Code)

Secretary:_____
          (Name)          (Number and Street)      (City)      (State)      (Zip Code)

IN TESTIMONY WHEREOF, the undersigned has (have) signed (and sealed) this registry statement

this_____day of_____, 19____.

_____
(INCORPORATOR OF PROPOSED DOMESTIC
BUSINESS CORPORATION)

Attest
                                   _____
                                   (NAME OF FOREIGN CORPORATION
                                   OR CORPORATE INCORPORATOR)

_____    By_____
(SECRETARY, ASSISTANT SECRETARY, ETC.)           (PRESIDENT, VICE PRESIDENT, ETC.)

(CORPORATE SEAL)

---

For Department use only: Certificate of Incorporation ☐, Certificate of Domestication ☐, Certificate of Authority ☐ issued by the Department of State on the_____day of _____, A.D. 19____.

---

NOTE:   All Pennsylvania Corporate Tax Reports must be filed with the Commonwealth of Pennsylvania on the same basis as used by the corporation in filing Income Tax Reports with the United States Government.

       In the case of a proposed business corporation, this Registry Statement shall be executed by an incorporator thereof, if a natural person, and in the case of a corporate incorporator or a foreign business corporation it shall be executed under the seal of the corporation by two duly authorized officers thereof. The Registry Statement shall be submitted in triplicate except that only one statement need include a copy of the stated purposes of a foreign corporation. Only one copy need be manually signed. The remaining copies may be either conformed or facsimile copies.

[B6689]

### 3. Incorporation Fees

All states require that a statutory fee be paid at the time the articles of incorporation are filed. Frequently, the fee is calculated on the number of shares which the articles of incorporation authorize the corporation to issue and may take into consideration the par value [9] of such shares. For example, the fee may be calculated as a percentage of the dollar amount determined by multiplying the authorized number of shares by the par value per share, or it may be calculated as a dollar amount per number of authorized shares.

**PROBLEM**

**If the fee is $\frac{1}{10}$ of 1% of the total par value of shares, what is the fee for 100,000 shares, par value $1.00 per share?**

In many states, there is a flat charge for filing the Articles of Incorporation and an additional "fee" (license fee or excise tax), which must be paid, calculated on the authorized number of shares. The MBCA, for example, suggests at Section 130(c) a fixed dollar amount as the fee for filing the articles, and an additional "license fee".

### 4. Other Formalities

In some states the signature(s) of the person(s) signing the articles of incorporation must be notarized.

## B.    OTHER STEPS IN THE INCORPORATION PROCEDURE

In addition to the preparation and filing of articles of incorporation, there are various other routine matters in forming a new corporation. The corporate law of the state of incorporation must be consulted to determine what additional steps are required. Some of the most commonly required steps are discussed below:

### 1. Publication

Several states require that the articles of incorporation be published in a newspaper of general circulation in the county in which the corporation's office designated in the articles (registered office) is located, or in some other manner. In other states, only a notice of the corporation's formation need be published. In many states, no publication at all is required. Section 205 of the Pennsylvania Business Corporation Law is illustrative of a statutory notice requirement:

> "The incorporators shall advertise their intention to file or the corporation shall advertise the filing of articles of incorporation with

---

9. The "par value" is the legal minimum that must be paid for shares of stock. The corporation may set any value—$.01, $1.00, $100.00. Ordinarily a low or nominal value is set.

the Department of State one time in two newspapers published in the English language, one of which shall be a newspaper of general circulation, and the other the legal newspaper, if any, designated by the rules of the court for the publication of legal notices; otherwise, in two newspapers of general circulation published in the county in which the initial registered office of the corporation is to be located. Where there is but one newspaper of general circulation published in any county, advertisement in such newspaper shall be sufficient. Advertisements may appear prior to or after the day the articles of incorporation are filed with the Department of State, and shall set forth briefly:

"(1) The name of the proposed corporation,

"(2) A statement that the corporation is to be or has been organized under the provisions of this act,

"(3) The purpose or purposes of the corporation,

"(4) The time when the articles will be or were filed with the Department of State."

A sample advertisement which would satisfy the foregoing statutory requirement and which would appear after the filing of articles of incorporation is as follows:

### EXAMPLE—Advertisement of Incorporation

"Articles of incorporation of SMITH, INC. were filed with the Pennsylvania Department of State on July 1, 19___. The corporation has been incorporated under the provisions of the Pennsylvania Business Corporation Law, Act of May 5, 1933, P.L. 364, as amended, for the purpose of selling groceries at retail, and shall have unlimited power to engage in and to do any lawful act concerning any or all lawful business for which corporations may be incorporated under such law."

### QUESTION

**Of what value is the requirement of a legal advertisement of incorporation?**

In many states there are service agencies which place these "legal" advertisements for a nominal charge. Where these services are available, lawyers and paralegals frequently use them to save time rather than placing an advertisement with the newspaper directly. After the required advertisement appears, the newspaper in which it appeared or the service agency, if one was used, will send notarized copies of "proof of publication". These proofs will be filed in the official corporate records of the corporation. A sample form of proof of publication appears on Page 31.

# Bucks County Law Reporter

### DOYLESTOWN, PA.

Owned and Published by the Bucks County Bar Association

STATE OF PENNSYLVANIA,   }
COUNTY OF BUCKS      ss :

John F. O'Neill, Jr., being duly sworn according to law deposes and says that he is the editor of the Bucks County Law Reporter, the legal publication designated by the several Courts of Bucks County, Pennsylvania, as the official newspaper for the publication of legal notices in Bucks County, Pennsylvania, which was established in 1951; that the printed notice, a copy of which is attached hereto was published in said paper on the following dates:—

December 20, 1973

that your deponent is not interested in the subject matter of the notice so published and that all of the allegations of this statement as to the time, place and character of the publication are true.

_____
Editor

Sworn to and subscribed before me this
____21st____ day of __December,__
A.D. 19 73.

[Seal]

*Elizabeth G. Lawfer*

NOTARY PUBLIC, DOYLESTOWN, BUCKS COUNTY
MY COMMISSION EXPIRES OCTOBER 25, 1977

NOTICE IS HEREBY GIVEN THAT Articles of Incorporation have been filed with and approved by the Department of State of the Commonwealth of Pennsylvania at Harrisburg, Pa., on November 16, 1973, for the purpose of obtaining a Certificate of Incorporation pursuant to the provisions of the Business Corporation Law of the Commonwealth of Pennsylvania, approved May 5, 1933, as amended.

The name of the corporation is PHOTO WORLD LTD.

The purpose or purposes for which it was organized are as follows: To buy, sell, lease and repair all forms of cameras and other forms of photographic equipment and supplies; and to have the unlimited power to engage in and to do any lawful act concerning any or all lawful business for which corporations may be organized under the Business Corporation Law, Act of May 5, 1933, P.L. 364, as amended.

COHEN, SHAPIRO, POLISHER, SHIEKMAN & COHEN, Solicitors
22nd Floor, Philadelphia Saving Fund Building
Philadelphia, Pa. 19107

[B6692]

## 2. Payment of Capital

In many states, the formation of the corporation is not complete, or the corporation is prohibited from commencing business until some minimum amount of capital contribution of money or property is paid in by shareholders.

## 3. Organization Meeting

The organization meeting at which action is taken to adopt by-laws, elect directors and/or officers, accept subscriptions for shares and approve other matters is required in several states to complete formation of the corporation.[10]

## 4. Recording

In several states (e. g., Delaware), a certified copy of the articles of incorporation must be filed in a local office, i. e., in the county in which the corporation's registered office is located.

## 5. Corporate Seal, Minute Book and Stock Certificate Book

These three items are generally referred to as the "corporate kit" and must be ordered, for each new corporation, from a local supplier who is listed under "Corporate Supplies" in the yellow pages of the telephone directory. Each law office has its own favorite supplier.

To order the corporate seal, the supplier must be told the name of the corporation and the state and year of incorporation. The use of corporate seals is discussed in Chapter Seven.

The minute book will contain the written notes of proceedings at corporate meetings and official corporate documents. The only decision involved in ordering a minute book is whether it is to be an inexpensive or expensive one. When ordering the stock certificate book, the supplier must be told the name of the corporation, state of incorporation, number of shares of authorized stock and its par value and the number of certificates to be printed. It is customary to order only 25 certificates for the typical corporation with a small number of shareholders. Corporations with large numbers of shareholders, such as General Motors Corporation, usually order certificates from a specialized financial printer such as Security-Columbian Banknote Company (United States Banknote Corp.).

## 6. Securities Law Clearance

Many states regulate the offer and sale of securities even to only a few shareholders. In some states, depending on the number of subscribers to the corporation's stock, clearance from the state securities commission, which is the state regulator of issuance of securities, will

---

10. The matter will be discussed below in Section IV of Chapter Seven.

be required before any shares are actually sold. The requirements of State Securities Laws ("Blue Sky Laws") are complex and vary considerably from state to state. You should become familiar with those laws relevant to your state of employment so that you are certain to comply with the statute and the regulations thereunder issued by the local blue sky commission prior to issuing securities.

### 7. Restrictions on Transfer

Prior to or shortly after incorporation, the persons organizing the corporation often agree to the imposition of some restrictions upon the transfer of the shares of the corporation for which they are subscribing and will enter into a Shareholders' Agreement.[11]

### C. EVIDENCE OF INCORPORATION SENT BY STATE

Some states acknowledge the filing of articles of incorporation by returning a duplicate copy of the articles with the signature of the Secretary of State and the filing date. The filing date is quite important because it is the date of incorporation and will be referred to later in many documents and agreements involving the corporation, such as income tax returns and contracts.

All states, either in addition to, or in lieu of, the signed duplicate copy of the articles referred to above, issue a formal looking document, sometimes with the state seal attached, called a "Certificate of Incorporation". The certificate will also indicate the date of incorporation. A copy of such a certificate appears on Page 34.

11. The subject is covered in detail in Chapter Ten.

**EXAMPLE—Certificate of Incorporation**

## Commonwealth of Pennsylvania

3-1-73.52 _880_

### Department of State

#### Office of the
#### Secretary of the Commonwealth

### To all to whom these Presents shall come, Greeting:

WHEREAS, Under the provisions of the Business Corporation Law, approved the 5th day of May, Anno Domini one thousand nine hundred and thirty-three, P. L. 364, as amended, the Department of State is authorized and required to issue a

CERTIFICATE OF INCORPORATION

evidencing the incorporation of a business corporation organized under the terms of that law.

AND WHEREAS, The stipulations and conditions of that law have been fully complied with by the persons desiring to incorporate as

PHOTO WORLD LTD.

THEREFORE, KNOW YE, That subject to the Constitution of this Commonwealth and under the authority of the Business Corporation Law, I do by these presents, which I have caused to be sealed with the Great Seal of the Commonwealth, create, erect, and incorporate the incorporators of and the subscribers to the shares of the proposed corporation named above, their associates and successors, and also those who may thereafter become subscribers or holders of the shares of such corporation, into a body politic and corporate in deed and in law by the name chosen hereinbefore specified, which shall exist
    perpetually    and shall be invested with and have and enjoy all the powers, privileges, and franchises incident to a business corporation and be subject to all the duties, requirements, and restrictions specified and enjoined in and by the Business Corporation Law and all other applicable laws of this Commonwealth.

GIVEN under my Hand and the Great Seal of the Commonwealth, at the City of Harrisburg, this _16th_ day of _November_ in the year of our Lord one thousand nine hundred and _seventy-three_ and of the Commonwealth the one hundred and _ninety-eighth_

'Seal]

C. _DeLores Tucker_

Secretary of the Commonwealth

as       [B6693]

It may take several weeks to receive any evidence of incorporation from the state. A telephone call to the corporation bureau or department will often confirm that the articles were in fact filed. The telephone information is not official. It is advisable, if possible, not to rely on the date provided by telephone.

All evidence of incorporation received from the state should be filed in the corporate minute book.

## D. TRANSFER OF PRE–INCORPORATION SUBSCRIPTION AGREEMENT

After the articles of incorporation have been filed, any person who, while acting as incorporator, executed a pre-incorporation subscription agreement but who does not intend to be an initial shareholder of the corporation should assign such subscription right to one of the persons who will in fact be a shareholder of the corporation. The form of such a subscription assignment is set forth below.

**EXAMPLE—Transfer of Subscription**

### [*NAME OF CORPORATION*]

### TRANSFER OF SUBSCRIPTION

I, the undersigned, in consideration of the sum of One Dollar to me paid, the receipt of which is hereby acknowledged, and for other good and valuable consideration, hereby sell, assign and transfer all my right, title and interest as subscriber to and incorporator of the above named _____ corporation with respect to the shares subscribed to by me, as follows:

| **To** | **No. and Class of Shares** |
| --- | --- |

and I do hereby direct said corporation to issue certificate(s) for said shares of stock to and in the names of the aforesaid assignee(s) or his, her, their or its nominees, or assigns.

IN WITNESS WHEREOF, intending to be legally bound hereby, I have hereunto set my hand and seal this _____ day of _____, 19__.

_____ [*Seal*]

## IV. ARTICLES OF INCORPORATION

Each state requires specific information in the articles of incorporation. Refer to Section 54 of the MBCA, for example. It establishes a sample set of requirements for articles of incorporation. The individual concepts will be discussed immediately below.

The following is an analysis of certain elements generally required in the articles of incorporation:

## A. NAME

The requirements imposed upon the name of a new corporation have already been discussed.[12]   Again, remember that the names must be inserted exactly in the form desired by the client.

## B. REGISTERED OFFICE WITHIN THE STATE

All states require that corporations incorporated under their law maintain a "registered office" within the state.  This office need not be the executive offices of the corporation, or a principal place of business; indeed it normally need not be an actual business office of the corporation at all.  For corporations which are just commencing operations, the address of the attorney forming the corporation or the residence address of one of the organizers has been frequently used as the registered office.  This is not a recommended procedure, as all tax returns and other communications from the state are directed to the registered office.  It is a costly and time-consuming process for the attorney to forward such papers to the client and the papers may be lost.  A corporation may choose to use a corporate service company, such as CT Corporation and its affiliates or United States Corporation Company, for its registered office.  These companies specialize in performing the service for a fee.  They will be responsible for forwarding documents issued by the state to the corporation.  Moreover, the law firm, perhaps, should not be the place where service of process in a lawsuit may be made.  Why not?

The significant features of a corporation's registered office are the following:

(a) State statutes deem it sufficient notice to a corporation for certain information to be delivered to a corporation's registered office.  Legal notice, service of process in a lawsuit, tax returns, and changes in state statutes are among those things of which the corporation has notice if it has been delivered to its registered office.

(b) It is generally required that certain records of the corporation be maintained at its registered office.  Section 52 of the MBCA, for example, requires a corporation to keep, either at its registered office, its principal place of business or at the office of its transfer agent and registrar,[13] a record of the shareholders of the corporation.

(c) The location of the registered office may be relevant to determine what courts in a state have authority to handle matters relating to the corporation.  Some states give authority to the court within the county in which the registered office is located to hear suits by shareholders seeking to remove a director for cause.[14]

---

12.  See Section II.B, above.

13.  Persons appointed for the purpose of recording stock transfers for the corporation.

14.  For example, Section 405(c) of the Pennsylvania Business Corporation Law.

## C. REGISTERED AGENT

While all states require a corporation to have a registered office or its equivalent, many do not require a registered agent. When a corporation is required to have a registered agent, the function of the agent is to permit persons to commence legal action against the corporation by notice to the agent:

> "The registered agent so appointed by a corporation shall be an agent of such corporation upon whom any process, notice or demand required or permitted by law to be served upon the corporation may be served."

Section 14, MBCA.

The registered agent must be a person who can be relied upon to forward documents relating to lawsuits to the corporation.

### PROBLEMS

**Under the MBCA**

1. Is the registered agent the sole person on whom service of process in a lawsuit may be made?

2. What if service is made on a sole shareholder?

## D. PURPOSE OF THE CORPORATION

A corporation may engage only in the activities authorized in its articles of incorporation. At one point in the development of corporate law, these purposes were required to be set forth in detail and required careful draftsmanship on the part of the incorporators. Under most modern corporation statutes, however, it is generally acceptable to simply authorize the corporation to do any lawful act concerning any or all lawful business for which corporations may be incorporated under the law of that particular state, commonly called a full purpose or general purpose clause. For example, Section 204(3) of the PBCL requires the following in the articles of incorporation.[15]

> "A brief statement: (i) of the purpose or purposes for which the corporation is incorporated which may consist of or include a statement that the corporation shall have unlimited power to engage in and to do any lawful act concerning any or all lawful business for which corporations may be incorporated under this act, and (ii) that the corporation is incorporated under the provisions of this act."

If, for any reason, the incorporators feel that it is desirable to limit the corporation with respect to the activities in which it may engage, the purpose clause in the articles will require careful attention in or-

---

15. Also see MBCA, Section 54(c).

der to accomplish the desired limitation without unnecessarily restricting the corporation in the exercise of its intended business. A typical example of a "full purpose" corporation follows:

**EXAMPLE:**

> "The Corporation shall have unlimited power to engage in and to do any lawful act concerning any or all lawful business for which corporations may be incorporated under the Act of May 5, 1933, P.L. 364, as amended, under the provisions of which the Corporation is incorporated."

## E.   TERM OF EXISTENCE

An ordinary business corporation is generally permitted to have perpetual existence. Absent very unusual and special circumstances where the incorporators know the corporate purpose will be completed at a specified time, a perpetual term is ordinarily specified in the articles when the term must be indicated. In some states, absent a contrary provision in the articles, the corporation is deemed to have perpetual existence.

## F.   AUTHORIZED CAPITAL

The authorized capital of a business corporation consists of the total number of shares of all classes and series of stock authorized for issuance in the articles of incorporation. Many factors must be considered in each case to determine the numbers and classes of shares which should be authorized, the par value of such shares and the relative powers, preferences and rights of each such class.[16]

## G.   INITIAL DIRECTORS

In some states, the articles of incorporation must specify the number and names of those individuals who will serve as the initial directors of the corporation. For example, Section 54(j), MBCA, would require a statement in the articles of incorporation of:

> "The number of directors constituting the initial board of directors and the names and addresses of the persons who are to serve as directors until the first annual meeting of shareholders or until their successors be elected and qualify."

When the statute requires the names of directors, it is common practice to name attorneys, paralegals and secretaries as original directors. This is done because they are convenient for signing documents. Whenever these nominal directors are used, it is desirable to obtain their resignations in advance in the event their services no

---

16. This subject is covered extensively in Chapter Eight, "Corporate Equity and Debt Securities".

longer are available or required. A sample form of resignation is set forth below:

**EXAMPLE—Resignation of Directors**

[NAME OF CORPORATION]

RESIGNATIONS

We hereby resign as members of the Board of Directors of [*Name of corporation*] effective immediately.

Dated: _____

/s/ _____
　　Director

/s/ _____
　　Director

/s/ _____
　　Director

In other states, the incorporator is given the option of naming the initial directors. In such a state, it is wise to name the initial directors in the articles only if a decision has been made as to who they will be. By so naming the initial directors, the necessity of having both an organization meeting of the incorporators and of the initial directors is eliminated.[17]

## H.　OTHER PROVISIONS OF ARTICLES

Virtually any provision relevant to the operation of the corporation may, if the organizers desire, be included in the articles of incorporation. In addition, the corporation laws of many states provide that certain powers, rights, privileges and procedures are permissible or appropriate only if provided for in the articles of incorporation. There are several similar privileges or powers which are conferred automatically unless expressly denied by the articles. It is essential for this reason that the specific state corporation law be considered at the outset of the incorporation procedure. Some of the more important provisions which must be provided for, if at all, in the articles of incorporation are as follows:

### 1.　Shareholders' Pre-emptive Rights

A pre-emptive right is the right of a shareholder to have the opportunity to purchase shares which the corporation may desire to sell at a future date before any such shares may be sold to persons who are not then shareholders. It is designed to allow shareholders to maintain their proportionate interest in the corporation. For example, if a corporation desires to sell more stock to raise cash, pre-emp-

---

17.　See Chapter Seven, Section IV for a discussion of the organization meeting of the corporation.

tive rights would require to give shareholders an opportunity to purchase the stock first on a pro rata basis before the corporation sold stock to non-stockholders.

Consider how a corporation may be inhibited in acquiring a desired piece of specific real estate owned by a non-shareholder for stock if shareholders have pre-emptive rights.   Modern corporation statutes deal with pre-emptive rights in one of two ways: Either the articles must expressly provide for pre-emptive rights, or there are no such rights; or, alternatively, pre-emptive rights exist unless the corporation expressly provides otherwise.   The present trend is to provide that no pre-emptive rights exist unless expressly provided for in the articles of incorporation.   This is in line with permitting corporations latitude in determining on what basis to issue stock.

The MBCA reflects this dual approach of state laws to pre-emptive rights by suggesting alternative possible sections on the subject:

> "The shareholders of a corporation shall have no pre-emptive right to acquire   .   .   .   shares of the corporation,   .   .   .   except to the extent, if any, that such right is provided in the articles of incorporation."

> Section 26, MBCA.

### (ALTERNATIVE)

> "Except to the extent limited or denied by this section or by the articles of incorporation, shareholders shall have a pre-emptive right to acquire unissued   .   .   .   shares or securities   .   .   .   .

> "Unless otherwise provided in the articles of incorporation,

>> "(a) No pre-emptive right shall exist

>>> "(1) to acquire any shares issued to directors, officers or employees pursuant to approval by the affirmative vote of the holders of a majority of the shares entitled to vote thereon or when authorized by and consistent with a plan theretofore approved by such a vote of shareholders; or

>>> "(2) to acquire any shares sold otherwise than for cash.

>> "(b) Holders of shares of any class that is preferred or limited as to dividends [18] or assets shall not be entitled to any pre-emptive right.

>> "(c) Holders of shares of common stock shall not be entitled to any pre-emptive right to shares of any class that is preferred or limited as to dividends or assets or to any obligations, unless convertible into shares of common stock or carrying a right to subscribe to or acquire shares of common stock.[19]

---

18.  "Dividends" are shares of profits of corporations distributed to shareholders.

19.  Common stock is generally the stock which has the residual rights in the corporation after all creditors and other classes of stock have received their share of assets. Chapter Eight will provide a discussion of different classes of stock.

### 2.　Cumulative Voting

Cumulative voting is the right of a shareholder, voting in the election of directors, to multiply the number of votes to which the shareholder is entitled by the number of directors to be elected, and to cast the whole number of such votes for one candidate or to distribute them among any two or more candidates. The effect of cumulative voting is to enable the owners of a sizable minority of shares to elect a representative to a corporation's board of directors. This effect can be illustrated as follows:

**EXAMPLE:** X Corp. has 100 shares of voting common stock issued and outstanding.[20] A and B each own 30 shares; C and D each own 20 shares. X Corp. has no other stock outstanding. There are three vacancies to be filled on the X Corp. board of directors. A and B nominate $D_1$, $D_2$ and $D_3$. C and D nominate $D_4$.

**(a)** Without cumulative voting and with one vote per share, $D_1$, $D_2$ and $D_3$ are elected since A and B outvote C and D, 60 votes to 40 on each vacancy to be filled.

**(b)** With cumulative voting, A and B cannot prevent C and D from electing $D_4$. C and D cumulate their votes (3 vacancies x 40 shares equals 120 votes) and cast all votes for $D_4$. A and B have 180 votes available (60 shares x 3 vacancies). In order to cast more than 120 votes for $D_1$, $D_2$ and $D_3$, A and B would need a minimum of 363 votes (121 for each). Obviously, they are far short.

To determine how many shares one must hold or control under cumulative voting to insure the election of a certain number of directors, the following method may be used:

1. *Multiply* total number of shares entitled to vote by number of directors it is desired to elect.

2. *Divide* the product of (1) by a number equal to one more than the number of directors to be elected. Disregard all fractional shares in the computation.

3. *Add* one to the quotient of (2) and the result will be the least number of shares it is necessary to hold or control to elect the desired number of directors.

Algebraic Formula

　　x = shares required

　　a = total voting shares

　　c = number of directors desired to be elected

　　b = number of directors to be elected

$$x = \frac{ac}{b + 1} + 1$$

**20.** Outstanding shares are those which have been issued and are in the hands of shareholders.

## PROBLEMS

1.  What is the number of shares required to elect with cumulative voting two directors on a seven-person board of directors if there are 100 shares outstanding?

2.  Can Smith be sure of electing three directors if he owns 38 shares?

3.  If there is no cumulative voting can Smith be sure of electing two directors if he owns 38 shares?

4.  If a corporation has 600 shares outstanding and the shareholders have cumulative voting in the election of nine (9) directors, what is the minimum number of votes required to elect a majority of the Board?

5.  Can you change the formula to enable you to calculate the number of shares which must be owned to elect a specific number of directors under cumulative voting?

As in the case of pre-emptive rights, the modern corporate statutes deal with the question of cumulative voting in one of two ways. Either cumulative voting exists unless expressly denied in the articles of incorporation; or, if the articles are silent on the subject, no cumulative voting rights exist. In some states, however, cumulative voting is mandatory, either under statute or the state's constitution.

For example, Section 505 of the Pennsylvania Business Corporation Law states that cumulative voting exists unless abolished by specific provision in the corporation's articles.

Section 214 of the General Corporation Law of Delaware, on the other hand, does not grant cumulative voting unless it is specifically provided by the certificate of incorporation.

## PROBLEM

In your state what is the status of cumulative voting?

## 3. Informal Action of Shareholders

Modern corporation statutes allow shareholders to take action without the necessity of a formal meeting by consenting in writing to various proposals.[21] (See, e. g., Section 145, MBCA). Several states now permit informal shareholder action with less than unanimous consent. In some states, informal action with less than unanimous consent must be specifically authorized in the articles.

---

21. A formal meeting is generally required to take action by the directors collectively or the shareholders. The requisites of a meeting include notice, quorum, and a vote of the majority of the persons entitled to vote. See Chapter Seven for further information.

A sample provision to be inserted in the articles of incorporation of a corporation to permit written consents by less than all shareholders is as follows:

**EXAMPLE:**

"Except as otherwise provided by and subject to the provisions of applicable law, any action which may be taken at a meeting of the shareholders or of a class of shareholders of the corporation may be taken without a meeting if a consent or consents in writing to such action, setting forth the action so taken, shall be (i) signed by shareholders entitled to cast a majority (or such larger percentage as may be required by law) of the number of votes which all such shareholders are entitled to cast thereon, and (ii) filed with the secretary of the corporation."

## PROBLEM

**Draft a provision for inclusion in the articles of incorporation of a MBCA corporation requiring the approval of 2/3 of all outstanding shares in order to amend the articles.**

## V. SAMPLE FORMS OF ARTICLES OF INCORPORATION

In this section, two sample forms of articles of incorporation of a hypothetical corporation are set forth. In addition to illustrating the general makeup of the articles, the purpose of setting forth these samples in the text is to illustrate the importance of the corporation law of the state of incorporation as it pertains to the content of the articles. The "structure" of the corporation formed by both sample articles (one a Delaware corporation and one a Pennsylvania corporation) is identical. Due to differences in the corporation laws of the two states, the contents of the articles differ. The contents of articles of other states have their own requirements.

**EXAMPLE—Pennsylvania Articles**

COMMONWEALTH OF PENNSYLVANIA
DEPARTMENT OF STATE
CORPORATION BUREAU

ARTICLES OF INCORPORATION

OF

FUN CITY FRANCHISE CORP.

The undersigned, being of full age, desiring to incorporate a business corporation under the provisions of the Business Corporation Law, approved May 5, 1933, P.L. 364, as amended, does hereby certify:

1. The name of the corporation is:

FUN CITY FRANCHISE CORP.

2. The location and post office address of its initial registered office in the Commonwealth of Pennsylvania is:

4455 Main Street

Philadelphia, Pennsylvania    19103

3. The purpose or purposes for which the corporation is incorporated are to engage in manufacturing and to engage in and do any lawful act concerning any or all lawful business for which corporations may be incorporated under the Pennsylvania Business Corporation Law.

4. The term for which the corporation is to exist is perpetual.

5. The aggregate number of shares which the corporation shall have authority to issue is:

2,000,000 shares of Common Stock, par value $.01 per share.

6. The name and post office address of the incorporator and the number and class of shares subscribed by him are:

| Name | Address | Number & Class of Shares |
|---|---|---|
| [*Name and address of person preparing Articles of Incorporation*] | | One share of common stock |

7. Unless the Board of Directors shall otherwise direct, any action which may be taken at a meeting of the shareholders or of a class of shareholders may be taken without a meeting, if a consent or consents in writing to such action, setting forth the action so taken, shall be (1) signed by shareholders entitled to cast such a percentage of the number of votes which all such shareholders are entitled to cast thereon as is required by law for the taking of action at a meeting of the shareholders or of a class of shareholders and (2) filed with the secretary of the corporation. In no case, however, shall such percentage be less than the larger of (1) two-thirds of the total number of votes which all shareholders of the corporation or of a class of shareholders are entitled by the Articles to cast upon such action, or (2) the minimum percentage of the vote required by law, if any, for

the proposed corporate action. Such action shall not become effective until after at least ten days' written notice of such action shall have been given to each shareholder of record entitled to vote thereon. This paragraph shall not be applicable to any action with respect to any plan or amendment of articles to which Section 515 of the Pennsylvania Business Corporation Law is applicable.

Signed on February 6, 19___.

_____
[*Signature of person named in paragraph 6*]
Incorporator

Filed in the Department of State on _____, 19___.

_____
Secretary of the Commonwealth

### EXAMPLE—Delaware Articles of Incorporation

## CERTIFICATE OF INCORPORATION

### OF

## FUN CITY FRANCHISE CORP.

1. The name of the corporation is:

FUN CITY FRANCHISE CORP.

2. The address of its registered office in the State of Delaware is 901 Market Street, in the City of Wilmington, County of New Castle. The name of its registered agent at such address is Corporation Guarantee and Trust Company.

3. The nature of the business or purposes to be conducted or promoted is:

To engage in manufacturing and any lawful act or activity for which corporations may be organized under the General Corporation law of Delaware.

4. The total number of shares of stock which the corporation shall have authority to issue is:

2,000,000 shares of Common Stock par value $.01 per share.

5. At all elections of directors of the corporation, each stockholder shall be authorized to as many votes as shall equal the number of votes which he would be entitled to cast for the election of directors with respect to his shares of stock multiplied by the number of directors to be elected, and he may cast all of such votes for one single director

or may distribute them among the number to be voted for, or for any two or more of them as he may see fit.

6.  The name and mailing address of the incorporator is as follows:

**Name**                              **Address**

[*Name and address of person preparing the Articles*]

7.  In furtherance and not in limitation of the powers conferred by statute, the board of directors is expressly authorized to make, alter or repeal the by-laws of the corporation.

IN WITNESS WHEREOF, I have hereunto set my hand this 6th day of February, 19___.

_____

Incorporator

### Analysis of Sample Forms

In reviewing the above forms, note the following:

**Paragraph 2 (of both forms):** Because the only business office of the corporation is in Pennsylvania, this business address has been used in the Pennsylvania articles. The PBCL does not provide for a "registered agent", and therefore, no agent is named in the Articles. If the same Pennsylvania business incorporates in Delaware, perhaps to take advantage of favorable Delaware business laws, the Delaware General Corporation Law ("DGCL"), requires that the Articles designate a registered office within the State of Delaware *and* a registered agent at that address. (See Section 102(2), DGCL). Since it is assumed the corporation has no offices or employees in Delaware, the hypothetical corporation has designated a corporation service company as its agent and used this service company's address as its registered office in Delaware.[22]

**Paragraph 3 (of both forms):** In both forms, a general purpose clause has been utilized.

**Paragraph 4 (Pennsylvania form):** Under PBCL Section 204, the articles must state the term for which the corporation is to exist. The Pennsylvania form provides for perpetual existence. Under DGCL Section 102(b)(5) the corporation automatically has a perpetual term unless the articles limit the term; thus, no statement to that effect has been included in the Delaware form.

**Paragraph 5 (Pennsylvania form) and Paragraph 4 (Delaware form):** The authorized capitalization is set forth in identical terms on both forms. However, the absence of any provision in the Pennsylvania form abolishing cumulative rights means that shareholders will be entitled to cumulate their votes.[23] To accomplish this in Dela-

---

**22.** See Section IV.B, *supra.*

**23.** See Section IV.H.2, *supra*, for a discussion of cumulative voting.

ware, a provision specifically providing for cumulative voting (Paragraph 5) is necessary.

**Paragraph 6 (both forms):** Both the PBCL and the DGCL require that the name and address of the incorporator be set forth in the articles. Under Section 204(A) of the PBCL, however, the number of shares of the corporation's stock for which the incorporator has subscribed must be set forth, and it is necessary that the incorporator subscribe for at least one share of stock.[24] No such requirement exists under Delaware law.

**Paragraph 7 (Pennsylvania form):** Under Section 513 of the PBCL[25] informal shareholder action by less than unanimous consent must be specifically authorized in the articles. No similar provision is necessary in the Delaware form of articles since this authority is automatically available to Delaware corporations unless prohibited by the articles.[26]

**Paragraph 7 (Delaware form):** Under Section 109 of the DGCL, the by-laws of a corporation may only be amended by shareholder action unless the articles expressly confer authority to amend on the Board of Directors.[27] Under Section 304 of the PBCL, the authority may be conferred on the Board in the initial by-laws of the corporation; hence, there is no similar provision in the Pennsylvania form of Articles.

Below is a sample of the letter transmitting the articles of incorporation to the Secretary of State for the Pennsylvania corporation.

**EXAMPLE—Letter of Transmittal**

(The following letter is designed to be used in transmitting the required documents and fees to the Secretary of State of Pennsylvania to incorporate Fun City Franchise Corp., the hypothetical Pennsylvania corporation discussed in the text.)

Corporation Bureau
Department of State
Harrisburg, Pennsylvania    17111

Re: FUN CITY FRANCHISE CORP.

Gentlemen:

Enclosed for filing for the above-named proposed business corporation are the following:

1. Articles of Incorporation in duplicate.
2. Registry Statement in triplicate.

---

24. See Section II.D., *supra*, for a discussion of subscriptions.

25. See Section IV.H.3.

26. Section 228 of the DGCL is the relevant provision.

27. A discussion of by-laws is contained in Section VI.

3.   Check in the amount of $75.00 for filing fee.

Please forward the appropriate certificate and the certified copy of the articles of incorporation to the undersigned.

Sincerely,

Below is the Form of articles of incorporation utilized under the MBCA.

**EXAMPLE—Articles of Incorporation Under MBCA**

Filing fee: $_____

ARTICLES OF INCORPORATION

OF

_____

The undersigned, acting as incorporator(s) of a corporation under the _____ Business Corporation Act, adopt(s) the following Articles of Incorporation for such corporation:

(Note 1)

FIRST:  The name of the corporation is _____
_____.

SECOND:  The period of its duration is _____.

THIRD:  The purpose or purposes for which the corporation is organized are:  _____
_____.

FOURTH:  The aggregate number of shares which the corporation shall have authority to issue is _____
_____.

(Note 2)

FIFTH:  Provisions granting preemptive rights are:

(Note 3)

SIXTH: Provisions for the regulation of the internal affairs of the corporation are:

(Note 4)

SEVENTH: The address of the initial registered office of the corporation is _____,
and the name of its initial registered agent at such address is _____.

EIGHTH: The number of directors constituting the initial board of directors of the corporation is _____, and the names and addresses of the persons who are to serve as directors until the first annual meeting of shareholders or until their successors are elected and shall qualify are:

**Name** **Address**

_____

NINTH: The name and address of each incorporator is:

**Name** **Address**

_____

Dated, _____, 19___.

Incorporator(s) (Note 5)

Notes: 1. One or more persons or domestic or foreign corporations may be the incorporator or incorporators.

2. If the authorized shares are to consist of one class only, insert a statement of the par value of such shares or a statement that all of such shares are to be without par value.

If the authorized shares are to be divided into classes, insert a statement of the number of shares of each class, a statement of the par value of the shares of each such class or that such shares are to be without par value, and a statement of the preferences, limitations and relative rights in respect of the shares of each class.

If the authorized shares of any preferred or special class are to be issued in series, insert a statement of the designation of each series, a statement of the variations in the relative rights and preferences as between series in so far as the same are to be fixed in the articles of incorporation, and a statement of any authority to be vested in the board of directors to establish series and fix and determine the variations in the relative rights and preferences as between series.

3. If preemptive rights are not to be granted, omit this article or insert "None."

4.  If no provisions for the regulation of the internal affairs of the corporation are to be set forth, omit this article or insert "None."

5.  Corporate incorporators should sign by a duly authorized officer.

### PROBLEM

**Prepare a draft of articles of incorporation for the following corporation which is to be incorporated under the laws of the state of Ohio, which for purposes of this assignment will be deemed to have adopted the MBCA:**

Name: Abjac Enterprises, Inc.

Address: 123 North Front Street
Cleveland, Ohio

Name of Registered Agent, if required: George Smith

Term of Existence: Perpetual

Purpose Clause: General

Authorized Capital: 1,000,000 shares of Common Stock, par value $1.00 per share

Name of incorporator: Henry S. Smith

Names and addresses of initial directors:

Alan Brandon, 1480 Wilson Street
Cleveland, Ohio

Charlene Dann, 1851 North Lake Road
Cleveland, Ohio

Edgar Frank, 931 Flower Road
Shaker Heights, Ohio

Initial directors are to be named in articles.

Special Features:

(a)  Shareholder action by less than unanimous consent in writing.

(b)  No pre-emptive rights for shareholders.

Note the checklist for incorporations at Section IIA of this Chapter.

## VI.  CORPORATE BY-LAWS

### A.  INTRODUCTION

The by-laws [28] of a corporation provide, in conjunction with the articles of incorporation, the standards and procedures for the legal operation of a corporation. Those of you who have been in clubs or organizations have previously encountered by-laws as the governing

---

**28.** Note that some states spell "by-laws" without a hyphen as "bylaws".

rules of procedure. There are many significant areas where the state corporation law provides that a specific governing standard of the corporation may be provided in either the articles of incorporation or by-laws. However, the articles require shareholder action for an amendment. Therefore, because the articles or by-laws can usually provide that the by-laws are amendable by the Board of Directors without shareholder approval, and, because the corporation's by-laws are not a public document which can be readily obtained by anyone (unlike the articles), it is preferable to deal with these matters in the by-laws. The opposite would be true, however, if, for some reason, the presence of an extensive amount of management flexibility would be undesirable from the viewpoint of the shareholders of the corporation. For example, shareholders may not desire the Board to issue additional stock because they desire to control the ownership of the corporation closely. In such a case, much of the material ordinarily found in the by-laws could be set forth in the articles. Any change would then require an amendment to the articles of incorporation which, in all states, is an action requiring shareholder approval.

In those states which require the initial directors of a corporation to be named in the articles of incorporation ( e. g., Section 54(j), MBCA), the by-laws will be adopted by the initial board of directors at the organization meeting.[29]

"The initial by-laws shall be adopted by its board of directors."
Section 27, MBCA.

A corporation's by-laws may provide for the following:

**1. With respect to the Board of Directors, the by-laws generally provide for:** (1) the number of directors which constitute the Board; (2) the procedure for the filling of vacancies on the Board; (3) the manner in which nominations to the Board are made; (4) rules on the place, frequency and notice of directors' meetings; (5) the formation of special committees of directors and the powers which may be delegated to such committees; (6) the classification of the board,[30] if any, and the term which each class shall serve; (7) special qualifications of directors, if any; (8) and the determination of a quorum at directors' meetings;

**2. With respect to shareholders and shareholders' meetings, the by-laws provide for:** the place, frequency and notice of share-

---

**29.** Organization and other meetings of the corporation are discussed in detail in Chapter Seven.

**30.** Classification of directors is a method whereby some corporations provide for election of only a portion of the Board each year. For example, a Board of six directors might have three classes with one class consisting of two directors being elected each year. In such a case, a director will ordinarily serve for a three year term until his class is up for reelection. Such a classification prevents a sudden takeover of corporations by outsiders by requiring several years to accomplish the election of a majority of the Board.

holders' meetings; and may also provide for shareholder procedures with respect to approval of certain corporate actions, and rights and privileges pertaining to certain classes of shareholders;

**3. With respect to officers, the by-laws define:** the positions which shall constitute corporate officers, the manner of election of officers and the duties of officers;

**4. The by-laws describe indemnification of officers and directors of the corporation;** [31]

**5. The by-laws detail the form of stock certificates;**

**6. The by-laws set forth the procedure for amending by-laws.**

It must be emphasized that the provisions contained in the by-laws must be consistent with the articles of incorporation and the corporation law of the state of incorporation. The statute is first in order of control, followed by the articles. For example, if a corporate statute requires cumulative voting unless the articles provide otherwise, the by-laws cannot eliminate cumulative voting if the articles do not eliminate it. Similarly the by-laws cannot provide for pre-emptive rights if the articles deny such rights because the by-laws cannot prevail over provisions in the articles. It is important to remember that, in the absence of a specific provision in a corporation's by-laws (or articles) dealing with a particular matter, the statutory provision on the matter will "fill the void". In any event, the statute will always control unless it permits the articles or by-laws to provide otherwise, and they do so. The articles, where they comply with statutory authority, will control the by-laws.

## PROBLEM

Under your state law, how do you know if a quorum is present at a meeting? If no quorum exists can any action be taken at the meeting?

## B.   FORM OF BY–LAWS

The following is a *short* form of "Model By-Laws" for use in states which have enacted the Model Business Corporation Act. The numbers in brackets are references to sections in the MBCA. It is suggested that the student analyze carefully the form and content to comprehend the purpose and structure of by-laws. It is probable that any law firm for which you may work will have its own form of by-laws that it generally uses.

---

31. Most corporate statutes permit the by-laws to provide for the corporation to defend a director or officer in a lawsuit which involves the director or officer and pay for losses incurred by the director or officer respecting actions on behalf of the corporation if such person acted in good faith in the best interests of the corporation. See Section 5 of the MBCA, for example.

**EXAMPLE—By-Laws ***

## BY-LAWS OF
## [*NAME OF CORPORATION*]

### Article I.  Shareholders

Meetings of shareholders shall be held at the registered office of the corporation unless another place shall have been determined by the directors and stated in the notice of meeting.  Annual meetings shall be held at _____ P.M. on the _____ of _____ unless a holiday and then on the next business day.  [§ 28]

*notice is very important*

### Article II.  Directors

*Section 1.*  The number of directors shall be _____.  [§ 36]

*Section 2.*  A regular meeting of the board of directors shall be held without notice immediately following the annual meeting of shareholders and at the same place.  The board of directors may provide for the holding without notice of additional regular meetings.  [§ 43]

*Section 3.*  Special meetings of the board of directors may be called by the president or any two directors on 24 hour notice given personally or by telephone or telegraph, or on four days' notice given by mail.  Special meetings shall be held at the place fixed by the board of directors for the holding of meetings, or if no such place has been fixed, at the principal business office of the corporation.  [§ 43]

### Article III.  Officers

*Section 1.*  The officers of the corporation shall be a president, a vice president, a secretary and a treasurer, who shall be elected annually at the regular meeting of the board of directors held after the annual meeting of shareholders and shall hold office only so long as they are satisfactory to the board of directors.  [§ 50, § 51]

*Listed officers*

*Section 2.*  The president shall be the principal executive officer of the corporation to put into effect the decisions of the board of directors.  Subject to such decisions, he shall supervise and control the business and affairs of the corporation.  He shall preside at meetings of the shareholders and directors.  [§ 35, § 50]

*Duties*

---

* Numbers in [brackets] are references to Sections of the Model Business Corporation Act.

*Section 3.* Subject to any specific assignments of duties made by the board of directors, the vice president, secretary and treasurer shall act under the direction of the president. The vice president shall perform the duties of the president when the president is absent or unable to act. The secretary shall prepare and keep minutes of the meetings of the shareholders and the directors and shall have general charge of the stock records of the corporation. [§ 31, § 52] The treasurer shall have custody of the funds of the corporation and keep its financial records. [§ 52]

### Article IV.  Miscellaneous

*Section 1.* The board of directors may authorize any officer or agent to enter into any contract or to execute any instrument for the corporation. Such authority may be general or be confined to specific instances. [§ 35, § 50]

*Section 2.* Certificates representing shares of the corporation shall be in such form as the board of directors shall determine. [§ 23] Transfers of shares shall be made only on the stock transfer books of the corporation. [§ 52]

### Article V.  Action Without Meeting

Any action required or permitted to be taken by the board of directors or the shareholders at a meeting may be taken without a meeting if a consent in writing, setting forth the action so taken, shall be signed by all directors or shareholders, as the case may be. [§ 44, § 145]

### Article VI.  Amendments

These by-laws may be altered, amended or repealed and new by-laws may be adopted by the board of directors or by the shareholders. [§ 27]

The following is a long form of by-laws under the MBCA which comprehensively spells out corporate regulations:

### PROBLEM

Compare the short form with the long form and point out the most salient points of difference.

### EXAMPLE—Model By-Laws—A Long Form *

BY-LAWS

OF

---

* Numbers in [brackets] are references to Sections of the Model Business Corporation Act.

### Article I. Offices

The principal office of the corporation in the State of _____ shall be located in the City of _____, County of _____. The corporation may have such other offices, either within or without the State of _____, as the board of directors may designate or as the business of the corporation may require from time to time.

The registered office of the corporation required by The _____ Business Corporation Act to be maintained in the State of _____ may be, but need not be, identical with the principal office in the State of _____, and the address of the registered office may be changed from time to time by the board of directors. [§ 12, § 13(g)]

### Article II. Shareholders

Section 1. *Annual Meeting.* The annual meeting of the shareholders shall be held on the _____ in the month of _____ in each year, beginning with the year 19__, at the hour of _____ o'clock __.M., or at such other time on such other day within such month as shall be fixed by the board of directors, for the purpose of electing directors and for the transaction of such other business as may come before the meeting. If the day fixed for the annual meeting shall be a legal holiday in the State of _____, such meeting shall be held on the next succeeding business day. If the election of directors shall not be held on the day designated herein for any annual meeting of the shareholders, or at any adjournment thereof, the board of directors shall cause the election to be held at a special meeting of the shareholders as soon thereafter as conveniently may be. [§ 28, § 36]

Section 2. *Special Meetings.* Special meetings of the shareholders, for any purpose or purposes, unless otherwise prescribed by statute, may be called by the president or by the board of directors, and shall be called by the president at the request of the holders of not less than one-tenth of all outstanding shares of the corporation entitled to vote at the meeting. [§ 28]

Section 3. *Place of Meeting.* The board of directors may designate any place, either within or without the State of _____, as the place of meeting for any annual meeting or for any special meeting called by the board of directors. A waiver of notice signed by all shareholders entitled to vote at a meeting may designate any place, either within or without the State of ———, as the place for the holding of such meeting. If no designation is made, or if a special meeting be otherwise called, the place of meeting shall be the principal office of the corporation in the State of ———. [§ 28]

Section 4. *Notice of Meeting.* Written notice stating the place, day and hour of the meeting, and in case of a special meeting, the purpose or purposes for which the meeting is called, shall, unless otherwise prescribed by statute, be delivered not less than ten nor more than fifty days before the date of the meeting, either personally or by mail, by or at the direction of the president, or the secretary, or the officer or other persons calling the meeting, to each shareholder of record entitled to vote at such meeting. If mailed, such notice shall be deemed to be delivered when deposited in the United States mail, addressed to the shareholder at his address as it appears on the stock transfer books of the corporation, with postage thereon prepaid. [§ 29]

Section 5. *Closing of Transfer Books or Fixing of Record Date.* For the purpose of determining shareholders entitled to notice of or to vote at any meeting of shareholders or any adjournment thereof, or shareholders entitled to receive payment of any dividend, or in order to make a determination of shareholders for any other proper purpose, the board of directors of the corporation may provide that the stock transfer books shall be closed for a stated period but not to exceed, in any case, fifty days. If the stock transfer books shall be closed for the purpose of determining shareholders entitled to notice of or to vote at a meeting of shareholders, such books shall be closed for at least ten days immediately preceding such meeting. In lieu of closing the stock transfer books, the board of directors may fix in advance a date as the record date for any such determination of shareholders, such date in any case to be not more than fifty days and, in case of a meeting of shareholders, not less than ten days prior to the date on which the particular action, requiring such determination of shareholders, is to be taken. If the stock transfer books are not closed and no record date is fixed for the determination of shareholders entitled to notice of or to vote at a meeting of shareholders, or shareholders entitled to receive payment of a dividend, the date on which notice of the meeting is mailed or the date on which the resolution of the board of directors declaring such dividend is adopted, as the case may be, shall be the record date for such determination of shareholders. When a determination of shareholders entitled to vote at any meeting of shareholders has been made as provided in this section, such determination shall apply in any adjournment thereof. [§ 30]

Section 6. *Voting Record.* The officer or agent having charge of the stock transfer books for shares of the corporation shall make a complete record of the shareholders entitled to vote at each meeting of shareholders or any adjournment thereof arranged in alphabetical order, with the address of and the number of shares held by each. Such record shall be produced and kept open at the time and place of meeting and shall be subject to the inspection of any shareholder during the whole time of the meeting for the purposes thereof. [§ 31]

Section 7. *Quorum.* A majority of the outstanding shares of the corporation entitled to vote, represented in person or by proxy, shall constitute a quorum at a meeting of shareholders. If less than a majority of the outstanding shares are represented at a meeting, a majority of the shares so represented may adjourn the meeting from time to time without further notice. At such adjourned meeting at which a quorum shall be present or represented, any business may be transacted which might have been transacted at the meeting as originally noticed. The shareholders present at a duly organized meeting may continue to transact business until adjournment, notwithstanding the withdrawal of enough shareholders to leave less than a quorum. [§ 32]

Section 8. *Proxies.* At all meetings of shareholders, a shareholder may vote in person or by proxy executed in writing by the shareholder or by his duly authorized attorney in fact. Such proxy shall be filed with the secretary of the corporation before or at the time of the meeting. No proxy shall be valid after eleven months from the date of its execution, unless otherwise provided in the proxy. [§ 33]

Section 9. *Voting of Shares.* Subject to the provisions of Section 12 of this Article II, each outstanding share entitled to vote shall be entitled to one vote upon each matter submitted to a vote at a meeting of shareholders. [§ 33]

Section 10. *Voting of Shares by Certain Holders.* Shares standing in the name of another corporation may be  voted by such officer, agent or proxy as the by-laws of such corporation may prescribe, or, in the absence of such provision, as the board of directors of such other corporation may determine. [§ 33]

Shares held by an administrator, executor, guardian or conservator may be voted by him, either in person or by proxy, without a transfer of such shares into his name.

Shares standing in the name of a trustee may be voted by him, either in person or by proxy, but no trustee shall be entitled to vote shares held by him without a transfer of such shares into his name. [§ 33]

Shares standing in the name of a receiver may be voted by such receiver, and shares held by or under the control of a receiver may be voted by such receiver without the transfer thereof into his name if authority so to do be contained in an appropriate order of the court by which such receiver was appointed. [§ 33]

A shareholder whose shares are pledged shall be entitled to vote such shares until the shares have been transferred into the name of the pledgee, and thereafter the pledgee shall be entitled to vote the shares so transferred. [§ 33]

Neither treasury shares of its own stock held by the corporation, nor shares held by another corporation if a majority of the shares entitled to vote for the election of directors of such other corporation are held by the corporation, shall be voted at any meeting or counted in determining the total number of outstanding shares at any given time for purposes of any meeting. [§ 33]

Section 11. *Informal Action by Shareholders.* Any action required or permitted to be taken at a meeting of the shareholders may be taken without a meeting if a consent in writing, setting forth the action so taken, shall be signed by all of the shareholders entitled to vote with respect to the subject matter thereof. [§ 145]

[Optional Section.] Section 12. *Cumulative Voting.* At each election for directors every shareholder entitled to vote at such election shall have the right to vote, in person or by proxy, the number of shares owned by him for as many persons as there are directors to be elected and for whose election he has a right to vote, or to cumulate his votes by giving one candidate as many votes as the number of such directors multiplied by the number of his shares shall equal, or by distributing such votes on the same principle among any number of such candidates. [§ 33]

### Article III. Board of Directors

Section 1. *General Powers.* The business and affairs of the corporation shall be managed by its board of directors. [§ 35]

Section 2. *Number, Tenure and Qualifications.* The number of directors of the corporation shall be _____. Each director shall hold office until the next annual meeting of shareholders and until his successor shall have been elected and qualified.  Directors need not be residents of the State of ———— or shareholders of the corporation.  [§ 35, § 36]

Section 3.  *Regular Meetings.*  A regular meeting of the board of directors shall be held without other notice than this by-law immediately after, and at the same place as, the annual meeting of shareholders.  The board of directors may provide, by resolution, the time and place, either within or without the State of ————, for the holding of additional regular meetings without other notice than such resolution.  [§ 43]

Section 4.  *Special Meetings.*  Special meetings of the board of directors may be called by or at the request of the president or any two directors.  The person or persons authorized to call special meetings of the board of directors may fix any place, either within or without the State of ————, as the place for holding any special meeting of the board of directors called by them.  [§ 43]

Section 5.  *Notice.*  Notice of any special meeting shall be given at least two days previously thereto by written notice delivered personally or mailed to each director at his business address, or by telegram.  If mailed, such notice shall be deemed to be delivered when deposited in the United States mail, so addressed, with postage thereon prepaid.  If notice be given by telegram, such notice shall be deemed to be delivered when the telegram is delivered to the telegraph company.  Any director may waive notice of any meeting.  The attendance of a director at a meeting shall constitute a waiver of notice of such meeting, except where a director attends a meeting for the express purpose of objecting to the transaction of any business because the meeting is not lawfully called or convened.  Neither the business to be transacted at, nor the purpose of, any regular or special meeting of the board of directors need be specified in the notice or waiver of notice of such meeting.  [§ 43]

Section 6.  *Quorum.*  A majority of the number of directors fixed by Section 2 of this Article III shall constitute a quorum for the transaction of business at any meeting of the board of directors, but if less than such majority is present at a meeting, a majority of the directors present may adjourn the meeting from time to time without further notice.  [§ 40]

Section 7.  *Manner of Acting.*  The act of the majority of the directors present at a meeting at which a quorum is present shall be the act of the board of directors.  [§ 40]

Section 8. *Action Without a Meeting.* Any action required or permitted to be taken by the board of directors at a meeting may be taken without a meeting if a consent in writing, setting forth the action so taken, shall be signed by all of the directors. [§ 44]

Section 9. *Vacancies.* Any vacancy occurring in the board of directors may be filled by the affirmative vote of a majority of the remaining directors though less than a quorum of the board of directors. A director elected to fill a vacancy shall be elected for the unexpired term of his predecessor in office. Any directorship to be filled by reason of an increase in the number of directors may be filled by election by the board of directors for a term of office continuing only until the next election of directors by the shareholders. [§ 38]

Section 10. *Compensation.* By resolution of the board of directors, each director may be paid his expenses, if any, of attendance at each meeting of the board of directors, and may be paid a stated salary as director or a fixed sum for attendance at each meeting of the board of directors or both. No such payment shall preclude any director from serving the corporation in any other capacity and receiving compensation therefor. [§ 35]

Section 11. *Presumption of Assent.* A director of the corporation who is present at a meeting of the board of directors at which action on any corporate matter is taken shall be presumed to have assented to the action taken unless his dissent shall be entered in the minutes of the meeting or unless he shall file his written dissent to such action with the person acting as the secretary of the meeting before the adjournment thereof or shall forward such dissent by registered mail to the secretary of the corporation immediately after the adjournment of the meeting. Such right to dissent shall not apply to a director who voted in favor of such action. [§ 48]

### Article IV. Officers

Section 1. *Number.* The officers of the corporation shall be a president, one or more vice-presidents (the number thereof to be determined by the board of directors), a secretary, and a treasurer, each of whom shall be elected by the board of directors. Such other officers and assistant officers as may be deemed necessary may be elected or appointed by the board of directors. Any two or more offices may be held by the same person, except the offices of president and secretary. [§ 50]

Section 2. *Election and Term of Office.* The officers of the corporation to be elected by the board of directors shall be elected annually by the board of directors at the first meeting of the board of directors held after each annual meeting of the shareholders. If the election of officers shall not be held at such meeting, such election shall be held as soon thereafter as conveniently may be. Each officer shall hold office until his successor shall have been duly elected and shall have qualified or until his death or until he shall resign or shall have been removed in the manner hereinafter provided. [§ 50]

Section 3. *Removal.* Any officer or agent may be removed by the board of directors whenever in its judgment, the best interests of the corporation will be served thereby, but such removal shall be without prejudice to the contract rights, if any, of the person so removed. Election or appointment of an officer or agent shall not of itself create contract rights. [§ 51]

Section 4. *Vacancies.* A vacancy in any office because of death, resignation, removal, disqualification or otherwise, may be filled by the board of directors for the unexpired portion of the term. [§ 50]

Section 5. *President.* The president shall be the principal executive officer of the corporation and, subject to the control of the board of directors, shall in general supervise and control all of the business and affairs of the corporation. He shall, when present, preside at all meetings of the shareholders and of the board of directors. He may sign, with the secretary or any other proper officer of the corporation thereunto authorized by the board of directors, certificates for shares of the corporation any deeds, mortgages, bonds, contracts, or other instruments which the board of directors has authorized to be executed, except in cases where the signing and execution thereof shall be expressly delegated by the board of directors or by these By-Laws to some other officer or agent of the corporation, or shall be required by law to be otherwise signed or executed; and in general shall perform all duties incident to the office of president and such other duties as may be prescribed by the board of directors from time to time. [§ 23, § 50]

Section 6. *The Vice-Presidents.* In the absence of the president or in the event of his death, inability or refusal to act, the vice-president (or in the event there be more than one vice-president, the vice-presidents in the order designated at the time of their election, or in the absence of any designation, then in the order of their election) shall perform the duties of the president, and when so acting, shall have all the powers of and be subject to all the restrictions upon the president. Any vice-president may sign, with the secretary or an assistant secretary, certificates for shares of the corporation; and shall perform such other duties as from time to time may be assigned to him by the president or by the board of directors. [§ 23, § 50]

Section 7. *The Secretary.* The secretary shall: (a) keep the minutes of the proceedings of the shareholders and of the board of directors in one or more books provided for that purpose; (b) see that all notices are duly given in accordance with the provisions of these By-Laws or as required by law; (c) be custodian of the corporate records and of the seal of the corporation and see that the seal of the corporation is affixed to all documents the execution of which on behalf of the corporation under its seal is duly authorized; (d) keep a register of the post office address of each shareholder which shall be furnished to the secretary by such shareholder; (e) sign with the president, or a vice-president, certificates for shares of the corporation, the issuance of which shall have been authorized by resolution of the board of directors; (f) have general charge of the stock transfer books of the corporation; and (g) in general perform all duties incident to the office of secretary and such other duties as from time to time may be assigned to him by the president or by the board of directors. [§ 23, § 31, § 50, § 52]

Section 8. *The Treasurer.* The treasurer shall: (a) have charge and custody of and be responsible for all funds and securities of the corporation; (b) receive and give receipts for moneys due and payable to the corporation from any source whatsoever, and deposit all such moneys in the name of the corporation in such banks, trust companies or other depositaries as shall be selected in accordance with the provisions of Article V of these By-Laws; and (c) in general perform all of the duties incident to the office of treasurer and such other duties as from time to time may be assigned to him by the president or by the board of directors. If required by the board of directors, the treasurer shall give a bond for the faithful discharge of his duties in such sum and with such surety or sureties as the board of directors shall determine. [§ 50]

Section 9. *Assistant Secretaries and Assistant Treasurers.* The assistant secretaries, when authorized by the board of directors, may sign with the president or a vice-president certificates for shares of the corporation the issuance of which shall have been authorized by a resolution of the board of directors. The assistant treasurers shall respectively, if required by the board of directors, give bonds for the faithful discharge of their duties in such sums and with such sureties as the board of directors shall determine. The assistant secretaries and assistant treasurers, in general, shall perform such duties as shall be assigned to them by the secretary or the treasurer, respectively, or by the president or the board of directors. [§ 23, § 50]

Section 10. *Salaries.* The salaries of the officers shall be fixed from time to time by the board of directors and no officer shall be prevented from receiving such salary by reason of the fact that he is also a director of the corporation. [§ 2(k), § 35]

### Article V. Contracts, Loans, Checks and Deposits

Section 1. *Contracts.* The board of directors may authorize any officer or officers, agent or agents, to enter into any contract or execute and deliver any instrument in the name of and on behalf of the corporation, and such authority may be general or confined to specific instances. [§ 4(g), § 35]

Section 2. *Loans.* No loans shall be contracted on behalf of the corporation and no evidences of indebtedness shall be issued in its name unless authorized by a resolution of the board of directors. Such authority may be general or confined to specific instances. [§ 4(h), § 35]

Section 3. *Checks, Drafts, etc.* All checks, drafts or other orders for the payment of money, notes or other evidences of indebtedness issued in the name of the corporation, shall be signed by such officer or officers, agent or agents of the corporation and in such manner as shall from time to time be determined by resolution of the board of directors. [§ 35]

Section 4. *Deposits.* All funds of the corporation not otherwise employed shall be deposited from time to time to the credit of the corporation in such banks, trust companies or other depositaries as the board of directors may select. [§ 35]

### Article VI. Certificates for Shares and Their Transfer

Section 1. *Certificates for Shares.* Certificates representing shares of the corporation shall be in such form as shall be determined by the board of directors. Such certificates shall be signed by the president or a vice-president and by the secretary or an assistant secretary and sealed with the corporate seal or a facsimile thereof. The signatures of such officers upon a certificate may be facsimiles if the certificate is manually signed on behalf of a transfer agent or a registrar, other than the corporation itself or one of its employees. Each certificate for shares shall be consecutively numbered or otherwise identified. The name and address of the person to whom the shares represented thereby are issued, with the number of shares and date of issue, shall be entered on the stock transfer books of the corporation. All certificates surrendered to the corporation for transfer shall be cancelled and no new certificate shall be issued until the former certificate for a like number of shares shall have been surrendered and cancelled, except that in case of a lost, destroyed or mutilated certificate a new one may be issued therefor upon such terms and indemnity to the corporation as the board of directors may prescribe. [§ 23, § 52]

Section 2. *Transfer of Shares.* Transfer of shares of the corporation shall be made only on the stock transfer books of the corporation by the holder of record thereof or by his legal representative, who shall furnish proper evidence of authority to transfer, or by his attorney thereunto authorized by power of attorney duly executed and filed with the secretary of the corporation, and on surrender for cancellation of the certificate for such shares. The person in whose name shares stand on the books of the corporation shall be deemed by the corporation to be the owner thereof for all purposes. [§ 23]

### Article VII.  Fiscal Year

The fiscal year of the corporation shall begin on the first day of January and end on the thirty-first day of December in each year. [§ 2]

### Article VIII.  Dividends

The board of directors may, from time to time, declare and the corporation may pay dividends on its outstanding shares in the manner, and upon the terms and conditions provided by law and its Articles of Incorporation. [§ 45]

### Article IX.  Corporate Seal

The board of directors shall provide a corporate seal which shall be circular in form and shall have inscribed thereon the name of the corporation and the state of incorporation and the words, "Corporate Seal". [§ 4(c)]

### Article X.  Waiver of Notice

Whenever any notice is required to be given to any shareholder or director of the corporation under the provisions of these By-Laws or under the provisions of the Articles of Incorporation or under the provisions of the _____ Business Corporation Act, a waiver thereof in writing signed by the person or persons entitled to such notice, whether before or after the time stated therein, shall be deemed equivalent to the giving of such notice. [§ 144]

### Article XI. Amendments *with Notice*

These By-Laws may be altered, amended or repealed and new By-Laws may be adopted by the board of directors or by the shareholders at any regular or special meeting. [§ 27]

### [Optional] Article XII. Executive Committee — *Outside of Board & Directors*

Section 1. *Appointment.* The board of directors by resolution adopted by a majority of the full board, may designate two or more of its members to constitute an executive committee. The designation of such committee and the delegation thereto of authority shall not operate to relieve the board of directors, or any member thereof, of any responsibility imposed by law. [§ 42]

Section 2. *Authority.* The executive committee, when the board of directors is not in session shall have and may exercise all of the authority of the board of directors except to the extent, if any, that such authority shall be limited by the resolution appointing the executive committee and except also that the executive committee shall not have the authority of the board of directors in reference to amending the articles of incorporation, adopting a plan of merger or consolidation, recommending to the shareholders the sale, lease or other disposition of all or substantially all of the property and assets of the corporation otherwise than in the usual and regular course of its business, recommending to the shareholders a voluntary dissolution of the corporation or a revocation thereof, or amending the By-Laws of the corporation. [§ 42]

Section 3. *Tenure and Qualifications.* Each member of the executive committee shall hold office until the next regular annual meeting of the board of directors following his designation and until his successor is designated as a member of the executive committee and is elected and qualified. [§ 42]

Section 4. *Meetings.* Regular meetings of the executive committee may be held without notice at such times and places as the executive committee may fix from time to time by resolution. Special meetings of the executive committee may be called by any member thereof upon not less than one day's notice stating the place, date and hour of the meeting, which notice may be written or oral, and if mailed, shall be deemed to be delivered when deposited in the United States mail addressed to the member of the executive committee at his business address. Any member of the executive committee may waive notice of any meeting and no notice of any meeting need be given to any member thereof who attends in person. The notice of a meeting of the executive committee need not state the business proposed to be transacted at the meeting. [§ 42, § 144]

Section 5. *Quorum.* A majority of the members of the executive committee shall constitute a quorum for the transaction of business at any meeting thereof and action of the executive committee must be authorized by the affirmative vote of a majority of the members present at a meeting at which a quorum is present. [§ 42]

Section 6. *Action Without a Meeting.* Any action required or permitted to be taken by the executive committee at a meeting may be taken without a meeting if a consent in writing, setting forth the action so taken, shall be signed by all of the members of the executive committee. [§ 44]

Section 7. *Vacancies.* Any vacancy in the executive committee may be filled by a resolution adopted by a majority of the full board of directors. [§ 42]

Section 8. *Resignations and Removal.* Any member of the executive committee may be removed at any time with or without cause by resolution adopted by a majority of the full board of directors. Any member of the executive committee may resign from the executive committee at any time by giving written notice to the president or secretary of the corporation, and unless otherwise specified therein, the acceptance of such resignation shall not be necessary to make it effective. [§ 42]

Section 9. *Procedure.* The executive committee shall elect a presiding officer from its members and may fix its own rules of procedure which shall not be inconsistent with these By-Laws. It shall keep regular minutes of its proceedings and report the same to the board of directors for its information at the meeting thereof held next after the proceedings shall have been taken. [§ 42]

### Article XIII.  Emergency By-Laws [§ 27A]

The Emergency By-Laws provided in this Article XIII shall be operative during any emergency in the conduct of the business of the corporation resulting from an attack on the United States or any nuclear or atomic disaster, notwithstanding any different provision in the preceding Articles of the By-Laws or in the Articles of Incorporation of the corporation or in the _____ Business Corporation Act. To the extent not inconsistent with the provisions of this Article, the By-Laws provided in the preceding Articles shall remain in effect during such emergency and upon its termination the Emergency By-Laws shall cease to be operative.

During any such emergency:

(a) A meeting of the board of directors may be called by any officer or director of the corporation. Notice of the time and place of the meeting shall be given by the person calling the meeting to such of the directors as it may be feasible to reach by any available means of communication. Such notice shall be given at such time in advance of the meeting as circumstances permit in the judgment of the person calling the meeting.

(b) At any such meeting of the board of directors, a quorum shall consist of _____ [here insert the particular provisions desired].

(c) The board of directors, either before or during any such emergency, may provide, and from time to time modify, lines of succession in the event that during such an emergency any or all officers or agents of the corporation shall for any reason be rendered incapable of discharging their duties.

(d) The board of directors, either before or during any such emergency, may, effective in the emergency, change the head office or designate several alternative head offices or regional offices, or authorize the officers so to do.

No officer, director or employee acting in accordance with these Emergency By-Laws shall be liable except for willful misconduct.

These Emergency By-Laws shall be subject to repeal or change by further action of the board of directors or by action of the shareholders, but no such repeal or change shall modify the provisions of the next preceding paragraph with regard to action taken prior to the time of such repeal or change. Any amendment of these Emergency By-Laws may make any further or different provision that may be practical and necessary for the circumstances of the emergency.

---

It is a matter of judgment by the lawyer as to whether a long form or a short form is used. The paralegal should be able to understand both types and know how to modify them for a specific new corporation.

Chapter Three

# QUALIFICATION OF CORPORATIONS IN FOREIGN JURISDICTIONS

## I. INTRODUCTION

A corporation, depending upon the nature of its activities, may not confine its business to the state of its incorporation. In some instances the state of incorporation may have been chosen for reasons totally unrelated to the company's activities, such as favorable corporate statutes or tax laws, and no business will be conducted there. This fact is emphasized when we consider that approximately one-third of the largest corporations in the United States are Delaware corporations. Yet such corporations may conduct little or no business in Delaware. When a corporation conducts affairs outside of the state of its incorporation, the question arises as to what additional requirements are imposed upon such corporations by states other than the state of incorporation. Such states are normally referred to as "foreign jurisdictions", and a corporation which was not incorporated under the laws of that state is normally referred to as a "foreign corporation" with respect to such state.[1]

When can a state regulate, control or tax a foreign corporation? The simple answer is when the corporation is "doing business" in that state. Unfortunately there is no simple definition of what constitutes "doing business" in a foreign jurisdiction. Each state differs as to the definition. In addition, the definition may vary within a single state depending upon the nature of the statutes and court decisions. "Doing business" may also mean one thing if the issue is the ability of a state to tax a foreign corporation and quite another if the issue is whether a resident of the foreign state may sue the corporation in the courts of that state.

### QUESTION

Which do you think would require a greater degree of "doing business" in a state—a corporation's subjection to taxation or to suit in that state's courts?

Statutory law may not define the term "doing business". Therefore a corporation seldom has a clear idea when it must obtain a certificate to conduct its business in the state, a procedure known as "qualifying" as a foreign corporation. Typically, the applicable law will make a general statement that it covers all foreign corporations

---

1. A corporation that is incorporated in a specific state is said to be a domestic corporation with respect to that state.

"doing" or "transacting" business within its boundaries, and then list several exclusions from such terms.[2]

Because of the difficult legal issues involved in describing "doing business", no attempt is made in these materials to give this concept a complete definition. A lawyer will make the decision as to whether qualification is necessary. The Supreme Court of the United States has wrestled with the problem on many occasions and in several different contexts, but the definition is still far from settled. It is sufficient to recognize the definitional problem and turn to an analysis of what requirements are imposed on foreign corporations, assuming that a determination has been made that the foreign corporation is "doing business" within the meaning of the corporate laws of a particular state.

### QUESTION

**If there is a doubt as to the need to qualify, why would a corporation be reluctant to do so even if the "safer" course would be to qualify?**

Because a decision to qualify as a foreign corporation in a jurisdiction imposes obligations on the corporation, including compliance with the laws of the foreign state, the board of directors of the corporation normally must approve such a qualification. This is so even though a corporation, by virtue of its "doing business" in a foreign jurisdiction, is required by the laws of that state to qualify as a foreign corporation.

A typical resolution of the board of directors of a corporation, approving such qualification, is as follows:

RESOLVED, that this Company qualify as a foreign corporation under the laws of the State of Connecticut; that the President or any Vice President, and the Secretary or any Assistant Secretary of this Company be and each of them is hereby authorized and empowered to execute, verify and deliver such documents and certificates, to pay all fees and charges and to take any other action as may be necessary or desirable in connection with the qualification of this Company as a foreign corporation under the laws of the State of Connecticut.

## II.  QUALIFICATION

### A.  APPLICATION FOR CERTIFICATE OF AUTHORITY

A foreign corporation is not permitted to transact business within a state until it has obtained a certificate of authority or qualifica-

---

**2.** See Section 106 of the MBCA, for example.

**QUESTIONS: Does the opening of a checking account in an MBCA-type** state require a corporation to qualify to do business? Holding shareholders' or directors' meetings? Issuing a promissory note to a creditor?

tion to do so. The procedure for qualification is very similar to that of incorporation in most states.

## QUESTIONS

Do individuals or partnerships have to qualify to do business in a state other than that of formation? Why or why not?

Section 110 of the MBCA describes the normal type of requirements imposed on a corporation to obtain a certificate.

## PROBLEM

Review this Section against the MBCA requirements for incorporation of a domestic corporation (Sections 8, 12 and 54) to identify similarities and differences between them.

Normally, an application for a certificate of authority must be accompanied by (a) the corporation's articles of incorporation and all amendments to the articles, duly authenticated or certified by the appropriate official of the state of incorporation of the foreign corporation,[3] (b) certificate attesting as to the existence and good standing of the foreign corporation from the state of its incorporation [4] and (c) the applicable fees and franchise taxes which are payable upon such qualification. The form of application is invariably provided by the state.

## B. FORM OF APPLICATION

Some states may require more than one form to be filed in connection with the application for qualification.[5] A sample of a Pennsylvania application follows:

**EXAMPLE—Application for Certificate of Authority**

COMMONWEALTH OF PENNSYLVANIA
DEPARTMENT OF STATE
CORPORATION BUREAU

APPLICATION FOR
CERTIFICATE OF AUTHORITY

1. The name of the corporation is
FUN CITY MARKETING, INC.

3. **QUESTION: What state official would be the usual certifying authority?**

4. **QUESTION: Who would ordinarily provide such a certificate? Does it cost anything?**

5. In Pennsylvania, for example, it is necessary to submit both an application for a certificate of authority as well as a registry statement. See Section 1004 of the Pennsylvania Business Corporation Law and Section III.A of Chapter Two for an example of a registry statement.

2. The name of the State or Country under the laws of which the corporation was formed is:
   DELAWARE

3. The address of its principal office in said State or Country is:
   4455 MAIN STREET
   DOVER, DELAWARE

4. The address of its proposed registered office within the Commonwealth of Pennsylvania is:
   1700 MARKET STREET
   PHILADELPHIA, PENNSYLVANIA   19103

5. The said corporation designates the Secretary of the Commonwealth of Pennsylvania, and his successor in office, as its true and lawful attorney upon whom all lawful process in any action or proceeding against it may be served, and agrees that service of process upon the Secretary of the Commonwealth shall be of the same legal force and validity as if served on the corporation, and that the authority for such service of process shall continue in force as long as any liability remains outstanding against the corporation in this Commonwealth.

6. The character and nature of the business the corporation proposes to do within this Commonwealth, said business being authorized by its Articles as the same remain of record in its state of incorporation is: to engage in the sale of franchises for amusement centers and to supply such franchises with equipment, supplies and management assistance.

7. The said corporation is duly incorporated for a purpose or purposes involving pecuniary profit, incidental or otherwise, to its shareholders.

   IN WITNESS WHEREOF, the applicant has caused this Application to be signed by its President or Vice President and its corporate seal, duly attested by its Secretary or Treasurer, to be hereunto affixed this 15th day of May, 19__.

                              FUN CITY MARKETING, INC.

[*Corporate Seal*]     By: /s/John Doe
                           _____
                           President
                    Attest: /s/Jane Doe
                           _____
                           Secretary

Approved and filed in the Department of State on _____ 19__.

                           _____
                           Secretary of the Commonwealth

**EXAMPLE: Registry Statement**

## REGISTRY STATEMENT

TO THE COMMONWEALTH OF PENNSYLVANIA
DEPARTMENT OF STATE
CORPORATION BUREAU
HARRISBURG, PENNSYLVANIA              May 15, 19__

In compliance with the requirements of the Business Corporation Law, approved May 5, 1933, P.L. 364, as amended, the following information concerning the Corporation hereinafter named is hereby certified for registration:

1.  Name of Corporation: FUN CITY MARKETING, INC.

2.  Address to which Corporation desires correspondence to be directed by Department of Revenue and other Commonwealth agencies:

    1700 MARKET STREET, PHILADELPHIA, PENNSYLVANIA 19103

3.  Date of incorporation: January 1, 19__

4.  Act of Assembly or authority under which incorporated:

    DELAWARE BUSINESS CORPORATION LAW

5.  Kind or kinds of business the Corporation intends to engage in this Commonwealth within one year from execution of this registry statement:

    SALE OF FRANCHISES FOR AMUSEMENT CENTERS AND TO SUPPLY SUCH FRANCHISES WITH EQUIPMENT, SUPPLIES AND MANAGEMENT ASSISTANCE.

6.  Name and residence address of its Treasurer:

    MARY M. AJAX, 4 WOODED LANE, BRYN MAWR, PENNSYLVANIA

7.  Text of purposes as stated in its Articles:

    TO ENGAGE IN ALL LAWFUL FORMS OF BUSINESS ACTIVITY AS PERMITTED BY THE DELAWARE BUSINESS CORPORATION LAW.

[*Corporation Seal*]

_____

President or Vice President

_____

Secretary or Treasurer

A sample form of an application for Certificate of Authority under the MBCA is set forth below:

**EXAMPLE—Application for Certificate of Authority**

Filing fee: $_____

APPLICATION FOR

CERTIFICATE OF AUTHORITY

OF

_____

To the Secretary of State

    of the State of _____ :

    Pursuant to to the provisions of Section 110 of the _____ Business Corporation Act, the undersigned corporation hereby applies for a Certificate of Authority to transact business in your State, and for that purpose submits the following statement:

    FIRST: The name of the corporation is _____.

    SECOND: The name which elects to use in your State is _____ (Note 1).

    THIRD: It is incorporated under the laws of _____.

    FOURTH: The date of its incorporation is _____ and the period of its duration is _____.

    FIFTH: The address of its principal office in the state or country under the laws of which it is incorporated is _____.

    SIXTH: The address of its proposed registered office in your State is _____, and the name of its proposed registered agent in your State at that address is _____.

    SEVENTH: The purpose or purposes which it proposes to pursue in the transaction of business in your State are _____.

EIGHTH: The names and respective addresses of its directors and officers are:

| Name | Office | Address |
|------|--------|---------|
| ———————— | ———————— | ———————— |
| ———————— | ———————— | ———————— |
| ———————— | ———————— | ———————— |
| ———————— | ———————— | ———————— |
| ———————— | ———————— | ———————— |
| ———————— | ———————— | ———————— |
| ———————— | ———————— | ———————— |

NINTH: The aggregate number of shares which it has authority to issue, itemized by classes, par value of shares, shares without par value, and series, if any, within a class, is:

| Number of Shares | Class Series | Par Value per Share or Statement that Shares are without Par Value |
|------|------|------|

TENTH: The aggregate number of its issued shares, itemized by classes, par value of shares, shares without par value, and series, if any, within a class, is:

| Number of Shares | Class | Series | Par Value per Share or Statement that Shares are without Par Value |
|------|------|------|------|

ELEVENTH: The amount of its stated capital, as defined in the ———— Business Corporation Act, is $————.

TWELFTH: An estimate of the value of all property to be owned by it for the following year, wherever located, is $————.

THIRTEENTH: An estimate of the value of its property to be located within your State during such year is $————.

FOURTEENTH: An estimate of the gross amount of business to be transacted by it during such year is $————.

FIFTEENTH: An estimate of the gross amount of business to be transacted by it at or from places of business in your State during such year is $————.

SIXTEENTH: This Application is accompanied by a copy of its articles of incorporation and all amendments thereto, duly authenticated by the proper officer of the state or county under the laws of which it is incorporated.

Dated _____, 19\_\_.

_____ (Note 2)

By _____

Its _____ President

and _____    (Note 3)

Its _____ Secretary

(Add Verification Form A)

Notes: 1.   If the name of the corporation does not contain the word "corporation," "company," "incorporated," or "limited," or an abbreviation of one of such words, insert the name of the corporation with the word of abbreviation which it elects to add thereto for use in this State.

2.   Exact corporate name of corporation making the application.

3.   Signatures and titles of officers signing for the corporation.

In contrast to the requirements of the MBCA, some states do not require the designation of a registered agent in an application for a certificate of authority. However, they may require a registered office. In order, however, to provide a method by which lawsuits may be initiated against a foreign corporation registered in such a state, the law requires the application for the certificate of authority to provide for the designation of the secretary of the state as its agent upon whom service of process may be served. The form above provides for such a designation.

Once a certificate of authority is issued, the foreign corporation is given certain rights to operate in the state:

"Upon the issuance of a certificate of authority by the Secretary of State, the corporation shall be authorized to transact business in this State for those purposes set forth in its application, subject, however, to the right of this State to suspend or to revoke such authority as provided in this Act."

Section 112, MBCA.

A copy of the certificate of authority recommended by the MBCA appears as below:

**EXAMPLE—Certificate of Authority**

STATE OF _____

OFFICE OF THE SECRETARY OF STATE

CERTIFICATE OF AUTHORITY

OF

_____

The undersigned, as Secretary of State of the State of _____, hereby certifies that duplicate originals of an Application of _____ for a Certificate of Authority to transact business in this State, duly signed and verified pursuant to the provisions of the _____ Business Corporation Act, have been received in this office and are found to conform to law.

ACCORDINGLY the undersigned, as such Secretary of State, and by virtue of the authority vested in him by law, hereby issues this Certificate of Authority to _____, to transact business in this State under the name of _____ and attaches hereto a duplicate original of the Application for such Certificate.

Dated _____, 19__

_____
Secretary of State

The certificate of authority should be filed in the minute book of the corporation.

## C.  NAME

As discussed above,[6] most state laws control the name that may be used by a foreign corporation by restricting the issuance of a certificate of authority in a manner similar to that of Section 108 of the MBCA.

### PROBLEMS

**What MBCA procedures allow a foreign corporation with a deceptively similar name to a domestic corporation to obtain a certificate of authority?  What does the name limitation indicate that a paralegal must do if it is known that a corporation being incorporated must immediately qualify in other states?**

Similarly, a foreign corporation is not permitted to change its name, unless the new name would also be acceptable under state law as in the MBCA provision at Section 109.

**6.** See Section II.B of Chapter Two.

Since corporations with identical names can create unnecessary problems of confusion in taxing and regulatory authorities, it is obvious why state law attempts to control the names used by both domestic and foreign corporations. For a corporation which plans to conduct a business in many states, such controls pose a serious problem. A corporation must (a) determine if its name is available in every state in which it may decide to transact business, and (b) reserve its name in states in which it is currently not transacting business. Normally, the availability of a name can be checked by contacting the Department of State or the Secretary of State of each state in question directly or by having CT Corporation System, United States Corporation Company, or an equivalent organization conduct the check through its branch offices in each state. Reserving a name is a more difficult process. Many states have a procedure, either formally embodied in a statute [7] or established by administrative practice, to permit the reservation of a name. These procedures normally permit reservation of a name for a limited period of time (e. g., not more than 3 or 6 months).

### QUESTION

**How long a period of time is a reservation effective under the MBCA?**

Corporations are therefore confronted with the alternatives of (a) doing nothing, in the hope that no one else will preempt a particular name, (b) attempting to qualify as a foreign corporation, even if no business activity is contemplated at present in a particular state, or (c) creating a "name-holding" corporation in the state in question whose only purpose is to protect the availability of a name. The statutes and administrative procedures of states vary on the question of whether a foreign corporation may qualify without intending in the near future to transact any business within the state. Particular care must be taken before deciding that a corporation should qualify in a foreign jurisdiction simply as a means of reserving a corporate name. As will be shown below, the obligations imposed upon foreign corporations are considerable, and qualification is not a step to be taken casually.

### D.   REGISTERED OFFICE

The application for a certificate of authority requires information concerning the foreign corporation's registered office and, if required, a registered agent in such state.[8] In effect, state law requires the "presence" of the foreign corporation in its jurisdiction.[9]

7. See, e.g., Section 9 of the MBCA and Section II.C of Chapter Two.

8. Compare this requirement to similar requirements of incorporation.

9. See Section 113 of the MBCA.

Changes in the registered office or registered agent of a foreign corporation require appropriate notification to the state as in the MBCA example at Section 114.

## QUESTIONS

How is a registered agent for a foreign corporation terminated under the MBCA? How does a registered agent of a foreign corporation change an address?

Often, a foreign corporation desiring to qualify in a given state will not have an office or an employee in the state suitable to act as its registered office or registered agent. For this reason, as well as for reasons of administrative convenience, a corporation often uses specialized companies, such as CT Corporation System and United States Corporation Company, to serve as its registered office and agent within foreign jurisdictions.

## E. ADVERTISEMENT

As is true of initial incorporations,[10] many state laws require a foreign business corporation to advertise its intention to apply for a certificate of authority. Under the Pennsylvania Business Corporation Act, the advertising requirements are imposed upon a foreign corporation which are similar to those for initial incorporations.

Under the Pennsylvania statute, a typical form of advertisement would be as follows:

Fun City, Inc., a Delaware corporation, with its principal office in Delaware at 120 Main Street, Wilmington, Delaware, has applied for a certificate of authority under the provisions of the Pennsylvania Business Corporation Act, Act of May 5, 1933, P.L. 364, as amended, by the filing of an application for a certificate of authority with the Department of State of the Commonwealth of Pennsylvania of June 1, 19___.

The proposed registered office of Fun City, Inc., in the Commonwealth of Pennsylvania is 1700 Market Street, Philadelphia, Pennsylvania.

Fun City, Inc., proposes to operate one or more amusement parks in the Commonwealth of Pennsylvania.

The method of placing such an advertisement in the appropriate newspaper or newspapers and the proper procedure for obtaining proof of publication of such advertisement is identical with that which has been discussed under the advertisement requirements for an initial incorporation. The proof of publication is to be placed by the paralegal in the corporate minute book.

10. See Section III.B of Chapter Two.

## III. CONSEQUENCES OF QUALIFICATION AS A FOREIGN CORPORATION

### A. SERVICE OF PROCESS

Once a foreign corporation is qualified in a given state, its registered agent, if one is specified in its application, may be served as an agent of the corporation with any process, notice or demand required or permitted to be served by law. In effect, this means that a qualified foreign corporation becomes subject to the jurisdiction of the courts in the states in which it has qualified.

Some states provide, in addition to or in lieu of the use of a registered agent, for service of process on a foreign corporation to be accomplished by serving the Secretary of that State.[11]

### QUESTIONS

Is the possibility of subjection to a lawsuit in a foreign jurisdiction a consideration for not qualifying if there is a close question as to whether qualification is necessary? Why or why not? Is it possible that a corporation may be sued in a foreign jurisdiction even if it has not qualified?

### B. ANNUAL REPORTS

A foreign corporation qualified to do business in a state is normally required to file an annual report with the state.[12]

The basic function of the annual report filed by a foreign corporation is to supply the state with enough information to determine the amount of state taxes which should be paid. The form is normally supplied by the state and is required to be filed within a specific period of time after the end of the appropriate calendar of fiscal year.[13] A sample form of such a report appears below:

**EXAMPLE—Annual Report of Foreign Corporation**

ANNUAL REPORT

OF

_____

To the Secretary of State
    of the State of _____:

    Pursuant to the provisions of Section 125 of the _____ Business Corporation Act, the undersigned corporation hereby submits the following annual report:

    FIRST: The name of the corporation is _____

_____.

---

11. See Section 115 of the MBCA.

12. See Section 125 of the MBCA for a model of this type of requirement.

13. Section 126 of the MBCA contains such a provision.

SECOND: It is incorporated under the laws of _____.

THIRD: The address of its registered office in your State is _____
and the name of its registered agent in your State of such address is _____.

FOURTH: If a foreign corporation, the address of its principal office in the state or country under the laws of which it is incorporated is _____.

FIFTH: The character of the business in which it is actually engaged in your State, briefly stated, is _____
_____
_____.

SIXTH: The names and respective addresses of its directors and officers are:

| Name | Office | Address |
|------|--------|---------|
| _____ | _____ | _____ |
| _____ | _____ | _____ |
| _____ | _____ | _____ |
| _____ | _____ | _____ |
| _____ | _____ | _____ |
| _____ | _____ | _____ |
| _____ | _____ | _____ |

SEVENTH: The aggregate number of shares which it has authority to issue, itemized by classes, par value of shares, shares without par value, and series, if any, within a class, is:

| Number of Shares | Class | Series | Par Value per Share or Statement that Shares are without Par Value |
|------------------|-------|--------|-------------------------------------------------------------------|

EIGHTH: The aggregate number of its issued shares, itemized by classes, par value of shares, shares without par value, and series, if any, within a class, is:

| Number of Shares | Class | Series | Par Value per Share or Statement that Shares are without Par Value |
|------------------|-------|--------|-------------------------------------------------------------------|

NINTH: The amount of its stated capital, as defined in the _____ Business Corporation Act, as of the close of business on December 31 next preceding the date hereof, was $_____.

TENTH: It will _____ (Note 1) pay the annual franchise on the basis of its entire stated capital.   (Note 2)

Dated: _____, 19__.

_____ (Note 3)

By _____ (Note 4)

Its _____

(Add Verification Form C)

Notes: 1. Insert the word "not" unless all of the property of the corporation is located, and all of its business is transacted at or from places of business, within this State, or unless it elects to pay the annual franchise tax on the basis of its entire stated capital.

2. If the word "not" is inserted pursuant to Note 1, attach a supplemental statement in accordance with the requirements of subparagraph (h) of Section 125.

3. Exact corporate name of corporation making the report.

4. Signature and title of officer signing for the corporation.

## C.  TAXES

The taxes imposed upon a foreign corporation after it has qualified to do business in a given state vary enormously from state to state.   The following is only a general analysis of the typical kinds of taxes levied upon qualified foreign corporations:

### 1.  Initial Franchise Tax

A state may impose and collect a tax at the time that the application for a certificate of authority is filed or shortly thereafter. The tax is normally computed on the number of shares of the corporation which is authorized and will vary depending upon the par value of such shares, or the fact that such shares have no par value.   This tax is in addition to any filing fee that relates, at least theoretically, to the cost to the state of processing the application for a certificate of authority.

### 2.  Annual Franchise Tax

The annual franchise tax imposed on a foreign business corporation is normally imposed upon that portion of the business "capital" of the corporation which is present in the state.   The phrase "capital" is a defined term and recourse to the individual state tax law is necessary for the appropriate definition. The amount of "capital" which is present in a given state is typically determined by a formula.

In addition to state taxes, a foreign corporation might also be subject to taxes imposed by cities, counties and other political subdivisions. The subject of state and local taxation is a highly technical one which is normally the province of lawyers who are experts in the field. The foregoing discussion is intended to familiarize the student with the nature of the tax burden imposed upon a qualified foreign corporation and to suggest to the student reasons why corporations are sometimes unwilling to qualify to do business in a given jurisdiction if there is any remote possibility that qualification is not required by law.

### D. AMENDMENT OF ARTICLES OF INCORPORATION

If a foreign corporation amends its articles of incorporation,[14] the foreign corporation is required to file the amendment with the Secretary of State of the states in which it is qualified.[15]

### E. AMENDMENT OF CERTIFICATE OF AUTHORITY

Once a foreign corporation obtains a certificate of authority, it is permitted to amend the certificate of authority in the event it changes its corporate name or desires to pursue other forms of business activity within the state.[16]

### IV. CONSEQUENCES OF TRANSACTING BUSINESS WITHOUT A CERTIFICATE OF AUTHORITY

Not only does state law require a corporation doing business within the state to obtain a certificate of authority and impose requirements and obligations on such corporations, but state law also covers the contingency of a corporation which is transacting business within a state without a certificate of authority.[17] In most states, a foreign corporation improperly failing to obtain a certificate of authority is denied the right to sue in the courts of that state.

### QUESTION

**Can an unqualified foreign corporation defend itself in a lawsuit in a state in which it has improperly failed to qualify?**

Some states also impose fines and penalties on unqualified corporations which are improperly doing business in the state.

---

14. See Chapter Four for a description of the amendment process.

15. See, for example, Section 116 of the MBCA.

16. See Section 118 of the MBCA, which is a model of requirements for amendment. Note that the amendment must result in a certificate of authority which meets all requirements for an original certificate of authority.

17. See Section 124 of the MBCA.

## V. WITHDRAWAL OF QUALIFICATION

A foreign corporation which has qualified to do business within a given state may, after it has ceased doing business within that state, withdraw its qualification by filing an application for withdrawal.[18]

The proof of publication and the certificate of withdrawal should be filed in the corporation's minute book.

The following form is suggested by the MBCA for withdrawals:

**EXAMPLE—Application for Certificate of Withdrawal**

Filing fee: $_____

APPLICATION FOR
CERTIFICATE OF WITHDRAWAL
OF

_____

To the Secretary of State
     of the State of _____:

Pursuant to the provisions of Section 119 of the _____ Business Corporation Act, the undersigned corporation hereby applies for a Certificate of Withdrawal from your State, and for that purpose submits the following statement:

FIRST: The name of the corporation is _____. It is incorporated under the laws of _____.

SECOND: It is not transacting business in your state.

THIRD: It hereby surrenders its authority to transact business in your state.

FOURTH: It revokes the authority of its registered agent in your State to accept service of process, and consents that service of process in any action, suit or proceeding based upon any cause of action arising in your State during the time the corporation was authorized to transact business in your State may thereafter be made on the corporation by service thereof on the Secretary of State of your State.

FIFTH: The post-office address to which the Secretary of State may mail a copy of any process against the corporation that may be served on him is _____.

SIXTH: The aggregate number of shares which it has authority to issue, itemized by classes, par value of shares,

18. Section 119 of the MBCA provides an example of the information which must be contained in an application for withdrawal.

shares without par value, and series, if any, within a class, as of this date is:

| Number of Shares | Class | Series | Par Value per Share or Statement that Shares are without Par Value |
|---|---|---|---|
| | | | |

SEVENTH: The aggregate number of its issued shares, itemized by classes, par value of shares, shares without par value, and series, if any, within a class, as of this date is:

| Number of Shares | Class | Series | Par Value per Share or Statement that Shares are without Par Value |
|---|---|---|---|
| | | | |

EIGHTH: The amount of its stated capital as of this date is $_____.

Dated _____, 19__.

_____ (Note 1)

By _____

    Its _____ President

                                } (Note 2)

and _____

    Its _____ Secretary

(Add Verification Form A)

Notes: 1. Exact corporate name of corporation making the statement.

        2. Signatures and titles of officers signing for the corporation.

## PROBLEM

Compare the form for withdrawal with the MBCA's suggested forms used in dissolution of a domestic corporation.[19]

If a state permitted a qualified foreign corporation to withdraw simply by filing an application for a certificate of withdrawal, the state might discover subsequently that the corporation still owed taxes from its prior activities. Since a corporation would like to remove

---

19. See Chapter Eleven for MBCA forms of dissolution.

any continuing burden by withdrawing from qualification, the state considers it an appropriate time to make certain that the corporation's tax payments to the state are current. The office of the state government in which the application for withdrawal has been filed normally will not approve the application until it has received notice from the various state taxing departments that all fees and franchise taxes have been paid. This notice is usually referred to as a "clearance certificate".

## PROBLEMS

In what office is the application for certificate of withdrawal (or its equivalent) filed in your state? Does your state require a clearance certificate or similar document prior to withdrawal? How long does it take ordinarily to obtain a clearance certificate?

To obtain a clearance certificate, a corporation normally must file tax returns to the date of withdrawal and all taxes which the corporation may owe the state through the date of withdrawal. Only after the corporation has filed such a tax return and paid all the taxes and fees required will the state issue the clearance certificate. The accountant for the corporation ordinarily has the responsibility to file tax returns and obtain the clearance certificate.

Once a clearance certificate (or its equivalent) has been obtained and forwarded to the appropriate office of the state in which the application for withdrawal has been filed, the state will grant the application for withdrawal.[20]

In some states, a foreign corporation which intends to apply or applies for a certificate of withdrawal must advertise this fact.

The following is a sample of an advertisement which will satisfy the advertising requirement:

Fun City, Inc., a Delaware corporation, with its principal office in Delaware located at 120 Main Street, Wilmington, Delaware, and with a registered office in the Commonwealth of Pennsylvania at 1700 Market Street, Philadelphia, Pennsylvania, has filed with the Department of State of Commonwealth of Pennsylvania, an application for a certificate of withdrawal on December 31, 19___.

## PROBLEMS

1. Does your state have an advertising requirement? If so, when and where must the advertising take place?

2. Compare the advertising requirements for a certificate with the requirements of advertising a dissolution of a domestic corporation described in Chapter Eleven.

***

20. See Section 120 of the MBCA.

## QUALIFICATION PROBLEM
### MEMORANDUM

TO: Lawyer's Assistant

FROM: Abbie Kanter

A client of ours, State Street, Inc., is a Delaware corporation formed for the purpose of selling paint at retail through its own stores. As a means of insuring supply, it has recently begun to produce its own paint, at its various locations through a wholly-owned subsidiary, State Street Paint Bank, Inc. New stores are about to be opened in Lexington, Kentucky (assume that it has adopted the MBCA).

(a) I think the corporation needs to qualify in Kentucky. Do you agree?

(b) If so, what further information do you need?

(c) Do you foresee any problems in qualifying?

(d) In any event please prepare sample resolutions authorizing qualification of each corporation.[21]

## VI. QUALIFICATION CHECKLIST

A checklist of information required in qualifying a foreign corporation appears below.

### Checklist of Information Required in Connection with Foreign Qualification

I. **Qualification**

    A. *Basic Information*

The following information, depending on the state statute, may be required:

1. Name of corporation.

2. State of incorporation.

3. Address, including street and number, of principal office in state of incorporation.

4. Address, including street and number, of proposed registered office in foreign jurisdiction.

5. Name and address, including street and number, of proposed registered agent in foreign jurisdiction.

6. The statute under which the corporation was incorporated.

7. Date of incorporation.

8. "Purpose" clause of articles of incorporation.

---

21. See Chapter Seven, Section IV.

I. **Qualification**—Continued

    A. *Basic Information*—Continued

    The following information, depending on the state statute, may be required:—Continued

        9. Actual business activity which corporation is to pursue in the state in which it wishes to qualify.

       10. Names and addresses of the directors and officers of the corporation.

       11. Number of shares which the corporation has authority to issue, itemized by classes and series, if any.

       12. Number of shares which the corporation has issued, itemized by classes and series, if any.

    B. *Name*

    Is the name of the corporation available for use in the foreign jurisdiction? If so, must action be taken to reserve the name?

    C. *Filing*

    After ascertaining the appropriate state office (e. g., Department of State) in which documents must be filed, decide which of the following, and how many copies of each, must be filed:

        1. Application for Certificate of Authority?

        2. Any other forms?

        3. Certified copy of Articles of Incorporation?

        4. Good Standing Certificate?

    D. *Fees*

    What fees and/or taxes must be paid in connection with the application for a certificate of authority?

    E. *Advertisement*

    What advertising requirements, if any, must be satisfied in connection with qualification as a foreign corporation?

II. **Later Requirements**

    A. *Annual Reports*

        1. When must they be filed?

        2. With whom must they be filed?

        3. What information must be contained in such reports?

    B. *Tax Returns*

        1. When must they be filed?

        2. With whom must they be filed?

        3. What is the form of tax return and what information is required?

II. **Later Requirements**—Continued

C. *Report Certain Changes*

If any one of the following events occur, it may be necessary to make an appropriate filing with a state in which the corporation is qualified to do business:

1. Change of Name.
2. Change of Articles of Incorporation.
3. Change of Registered Office.
4. Change of Registered Agent.
5. Change of business activity carried on within the state.
6. Merger of Corporation.

III. **Withdrawal from Qualification**

When a corporation is no longer "doing" or "transacting" business within a state, it will probably desire to withdraw from qualification and thereby eliminate the various obligations imposed upon it as a qualified foreign corporation.

A. *Certificate of Withdrawal*

What information must be set forth in the certificate of withdrawal and with whom must it be filed?

B. *Clearance Certificate*

What taxes, fees or charges must be paid in order to obtain from the Department of Revenue a statement that all taxes, fees, etc., have been paid?

C. *Advertising*

What advertising requirements, if any, must be satisfied?

D. *Fees*

What are the filing fees for the certificate of withdrawal?

### PROBLEM

Compare the foregoing checklist with the checklist for incorporation contained in Chapter Two, Section II.

## Chapter Four

# AMENDMENT OF ARTICLES OF INCORPORATION AND BY–LAWS

## I. INTRODUCTION

Once a corporation has been created by the filing of Articles of Incorporation, the corporation has the right to amend its Articles of Incorporation. For example, the MBCA provides the following:

> "A corporation may amend its articles of incorporation, from time to time, in any and as many respects as may be desired, so long as its articles of incorporation as amended contain only such provisions as might be lawfully contained in original articles of incorporation at the time of making such amendment, and, if a change in shares or the rights of shareholders, or an exchange, reclassification or cancellation of shares or rights of shareholders is to be made, such provisions as may be necessary to effect such change, exchange, reclassification or cancellation."

*may have to give Notice*

Section 58, MBCA.

### PROBLEMS

1. Why would a corporation want to amend its articles?

2. Would a corporation (a) change its name by an amendment? (b) increase the number of authorized shares? (c) change the number of directors? (d) modify its fiscal year?[1] (e) adopt a different date for its annual meeting of shareholders? (f) adopt a new business purpose for the corporation? (g) adopt a new registered office?

There are a number of steps which must be followed to amend articles of incorporation. The following sections outline these steps.

## A. PROPOSAL OF AMENDMENT

Typically, amendments to the articles of incorporation are initially proposed by the board of directors:

> "The board of directors shall adopt a resolution setting forth the proposed amendment and . . . directing that it be submitted to a vote at a meeting of shareholders, which may be either the annual or a special meeting."

*ps 4/34*

Section 59(a), MBCA.

---

1. The fiscal year of a company is twelve consecutive calendar months that a corporation elects as its accounting and financial reporting year. It starts at the beginning of a month, e.g., January 1, October 1, or December 1, and ends on the last day of the twelfth calendar month thereafter.

In some states, provision is also made for amendments to be proposed by a petition of shareholders entitled to cast a specified percentage of the votes which all shareholders are entitled to cast for the amendment.

A form of the resolutions of a board of directors of an MBCA corporation proposing an amendment to the articles of incorporation is set forth below:

**EXAMPLE—Board of Directors Proposal to Amend the Articles of Incorporation**

### [NAME OF CORPORATION]

### ACTION BY THE BOARD OF DIRECTORS

The Board of Directors of [Name of Corporation], a [State of Incorporation] corporation, hereby adopt the following action of this corporation:

RESOLVED:

1. That paragraph 1 of the Articles of Incorporation of the corporation be amended so as to read in its entirety as follows:

The name of the corporation is: XYZ CORP.

2. That upon shareholder approval of the above amendment, the President or any Vice President and the Secretary or any Assistant Secretary of the corporation are authorized and directed to execute, under the corporate seal of the corporation, Articles of Amendment to the Articles of Incorporation and to file such Articles of Amendment with the Secretary of State of the State of _____, and take such other action as is required to implement the Amendment.

3. That the approval of the shareholders to this amendment be obtained by a vote of the shareholders entitled to vote thereon either at a special meeting of the shareholders or by such written consent as is required for approval of this Amendment without a meeting in accordance with the Corporation's By-Laws and the Business Corporation Law of the State of _____.

### B. SUBMISSION TO SHAREHOLDERS

Once a proposal for an amendment has been made, the shareholders must vote on the amendment or agree to it by written consent, if state law permits written consents in lieu of a meeting. If a meeting is desired or required, either because of state law or the impracticality of obtaining written consents where the number of shareholders is very large, shareholders must receive notice of the meeting containing certain information.   An example of such a statute for a state that has adopted the MBCA approach follows:

"Written notice setting forth the proposed amendment or a summary of the changes to be effected thereby shall be given to each shareholder of record entitled to vote thereon within the time and in the manner provided in this Act for the giving of notice of meetings of shareholders.   If the meeting be an annual meeting, the proposed amendment or such summary may be included in the notice of such annual meeting."

Section 59(b), MBCA.

Note that provisions in different states may differ.

## C.   SHAREHOLDER APPROVAL

Unless the corporation's articles (or in some states the by-laws) provide for a higher percentage, proposed amendments only need be approved by a statutory percentage of votes entitled to be cast on the particular action, usually a majority or two-thirds.   The MBCA provision provides for a majority vote:

"At such meeting (i.e., the meeting specified in the notice to shareholders), a vote of the shareholders entitled to vote thereon shall be taken on the proposed amendment.   The proposed amendment shall be adopted upon receiving the affirmative vote of the holders of a majority of the shares entitled to vote thereon, unless any class of shares is entitled to vote thereon as a class, in which event the proposed amendment shall be adopted upon receiving the affirmative vote of holders of a majority of the shares of each class of shares entitled to vote thereon as a class and of the total shares entitled to vote thereon.

"Any number of amendments may be submitted to the shareholders, and voted upon by them, at one meeting."

Section 59(c), MBCA.

## PROBLEM

Is there any difference between the number of votes constituting (i) a majority of the outstanding shares and (ii) a majority of shares present at a duly organized meeting?

When more than one class of stock is outstanding, e. g., preferred and common, approval of the holders of a specified percentage of each class of stock may be required.   Such approval may be necessary because of the voting rights established in the corporation's articles of incorporation.   In addition, or in the alternative, approval may be required by state law.[2]

The purpose of such a provision is to give holders of a specific class of stock an opportunity to vote where a proposed amendment to

2.   See, for example, Section 242(c)(2) of the Delaware General Corporation Law.

the articles would adversely affect their class of stock. For example, a new class of preferred stock with priority over an existing preferred stock would adversely affect an existing class. The existing class may, therefore, have the right to vote on the amendment.

As was mentioned above, shareholder approval may be obtained at a duly called meeting or by unanimous written consent. In states in which informal consent by less than all shareholders is authorized for certain corporate actions, this method may be used to obtain the requisite shareholder approval provided that the nature of the amendment is not one for which such informal action is expressly prohibited.[3]

## D.  ARTICLES OF AMENDMENT

Once the appropriate shareholder approval has been obtained, articles of amendment must be prepared and executed. The contents of the articles of amendment are ordinarily limited to the text of the amendment itself. Section 61 of the MBCA, provides for the simple contents of the articles of amendment.

A sample form of Articles of Amendment designed for use in states which have adopted the MBCA is set forth below:

**EXAMPLE—Articles of Amendment (MBCA)**

Filing fee: $_____

ARTICLES OF AMENDMENT

TO THE

ARTICLES OF INCORPORATION

OF

_____

Pursuant to the provisions of Section 61 of the _____ Business Corporation Act, the undersigned corporation adopts the following Articles of Amendment to its Articles of Incorporation:

FIRST:  The name of the corporation is _____
_____.

SECOND:  The following amendments of the Articles of Incorporation were adopted by the shareholders (Note 1) of the corporation on _____, 19__, in the manner prescribed by the _____ Business Corporation Act:

(Insert Amendments)

THIRD:  The number of shares of the corporation outstanding at the time of such adoption was _____; and the number of shares entitled to vote thereon was _____.

---

3.  See paragraph 7 of the Articles of Incorporation of Fun City Franchise Corp. in Chapter Two for an example of such a provision.

FOURTH: The designation and number of outstanding shares of each class entitled to vote thereon as a class were as follows:

**Class**                                   **Number of**
                                              **Shares**

(Note 2)

FIFTH: The number of shares voted for such amendment was _____; and the number of shares voted against such amendment was _____.

(Note 2)

SIXTH: The number of shares of each class entitled to vote thereon as a class voted for and against such amendment, respectively, was:

**Class**                          **Number of Shares Voted**
                                    **For**            **Against**

(Note 2)

SEVENTH: The manner in which any exchange, reclassification, or cancellation of issued shares provided for in the amendment shall be effected is as follows:

(Note 3)

EIGHTH: The manner in which such amendment effects a change in the amount of stated capital, and the amount of stated capital as changed by such amendment, are as follows:

(Note 2)

Dated _____, 19__.

_____ (Note 4)

By _____
    Its _____ President          (Note 5)
and _____
    Its _____ Secretary

(Add Verification Form A)

Notes: 1.  Change to "board of directors" if no shares have been issued.

2.  If applicable, omit.

3.  This article may be omitted if the subject matter is set forth in the amendment or if it is inapplicable.

4. Exact corporate name of corporation adopting the Articles of Amendment.

5. Signatures and titles of officers signing for the corporation.

The following articles of amendment effect a change in the name of FUN CITY FRANCHISE CORP., to which you were first introduced in Chapter Two.

**EXAMPLE:**

CERTIFICATE OF AMENDMENT

OF

CERTIFICATE OF INCORPORATION

FUN CITY FRANCHISE CORP., a corporation organized and existing under and by virtue of the General Corporation Law of the State of Delaware,

DOES HEREBY CERTIFY:

FIRST: That at a meeting of the Board of Directors of FUN CITY FRANCHISE CORP. resolutions were duly adopted setting forth a proposed amendment to the Certificate of Incorporation of said corporation, declaring said amendment to be advisable and calling a meeting of the stockholders of said corporation for consideration thereof. The resolution setting forth the proposed amendment is as follows:

RESOLVED, that the Certificate of Incorporation of this corporation be amended by changing the Article thereof number "ONE" so that, as amended, said Article shall be and read as follows:

"The name of the corporation is: FRANCHISE MARKETING ASSOCIATES, INC."

SECOND: That thereafter, pursuant to resolution of its Board of Directors, a special meeting of the stockholders of said corporation was duly called and held, upon notice in accordance with Section 222 of the General Corporation Law of the State of Delaware, at which meeting the necessary number of shares as required by statute were voted in favor of the amendment.

THIRD: That said amendment was duly adopted in accordance with the provisions of Section 242 of the General Corporation Law of the State of Delaware.

FOURTH: That the capital of said corporation shall not be reduced under or by reason of said amendment.

IN WITNESS WHEREOF, said FUN CITY FRAN-CHISE CORP. has caused its corporate seal to be hereunto affixed and this certificate to be signed by    [name]

its President, and Attested by its Secretary, this 15th day of June, 19___.

By: /s/ _____

President

Attest: /s/ _____

Secretary

## PROBLEM

Prepare articles of amendment for Fun City Franchise Corp., a corporation, the Pennsylvania articles of incorporation of which appear in Section V of Chapter Two.  To accomplish the following utilize the MBCA form of articles of amendment:

    (a) **Increase the authorized capital to 5,000,000 shares of Common Stock, par value $.02 per share;  and**

    (b) **Require the affirmative vote of the holders of 75% or more of the outstanding common stock of the Company to merge or consolidate the Company with any other corporation.**

**Additional Information:**

**Date of Shareholders' Meeting: November 29, 19___**

**Number of Shares Outstanding: 1,500,000**

**Number of shares Represented in person or by proxy at the Shareholders' Meeting: 1,287,500**

**Number of Shares Voting for and against the amendment:**

**For—1,198,500**

**Against—89,000**

## E.  FILING OF ARTICLES OF AMENDMENT

Section 62, MBCA, sets forth a typical procedure for filing of Articles of Amendment:

"Duplicate originals of the articles of amendment shall be delivered to the Secretary of State.  If the Secretary of State finds that the articles of amendment conform to law, he shall, when all fees and franchise taxes have been paid as in this Act prescribed:

"(a) Endorse on each of such duplicate originals the word 'Filed', and the month, day and year of the filing thereof.

"(b) File one of such duplicate originals in his office.

"(c) Issue a certificate of amendment to which he shall affix the other duplicate original.

"The certificate of amendment, together with the duplicate original of the articles of amendment affixed thereto by the Secretary of State, shall be returned to the corporation or its representative."

A copy of the Amendment should be placed in the minute book of the corporation.

The filing is necessary to consummate the amendment to the articles and makes the amendment a document of public record as are the articles. A document of public record is one which may be inspected by any person at the official office where the document was filed. Any person may obtain a copy of a public document by paying the required copying fee.

### PROBLEM

**What happens if one fails to file the amendment?**

In some states (e. g., Delaware) a certified copy of the articles of amendment (as was true with respect to the duplicate copy of the Certificate of Incorporation) must be recorded in the county in which the corporation's registered office is located.[4]

### PROBLEM

**If there is such a requirement, is the amendment effective if the articles of amendment are not filed in the county office?**

### F. ADVERTISEMENT

Many states require publication of the filing of articles of amendment. The theory of requiring advertising of the filing is to notify the legal community and creditors of the corporate action. As a practical matter the advertising is little more than an economic benefit for the newspapers in which the advertisements are placed because few persons pay attention to them.

A sample advertisement, relating to an amendment changing the name of a corporation, which would satisfy a statutory advertising requirement is as follows:

"Articles of Amendment of FUN CITY FRANCHISE CORP., a Pennsylvania corporation with its registered office at 4455 Main Street, Philadelphia, Pennsylvania, were filed with the Department of State of the Commonwealth of Pennsylvania on July 1, 19__. The purpose of the Articles of Amendment was to change the name of the corporation to 'FRANCHISE MARKETING ASSOCIATES, INC.' "

As in the case of the initial advertisements that appeared at the time of incorporation, a proof of publication should be inserted in the corporate minute book.[5]

---

4. See Section IV.B of Chapter Two.   5. See Section III.B of Chapter Two, *supra.*

## G.   FEES AND TAXES

Typically, a state will impose a filing fee on a corporation filing articles of amendment.  In addition, if the amendment is to increase the corporation's authorized capital, states which impose a tax upon the amount of a corporation's capital initially also impose a similar levy on the amount of the increase in the capital.

## H.   EFFECTIVENESS OF AMENDMENT

As is true of the procedure for incorporation, an amendment to the articles of incorporation under modern corporation statutes is generally effective either upon the filing of articles of amendment, or, if applicable, upon the issuance of a certificate of amendment by the appropriate state agency after receipt of the articles of amendment. Section 63 of the MBCA is typical of many statutes in providing the following:

"Upon the issuance of the certificate of amendment by the Secretary of State, the amendment shall become effective and the articles of incorporation shall be deemed to be amended accordingly.

"No amendment shall affect any existing cause of action [6] in favor of or against such corporation, or any pending suit to which such corporation shall be a party, or the existing rights of persons other than shareholders; and, in the event the corporate name shall be changed by amendment, no suit brought by or against such corporation under its former name shall abate for that reason."

## PROBLEMS

1.   What does the preceding paragraph say about the effect of an amendment on third parties?

2.   Can a corporation amend its articles to extinguish a debt to a third party?

3.   Does the change in a corporation's name require amendments in its existing leases or other contracts?

4.   Does the change in corporate name cause the corporation to lose any rights to property titled in its old name, e.g., vehicles or real estate?  If not, why not?

5.   Besides the filing of the articles of amendment, what must a paralegal do for a corporation that has changed its name?

6.   Is there any other way that a corporation may operate under a desired name without amending its articles of incorporation?  (See Chapter Six.)

6.   A "cause of action" is a set of facts which can be asserted by a plaintiff sufficient to support a valid lawsuit.

## I. AMENDMENTS PRIOR TO ISSUANCE OF SHARES

Most corporate laws now establish a procedure for a corporation to amend its articles of incorporation prior to the issuance of its shares. For example, the following is the Delaware provision:

"(a) Before a corporation has received any payment for any of its stock, it may amend its certificate of incorporation at any time or times, in any and as many respects as may be desired, so long as its certificate of incorporation as amended would contain only such provisions as it would be lawful and proper to insert in an original certificate of incorporation filed at the time of filing the amendment.

"(b) The amendment of a certificate of incorporation authorized by this section shall be adopted by a majority of the incorporators, if directors were not named in the original certificate of incorporation or have not yet been elected, or, if directors were named in the original certificate of incorporation or have been elected and have qualified, by a majority of the directors. A certificate setting forth the amendment and certifying that the corporation has not received any payment for any of its stock and that the amendment has been duly adopted in accordance with the provisions of this section shall be executed, acknowledged, filed and recorded in accordance with section 103 of this title. Upon such filing, the corporation's certificate of incorporation shall be deemed to be amended accordingly as of the date on which the original certificate of incorporation became effective."

Section 241, Delaware General Corporation Law.

The states utilizing the MBCA have a similar procedure:

"If no shares have been issued, the amendment shall be adopted by resolution of the board of directors and the provisions for adoption by shareholders shall not apply."

Section 59(a), MBCA.

In contrast, other states such as Pennsylvania have no such provision. Nevertheless, the articles of incorporation of a Pennsylvania corporation may be amended prior to the issuance of shares because, under Section 207, PBCL, "those persons who subscribed for shares prior to the filing of the articles of incorporation, or their assignees, shall be shareholders in the corporation." Pennsylvania's approach to the problem is to provide for "shareholders" (by providing for the incorporators to subscribe nominally for shares) before any shares are issued; as a consequence, an amendment must be approved not only by the initial directors of the corporation but also by the subscribers.

## J. RESTATED ARTICLES OF INCORPORATION

A corporation may have many amendments to its articles, all of which are required to determine the current status of the articles, as amended.  The state corporate laws usually provide for a method of allowing the amended articles to be set forth and consolidated in one document by a "restatement" of the articles.  "Restatement" of the articles of incorporation may take one of two forms:

1.  Setting forth a revised articles of incorporation which incorporates all changes made, including current amendments.

2. Consolidating all prior amendments in one form without making any current amendments to the articles of incorporation.

In the former case, the board of directors may decide that it would be simpler, for future reference, to amend the articles of incorporation by restating them in their entirety, rather than changing several different provisions.  This is especially true when a corporation has previously amended its articles of incorporation and new additional amendments are proposed.  In such cases, the procedure for restating articles of incorporation is identical to that of making any amendment to the articles of incorporation.

In the latter case, the desire is simply to "clean up" the articles of incorporation by consolidating the original articles and all amendments into a single document: the restated articles of incorporation.  States which follow the MBCA approach permit this restatement without shareholder approval as set forth in Section 64 of the MBCA.

If no such provision existed, restatement of articles of incorporation (even though no substantive change was intended in the articles) would still require the same procedure as required for any current amendment to the articles of incorporation.

### PROBLEM

Utilizing (i) the articles of FUN CITY FRANCHISE CORP. in Chapter Two and (ii) the amendment to change its name that you made earlier in this Chapter, restate the articles in their entirety into one document.

## II.  INTRODUCTION TO AMENDMENT OF BY–LAWS

As indicated above, a corporation's articles of incorporation or its by-laws may provide for amendment of the by-laws by the board of directors.  For example, Section 109(a) of the Delaware General Corporation Law provides that:

"[T]he power to adopt, amend or repeal by-laws shall be in the stockholders entitled to vote, or, in the case of a non-stock corporation, in its members entitled to vote; provided, however, any corporation may, in its certificate of incorporation, confer that power to adopt, amend or repeal by-laws upon the directors or, in the case of a non-stock corporation, upon its governing body by whatever name designated."

### PROBLEM

**Can a Delaware corporation provide for amendment of the by-laws by the directors under the foregoing provision if the by-laws so provide but the articles are silent?**

Some states, such as Pennsylvania, permit either the articles or by-laws to vest power to amend the by-laws in the Board of Directors:

> "The shareholders shall have the power to make, amend, and repeal the by-laws of a business corporation, but except as otherwise provided in this act the authority to make, amend and repeal by-laws may be expressly vested by the articles or the by-laws in the board of directors, subject always to the power of the shareholders to change such action."

PBCL, Section 304.

## A.  PROCEDURE

When shareholder action is not required, the board of directors may amend the by-laws by resolution adopted at a duly constituted meeting or by unanimous consent in writing without a meeting when this type of informal action is permitted under the corporation law of the state of incorporation.[7]  A form of board resolution adopting an amendment to the by-laws by unanimous consent is as follows:

**EXAMPLE—Board of Directors Approval of Amendment to By-Laws**

[*NAME OF CORPORATION*]

ACTION BY UNANIMOUS CONSENT IN WRITING

OF THE

BOARD OF DIRECTORS

The undersigned, constituting the entire Board of Directors of [*Name of Corporation*], a [*State of Incorporation*] corporation, in accordance with the authority contained in the [*State of Incorporation*] Business Corporation Law, and in accordance with the by-laws of this corporation, without the formality of convening a meeting, hereby unanimously consent to the following action of this corporation:

RESOLVED: that Section 2.3(a) of the Corporation's by-laws be amended so as to read in its entirety as follows:

"(a) *Place.* Meetings of the board of directors shall be held at the corporation's ex-

---

7.  See Chapter Seven for a fuller discussion of actions by unanimous consent by the directors.

ecutive offices located at 1700 Market Street, Philadelphia, Pennsylvania, unless another location is designated in the notice of the meeting."

Dated: _____

*[Signature lines for all Directors]*

Filed with the undersigned on _____, 19__.

/s/ _____

Secretary of *[Name of Corporation]*

When shareholder action is required, a meeting of shareholders, or informal action of shareholders without a meeting, is required.[8]

### PROBLEM

Amend Article III, Section 2 of the long form of by-laws on pages 58–59 of Chapter Two to provide for a classified board of 6 directors with three classes of 2 directors each. Designate the three classes as A, B, and C. (Refer to footnote 30 of Chapter Two for an explanation of classification of a board of directors.)

### B.   RESTATEMENT OF BY–LAWS

Generally, no specific procedure is established by statute for the restatement of a corporation's by-laws since the by-laws are not usually a matter of public record. Since restatement is a method of amendment, by-laws may be restated in the same manner that they may be amended, i. e., by the board of directors, if properly permitted by the articles of incorporation or by-laws, or by the shareholders.

---

**8.**   The procedures for such meetings or actions are discussed in Chapter Seven.

Chapter Five

# CLOSE CORPORATIONS

## I.  INTRODUCTION

The generic term "close corporation" is usually applied to a corporation, all the stock of which is owned by a limited number of stockholders, where there is not "public" market for the stock of the corporation.[1] and, often, where the transfer of stock by any stockholder is subject to restrictions imposed by agreement among the stockholders.  The subject of such restrictive agreements is covered extensively in Chapter Ten of this book.

Several states provide for the formation of what is called a statutory "close corporation" which, in several respects, is treated differently under the state corporation law from corporations which do not follow the statutory requirements for a "close" corporation.[2]  The purpose of utilizing the close corporation structure is to enable the shareholders to run the corporation more like a partnership with less formality than is required of regular corporations and to preserve the intimate relationship between the shareholders.

The more important features of these statutory "close corporations" are discussed below.

## II.  PROVISIONS UNIQUELY APPLICABLE TO CLOSE CORPORATIONS

### A.  REQUISITE CONTENTS OF ARTICLES OF INCORPORATION

In states with statutory close corporations, the articles of such a corporation must state that the corporation is a "close corporation".  Generally the articles are required to include one or more specific provisions limiting the number of shareholders which the corporation may have.  The statutes usually prohibit "public offerings" of the corporation's stock,[3] and/or impose certain restrictions on the transfer of the corporation's stock.

1.  A public market exists for the stock of a corporation where the stock is owned by a large number of persons and where the stock may be easily bought and sold by the public at large through stockbrokers.  The stock of companies such as Xerox, General Motors, Exxon, U.S. Steel, American Telephone and Telegraph Company, etc., have a public market.  The trading in the stock of such companies is closely regulated by complex federal and state securities laws.  See Chapter One for a brief discussion of securities laws.

2.  See, e.g., Delaware General Corporation Law, Sections 341 to 356; Pennsylvania Business Corporation Law, Sections 371 to 386.

3.  A "public offering" of stock is the means by which the stock of a corporation acquires a "public market".  See footnote 1, *supra*.

As an example of a close corporation statute, Section 372 of the Pennsylvania Business Corporation Law, provides that, in addition to those statutory provisions applicable to the articles of an "ordinary" Pennsylvania business corporation, the articles of a close corporation must include additional information or statements. An example of the additional information or statements required of close corporations is set forth below:

"A. The articles of a close corporation, in addition to the provisions required by . . . of this act, shall provide that:

"(1) All of the issued shares of the corporation of all classes, exclusive of treasury shares,[4] shall be held of record by not more than a specified number of persons, not exceeding thirty; and

"(2) All of the issued shares of all classes shall be subject to one or more of the restrictions on transfer permitted by . . . this act; and

"(3) The corporation shall make no offering of any of its shares of any class which would constitute a "public offering"[5] within the meaning of the Securities Act of 1933.

"B. The articles of a close corporation may set forth the qualifications of shareholders, either by specifying classes of persons who shall be entitled to be holders of record of shares of any class, or by specifying classes of persons who shall not be entitled to be holders of shares of any class, or both.

"C. For purposes of determining the number of holders of record of the shares of a close corporation, shares which are held in joint[6] or common[7] tenancy or by the entireties[8] shall be treated as held by one shareholder."

## B. MANAGEMENT

The articles of incorporation of a close corporation may provide that the corporation shall have no directors and shall be managed directly by the shareholders. In such cases, no shareholders' meeting need be called to elect directors and, generally speaking, the shareholders are considered "directors" for most corporate purposes.

## C. DISSOLUTION

The articles may provide that the corporation can be dissolved at the option of any shareholder, much the same as a partnership.

---

4. Shares of stock that have been repurchased by the corporation that had originally issued them.

5. See footnotes 1 and 3.

6. A method of ownership by two or more persons where, when one owner dies, the survivor(s) gets the decedent's share directly rather than through the estate of the person who died.

7. Tenancy in common is a type of joint ownership in which one owner can sell or give away during life or by will at death his/her share.

8. Tenancy by the entireties is a joint tenancy where the two owners are husband and wife.

## III.   ARTICLES OF INCORPORATION FOR
## CLOSE CORPORATIONS

The following are sample Articles of Incorporation for a Pennsylvania "close corporation":

**EXAMPLE—Articles of a Close Corporation**

COMMONWEALTH OF PENNSYLVANIA
DEPARTMENT OF STATE
CORPORATION BUREAU

ARTICLES OF INCORPORATION

OF

FUN CITY FRANCHISE CORP.

(a Close Corporation)

The undersigned, being of full age, desiring to incorporate a business corporation under the provisions of the Business Corporation Law, approved May 5, 1933, P.L. 364, as amended, does hereby certify:

1.   The name of the corporation is:

FUN CITY FRANCHISE CORP.
(a Close Corporation)

2.   The location and post office address of its initial registered office in the Commonwealth of Pennsylvania is:

4455 Main Street
Philadelphia, Pennsylvania   19103

3.   The purpose or purposes for which the corporation is incorporated are to engage in manufacturing and to engage in and do any lawful act concerning any or all lawful business for which corporations may be incorporated under the Pennsylvania Business Corporation Law.

4.   The term for which the corporation is to exist is perpetual.

5.   The aggregate number of shares which the corporation shall have the authority to issue is:

100 shares of common stock, par value of $.01
per share.

6.   The corporation shall have no directors.  The business and affairs of the corporation shall be managed by its shareholders.  In such management, each shareholder shall be entitled to cast a number of votes equal to the number of shares held by him as a shareholder.  This provision shall

not be amended, repealed or modified except by the affirmative vote of holders of not less than ninety percent (90%) of all outstanding shares.

7. The names and addresses of each of the incorporators and the number and class of shares subscribed by each are:

| Name | Address | Number and Class of Shares |
|---|---|---|
| John Doe | 4455 Main Street<br>Philadelphia, Pa.<br>19103 | One common share, par value $.01 per share |

8. All of the issued shares of the corporation of all classes, exclusive of treasury shares, shall be held of record by not more than thirty (30) persons. For purposes of determining the number of holders of record under this provision, shares that are held in joint or common tenancy or by the entireties shall be treated as held by one shareholder.

9. No holder of any share of any class shall transfer any share to any person unless the corporation shall have consented to the transfer, or unless the transfer is in accordance with the terms and provisions of an agreement between the corporation and the transferor.

10. The corporation shall make no offering of any of its shares of any class which would constitute a "public offering" within the meaning of the federal statute known as the Securities Act of 1933.

Signed on May 1, 19__.

/s/John Doe
_____
Incorporator

Filed with the Department of State on _____, 19__.

_____

Secretary of the Commonwealth

### PROBLEM

Rewrite a draft of articles of incorporation for Abjac Enterprises, Inc., which is described in the problem in Section V of Chapter Two as an Ohio corporation, as a Pennsylvania close corporation.

# Chapter Six

## FICTITIOUS CORPORATE NAMES

### I.  INTRODUCTION

Many corporations conduct their business activities under one or more names that are different from their actual corporate name. This is a legitimate business practice where a specific name is familiar to the public or where the corporation is trying to develop public acceptance and awareness of the name. Another reason for using a fictitious name may be that the corporate name is too long or cumbersome to be used for general public acceptance. For example, Kraftco Corporation operates under the name "Kraft" or "Kraft Foods" in the sale of its cheeses and other foods because "Kraft" has acquired a secondary meaning for the public at large. Many states have laws, separate and apart from their general corporate laws, which govern the use of such "fictitious" names by corporations. In order to introduce the student to these laws, it is useful to review a typical "Fictitious Corporate Name Act".

### II.  FICTITIOUS NAME STATUTES

Registration under a "fictitious" name is usually defined as any "assumed or fictitious name, style or designation other than the proper corporate name of the corporation using such name".[1]

### QUESTIONS

**Who determines whether a corporation should adopt a fictitious name?  What corporate action must be taken to authorize the corporation to adopt a fictitious name?**

A corporation usually is not permitted to use a fictitious name in the state unless it first registers the name with the state and/or the county of location. In Pennsylvania, for example, a fictitious name is registered by filing an application under oath with the Secretary of the Commonwealth [2] and with the office of the Prothonotary [3] where the registered office of the corporation is located. The application contains the following information:

(a) Fictitious name being or to be used by the corporation.

(b) Nature of business to be conducted under the fictitious name.

(c) The full corporate name of, state and date of incorporation of, and the location of the principal place of business and the registered office of, the corporation filing the application.

---

1.  Pa. F.C.N.A. Section 2(7).

2.  Pennsylvania and a few other states, such as Massachusetts and Virginia, are officially called "commonwealths" rather than states.

3.  The prothonotary is the head clerk of the county courts in some states.

(d) The name and location of any other entity using the same fictitious name.

The Pennsylvania forms to be filed with the Secretary of the Commonwealth and the Prothonotary are as follows:

## EXAMPLE—Fictitious Name Registration—Commonwealth

APPLICANT'S ACC'T NO.
DSCB: 15-55 (Rev. 10-74)

Filing Fee: $40
CFN-28
Application for
Conducting Business by a
Corporation Under a
Fictitious Name

(Line for numbering)

COMMONWEALTH OF PENNSYLVANIA
DEPARTMENT OF STATE
CORPORATION BUREAU

Filed this _____ day of _____
_____ 19____
Commonwealth of Pennsylvania
Department of State

Secretary of the Commonwealth

(Box for Certification)

In compliance with the requirements of section 5 of the Fictitious Corporate Name Act, act of July 11, 1957 (P. L. 783) (15 P. S. § 55) the applicant corporation, desiring to register an assumed or fictitious name in the Office of the Secretary of the Commonwealth. hereby certifies:

1.    The fictitious name under which the business is being or will be carried on is:

_____

2.    A brief statement of the character or nature of the business is:

_____

3.    The name of the applicant corporation:

_____

4.    Its state and date of incorporation:

      State: _____ Date: _____

5.    The location, including street and number, if any, of the principal place of business in this Commonwealth:

      _____
      (STREET)                          (CITY)                          (ZIP CODE)

6.    The registered office of the applicant corporation in this Commonwealth:

      _____
      (STREET)                          (CITY)                          (ZIP CODE)

7.    (Strike out if inapplicable) the date on which the applicant was issued a certificate of authority by the Department of State to do business in this Commonwealth is _____.

                                                              (DATE)          [B6690]

M. BURR KEIM COMPANY, PHILADELPHIA

DSCB: 15-55 (Rev. 10-74)-2

8. The name and residence, including number and street, of any other entity, if any, in combination with which the applicant corporation seeks to conduct business under the fictitious name is or are:

(NAME)      (STREET)      (CITY)      (STATE)      (ZIP CODE)

IN TESTIMONY WHEREOF, all entities named within have signed this application or caused it to be signed by their Presidents or Vice Presidents and their corporate seals duly attested by their Secretaries or Treasurers to be hereunto affixed this _____ day of _____, 19_____.

COMMONWEALTH OF PENNSYLVANIA

SS:

COUNTY OF _____

Personally appeared before me, this _____ day of _____, 19____, _____

who, being duly sworn according to law, deposes and says that the statements contained in the foregoing application are true.

(SEAL) _____      _____
             (NOTARY PUBLIC)                            (SIGNATURE OF AFFIANT)

My Commission expires _____

INSTRUCTIONS FOR COMPLETION OF FORM:

     A.    Application must be signed in behalf of the applicant corporation and for all other entities listed with it in Paragraph 8.

     B.    If the applicant is a foreign corporation, the applicant must, prior to the filing of an application, be duly authorized to carry on or conduct the business described in Paragraph 2 under the laws of this Commonwealth. If the authorization to do business was issued by the Insurance Department or if no certificate of authority is required by law, Paragraph 7 of the form should be modified accordingly.

     C.    Where an individual is a member of a partnership or joint venture with one or more corporations under a fictitious name, Form DSCB: 15-55/54-28.1 (Application for conducting business under an Assumed or Fictitious Name—Individuals and Corporations) should be used.

     D.    Forms and information related to filing in the office of the prothonotary of the proper county shall be secured by direct inquiry addressed to the prothonotary.

     E.    All information shall be typed or printed, in black ink.

     F.    Make check payable to: Secretary of the Commonwealth. (CASH WILL NOT BE ACCEPTED).

     G.    Send application and check to: Corporation Bureau, Department of State, Room 308 North Office Bldg., Harrisburg, Pa. 17120.

[B6691]

## EXAMPLE—Fictitious Name Registration—County

C.P.-144½

**APPLICATION FOR REGISTRATION OF A CORPORATE FICTITIOUS NAME**

To the Prothonotary of Philadelphia County:
Application is hereby made to conduct a business by a corporation under an assumed or fictitious name under the Fictitious Corporate Name Act of 1957; 54 P.S. 81 et seq.; 15 P.S. 15 et seq. and as amended.

**PHILADELPHIA COUNTY
COURT OF COMMON PLEAS**

_____ Term, 19_____

No. _____

1. The Fictitious Name under which the business is being or will be carried on is:

_____

2. The character of the business so carried on or conducted is: _(Brief statement only):_

_____

_____

3. The name of the applicant corporation is:

_____

4. Its state of domicile and date of incorporation are:

_____

5. If the applicant is a foreign corporation, it avers that a Certificate of Authority to do business in this Commonwealth was issued by the Secretary of the Commonwealth on the_____day of_____ 19_____ ; or that no such Certificate is required by law: _(Strike out whichever is not applicable)._

6. The location including street and number, if any, of the principal place at which the business will be conducted under the proposed fictitious name is:

_____ , Philadelphia, Pa. _____

7. The registered office of the applicant corporation in this Commonwealth is:

_____

8. The name and residence, including number and street, of any other entity, if any, in combination with which the applicant corporation seeks to conduct business under the fictitious name is or are:

_____

_____

9. Applicant corporation avers that its last use in Pennsylvania of the name which it seeks to register commenced on a date prior to/subsequent to September 1, 1957. _(Strike out whichever is not applicable)._

IN TESTIMONY WHEREOF, the applicant has caused this Applicantion to be signed by its President or Vice President and its corporate seal, duly attested by its Secretary or Treasurer, to be hereunto affixed this_____ day of _____ , 19_____ .

ATTEST:

_____

_____    By_____
_(Secretary or Treasurer)_                      _(President or Vice President)_

(CORPORATE SEAL)

**COMMONWEALTH OF PENNSYLVANIA** ss:
**COUNTY OF PHILADELPHIA**

Before me, a_____in and for the State and County aforesaid, personally appeared
_____the _____ , and _____the
_____ of the above-named corporation who, being duly sworn, or affirmed, did depose and say that the foregoing Application was duly signed and sealed by them as the act and deed of the corporation; that the seal affixed thereto is the common and corporate seal of the corporation; and that the statements therein are true to the best of the knowledge and belief of each deponent.

Sworn to before me this _____ day
of_____ , 19_____ .

Certificate to be sent to:

SEAL     _____
                   _Notary Public_

My Commission expires_____

Filed in the office of the Prothonotary of Philadelphia County, Pa. on the_____day of_____ 19_____ .

5-47 (Rev. 1/76)

[B6696]

### PROBLEM

Locate the fictitious name registration act in your state and the forms to be filed and places to make a filing in order to register the name.

In Pennsylvania, a registration fee must be paid to the local Prothonotary and to the Secretary of the Commonwealth and must accompany the applications. When the applications have been filed and the required fees paid, the Prothonotary and the Secretary of the Commonwealth will each issue certificates of registration to the corporation.

## III. AMENDMENT OF FICTITIOUS NAMES

Corporations who have registered fictitious names are usually required to make supplemental filings in the event of a change in the location of their principal place of business or their registered office. These supplemental filings must usually be accompanied by additional filing fees. In Pennsylvania when the supplemental statements have been filed and the fees paid, the Prothonotary and the Secretary of the Commonwealth each issue certificates of amendment. A comparable procedure exists for any other amendment to the original application (e. g., a change in the character of the business conducted under the fictitious name); provided, however, that a corporation may not amend its fictitious name. If a corporation wishes to change its fictitious name, it must first follow the procedure described in the following paragraph for cancelling the registration of the initial fictitious name and then register a new fictitious name in the manner previously described. However, a corporation may file as many fictitious name registrations as it desires.

When, for whatever reason, a corporation ceases to conduct business under a registered fictitious name, the corporation is required to file with the Secretary of the Commonwealth and the Prothonotary a statement of cancellation, and pay the requisite filing fee. The Secretary of the Commonwealth and the Prothonotary will then issue certificates cancelling the registration.

### PROBLEM

Utilizing the Pennsylvania forms above, make the necessary fictitious name registration documents for FUN CITY FRANCHISE CORP., a Pennsylvania corporation, to operate under the fictitious name "Fun Rides". Do you need information other than that contained in the Articles of Incorporation in Chapter Two? If so, what information is needed?

## Chapter Seven

## SHAREHOLDERS' AND DIRECTORS' MEETINGS

### I. INTRODUCTION

Adherence to "formalities" is essential if the existence of a corporation is to withstand challenge. Cases exist which have held that the shareholder of a corporation cannot benefit from the corporation's limited liability if no efforts were made to operate the corporation "as a corporation" with the requisite meetings and actions by shareholders and directors. The authority of a corporation's officers to act on behalf of the corporation may have to be verified by reference to minutes of directors' and shareholders' meetings.

Despite the importance of accurate and complete records of actions by shareholders and directors, the proper maintenance of such records and the proper follow-up to insure timely corporate action may be neglected by lawyers as a result of the pressure of immediate problems. As a consequence, a lawyer's assistant is often charged with the responsibility of insuring the accurate and timely preparation of corporate minutes and of being certain that all corporations represented by the law firm are current in their shareholders' and directors' meetings and minutes.

In Chapter One the role of directors and shareholders of a corporation was outlined.[1] In the discussion of the powers of directors and shareholders, certain facts must be noted: (a) when a corporation has more than one director, a single director has no authority or rights relating to the management of the corporation in his individual capacity; rather, such authority and rights are vested in the "board of directors" and any action undertaken by directors must be done collectively as an action of the board of directors; and (b) no matter what the number of directors or shareholders, any action taken by the directors or shareholders must satisfy the formal requirements prescribed by state law and the articles of incorporation and by-laws of the corporation. This Chapter will examine the formal requirements imposed on the actions of shareholders and directors and provide examples of some of the more common types of actions.

### II. REQUIREMENTS OF MEETINGS

Historically, all actions by the directors and shareholders of a corporation were required to be taken at meetings. The following is a discussion of the customary statutory requirements which must be satisfied by such meetings and the methods of conducting meetings in

1. The basic role of directors and shareholders are outlined under Section II of this Chapter.

order that any action approved at a meeting is properly authorized. Preparation of notices, ballots and other meeting documents, including minutes, are tasks of paralegals. The forms included herein are only examples. The paralegal always must remember to make forms fit the matter at hand, not to try to make the matter at hand fit the forms! Forms are only useful tools, not a final product.

## A. SHAREHOLDERS' MEETINGS

### 1. Location

State law normally leaves it to the by-laws to specify the place at which shareholders' meetings are to be held. The Model Business Corporation Act sets forth a requirement which has been adopted in many states: [2]

"Meetings of shareholders may be held at such place within or without this state as may be stated in or fixed in accordance with the by-laws. If no other place is stated or so fixed, meetings shall be held at the registered office of the corporation."
Section 28, MBCA.

#### PROBLEM

**What is the registered office of the corporation? [3]**

An example of a possible by-law provision giving latitude to the board of directors to specify the location of a shareholders' meeting is as follows:

"Meetings of the shareholders shall be held at such place as may be designated by the board of directors."

### 2. Time and Calling of Meeting

Normally, state law requires that there be at least one regular meeting of the shareholders of the corporation each year (commonly called the "annual meeting"), at which meeting the directors of the corporation must be elected.

#### PROBLEM

**How does a shareholder go about calling a meeting under the MBCA if the corporation fails to do so in a calendar year? Who besides the board of directors and shareholders can call a shareholders' meeting under the MBCA?**

The by-laws of a corporation will ordinarily specify the time for the annual meeting. For example, a provision such as the following may be utilized:

"*Annual Meeting.* An annual meeting of the shareholders for the election of directors and for other business shall be held at such

---

**2.** See Chapter Two, Section II.B for an explanation of the MBCA.     **3.** See Chapter Two, Section IV.B if you need help.

time as may be fixed by the board of directors, on the first Monday in March of each year (or if such is a legal holiday, on the next following business day), or on such other day as may be fixed by the board of directors."

## PROBLEMS

**What time of the year should the annual meeting occur? Immediately before the end of the fiscal year?[4] Immediately thereafter? Three months thereafter? Why?**

In addition to annual meetings, there may also be special meetings of the shareholders. For example, Section 28 of the MBCA suggests the following provision:

"Special meetings of the shareholders may be called by the board of directors, the holders of not less than one-tenth of all shares entitled to vote at the meeting, or such other persons as may be authorized in the articles of incorporation or the by-laws."

Often, a by-law provision will grant to the president of the corporation the right to call a special meeting of shareholders:

"*Special Meetings.* Special meetings of the shareholders may be called at any time by the president, or the board of directors, or the holders of at least one-tenth of the outstanding shares of stock of the Company entitled to vote at the meeting."

## PROBLEMS

1. Why would a special meeting ever be necessary?

2. How do shareholders call a meeting?

## 3. Notice

Virtually every state provides some statutory procedure for giving notice of meetings of shareholders, to shareholders, including the time and place of the meeting. In the case of the annual meeting, the purpose of the meeting generally need not be given, but as a matter of practice and courtesy, most notices of shareholders' meetings do contain some description of the business to be transacted at the meeting. In the case of special meetings, the notice must also specify the purpose for which the meeting was called. Section 29 of the MBCA is fairly typical of the statutory notice provisions that states have adopted:

"Written notice stating the place, day and hour of the meeting and, in case of a special meeting, the purpose or purposes for which the meeting is called, shall be delivered not less than ten nor more than fifty days before the date of the meeting, either personally or by mail, by or at the direction of the president, the secre-

---

4. See footnote 1 of Chapter Four for an explanation of the meaning of "fiscal year".

tary, or the officer or persons calling the meeting, to each share-holder of record entitled to vote at such meeting. If mailed, such notice shall be deemed to be delivered when deposited in the United States mail addressed to the shareholder at his address as it appears on the stock transfer books of the corporation, with postage thereon prepaid."

A paralegal will often be asked to prepare the notice of the shareholders' meeting.

Examples of notices for an annual meeting of shareholders and a special meeting of shareholders are found below.

**EXAMPLE—Notice of Annual Meeting of Shareholders**

FUN CITY MARKETING, INC.
1700 Market Street
Philadelphia, Pennsylvania   19103

May 1, 19___

NOTICE OF ANNUAL MEETING

OF SHAREHOLDERS

To Our Shareholders:

Notice is hereby given that the Annual Meeting of shareholders will be held at the Corporation's offices located at 1700 Market Street, Philadelphia, Pennsylvania at 10:00 A.M., on May 26, 19___, for the purpose of considering the following matters:

1.   To elect five Directors pursuant to the by-laws of the Company. The following individuals have been nominated for election as directors by management in accordance with the Corporation's by-laws:

Joan Smith

James Green

Richard Thomas

William Jones

George Gray

2.   To ratify certain purchases and contracts made and entered into by the board of directors.

3.   To transact such other business as may properly come before the meeting.

/s/James Green

Secretary of FUN CITY MARKETING, INC.

**EXAMPLE—Notice of Special Meeting of Shareholders**

[*NAME AND ADDRESS OF CORPORATION*]

[*Date*]

### NOTICE OF SPECIAL MEETING
### OF SHAREHOLDERS

To Our Shareholders:

Notice is hereby given that a Special Meeting of Shareholders will be held at _____ at _____M., on _____, for the purpose of considering the following matters:

1. To consider and act upon a proposal to adopt an Amendment to the Articles of Incorporation to change the corporation's name to _____.

2. To transact such other business as may properly come before the meeting.

Secretary of [*Name of Corporation*]

### PROBLEM

XYX Corporation is calling a special meeting of shareholders on January 5, 19—, at 10:00 A.M. for the purpose of increasing the authorized capital of the corporation to 100,000 shares, par value $1.00 per share. The meeting will be held at the corporate headquarters at 125 Market Street, Milwaukee, Wisconsin. Draft a notice for the meeting.

An affidavit of the Secretary of a corporation establishing that notice of a shareholders' meeting was mailed to all shareholders is set forth below:

**EXAMPLE—Affidavit of Mailing**

I, James Green, Secretary of Fun City Marketing, Inc., a Delaware corporation (the "Corporation"), being duly sworn do depose and say that I caused notice of the annual meeting of the shareholders of the said Corporation, a copy of which is hereto attached and is hereby made a part of this affidavit, to be deposited in the United States Post Office at the City of Dover, Delaware, in a sealed envelope, postage prepaid, duly addressed to each shareholder of record of the said Corporation at his or her last-known post office address as the same appeared on the books of the Corporation.

/s/James Green

Secretary of FUN CITY MARKETING, INC.

BE IT REMEMBERED that on this 11th day of July, 19___, personally appeared before me, a Notary Public for the State of Delaware, James Green, who, being duly sworn, did depose and say that he is the Secretary of Fun City Marketing, Inc., and that the facts stated in the above Affidavit are true.

GIVEN under my hand and seal the day and year aforesaid.

/s/John Doe
───────────────
Notary Public

[*Seal*]

### PROBLEMS

**What is an affidavit?  Why is it necessary here?  What is a notary public?  Is it necessary to have a notary public execute all legal documents?**

The Securities Exchange Act of 1934, a federal statute, imposes substantial additional requirements on notices of shareholders' meetings given by certain corporations whose stock is publicly-held.[5] These requirements will not be discussed in this text.

### 4.   Who Is Entitled to Notice?

The names of the shareholders entitled to notice of a shareholders' meeting is complicated because the identity of the shareholders of a corporation may change as shares of stock are transferred from individual to individual.  Therefore, corporation laws generally provide for the board of directors either to (i) select a specific date (the "record date") before the meeting for determining the identity of the corporation's shareholders who are entitled to notice of and to vote at the meeting or (ii) to close the transfer books to prevent changes in ownership from a specified date to the date of the meeting.  See, for example, Section 30 of the MBCA.

The above provision provides for a third alternative if the board does not close the books or set a record date—the date of notice of the meeting is the record date in such a case.  The meaning of the foregoing provision may be illustrated as follows: If the board desires a meeting to be held on June 15 in a given year, it may determine the shareholders entitled to notice of and to vote at the meeting in a state that has adopted the MBCA in any of the following ways:

(a)  Close the transfer books to freeze the shareholders for any period commencing on or after April 26th until June 15, the meeting date.

---

5.   See Chapter One for a short discussion of the federal securities laws and "publicly-held corporations".

(b) Set a record date at any point from April 26th to June 5 of that year.

(c) Use the shareholders of record on the date of the mailing of notices to shareholders.

## PROBLEM

**If the meeting date is to be October 1, what alternatives under the MBCA do the directors have for determining the shareholders entitled to notice of and to vote at the meeting?**

For corporations whose stock is publicly-held and traded on national stock exchanges, the stock exchanges impose certain additional requirements relating to the timing of the record date. First of all, stock exchanges prohibit closing of the books as permitted by Section 30 of the MBCA. This is because stocks which are actively traded on exchanges, such as General Motors, should not be impeded or prevented from trading by closing of the transfer books. Additionally, the New York Stock Exchange requires that it be given at least ten days' notice of any record date, whether it is to determine shareholders entitled to vote at a shareholders' meeting, to receive dividends or to exercise some other right in their capacity as shareholders. Thus, when a board of directors of a corporation whose stock is listed on the New York Stock Exchange intends to call a meeting of shareholders, it must, in establishing the record date and meeting date, take into consideration not only the notice requirements of state law and the corporation's by-laws, but also the rules of the Exchange requiring sufficient notice of the record date.

It is also necessary to determine which classes of stock are entitled to vote on a particular matter.[6] Holders of common stock are generally entitled to vote on any matter for which shareholder approval is required. On the other hand, there are situations and particular matters on which another class of stock or all other classes of stock may have voting privileges. For example, if dividend rights or rights on dissolution of the corporation of a preferred class of stock were to be changed by an amendment to the articles, that preferred class would have the right to vote on the amendment. It would not ordinarily have such a right. Generally, the corporation's articles or by-laws will indicate which classes of stock are entitled to vote on any given question. However, if the holders of any class of stock could be uniquely affected as a class by certain corporate action, such as elimination of that class' dividend rights, they are entitled to have notice of the meeting and to vote on that matter, notwithstanding the fact that their stock is termed non-voting by the corporation's articles or by-laws.[7] The purpose of such a right is to grant fairness to

---

6. See Chapter Eight for a discussion of different classes of stock.

garding voting rights of classes other than common stock.

7. Section 60 of the MBCA provides a sample of a statutory provision re-

such shareholders and prevent the loss of rights without their consent.

### 5.  Maintenance of Shareholders' List

Most state laws require the officers of corporations to make available to the shareholders, prior to a meeting, a list of all shareholders at the record date who are entitled to vote at the meeting. The MBCA provides in Section 31 for the provision of a voting record of shareholders entitled to vote.  The requirement of producing a list before the meeting will enable shareholders who oppose management to contact the shareholders to campaign for their position.  It will also permit shareholders to verify independently of management who is entitled to vote at the meeting and their voting strength.  Paralegals may attend meetings and tally votes and take roll of shareholders present.  In the case of corporations which have many hundreds or thousands of shareholders, the shareholder list usually consists of a computer printout.  In such cases the record of shareholders' ownership is on computer programs.

### 6.  Proxies

State laws permit shareholders, who are not able to be present at a shareholders' meeting, to have their shares voted on their behalf by others by the use of "proxies".  For example, the MBCA suggests the following:

> "A shareholder may vote either in person or by proxy executed in writing by the shareholder or by his duly authorized attorney-in-fact.[8]  No proxy shall be valid after eleven months from the date of its execution, unless otherwise provided in the proxy."
> Section 33, MBCA.

A proxy is a written authorization to the person or persons named to vote shares at a shareholders' meeting with the same effect as if the holder of the shares were present in person at the meeting. A form of proxy appears below:

### EXAMPLE—Proxy Form for Annual Meeting of Shareholders

FUN CITY MARKETING, INC.

ANNUAL MEETING OF SHAREHOLDERS
JULY 31, 19__

KNOW ALL MEN BY THESE PRESENTS, that the undersigned shareholder of Fun City Marketing, Inc., here-

---

8.  An attorney-in-fact is a person who has been granted a power of attorney by another person.  A power of attorney is a writing which authorizes a person to act for the person signing the writing as described in the writing.  It is the creation of a formal "agency" relationship.

by appoints John Jones, William Smith and Ephraim Too and each of them the true and lawful attorney or attorneys of said shareholder, with full power of substitution and revocation to each of them (the action of a majority of them or their substitutes present and acting or, if only one be present and acting then the action of such one to be in any event controlling) for and in the name of the undersigned to vote all shares of stock which the undersigned would be entitled to vote if personally present at the annual meeting of the shareholders of said corporation, called to be held on Friday, July 31, 19___, and at any adjournment or adjournments thereof, with all the powers the undersigned would possess if personally present: 1. for the election of directors; 2. for the appointment of a firm of certified public accountants to act as auditors of the corporation; and 3. for the transaction of such other business as may come before the said meeting.

The undersigned hereby acknowledges receipt of the notice, dated July 1, 19___, of such annual meeting of shareholders and hereby revokes any proxy or proxies heretofore given.

_____

[Date]

_____

[Name of Registered Shareholder]

Shares _____

(Signature should correspond with name typed on the reverse hereof.   No witness is required.)

Return proxies to FUN CITY MARKETING, INC.,
Philadelphia, Pennsylvania   19103

### PROBLEM

Using the above form, draft a proxy card for XYC Corporation to be used at its January 15, 19___, meeting where (i) auditors are being appointed and (ii) a proposal to amend the articles of incorporation to change the corporate name to ABC Corporation is to be considered.  (Don't forget the general authorization provision.)

For publicly-held corporations with a large number of shareholders, the only way to obtain a sufficient number of votes (a "quorum") [9] to hold a valid shareholders' meeting is for the management of the corporation to solicit proxies.  The federal securities laws impose requirements on such corporations when they solicit proxies from their shareholders.

_____

9.  See Subsection 7 below for a discussion of "quorum".

## PROBLEMS

Can a shareholder give a proxy and later revoke it by sending another proxy with different instructions prior to the voting at the meeting? By revoking it and electing to vote in person? Can such revocation be effective if received by the corporation after the first proxy has been voted in accordance with its instructions?

A proxy card for companies with large numbers of shareholders is usually merely a printed computer card which may be addressed to shareholders and tallied by the computer.

## 7.    Quorum

No action may be taken at any meeting of shareholders unless a quorum is present. The MBCA provision is set forth in Section 32.

## PROBLEMS

Using the aforementioned Section of the MBCA, compute how many shares constitute a quorum if 1,000,000 shares are outstanding if the articles of incorporation are silent on the subject.

If the minimum required number of shares for a quorum is present, how many shares must vote affirmatively on a matter to approve the action?

Normally, the determination that a quorum exists is made by the secretary of the corporation. When there are judges of election such persons will perform this function.

## 8.    Judges of Election

Many corporation statutes provide for use of inspectors or judges of elections. They may be employees of the corporation who are not standing for election as directors of the corporation, or, if a company is large enough to have employed a separate transfer agent that keeps records of shareholders, an employee of the transfer agent may serve. These inspectors or judges, when utilized, are responsible for and have the authority to determine officially the number of shares entitled to vote at the meeting, the shares represented (in person or by proxy) at the meeting, the presence of a quorum, and to tabulate and determine the outcome of all shareholder votes. They are ordinarily only utilized by corporations which have a substantial number of shareholders or a corporation with a few shareholders when there is an election contest. Section 512 of the Pennsylvania Business Corporation Law is typical in setting forth the authority and responsibility of "judges of election" and the circumstances when there use is required or optional:

> "A.  In advance of any meeting of shareholders, the board of directors may appoint judges of election, who need not be shareholders, to act at such meeting or any adjournment thereof.  If judges of election be not so appointed, the chairman of any such meeting may, and on the request of any shareholder or his proxy shall, make such appointment at the meeting.  The number of judges shall be one or three.  If appointed at a meeting on the request of one or more shareholders or proxies, the majority of shares present and entitled to vote shall determine whether one or three judges are to be appointed.  No person who is a candidate for office shall act as a judge.

> "B.  In case any person appointed as judge fails to appear or fails or refuses to act, the vacancy may be filled by appointment made by the board of directors in advance of the convening of the meeting or at the meeting by the person or officer acting as chairman.

> "C.  The judges of election shall determine the number of shares outstanding and the voting power of each, the shares represented at the meeting, the existence of a quorum, the authenticity, validity, and effect of proxies, receive votes or ballots, hear and determine all challenges and questions in any way arising in connection with the right to vote, count and tabulate all votes, determine the result, and do such acts as may be proper to conduct the election or vote with fairness to all shareholders.  The judges of election shall perform their duties impartially, in good faith, to the best of their ability, and as expeditiously as is practical.  If there be three judges of election, the decision, act or certificate of a majority shall be effective in all respects as the decision, act or certificate of all.

> "D.  On request of the chairman of the meeting, or of any shareholder or his proxy, the judges shall make a report in writing of any challenge or question or matter determined by them, and execute a certificate of any fact found by them.  Any report or certificate made by them shall be prima facie evidence of the facts stated therein."

The corporation pays the judges who are appointed by the board of directors.  Note that the MBCA has no provision similar to the above Pennsylvania provision.

## QUESTION

**Does this mean that a shareholders' meeting in an MBCA state could not have judges of election appointed?**

Normally, the judges of election are required to execute an "Oath" which is filed with the minutes of the meeting. A form of Oath of Judge of Elections is set forth below:

### EXAMPLE—Oath of Judges of Election

We, John Able, Joan Baker and James Charley, duly appointed Judges of Election of Fun City Marketing, Inc., do solemnly swear that we will faithfully and impartially perform our duties as Judges of Election at the annual meeting of shareholders of the above named corporation to be held on July 31, 19__, and that we will fairly and diligently canvass the votes cast at such election and honestly and truthfully report the result of said election.

/s/John Able
_____
John Able

/s/Joan Baker
_____
Joan Baker

/s/James Charley
_____
James Charley

SWORN TO AND SUBSCRIBED BEFORE ME THIS 31st day of July, 19__.

/s/John Doe
_____
Notary Public


## 9. Voting

The simplest method of voting, and one that is only practical in corporations with a few shareholders, is for the shareholders present at the meeting, along with persons holding proxies for shareholders who are not present at the meeting, to indicate by voice or hand their approval or disapproval for any proposal presented and for the person presiding at the meeting to record which shareholders are for or against the proposal and the number of shares voted by each shareholder. If judges or inspectors are elected, they will tally the vote.

The more common method of voting is by ballot, even when not required by state law. Many states, however, require that the election of directors be conducted by ballot.  For example, Delaware law provides as follows: [10]

"All elections shall be by written ballot, unless otherwise provided in the certificate of incorporation."

Section 211(e), Delaware General Corporation Law.[11]

Ballots normally make specific reference to the matter to be voted upon so that no confusion can exist in their use.  Sample forms of ballots for use by a shareholder voting his or her own stock and by a person voting stock pursuant to a proxy are included below:

**EXAMPLE—Ballot for Shareholders**

XYZ CORPORATION

ANNUAL MEETING OF SHAREHOLDERS
HELD JULY 1, 19__

BALLOT

The undersigned, the holder of record on July 1, 19__, of _____ shares of the Common Stock of XYZ Corporation, a Pennsylvania corporation (the "Company"), and entitled to vote such shares at the above-mentioned meeting of shareholders of the Company, does hereby, for and on behalf of himself or herself, vote said shares with respect to the election of directors and the adoption of proposals attached hereto as follows:

Proposal 1—Election of Directors

**Shares**

[*Names
of
Directors*]

Proposal 2—Amendment of "Purpose" Clause

**For**                                    **Shares**

**Against**

10.  Compare the Pennsylvania Business Corporation Law at Section 505A, which does not require a ballot unless the by-laws otherwise provide.

11.  Note that a Delaware corporation can avoid the necessity of a ballot only if the certificate of incorporation so provides.  Even such a provision in the by-laws is not effective.  This points up the necessity of reading the statute of the state of incorporation.

Proposal 3—Elimination of Cumulative Voting

                                                    **Shares**
            **For**
        **Against**

Proposal 4—Approval of Auditors

            **For**                                 **Shares**
        **Against**

_____ (Signed)
_____ (Printed)
        *[Name of Registered Shareholder]*

**EXAMPLE—Ballot for Proxies**

### XYZ CORPORATION

### ANNUAL MEETING OF SHAREHOLDERS
### HELD JULY 31, 19__

### MANAGEMENT PROXY BALLOT

The undersigned, as attorneys and proxies of shareholders of XYZ Corporation, a Pennsylvania corporation (the "Company"), acting pursuant to written proxies executed by holders of record of an aggregate _____ shares of the Common Stock of the Company entitled to vote at the above-mentioned meeting of shareholders of the Company, which proxies have been filed with the Secretary of the Company, do hereby, for and on behalf of said shareholders, vote said shares with respect to the election of directors and the adoption of proposals attached hereto, as follows:

Proposal 1—Election of Directors

                                                    **Shares**
        *[Names
        of
        Directors]*

Proposal 2—Amendment of "Purpose" Clause

            **For**                                 **Shares**
        **Against**

Proposal 3—Elimination of Cumulative Voting

                                                    **Shares**
            **For**
        **Against**

Proposal 4—Approval of Auditors

**Shares**

**For**

**Against**

_____

[*Name of Proxy*]

_____

[*Name of Proxy*]

It should be noted that there must be a separate ballot or section of a ballot for each proposal that will be voted upon at the meeting.

Once all of the shareholders and holders of proxies who are present at the meeting have voted by ballot, the judges of election, if they have been appointed, or the Secretary of the meeting, if he or she is serving as the judge, will prepare a report setting forth the results of the voting.  A sample form of report of voting is found below:

**EXAMPLE—Report of Judge of Elections**

XYZ CORPORATION

ANNUAL MEETING OF SHAREHOLDERS
HELD JULY 31, 19__

REPORT OF JUDGE OF ELECTIONS

The undersigned, duly appointed and qualified Judge of Election at the Annual Meeting of Shareholders of XYZ Corporation (the "Company") held on July 31, 19__, American Trust Bank Building, Southwest Corner of Broad Street and 7th Avenue, New York, New York, does hereby certify:

1.    Before entering upon the discharge of my duties as Judge of Election at said Meeting, I took and subscribed to an oath to execute faithfully the duties of Judge of Election with strict impartiality in accordance with the best of my ability.

2.    At said Meeting, I examined the list of holders of the Common Stock of the Company as of the close of business on July 1, 19__, the record date for said meeting, and the written proxies and ballots presented to me;  and I determined that holders of record of _____ shares of the Common Stock of the Company were represented in person or proxy at the Meeting, out of a total of 1,000,000 shares of Common Stock which are outstanding.  Therefore, there were represented in person or by written proxies ___% of the Common Stock of the Company entitled to vote at the

Meeting, which percentage constituted a quorum pursuant to the requirements of law.

3. The result of a vote taken by ballot and conducted by me as Judge of Election on the resolutions and proposals attached hereto, duly moved and seconded at said Meeting, was as follows:

Proposal No. 1

**Votes Cast in Favor of**
**Nominees for Directors**

| Nominee | Number of Shares |
|---|---|
| [*Names of Directors*] | |

| | | |
|---|---|---|
| Proposal No. 2 | For: | Against: |
| Proposal No. 3 | For: | Against: |
| Proposal No. 4 | For: | Against: |

4. A majority of the outstanding shares of Common Stock having been voted at this Meeting, at which a quorum was present, in favor of all proposals and for the nominees for directors, such proposals have been duly adopted and such nominees have been duly elected directors of the Company.

IN WITNESS WHEREOF, I have made the foregoing report and subscribe my name hereto this 31st day of July, 19___.

_____

[*Name of Judge of Elections*]

## 10. Minutes

At every shareholders' meeting a record of the meeting is recorded and later placed in the minute book. The minutes are a summary of the proceedings and contain any formal resolutions of the shareholders.[12]

The minutes are not a transcription of the meeting but only a summary. They are often written by the paralegal initially and reviewed by the attorney in charge and corporate officials. The styles of preparing minutes vary greatly and the law firm or corporation with which the paralegal is affiliated will have its own style and preferences as to form.[13]

Resolutions, whether those of shareholders or directors, must do two things: (a) authorize the corporation to take an action and (b)

12. The form of resolution will follow the format of directors' resolutions discussed below under Section II.B.

13. See Section VI of this Chapter setting forth a form of minutes of a meeting of a corporation.

designate those officers or other persons who are entitled to consummate the transaction on behalf of the corporation and the amount of discretion that such persons shall have in consummating the transaction. Unless corporate resolutions carefully do those two things, it is not clear what the corporation is to do or who is to do it on behalf of the corporation. A corporation can only act through designated authorized persons.

### PROBLEMS

How does the requirement of formal resolutions for a corporation differ from the method of operation of a partnership or sole proprietorship?[14] Are minutes and resolutions necessary to authorize actions of the partnership or proprietorship? Why or why not? Can partners or proprietors act on behalf of the business without specific authorization by resolution?

## 11.  Summary

The following is a checklist of tasks for a paralegal prior to and after a shareholders' meeting.

(a) Preparation of notice of meeting (waiver of notice if possible).

   (1) Location of meeting.

   (2) Place of meeting.

   (3) Time of meeting.

   (4) Actions to take place at meeting.

   (5) Setting of record date.

(b) Preparation of shareholders' list.

(c) Mailing to shareholders.

   (1) Notice of meeting.

   (2) Annual report to shareholders.

   (3) Proxy statement and proxies (if solicited or required).

(d) Preparation of script of meeting.

(e) Attendance at meeting.

   (1) Notes of proceedings.

   (2) Identification of formal and informal actions.

(f) Preparation of draft of minutes and formal resolutions.

### B.   DIRECTORS' MEETINGS

Directors can only act as a body. The action of an individual director is meaningless unless there is only one director. This is

---

14. See Chapter One for a discussion of partnerships and sole proprietorships.

done by statute at meetings or by written consents.[15]   In contrast to shareholders' meetings, state laws normally impose fewer rigid requirements on directors' meetings, leaving the details to the by-laws of the corporation.   This is because the directors' meetings are ordinarily attended by fewer persons and the meetings are less formal to encourage free and open discussion.   This absence of specific formalities will be evident in the discussion which follows.

### 1.  Location

Normally, state law does not indicate the location of directors' meetings.   Typically, the by-laws of the corporation will allow the directors themselves to decide upon the location for their meetings.   A common type of by-law provision follows:

> "*Place.*   Meetings of the board of directors shall be held at such place as may be designated by the board or in the notice of the meeting."

### 2.  When

State law does not impose any requirement for the frequency of directors' meetings.   The by-laws of most corporations permit the board to designate a regular meeting date as in the following example:

> "*Regular Meetings.*   Regular meetings of the board of directors shall be held at such times as the board may designate by resolution.   Notice of regular meetings need not be given."

Acting under the authority given to it in the by-laws, the board of directors will adopt a resolution, such as the one that follows, specifying when regular meetings will be held:

> "RESOLVED, that regular meetings of the board of directors of this Company shall be held at the executive offices of the Company on the first Monday of the months of February, April, June, August, October and December, or, if such date shall be a legal holiday, on the next succeeding day which is not a legal holiday."

### PROBLEM

**Must regular meetings be provided for in the by-laws? Does the MBCA require them?**

In addition to regular meetings, by-laws will also provide for special meetings as the following example shows:

> "*Special Meetings.*   Special meetings of the board of directors may be called at any time by the president and shall be called by the president upon the written request of one-third of the directors.   Notice (which need not be written) of the time and place of

---

15.  Consents are discussed at Section III below.

each special meeting shall be given to each director at least two days before the meeting."

### 3. Notice

With no statutory requirements, it is typical to provide in the by-laws for no notice in the case of regular meetings and a short notice period in the case of special meetings. This distinction is illustrated in the by-law clauses above, relating to regular and special meetings.

#### PROBLEM

Must the purpose for a special meeting be stated in the notice? Why or why not?

### 4. Who Is Entitled to Notice?

As indicated in the by-law clause relating to the special meetings of directors above, each director is entitled to notice of a special meeting of directors.

#### PROBLEM

What if one director of seven is not properly notified before a meeting is held? Is action by the other six directors valid? If not, can the defect in notice be cured? What if the director who was not properly notified is present at the meeting? Use the MBCA in formulating your answers.

### 5. Quorum

While state laws do not impose many requirements in connection with directors' meetings, they normally do impose quorum requirements such as that suggested by the MBCA:

"A majority of the number of directors fixed by or in the manner provided in the by-laws or in the absence of a by-law fixing or providing for the number of directors, then of the number stated in the articles of incorporation, shall constitute a quorum for the transaction of business unless a greater number is required by the articles of incorporation or the by-laws. The act of the majority of the directors present at a meeting at which a quorum is present shall be the act of the board of directors, unless the act of a greater number is required by the articles of incorporation or the by-laws."

Section 40, MBCA.

#### PROBLEM

If X corporation has nine directors, and the by-laws and articles are silent as to a quorum at a directors' meeting, how many directors are required to do business at a directors' meeting under the MBCA statute? What is the minimum number of directors that can possibly take affirmative action at such a meeting?

The by-laws may also contain a clause covering quorum requirements, but this clause will not normally depart from the statutory requirement. A sample by-law provision follows:

"*Quorum.* A majority of all the directors in office shall constitute a quorum for the transaction of business at any meeting and, except as otherwise provided herein, the acts of a majority of the directors present at any meeting at which a quorum is present shall be the acts of the board of directors."

### 6. Proxies

Since statutes do not permit directors to be represented at directors' meetings by written proxies, directors must attend a meeting to be able to vote on the matters considered at the meeting. The reason for prohibition of proxies is that directors are "fiduciaries"[16] of a corporation and as such have been imposed with certain obligations. Therefore, they cannot delegate away their obligations to a proxy and must act personally.

### 7. Voting

No requirements are imposed by statute on the method by which directors vote. Normally, voting is done by a voice vote with one person, who is keeping the minutes of the meeting, keeping a record. As discussed earlier, it is often the paralegal who will be keeping the minutes.

### 8. Minutes

A paralegal often will make the initial draft of minutes which record the proceedings and resolutions of a meeting.[17]

### PROBLEMS

Why are minutes needed? Do partnerships hold meetings of partners to authorize partners to act? Can partners act without such meetings?[18] Can corporations act without such meetings? Must a directors' meeting be held to authorize every corporate action? Only major actions? If so, which major actions? If a corporation is in the business of selling real estate, must every sale of land be preceded by a directors' resolution? How about a sale of land by a manufacturing company? How

16. A "fiduciary" is a person in a position of trust with respect to another person such as the relationship of a director to the corporation. The law imposes duties on a fiduciary so that the director must not take advantage of the position or the law will make the director answerable for damages. There are many other fiduciary relationships on which the law imposes obligations and duties. For example: attorney-client, physician-patient, trustee-trust, spouse-spouse, parent-child. Can you think of others?

17. The discussion of minutes above is applicable to directors' meetings as well.

18. See Chapter One for a discussion of differences between partnerships and corporations.

about the sale by a corporation engaged in the sale of real estate of all its real estate at one time to one purchaser?

Often the directors will be asked to approve a transaction which has already taken place, perhaps because there was inadequate time to prepare for a directors' meeting. For example, the president of the company may enter into a lease on behalf of the corporation without board approval and later seek approval of the board. The process of confirming a previous act done on behalf of a corporation is called "ratification". Ordinarily any action that could have been authorized in advance by the directors can be ratified by them after the fact. An example of a resolution ratifying a lease is as follows:

> RESOLVED, that the entry into a lease in the form attached hereto between XYZ Corporation and this Corporation pursuant to which this Corporation shall lease Blackacre for a period of one year for $10,000, be and is hereby ratified, approved, confirmed and adopted.

PROBLEM

Can shareholders similarly ratify actions which have previously taken place?

## 9. Summary

Following is a summary of actions that paralegals may do prior to or after a directors' meeting:

(a) Preparation of notice of meeting (waiver of notice if available).

   (1) Location of meeting.

   (2) Place of meeting.

   (3) Time of meeting.

   (4) Actions to take place at meeting.

(b) Mailing of notice to directors.

(c) Attendance at meeting.

   (1) Notes of proceedings.

   (2) Identification of formal and informal actions.

(d) Preparation of draft of minutes and formal resolutions.

C. ‑OTHER MATTERS

## 1. Waiver of Notice

Under the corporation laws of many states, a "waiver of notice", signed by the person entitled to receive notice, is deemed to be the equivalent of actual notice. A waiver of notice may be used for both shareholders' and directors' meetings.  Section 8B of the Pennsylvania Business Corporation Law typifies this approach:

> "Whenever any written notice is required to be given under the provisions of this act or the articles or by-laws of any corporation, a waiver thereof in writing, signed by the person or persons entitled to such notice, whether before or after the time stated therein, shall be deemed equivalent to giving of such notice.  Except in the case of a special meeting of shareholders, neither the business to be transacted at nor the purpose of the meeting need be specified in the waiver of notice of such meeting."

A form "waiver of notice" is set forth below:

### EXAMPLE—Waiver of Notice

We, the undersigned, being shareholders of _____, a corporation organized under the laws of the State of _____, do hereby waive any and all notice required by the laws of the State of _____, or by the Articles of Incorporation or By-Laws of said Corporation, and do hereby consent to the holding of a _____ (insert "annual" or "special") meeting of shareholders of said Corporation, on _____, 19__, at _____.M., or any adjournment or adjournments thereof, at the principal office of the Corporation, _____, for the purpose of _____.

We do further consent to the transaction of any business, in addition to the business herein noticed to be transacted, that may come before said meeting.

Dated at the City of _____, State of _____, this _____ day of _____, 19__.

[*Signature lines for all shareholders*]

### 2.  Special Method of Participation at Meetings

Traditionally, for a shareholder or director to participate in and vote at a meeting, it was necessary to be physically present at the meeting or, in the case of a shareholders' meeting, to be represented by proxy.  In recent years, some states such as Pennsylvania have permitted persons to be present at meetings by way of telephone:

> "If the by-laws of a business corporation so provide, one or more directors or shareholders may participate in a meeting of the board, of a committee of the board or of the shareholders by means of conference telephone or similar communications equipment by means of which all persons participating in the meeting can hear each other."

Section 8E, PBCL.

Appropriate by-law provisions to permit conference telephone participation are as follows:

*Directors*:

"*Participation*. One or more directors may participate in a meeting of the board or a committee of the board by means of conference telephone or similar communications equipment by means of which all persons participating in the meeting can hear each other."

*Shareholders*:

"*Participation*. One or more shareholders may participate in a shareholders' meeting by means of conference telephone or similar communications equipment by means of which all persons participating in the meeting can hear each other."

## PROBLEMS

Why is it important that all persons at the meeting hear each other? Is a quorum determined the same way at a telephone meeting as at a meeting in one place? If the corporate laws of the state of incorporation are silent about the use of conference telephone calls for meetings, is a meeting valid if the articles or by-laws have authorized conference telephone meetings?

## III.  WRITTEN CONSENTS

For most corporations, the necessity of having a meeting in order for directors and shareholders to take action can prove cumbersome. The logistics of getting people together on a regular basis may be difficult. To eliminate the necessity of having an actual meeting, some state laws have created a procedure by which action may be taken if consented to in writing by all of the directors or shareholders. The MBCA suggested approach is set forth in Section 44 as to directors and Section 145 as to shareholders.

Forms of unanimous written consents by the board of directors and shareholders of a corporation are set forth below:

### EXAMPLE—Unanimous Written Consent of Directors

### [*NAME OF CORPORATION*]

### ACTION BY UNANIMOUS CONSENT IN WRITING
### OF THE
### BOARD OF DIRECTORS

The undersigned, constituting the entire Board of Directors of [*name of corporation*], a [*name of state*] corporation, in accordance with the authority contained in Section _____ of the _____ Business Corporation Law, without the formality of convening a meeting do hereby unanimously consent to the following action of this corporation:

RESOLVED, that _____

*[Set forth action taken]*

Dated: _____

*[Signature lines for all directors with their names under the respective signature lines]*

Filed with the undersigned on _____, 19___.

_____

Secretary of *[Name of Corporation]*

**EXAMPLE—Unanimous Written Consent of Shareholders**

*[NAME OF CORPORATION]*

ACTION BY UNANIMOUS CONSENT IN WRITING
OF THE
SHAREHOLDERS

The undersigned, being all the shareholders of *[name of corporation]*, a *[name of state]* corporation, in accordance with the authority contained in Section _____ of the _____ Business Corporation Law, without the formality of convening a meeting do hereby unanimously consent to the following action of this corporation:

RESOLVED, that _____

*[Set forth action taken]*

Dated: _____

*[Signature lines for all shareholders with their names under their respective lines]*

Filed with the undersigned on _____, 19___.

_____

Secretary of *[Name of Corporation]*

It must be noted that the written consent is the action itself. Therefore, until it has been *fully executed* by all of the consenters (directors or shareholders), no action has taken place.

### QUESTIONS

**How does this contrast with a meeting of directors or shareholders where the action is effectuated and the minutes of the meeting are later drawn up? Are the minutes of the meeting the action itself or only evidence thereof?**

Under some state laws, shareholder action is permitted to be taken by a written consent signed by less than all of the shareholders in certain circumstances.   For example, Delaware provides the following:

"(a) Unless otherwise provided in the certificate of incorporation, any action required by this chapter to be taken at any annual or special meeting of stockholders of a corporation, or any action which may be taken at any annual or special meeting of such stockholders, may be taken without a meeting, without prior notice and without a vote, if a consent in writing, setting forth the action so taken, shall be signed by the holders of outstanding stock having not less than the minimum number of votes that would be necessary to authorize or take such action at a meeting at which all shares entitled to vote thereon were present and voted   .   .   .

(c) Prompt notice of the taking of the corporate action without a meeting by less than unanimous written consent shall be given to those stockholders   .   .   .   who have not consented in writing. In the event that the action which is consented to is such as would have required the filing of a certificate under any other section of this title, if such action had been voted on by stockholders   .   .   .   at a meeting thereof, the certificate filed under such other section shall state, in lieu of any statement required by such section concerning any vote of stockholders   .   .   ., that written consent has been given in accordance with the provisions of this section, and that written notice has been given as provided in this section."

Section 228, DGCL.

This provision allows less than all shareholders to consent in writing to an action.

### PROBLEM

What if a Delaware corporation follows this procedure but fails to notify other shareholders of the action within a reasonable time?

A suggested form for use by paralegals evidencing written consent by less than all of the shareholders of a Delaware corporation and a special form of notice of such action which is required to be sent to all shareholders pursuant to Delaware law are included below:

### EXAMPLE—Less Than Unanimous Written Consent of Shareholders (Delaware)

[*NAME OF CORPORATION*]

ACTION BY CONSENT IN WRITING

OF THE

SHAREHOLDERS

The undersigned, being the holders of shares entitled to cast more than two-thirds of the votes which may be voted in approval of the corporate action hereafter set forth, and in accordance with the authority contained in Section 228 of the Delaware General Corporation Law, without the formality of convening a meeting do hereby consent to the following action of this corporation:

RESOLVED, that

_____

*[Set forth the action taken]*

Dated: _____

*[Signature lines for all shareholders whose consent will be obtained with their names under their respective signature lines]*

Filed with the undersigned on _____, 19__.

_____

Secretary of *[Name of Corporation]*

## EXAMPLE—Notice of Informal Action by Less Than Unanimous Consent of Shareholders (Delaware)

*[NAME OF CORPORATION]*

*[ADDRESS OF CORPORATION]*

*[Use the Corporation's stationery if available]*

TO ALL SHAREHOLDERS:

Pursuant to the provisions of Section 228 of the Delaware General Corporation Law, notice is hereby given of the following corporate action:

*[Set forth action taken]*

This action was approved by the [Board of Directors on _____,[1] and by the] holders of _____[2] of the Corporation's _____[3] voting shares in a written consent dated _____,[4] and filed with the Corporation on _____.[5]

Sincerely,

_____

Secretary of *[Name of Corporation]*

1. Date of Board Action, if Board approval was required.
2. Number of shares represented by the shareholders' written consent.
3. Number of voting shares outstanding.
4. Date of shareholder action by written consent.
5. Date shareholders' written consent was filed with Secretary.

## IV.  ORGANIZATION MEETING

### A.  GENERAL

The first meeting in a corporation's history is called the "organization meeting".  At this meeting certain matters are transacted which permit the corporation to proceed with its intended business. In most states, the requirement of an initial meeting of directors (if they are named in the articles) or incorporators (if no directors are named in the articles) is expressly set forth in the corporation law and the provisions of the law also indicate some of the matters that will be the subject of the meeting.  Section 57 of the MBCA (which Act *requires* that the articles name the initial directors of the corporation) provides the following:

"After the issuance of the certificate of incorporation [19] an organization meeting of the board of directors named in the articles of incorporation shall be held, either within or without this State, at the call of a majority of the directors named in the articles of incorporation, for the purpose of adopting by-laws, electing officers and transacting such other business as may come before the meeting.  The directors calling the meeting shall give at least three days' notice thereof by mail to each director so named, stating the time and place of the meeting."

### PROBLEMS

In view of the requirement of Section 57 of the MBCA, is a waiver of notice in lieu of notice of the organization meeting valid?  Can the meeting be by unanimous written consent in lieu of a meeting?

Section 210 of the Pennsylvania Business Corporation Law (which Act does not require that the initial directors be named in the articles) provides the following:

"After the filing of the articles of incorporation, an organization meeting of the board of directors named in the articles or of the incorporators if no directors are named in the articles, shall be held, either within or without this Commonwealth [20] at the call of a majority of the directors or incorporators for the purpose of adopting by-laws, which they shall have authority to do at such meeting, of electing directors if no directors are named in the arti-

---

19.  In a state following the MBCA format, the certificate of incorporation is the document issued by the state indicating that the articles of incorporation have been approved.  In other states, such as Delaware, the "certificate of incorporation" is the document filed by the incorporators which the MBCA-type states call the "articles of incorporation".

20.  Note that Pennsylvania (and a few other states such as Massachusetts and Virginia) are formally referred to as a "commonwealth" rather than a "state".  This is a formality only, not a matter of legal significance.

cles, and, in the case of a meeting of the board of directors, of electing officers, and of transacting such other business as may come before the meeting. The directors or incorporators calling the meeting shall give at least five days' written notice to each director or incorporator named in the articles, of the time and place of the meeting."

If state law permits directors to act by written consents,[21] the "organization meeting" can ordinarily be effected by such a written consent. If a meeting must be held, it is common to have a waiver of notice signed by all of the participants rather than waiting for the period required in the notice provision of the law.

## B.  ONE OR TWO ORGANIZATION MEETINGS

If the articles of incorporation have named directors, and if such persons are intended to serve as the actual directors of the corporation after operations have commenced, then only one organization meeting is necessary to transact all the required business. Sometimes, however, "nominal" directors, such as paralegals, attorneys or other employees will be named as directors. This is done to expedite formation of the corporation where the directors who are going to act after operations of the corporation have commenced either are unavailable or undetermined. If the named directors are not intended to serve as directors of the corporation after operations have commenced, then it is necessary to provide for their resignation and for the election of new directors. This can be done in one of two ways:

(1) After the organization meeting, and after shares have been issued, the nominal directors may resign and the shareholders of the corporation, either at a meeting or by a written consent, elect new directors; or

(2) At the organization meeting, nominal directors resign one at a time and new directors are elected to fill each of the vacancies at that meeting.

The following is an example of resolutions which would be used if this latter approach is utilized:

"RESOLVED, that the resignation of John Smith as a director of this Company be and hereby is accepted, effective immediately."

"RESOLVED, that Jennifer Jones be and hereby is elected a director of this Company to fill the vacancy created by the resignation of John Smith accepted in the preceding resolution and to serve in accordance with the Bylaws of this Company until the next annual meeting of this Company and her successor shall have been elected; and that Jennifer Jones be and hereby is requested to participate in this meeting of the Board of Directors."

(Similar resolutions would be adopted for each other resignation and replacement)

21.  See discussion under Section III of this Chapter above.

It should be noted that a majority of the directors who are elected must participate in the meeting to insure that a quorum will continue to exist throughout the meeting.

If no directors are named in the articles of incorporation, then two organization meetings will always be necessary: the first, a meeting of incorporators to elect directors and, if permitted by state law, to approve the bylaws and the second, a meeting of directors, to take all other appropriate action.

Included below is a set of minutes of an Organization Meeting of Incorporators at which the bylaws are adopted and directors are elected.

**EXAMPLE—Organization Meeting of Incorporators (Delaware)**

[*NAME OF CORPORATION*]

MINUTES OF MEETING OF INCORPORATORS

A meeting of the incorporators named in the Certificate of Incorporation of _____, a Delaware corporation, was held at _____ at _____ o'clock __M. on _____, pursuant to the foregoing waiver of notice.

The following persons were present, namely:

[*Names of all Incorporators*]

being all of the incorporators of the Corporation.

_____ called the meeting to order, and upon motion duly made and seconded, was chosen to act as Chairman of the meeting and _____ was chosen to act as Secretary thereof. The Secretary presented the waiver of notice of the meeting, and, there being no objection, the Chairman ordered that such waiver be filed with the records of the Corporation.

The Secretary reported that the Certificate of Incorporation had been filed in the Office of the Secretary of the State of Delaware on _____, and that a certified copy thereof had been recorded in the Office of the Recorder of _____ County in said State, being the County in which the principal office of the corporation in said State is located. There being no objection, the Chairman ordered that the Secretary cause a copy of the Certificate of Incorporation to be inserted in the Minute Book of the Corporation.

The Secretary presented a copy of the proposed bylaws for the regulation of the Corporation's affairs, and such proposed bylaws having been read, the same were, upon motion duly made and seconded, adopted and in all respects approved and confirmed as and for the bylaws of the Corporation. The Secretary was directed to cause a copy of the bylaws to be inserted in the Minute Book of the Corporation.

The Chairman then stated that it was in order to elect Directors of the Corporation as contemplated in the bylaws, and upon motion duly made and seconded, the following, namely:

were duly nominated as Directors of the Corporation to hold office, subject to the provisions of the bylaws, until their respective successors shall be elected and qualify.

There being no other nominations, a ballot was then taken, and, all of the incorporators having voted, the Chairman canvassed the ballots and declared that _____ had been duly elected, by unanimous vote of all the Incorporators, as Directors of the Corporation to hold office, subject to the provisions of the bylaws, until their respective successors should be elected and qualify.

Upon motion duly made and seconded, the following resolution was then unanimously adopted:

RESOLVED, that the Board of Directors of this corporation be and it hereby is authorized in its discretion, subject to the provisions of law and the Certificate of Incorporation and bylaws of this Corporation, to issue from time to time shares of the capital stock of this Corporation in such amounts and for such consideration permitted by laws as said Board shall from time to time determine.

There being no further business to come before the meeting, it was, upon motion duly made and seconded, adjourned.

_____
Secretary of the Meeting

A form of minutes of an organization meeting of directors at which all necessary initial action is taken follows:

**EXAMPLE—Organization Meeting of Directors (Following Incorporators' Meeting) (Pennsylvania)**

[*NAME OF CORPORATION*]

MINUTES OF FIRST MEETING
OF
BOARD OF DIRECTORS

The first meeting of the Board of Directors of the above corporation was held at _____ o'clock __M. on _____ at _____ pursuant to due notice.

The following directors, constituting all of the directors, were present, namely:

_____ called the meeting to order and upon motion duly made and seconded was chosen to act as Chairman of the meeting and _____ was chosen to act as Secretary of the meeting.

The Secretary then presented the Minutes of the Meeting of the Incorporators of the Corporation held at _____ o'clock __M., reciting that the Articles of Incorporation had been filed in the office of the Secretary of the Commonwealth of Pennsylvania on _____. He also presented a copy of the By-Laws of the Corporation adopted at said Incorporators' meeting and, upon motion duly made and seconded, the following resolution was unanimously adopted:

> RESOLVED, that the minutes of the meeting of the Incorporators of this Corporation presented to this meeting, be and hereby are in all respects approved; and that the by-laws adopted at said meeting of Incorporators be and hereby are in all respects also approved and adopted by the Board of Directors as the by-laws of this Corporation for the regulation of its business and affairs.

The Chairman then stated that it was in order to proceed to the election of officers of the Corporation, and, upon motion duly made and seconded, the following persons were duly elected to the offices set forth below opposite their respective names, each to serve, subject to the provisions of the by-laws, until their respective successors are elected and qualify:

Thereupon, upon motion duly made and seconded, the following resolution was duly adopted:

> RESOLVED, that the proper officers of this Corporation be and they hereby are authorized and directed for and on behalf of the Corporation and under its corporate seal, if required, to make, execute and file any certificates or reports required by law to be filed in any State or States in which the officers of the Corporation shall find it necessary or advisable to file them in order to authorize the Corporation to transact business in such State or States, or for any other lawful purpose whatsoever.[22]

22. A corporation, unlike individuals, cannot operate outside its state of incorporation, unless it "registers" or "qualifies" to do business in the other states in which it is doing business. This resolution authorizes such qualification in other states. A corporation is called a "foreign" corporation by states other than its state of incorporation. See Chapter Two, Section VI.

The Secretary presented a proposed corporate seal for the Corporation to the meeting, and upon motion duly made and seconded, the following resolution was duly adopted:

RESOLVED, that the seal in the form presented to this meeting, bearing the inscription "_____ Corporate Seal 19__ Pennsylvania" be and hereby is approved and adopted as the corporate seal of this Corporation.

The Chairman then presented a form of proposed stock certificate of the Corporation and a specimen copy thereof was directed by the Chairman to be filed with the records of the meeting. Thereupon, upon motion duly made and seconded, the following resolutions were duly adopted:

RESOLVED, that the form of stock certificate for shares of capital stock of this Corporation, presented to this meeting, be and hereby is approved and adopted as the stock certificate of this Corporation, and that stock certificates in such form appropriately filled in, may be signed by the President or any Vice President and the Treasurer or any Assistant Treasurer or the Secretary or any Assistant Secretary of this corporation.

RESOLVED, that all of the authorized common stock of this Corporation, none of which is now outstanding, shall be issued pursuant to the following Plan in accordance with the provisions of Section 1244 [23] of the Internal Revenue Code of 1954, as amended: namely, that this Board of Directors, in its discretion, shall offer out of the Corporation's authorized common stock, during the period beginning with the date of this resolution and expiring not later than two years from the date hereof, all or any part of such shares to the full amount or number authorized by the Articles of Incorporation, in such amounts and for such consideration, consisting of money or property (other than stock or securities), as it from time to time determines and as may be permitted by law, provided that the maximum consideration to be received for all such shares shall not exceed $500,000.

23. A discussion of Section 1244 Plans is contained below under Section IV. C.8.

RESOLVED, that the appropriate officers of this Corporation are each authorized to execute and file with the Pennsylvania Securities Commission and the corresponding regulatory bodies of other states and the District of Columbia, such applications or documents as may be required by applicable law.

RESOLVED, that the Corporation accepts the offers of the following persons to purchase the number of shares of the common stock of the Corporation at the prices indicated opposite their names, and the appropriate officers are authorized to issue certificates therefor upon payment of the total purchase price in cash as soon as the appropriate applications or documents have been filed and, if required, approved by the Pennsylvania Securities Commission or any corresponding regulatory body:

| Name | No. of Shares | Total Purchase Price |
|------|---------------|----------------------|

Upon motion duly made and seconded, the following resolution was unanimously adopted:

RESOLVED, that this Board of Directors does hereby adopt in their entirety the resolutions set forth in the certified copy of banking resolutions directed to The New Banking and Trust Company, a copy of which was presented to this meeting.

RESOLVED, that the Treasurer of this Company be and hereby is authorized and empowered to pay and discharge all taxes, fees and other expenses heretofore incurred or to be incurred in connection with the organization of this Corporation and to reimburse the officers of this Corporation and all other persons for all expenditures heretofore made by them in such connection.

RESOLVED, that the Secretary of this Corporation be and hereby is authorized and empowered to procure the necessary corporate books and records and to open and maintain stock transfer books in accordance with the laws of the Commonwealth of Pennsylvania as well as any other applicable laws.

RESOLVED, that the President, any Vice President, the Treasurer or the Secretary of this Corporation be, and each of them hereby is, authorized and empowered to sign for and on behalf of this Corporation and in its corporate name all documents necessary to be signed by this Corporation in the ordinary course of its business; and that the Secretary or any Assistant Secretary of this Corporation be, and hereby is, authorized and empowered to affix the corporate seal of this Corporation to any such document when so signed, to sign in attestation of such seal on all documents to which such seal is affixed, and to certify under such seal and issue copies of this or any other resolution adopted by the Board of Directors or shareholders of this Corporation.

There being no further business, on motion duly made and seconded, the meeting adjourned.

_____
Secretary of the Meeting

The minutes of an Organization Meeting in the form of a Written Consent in lieu of a meeting is set forth below:

**EXAMPLE—Organization Meeting by Written Consent (Directors Named in Articles of Incorporation)**

[*NAME OF CORPORATION*]

ACTION BY UNANIMOUS CONSENT IN WRITING
OF THE
BOARD OF DIRECTORS

The undersigned, being all of the directors of _____, a [*name of state*] corporation (the "Company"), hereby adopt, by this unanimous consent in writing in accordance with Section _____ of the [*name of state*] Business Corporation Law, the following resolutions with the same force and effect as if they had been unanimously adopted at a duly convened meeting of the board of directors of the Company:

RESOLVED, that the bylaws, a copy of which is attached hereto and incorporated herein by reference, are hereby approved and adopted as the bylaws of this Company;

RESOLVED, that the following persons are elected to the offices of this Company set opposite their respective names, to serve in accordance with the bylaws of this Company and at the discretion of the board:

| | |
|---|---|
| James Allen | President |
| Laura Bond | Vice President |
| Emmet J. Charles | Vice President |
| Raymond Dent, Jr. | Treasurer and Assistant Secretary |
| Joan Edwards | Secretary and Assistant Treasurer |

RESOLVED, that the seal impressed on the margin of this page is hereby adopted as the seal of this Company;

RESOLVED, that the form of share certificate for the common stock of this Company attached hereto and incorporated herein by reference is approved and adopted and that share certificates in such form, appropriately filled in, may be signed by the President or any Vice President and the Treasurer or any Assistant Treasurer or the Secretary or any Assistant Secretary of this Company.

RESOLVED, that this Company's fiscal year will end on December 31 of each year;

RESOLVED, that the Treasurer of this Company be and hereby is authorized and empowered to pay and discharge all taxes, fees and other expenses heretofore incurred or to be incurred in connection with the organization of the Company and to reimburse the officers of this Company and all other persons for all expenditures heretofore made by them in such connection.

RESOLVED, that the Secretary of this Company be and hereby is authorized and empowered to procure the necessary corporate books and records and to open and maintain stock transfer books in accordance with the laws of the State of [*name of state*] as well as any other applicable laws.

RESOLVED, that the President, any Vice President, the Treasurer or the Secretary of this Company be, and each of them hereby is, authorized and empowered to sign for and on behalf of this Company and in its corporate name all documents necessary to be signed by this Company in the ordinary course of its business; and that the Secretary or any Assistant Secretary of this Company be, and hereby is, authorized and empowered to affix the corporate seal of this Company to any such document when so signed, to sign in attestation of such seal on all documents to which such seal is affixed, and to certify under such seal and issue copies of this or any other resolution adopted by the Board of Directors or stockholders of this Company.

RESOLVED, that the following Plan for offering common stock under Section 1244 of the Internal Revenue Code is adopted:

## PLAN FOR OFFERING COMMON STOCK
### Adopted on [date]

The common stock ("Stock"), none of which has yet been issued, of the Company will be offered for sale only in accordance with the following plan, and no other stock of the Company will be offered for sale while this plan is in effect.

1.   Stock will be offered for sale commencing [date] at such price (payable in cash or property other than stock or securities) not less than the par value per share and not in excess of an aggregate of $500,000 as the board of directors of the Company may from time to time determine.

2.   Proceeds of the sale of Stock under this plan will be used by the Company for its general corporate purposes.

3.   This plan will terminate on [date—2 years from adoption], unless sooner withdrawn by the board of directors, and no Stock will be issued under it after that date.

4.   This plan is adopted under Section 1244 of the Internal Revenue Code of 1954.[24]

RESOLVED, that this Company accepts the offer of Mr. Bryan Good to purchase 250 shares of the common stock of this Company, par value $1 per share, at the price of $100 per share.

RESOLVED, that this Company issue and deliver to Mr. Bryan Good 250 shares of its common stock, par value $1 per share, against receipt of the full consideration for said shares, namely, $25,000; that the proper officers of this Company be and hereby are authorized and empowered to execute a common

---

**24.**  See Section IV.C.8.

stock certificate representing said 250 shares of common stock, registered in the name of Mr. Good, to affix thereto the seal of this Company, and to deliver same to Mr. Good against payment therefor; and that said 250 shares of this Company's common stock, when issued to Mr. Good, shall be fully paid and nonassessable common stock of this Company.

RESOLVED, that this Company open a bank account with Northern-Penn National Bank; and that the resolutions attached hereto and incorporated herein by reference relating to such bank account be and hereby are adopted and approved.

---
[*Name of Director*]

---
[*Name of Director*]

---
[*Name of Director*]

Dated: _____

## C.  BUSINESS CONDUCTED AT ORGANIZATION MEETING

The following points will be covered in resolutions adopted at an organization meeting of the directors who were named in the articles of incorporation.  The paralegal will often be assigned the task of preparing them as part of the original organization package.

### 1.  Approve Articles of Incorporation

While it is not essential to do so, the minutes of many organization meetings will reflect the filing of the articles of incorporation, the issuance of a certificate of incorporation from the state agency, the approval of the articles of incorporation and a statement that the articles and certificate should be filed in the minute book of the corporation as set forth in the following resolution:

"RESOLVED, that the Articles of Incorporation of this Company, having been filed with the Department of State of the State of New Jersey on June 26, 19___ and a Certificate of Incorporation having been issued by said Department of State, be and hereby are approved, and that the Secretary of this Company be and hereby is instructed to file said Articles of Incorporation and Certificate of Incorporation in the minute book of this Company."

### 2.  Adopt Bylaws

The bylaws of the Company will be adopted and approved in a manner similar to that set forth below:

"RESOLVED, that the bylaws in the form presented to this meeting are approved and adopted as the bylaws of this Company, and are to be filed and maintained in a current status in the minute book of the Company."

## 3. Elect Officers

Officers of the corporation will be elected as the following example indicates:

"RESOLVED, that the following persons are elected to the offices of this Company set opposite their respective names, to serve in accordance with the bylaws of this Company and at the discretion of the board:

| | |
|---|---|
| James Clark | President |
| Mary Dodd | Vice President |
| Helen Edwards | Vice President |
| John Frank | Treasurer |
| Jessica Good | Secretary" |

## 4. Approve Corporate Seal

A corporate seal for the corporation will be approved:

"RESOLVED, that the seal presented to this meeting, an imprint of which is affixed below, be and is hereby adopted as the seal of this Company."

It might be appropriate to digress for a moment to discuss the function of the corporate seal. The corporate statutes of all states authorize a corporation to have a corporate seal. The example used in the MBCA is as follows:

"Each corporation shall have power:

" .   .   . (c) To have a corporate seal which may be altered at pleasure, and to use the same by causing it, or a facsimile thereof, to be impressed or affixed or in any other manner reproduced."
Section 4, MBCA.

While a corporation may have a seal, most statutes do not require the use of a seal for the validity or effectiveness of any contract or agreement to which the corporation is a party. The following Pennsylvania provision is typical:

"Any form of execution provided in the by-laws to the contrary notwithstanding, any note, mortgage, evidence of indebtedness, contract, or any other instrument of writing   .   .   . when signed by the president or vice president and secretary or assistant secretary or treasurer or assistant treasurer of such corporation shall be held to have been properly executed for and in behalf of the corporation. Except as otherwise required by act of Assembly,[25] the affixation of the corporate seal shall not be neces-

---

25. The "act of Assembly" referred to is a statute of the state legislature.

sary to the valid execution, assignment or endorsement by a domestic or foreign business corporation of any instrument in writing." Section 305, PBCL.

Similarly, the Internal Revenue Service no longer requires corporate seals to be affixed to corporate tax returns and other filings. Typically, corporate laws will only require the use of the corporate seal on share certificates [26] and for certain filings by the corporation with the state.[27] In certain states, the corporate seal may be required on certain documents executed by a corporation; for example, a corporate seal may be required for the proper execution by a corporation of a mortgage or a deed conveying real estate. Such requirements may not be found in the state corporate laws but rather in those state laws relating directly to mortgages, real estate deeds, etc. In addition, institutions, such as banks may require a seal on documents even though they are not legally required. Be sure to check with the party on the other side of a transaction as to whether a corporate seal will be necessary.

### QUESTIONS

**What happens if a statute requires a seal in a particular case and it is not affixed to a document? What happens if the bylaws require a seal but it is not affixed to a document? Is the document binding on the corporation anyway? On the other party?**

While corporations are not required to use their corporate seals except in certain limited areas, the use of corporate seals is common and agreements which are of significance to the corporation may have the corporate seal impressed. In the typical case, the board of directors, in approving the execution of an agreement, will specify in a resolution the following:

> "RESOLVED, that the President or any Vice President be and each of them hereby is authorized and directed to execute in the name and on behalf of this Company the XYZ Agreement; and that the Secretary or any Assistant Secretary be and each of them hereby is authorized and directed to affix thereto and attest [28] the corporate seal of this Company."

Note again that the resolutions do two major things: (i) authorize the corporation to do a specific act and (ii) designate those persons who may effectuate the act on behalf of the corporation.[29]

---

26.  See, e.g., Section 23, MBCA.

27.  See, e.g., Sections 602, 806, 1004 and 1101 of the Pennsylvania Business Corporation Law.

28.  In the strictest sense, "attesting" means formally acting as a witness to the execution by another officer.

29.  See Section II.A.10 above for a discussion of resolutions.

Since a corporation can only act through designated individuals, resolutions must do both things. Where so authorized, the corporate seal will be affixed to the agreement and the secretary or assistant secretary of the corporation will sign, attesting to the fact that the seal affixed on the agreement is in fact the corporate seal of the corporation.

### 5.  Approve Form of Share Certificate

The form of share certificate may be approved by the following type of resolution: [30]

> "RESOLVED, that the form of share certificate for the common stock of this Company presented to this meeting is approved and adopted and that share certificates in such form, appropriately filled in, may be signed by the President or any Vice President and the Treasurer or the Secretary of this Company."

### 6.  Establish Fiscal Year [31]

The fiscal year (financial accounting year) for keeping the corporation's financial records may be established by resolution:

> "RESOLVED, that this Company's fiscal year will end on November 30 of each year."

Note that a corporation may adopt a fiscal year other than the calendar year, e. g., July 1 to June 30, but it must ordinarily start at the beginning of a month and end at the end of a month.

### 7.  Adopt Bank Resolutions

Since the corporation will need to open and maintain a checking account at a bank for deposits and paying bills, it must adopt resolutions authorizing the bank account and establishing which persons will have authority to sign for the corporation with respect to the account. The form of resolutions to open the account are normally prescribed and supplied by the bank in which the account will be opened and maintained, and corporations typically adopt bank resolutions in the form established by the bank:

> "RESOLVED, that this Company open a bank account with First National Bank of Iowa; and that the resolutions presented to this meeting relating to such bank account be and hereby are adopted and approved."

---

30.  The statutory requirements for share certificates are discussed in Chapter Two.

31.  Chapter Three shows that the by-laws may be an alternative method of establishing the fiscal year.

Below is a typical form of resolution required by a bank:

**EXAMPLE:**

AUTHORITY FOR CORPORATION TO OPEN A BANK
ACCOUNT, BORROW MONEY, GUARANTEE LETTERS
OF CREDIT, AND PROVIDE SECURITY

CERTIFIED COPY OF RESOLUTION(S) [32] OF

Fine Art, Inc.

AUTHORIZING: (1) OPENING AND KEEPING A BANK
ACCOUNT,

(2) THE BORROWING OF MONEY,

(3) GUARANTEE OF LETTERS OF
CREDIT, AND

(4) PROVIDING SECURITY.

I, the undersigned Secretary of Fine Art, Inc., a Corporation duly organized and existing under the laws of Iowa, having its place of business at 211 S. Broad St., Des Moines, Iowa, hereby certify that the following is a true copy of certain Resolution(s) duly adopted by the Board of Directors of the Corporation in accordance with the By-Laws at, and recorded in the minutes of, a duly convened meeting of the said Board on July 21, 19___, and not subsequently rescinded or modified:

RESOLVED

1. "That an account of deposit and discount be opened and maintained with First National Bank of Iowa, the said account to be subject to the rules and regulations set forth in the deposit receipt folder furnished by the Bank, as well as to the rules and regulations of the Iowa Clearing House Association, to the regulations and operating letters of the Federal Reserve System and the Federal Reserve Bank of Chicago, to the Uniform Commercial Code (Ia.), and to such amendments to any of the foregoing as may hereafter be made.

That funds of this Corporation on deposit with the said Bank be subject to withdrawal by checks, notes, drafts,

---

32. Note that this form is the certificate of the secretary of the corporation to be presented to the bank stating that the resolution has been adopted.

PROBLEMS: Why is the certificate of an officer as to adoption of the resolution required? How else would the bank know that the resolution was adopted?

bills of exchange, acceptances, orders and/or other instruments made in the corporate name, when signed by any

two       of the following: [33]
_____
(insert number)

President
_____
Any Vice-President
_____
Secretary
_____
Treasurer
_____

(Type or print title(s) of officer(s) or name(s) of person(s) authorized to sign; it is suggested that title(s) only be inserted)

and all such checks, notes, drafts, bills of exchange, acceptances, orders and other instruments signed by the Corporation as aforesaid drawn upon said Bank, as drawee or made payable at the Bank, including instruments drawn to cash or bearer or to the individual order of any officer of the Corporation (whether signed by such officer or otherwise), shall be honored and paid by the said Bank and charged to the account of this Corporation, without any obligation upon the Bank to make any inquiry thereabout whatever.

That any and all checks, drafts, notes, and other orders and items of every kind deposited or to be deposited for the account of this Corporation for credit or for collection or otherwise, requiring endorsement in the name of this Corporation, shall be sufficiently endorsed when they bear the name of the Corporation stamped or in writing endorsed thereon, without any signature or countersignature thereto affixed."

2.    "That the officers of this Corporation are hereby authorized from time to time to borrow money and to obtain credit for this Corporation from the said Bank on such terms as may seem to them advisable and to make and deliver notes, drafts, acceptances, assignments, agreements, and/or any other obligations of this Corporation therefor in form satisfactory to the said Bank, any of said obligations to be signed by any       two       of the following:
_____
(insert number)

President
_____
Any Vice-President
_____
Secretary
_____
Treasurer
_____

(Type or print title(s) of officer(s) or name(s) of person(s) authorized to sign; it is suggested that title(s) only be inserted)"

33.  PROBLEMS: What if only one officer signs a check on Fine Art's bank account?  Can the bank honor it? What if the bank does honor it?

3. "That the officers of this Corporation are hereby authorized to execute on behalf of this Corporation its guarantee of Letters of Credit issued or to be issued at its request and on its behalf by or through said Bank and also to execute on behalf of this Corporation any and all agreements relating to drafts drawn under such Letters of Credit, said guarantee and agreements to be signed by any _____two_____

(insert number)

of the following:

President, Any Vice-President,
_____

Secretary or Treasurer
_____

_____

(Type or print title(s) of officer(s) or name(s) of person(s) authorized to sign; it is suggested that title(s) only be inserted)"

4. "As security for money borrowed and credit obtained, and as security for said Letters of Credit, the aforesaid officers of this Corporation, and any one or more attorneys-in-fact appointed by them in writing for such purpose, are hereby authorized to pledge, assign, transfer, endorse and deliver, either originally or in addition or substitution, any stocks, bonds, bills receivable, accounts receivable, contracts, bills of lading, warehouse receipts and commodities covered thereby, trust receipts and commodities and/or chattels covered thereby, mortgages, deeds to real property, policies of life insurance, other choses in action or evidences thereof, and/or any other property of this Corporation; with full authority to the officers of this Corporation having authority to sign or countersign notes, and to any such attorney-in-fact, to endorse and/or assign the same in the name of this Corporation, to execute trust receipts, security agreements, financing statements, and generally to execute any other documents or do any other act that may be necessary or required in connection with the Corporation's account or dealings with the said Bank, including the sale, discount or rediscount of any and all commercial paper, bills receivable and other instruments and evidences of debt at any time held by this Corporation, and to that end to endorse, transfer and deliver the same." [34]

5. "That the foregoing resolutions shall continue in full force and effect until written notice of revocation, duly signed by any officer of this Corporation in the name of the Corporation, or a certified copy of a subsequent resolution

34. This paragraph permits the officers of the corporation to pledge or otherwise provide collateral of the corporation (generally, money or property put up to back up the promise of the corporation to pay) to secure any borrowing from the bank.

of the Corporation pertaining to matters herein contained, shall have been received by the said Bank."

I further certify that the foregoing resolutions are fully in accord with and pursuant to the By-Laws of this Corporation.

I further certify that the following persons have been duly elected to the offices of this Corporation set opposite their respective names and now hold said offices respectively:

| | |
|---|---|
| James Hill | President |
| Dolores Coburn | Executive Vice President |
| Oliver Sinclair | Financial Vice President [35] |
| T. Baird Silton | Secretary |
| Jennifer Simpson | Treasurer |

IN WITNESS WHEREOF I have hereunto set my hand, and affixed the Corporate Seal of this Corporation this 2nd day of August, 19___.

/s/ Jennifer Simpson
_____
(Manual Signature)          Secretary

[*Corporate Seal*]     /s/_____

(If the Secretary is authorized to act alone by any of the foregoing resolutions and such Secretary signs this certification, the President must also sign manually)

## 8.   Adopt Section 1244 Plan

Section 1244 of the Federal Internal Revenue Code provides special tax treatment to certain shareholders of a corporation that has satisfied all of the requirements of such Section. When such a plan has been adopted, eligible shareholders may treat any loss (up to a specified maximum amount) realized upon the sale of the corporation's stock or when the stock becomes worthless as an "ordinary" loss for federal tax losses, and not a "capital" loss (which a sale of stock would ordinarily be). An "ordinary" loss may be used to offset other "ordinary" income of a taxpayer (e. g., wages, interest, income, dividends) for the purposes of computing taxable income while a "capital" loss may be generally used only to offset capital gains (e. g., sales of other stock) and, to the extent there are more capital losses than capital gains, the excess loss may be offset against ordinary income only to a very limited extent. For example, if a shareholder of a corporation with a Section 1244 Plan has salary of $25,000 and a loss in the same year on a sale of his Section 1244 stock of $15,000, the taxable income of such shareholder for federal income tax pur-

---

**35.**  Note the different titles which may be available for officers.

poses will be reduced to $10,000 for that year. However, had the loss on the sale of the stock not been 1244 stock the taxable income would have been approximately $23,000 because of the limitations in offset of capital losses against ordinary income.

One requirement which must be satisfied to achieve Section 1244 tax treatment is that the corporation has to adopt a Section 1244 Plan on a timely basis before the issuance of stock. Ordinarily *all* new corporations should establish a Section 1244 Plan as part of their initial minutes even if their shareholders may not qualify for Section 1244 treatment. It costs nothing to adopt the Plan. A form of resolutions adopting such a Plan may be as follows:

"RESOLVED, that the following Plan for offering common stock under Section 1244 of the Internal Revenue Code is adopted:

Plan for Offering Common Stock
Adopted on July 1, 19___

The common stock ('Stock'), none of which has as yet been issued, of SMITH CORPORATION (the 'Company'), will be offered for sale only in accordance with the following plan, and no other stock of the Company will be offered for sale while this plan is in effect.

1.  Stock will be offered for sale commencing July 1, 19— at such price (payable in cash or property other than stock or securities) not less than the par value per share and not in excess of an aggregate of $500,000 [36] as the board of directors of the Company may from time to time determine.

2.  Proceeds of the sale of Stock under this plan will be used by the Company for its general corporate purposes.

3.  This plan will terminate on June 30, 19___,[37] unless sooner withdrawn by the board of directors, and no Stock will be issued under it after that date.

4.  This plan is adopted under Section 1244 of the Internal Revenue Code of 1954."

This Plan need not be filed with the Internal Revenue Service, but it should be filed with the minutes of the corporation.

## 9.  Authorize Issuance of Stock

At the organization meeting, the directors will authorize the issuance of stock to designated persons at a specified price. The board may set any price for issuance of stock.

---

36.  No more than $500,000 in stock may be issued under a valid Section 1244 Plan.

37.  The stock must be issued within 2 years after adoption of the Plan.

## QUESTIONS

**Use the MBCA as a model statute for your answers.**

1. **Can stock be issued for property?**

2. **What method should directors use to value property received in exchange for stock?**

3. **Can stock be issued for services?**

Stock should not be issued for less than its "par value", if any.[38] However, the shares may, and often are, issued at greater than par value. The par value may be designated at any amount in the articles of incorporation. The example which follows assumes that there will be only one shareholder of the corporation:

"RESOLVED, that this Company accepts the offer of John Smith ('Smith') to purchase 250 shares of the common stock of this Company, par value $1 per share, at the price of $100 per share.

"RESOLVED, that this Company issue and deliver to Smith 250 shares of its common stock, par value $1 per share, against receipt of the full consideration for said shares, namely $25,000; that the proper officers of this Company be and hereby are authorized and empowered to execute a common stock certificate representing said 250 shares of common stock, registered in the name of Smith, to affix thereto the seal of this Company, and to deliver same to Smith against payment therefor; and that said 250 shares of this Company's common stock, when issued to Smith pursuant to this resolution, shall be fully paid and nonassessable [39] common stock of this Company."

## 10. General Authorization to Officers

The following resolutions provide for ongoing general authorization to certain officers of the corporation, as well as authorization to pay expenses in connection with the formation of the corporation:

"RESOLVED, that the Treasurer of this Company be and hereby is authorized and empowered to pay and discharge all taxes, fees and other expenses heretofore incurred or to be incurred in connection with the organization of this Company and to reimburse the officers of this Company and all other persons for all expenditures heretofore made by them in such connection.

"RESOLVED, that the Secretary of this Company be and hereby is authorized and empowered to procure the necessary corporate books and records and to open and maintain stock transfer books in accordance with the laws of the State of Iowa as well as any other applicable laws.

---

38. "Par value" is the minimum that may legally be paid in for stock upon issuance. A discussion of par value is contained in Chapter Eight, Section II.C.

39. Nonassessable stock is stock which has been issued for not less than par value, if any, and the owner cannot be charged for any further amount. This confers limited liability on the shareholder.

"RESOLVED, that the President, any Vice President, the Treasurer or the Secretary of this Company be, and each of them hereby is, authorized and empowered to sign for and on behalf of this Company and in its corporate name all documents necessary to be signed by this Company in the ordinary course of its business; and that the Secretary or any Assistant Secretary of this Company be, and hereby is, authorized and empowered to affix the corporate seal of this Company to any such document when so signed, to sign in attestation of such seal on all documents to which such seal is affixed, and to certify under such seal and issue copies of this or any other resolution adopted by the Board of Directors or stockholders of this Company."

## 11.  Form of Resolutions

It is important to note that when the above resolutions refer to the corporate seal, the form of share certificate, etc., the reference makes it clear that the items are being presented to the meeting.  In such an event the attending persons would physically observe such documents and objects.  If the same resolutions were adopted by a unanimous written consent, the items should be physically attached to the minutes.  Each resolution should then state that the document is "attached hereto and incorporated herein by reference as if set forth herein in full", or, in the case of the seal, "imprinted hereon", and such items should in fact be attached to or imprinted on the written consent.  For example, the following would be used for ratifying the form of the share certificates by unanimous consent:

"RESOLVED, that the form of share certificate for the common stock of this Company attached to these minutes and incorporated herein as if set forth herein in full is approved and adopted and that share certificates in such form, appropriately filled in, may be signed by the President or any Vice President and the Treasurer or Secretary of this Company."

### PROBLEM

Prepare an approval of the corporate seal in appropriate form for unanimous written consent.

## V.  CONDUCT OF MEETINGS

### A.  INTRODUCTION

While state laws impose many requirements on the shareholders' and directors' meetings and specify certain voting procedures, they contain no guidelines on the actual mechanics of the meeting itself. Corporate laws do not address themselves to such questions as who should preside at a meeting, what should be the order of business, what are the rights of persons to participate in the meeting, etc.  In some instances, the bylaws of a corporation will answer some of these questions but very seldom all of them.   The mechanics are largely determined by general rules of "parliamentary procedure" and by standards of a "reasonable" method of conducting a meeting.

The following sections provide a discussion of some of the more usual procedures used in conducting shareholders' and directors' meetings.

## B.   CHAIRMAN AND SECRETARY OF THE MEETING

Someone must preside over a meeting of shareholders and directors and someone must record the business transacted.   The function of "presiding" is normally performed, in the absence of any bylaw provision, by the senior officer of the corporation, who is usually the President.   The "recording" function is normally performed by the Secretary of the corporation.

Some corporations have bylaw provisions indicating which officers of the corporation preside and keep minutes of the meetings.   If the corporation has designated a "chairperson of the board", that person will typically, as the title would suggest, serve at least as chairperson of all directors' meetings and perhaps as chairperson of all shareholders' meetings.   An example of bylaw provisions governing this subject follow:

"(a) The Chairperson of the Board, if elected or appointed, shall preside at all meetings of the shareholders and of the Board of Directors and shall have such powers and duties as the Board may prescribe.

"(b) The President shall be the chief executive officer of the corporation and shall have general charge and supervision of the business of the corporation and shall exercise or perform all the powers and duties usually incident to the office of President.   In the absence of the Chairperson of the Board, the President shall preside at all meetings of the shareholders and of the Board of Directors, shall from time to time make such reports of the affairs of the corporation as the Board may require and shall annually present to the annual meeting of the shareholders a report of the business of the corporation for the preceding fiscal year.

"(c) The Secretary shall attend all sessions of the Board and all meetings of the shareholders and act as clerk thereof, and record all the votes and minutes thereof in books to be kept for that purpose; and shall perform like duties for the executive committee of the Board of Directors when required.   The Secretary shall give, or cause to be given, notice of all meetings of the shareholders and of the Board of Directors, shall perform such other duties as may be prescribed by the Board or by the President, shall keep in safe custody the corporate seal of the corporation, and may affix the same to any instrument requiring it and attest the same."

## C.  ORDER OF BUSINESS

Both shareholders' and directors' meetings are held for specific purposes—normally, the approval of corporate action or the election of officers or directors.

### PROBLEMS FOR REVIEW

1.  Who elects the directors?

2.  Who elects the officers?

3.  Who would vote on an amendment to the articles to change the corporate name?

Before such meetings are held, the person who will act as chairperson of the meeting will usually have an agenda (a list) of the specific matters to be considered at the meeting.  In addition, in the case of shareholders' meetings, the agenda may list those procedural requirements which must be satisfied in order for any action to be properly approved (e.g., determination that proper notice has been given, that a quorum exists, etc.).  In deciding upon the order, most corporate officers rely upon general rules of "parliamentary procedure".  The following is an outline summary of the events which might occur in a routine meeting:

### 1.  Shareholders' Meeting

(a)  Chairperson calls the meeting to order.

(b)  Chairperson designates secretary of the meeting and Judge of Election, if appropriate.

(c)  Chairperson determines whether proper notice for the meeting was given.

(d)  Secretary (or Judge of Election) reports on number of shares entitled to vote at meeting and number of shares represented at the meeting to determine if a quorum is present.

(e)  Minutes of last meeting read or a motion is adopted to dispense with reading.

(f)  Proposal for action presented to the meeting.

(g)  Discussion of proposal.

(h)  Voting on proposal.

(i)  Report of Judge of Election.

(j)  Adjournment.

### 2.  Directors' Meeting

Directors' meetings are more informal than shareholders' meetings.  There are usually fewer persons in attendance and they have more familiarity with each other.  Many times, a meeting of directors will review generally the business operations of the corporation and no specific proposal will be acted upon. When a specific proposal is to be acted upon, the following might represent an outline summary of the meeting:

(a) Chairperson calls the meeting to order.

(b) Chairperson designates the secretary of the meeting.

(c) Minutes of last meeting read or dispensed with by motion.

(d) Proposal for action presented to the meeting.

(e) Discussion of proposal.

(f) Voting on proposal.

(g) Adjournment.

### 3. Bylaw Provision

If a corporation deemed it desirable to do so, it might include a provision in the bylaws covering the order of business at a shareholders' meeting. A sample of such a bylaw provision follows:

"The following order of business shall be observed at all meetings of stockholders, unless otherwise determined by the holders of a majority of the outstanding stock entitled to vote, present in person or represented by proxy; or unless the Chairperson of the meeting determines that this order is impracticable or inconsistent with the purposes of the meeting, in which event the Chairperson may make appropriate changes in this order of business, which changes shall be announced by the Chairperson upon the determination of a quorum:

1. Call meeting to order.

2. Appoint temporary secretary, if necessary.

3. Appoint Judges of Election, if necessary.

4. Present proof of notice of the meeting.

5. Present list of stockholders.

6. Determine that a quorum is present.

7. Read minutes of last previous meeting.

8. Reports of officers and committees.

9. Elect directors, if the meeting is an annual meeting or a meeting called for that purpose.

10. All other business that must be considered.

11. Adjourn."

## D.   SCRIPT OF MEETING

Prior sections in this Chapter have given a bare outline of the events at a shareholders' or directors' meeting. A more complete picture may be obtained by reading a sample "script" of a shareholders' meeting which is set forth below.

## EXAMPLE—Script of Shareholders' Meeting

### XYZ CORPORATION

### ANNUAL MEETING OF SHAREHOLDERS
### JULY 31, 19__

North Trust Bank Building
Southwest Corner of Ninth Street
and South Henry Square
Sacramento, California

**Mr. Anderson (President and Chairperson):** This annual meeting of the shareholders of XYZ Corporation is now called to order.

On behalf of your board of directors and officers, I wish to express my sincere thanks to the shareholders who mailed their proxies, as well as to those of you who are here today, for their interest in the affairs of the Company.

I shall now ask Ms. Brown, the Secretary of the Company, to report whether the requirements for the holding of this meeting have been fulfilled.

**Ms. Brown (Secretary):** In compliance with the provisions of the by-laws of the Company, the board of directors of the Company by resolutions adopted on June 25, 19__, called this annual meeting of shareholders and established July 1, 19__, as the record date for the determination of shareholders entitled to notice of and to vote at this meeting.

At least 10 days prior to the date fixed for the holding of this meeting, there was mailed to all shareholders of record on July 1, 19__ a notice of meeting, a proxy statement and a proxy.[40] My affidavit indicating that such mailing occurred has been filed with the Company.

An alphabetical list of the shareholders of the Company, showing the name, address and number of shares held by each shareholder as of the record date is now on file at this meeting for reference and has been available for inspection at the principal office of the Company for at least the last ten days.[41]

---

40. A proxy is a piece of paper designating another person to vote in the absence of the first from the meeting (see Section II.A.6). This is in contrast to a "proxy statement" which is a document that public companies mail to their shareholders which describes the actions to be taken at the meeting.

41. See Section II.A.5 of this Chapter for the reason for this procedure.

Of the 1,000,000 shares of Common Stock of the Company which were outstanding on the record date for this meeting, there are proxies on file with the Company representing 800,000 shares of such stock, or 80% of the total number of shares outstanding. This constitutes a quorum for the transaction of business.[42]

**Mr. Anderson:** Thank you Ms. Brown. Since requirements for calling this meeting have been duly observed and there is represented here considerably more than the necessary number of shares of the outstanding stock of the Company to constitute a quorum, I hereby declare this meeting to be duly constituted for the transaction of all business. Are there any additional proxies to be submitted to the Secretary of the Company at this time? (Pause)

I hereby designate Mr. Charles of the North Trust Bank to act as judge of election for this meeting. Mr. Charles has already signed an Oath of Judge of Election and presented it to the Secretary of the meeting. The Secretary is instructed to file it with the minutes of this meeting.

As I am sure you recognized from the proxy material which was sent to each shareholder of the Company, there are a number of things to be considered by the shareholders of the Company at this meeting and I propose that we now take up the matters listed in the proxy statement in the order in which they are listed. In order to expedite matters, we will defer discussion and voting on any of the proposals until all of the proposals have been presented. After the proposals have been presented, I will endeavor to answer all questions which you might have.

The first matter set forth in the proxy material is the election of five directors to serve until the next annual meeting of shareholders and until their respective successors shall be elected and have qualified. I would like now to introduce to you the management nominees for directors of the Company, who are all present today: Ms. Kay, Mr. Mark, Mr. Nocks, Mr. Brown and me. Are there any other nominations for the board of directors?

**Shareholder in audience:** I move that the nominations for directors be closed.

**Second Shareholder in audience:** I second such motion.

**Mr. Anderson:** Will all those in favor of the motion to close the nominations for directors please so indicate. Will all

---

42. How does Ms. Brown know that 80% is enough for a quorum?

those opposed please so indicate. The motion is carried and nominations for directors of the Company are closed.

As I indicated, we are postponing the voting on this and other matters until all management proposals are before this meeting.

The second proposal before us is the amendment of Article III of the Articles of Incorporation of the Company in order to modernize the Articles to conform to current corporate practice of giving to the Company the greatest authority permitted under state law to engage in all forms of lawful business activities.

The following resolutions are hereby offered to amend Article III of the Articles of Incorporation of the Company and have been recommended by the Board of Directors for adoption by the shareholders:

> RESOLVED, that Article III of the Articles of Incorporation of the Company shall be restated in its entirety to read as follows:
>
>> "The Company shall have unlimited power to engage in and to do any lawful act concerning any or all lawful business, including manufacturing, processing, research and development, for which corporations may be incorporated under the Act under the provisions of which the Company was incorporated.[43]
>
> RESOLVED, that the proper officers of this Company be and each of them hereby is authorized and empowered to take all such action as any one of them may deem necessary or desirable to effect said amendment of the Articles of Incorporation of the Company.

The next proposal to be submitted to this meeting is the proposal to amend the Articles of Incorporation and by-laws of the Company to eliminate cumulative voting in the election of directors.[44] At present, directors of the Company are elected by cumulative voting and today's election of directors will be so conducted. Under cumulative voting, each shareholder has that number of votes in the election of directors equal to the number of shares owned by him multiplied by the number of directors to be elected. Each shareholder is entitled to cast the whole number of such votes for

---

43. As the reader can tell from comparing this form to the form in Section IV.D of Chapter Two, there is no magic in the exact style of the purpose clause.

44. See Section IV.H.2 of Chapter Two for a discussion of cumulative voting and its consequences.

one candidate or to distribute them among any two or more candidates. The candidates receiving the highest number of votes are elected. Upon the elimination of cumulative voting, shareholders of the Company will only be entitled to one vote per share in the election of directors and it will therefore require the vote of a majority of the outstanding shares represented at annual meetings of shareholders to elect a person to the board of directors.

The following resolutions are offered to effect the elimination of cumulative voting.

> RESOLVED, that paragraph B of Section 5 of Article Fifth of the Articles of Incorporation of this Company shall be restated in its entirety to read as follows:
>
>> "B. Such voting rights of the Common Stock shall be non-cumulative on all matters submitted to the shareholders, including the election of directors."
>
> RESOLVED, that Section 3–09 of the by-laws of the Company shall be amended and restated in their entirety to read as follows:
>
>> "*Election of Directors. Non-Cumulative Voting.* Elections for directors need not be by ballot except by written demand by shareholders at the meeting and before the voting begins. In all elections for directors, each shareholder entitled to vote shall have the right by person or by proxy to one vote for each share standing in the name of the shareholder on the record date."
>
> RESOLVED, that the proper officers of this Company be and each of them hereby is authorized and empowered to take such action as any one of them may deem necessary or desirable to effect the foregoing amendments to the Articles of Incorporation and by-laws of this Company.

The final management proposal to be considered at this meeting is the ratification of the recommendation of the Board to appoint Jones & Co. as auditors for the Company. Jones & Co. has been acting as auditors for the Company since May 1, 19__, is familiar with the affairs of the Company and has been of great assistance to us in our period of growth. The following resolution is offered in connection with the approval of the appointment of Jones & Co. as auditors of the Company:

> RESOLVED, that the appointment of Jones & Co., independent certified accountants, as auditors for

the Company in connection with the fiscal year of the Company beginning May 1, 19___, and ending April 30, 19___, be and hereby is approved.

**Shareholder in audience:** I move that Messrs. Anderson, Mark and Nocks and Ms. Brown and Kay be elected directors of the Company and that all of the resolutions just presented to this meeting by Mr. Anderson be adopted.

**Second Shareholder in audience:** I second the motion.

**Mr. Anderson:** I will now attempt to answer any questions which are asked by shareholders at our meeting today. (Entertain questions)

If there are no further questions, I suggest that we proceed to a vote on these matters. As I indicated to you, the election of directors shall be by cumulative voting.[45] The proposals for Amendment of the Articles of Incorporation require the affirmative vote of the holders of a majority of the outstanding stock to be approved.[46] The proposal for the approval of Jones & Co. as the Company's auditors requires only the affirmative vote of the holders of a majority of the shares present in person or proxy at this meeting to be approved.[47] The voting shall be by ballot and separate votes may be cast on each proposal before this meeting. Ballots are available and anyone so wishing to vote by ballot should now so indicate so that he or she may receive a ballot. All persons voting by ballot should deliver their ballots to our Judge of Election.

Are there any persons who wish to vote and who have not had an opportunity to do so?

If there are no persons who have not yet voted, I hereby declare the polls closed and request the Judge of Election to determine the votes cast and to submit his report.

While waiting for the results of the voting, I would like to take this opportunity to discuss the results of the Company's operations for the last year (Brief report of results). I now have the report of the Judge of Elections covering all of the proposals presented to this meeting and I would like to summarize it for you.

---

**45.** Would it have been possible to vote on the amendments to the Articles *before* the election of directors and, if the amendments passed, elect directors by non-cumulative voting ?

**46.** Note that the correct way of expressing the vote required is *not* the "affirmative vote of a majority of the outstanding stock" but rather "the affirmative vote of *holders* of a majority of the outstanding stock".

**47.** How does the required number of votes for approval of Jones and Co. differ from that required for the Amendment to the Articles of Incorporation ?

I am happy to announce that the holders of 790,000 shares voted for the election of each of Messrs. Anderson, Mark and Nocks, and Ms. Brown and Kay as directors of the Company. Since more than a majority of the shares were voted in favor of the election of each nominee, I am happy to announce that these persons will continue to serve your Company as directors for the ensuing year.

The second proposal, which concerned the revision of the purpose clause of the Articles of Incorporation of the Company, was approved by a vote of the holders of 795,000 shares in favor of such amendment and 5,000 shares against such amendment.

The shareholders of the Company have also approved the proposal which provided for the elimination of cumulative voting in the election of directors by a vote of the holders of 790,000 shares for the proposal and 10,000 shares against the proposal.

Finally, the shareholders of the Company have approved the appointment of Jones & Co. as auditors of the Company, by a vote of the holders of 800,000 shares for the proposal and no shares against the proposal.

Since shares constituting more than 79% of the outstanding stock of the Company were voted in favor of all the matters presented to this meeting, I therefore declare that all of the resolutions presented to this meeting have been duly approved by the shareholders of this Company. The report of the Judge of Elections will be filed in the Company's minute book by the Secretary of the meeting.

If there is no other business, I would entertain a motion that this meeting be adjourned.

**Shareholder in audience:** I move that this meeting be adjourned.

**Second Shareholder in audience:** I second such motion.

**Mr. Anderson:** All in favor so indicate. All opposed please so indicate. Ladies and Gentlemen, thank you for your cooperation at this meeting, and I declare this meeting to be adjourned.

Normally scripts are prepared *prior* to meetings to be used when there are a large number of shareholders expected to be present. Lawyers or paralegals will prepare the script for use at the meeting and the chairperson of the meeting will not depart from it to any degree. The script provides for certain persons to make and second motions and helps insure a smooth flow of business at the meeting. Participating persons are invariably asked in advance to perform these functions, and they, too, will have a copy of the "script". Note that the script is very different from the minutes of the meeting which is a summarized record of events occurring at the meeting.[48]

## VI.  MINUTES

The record of events that occur at meetings of shareholders and directors are maintained in the form of minutes.  State laws generally require such records as set forth in the following MBCA example:

> "Each corporation  .  .  .  shall keep minutes of the proceedings of its shareholders and board of directors  .  .  .  Any books, records and minutes may be in written form or in any other form capable of being converted into written form within a reasonable time."

Section 52, MBCA.

Corporate minutes are usually written by lawyers and paralegals. The language used follows a characteristic form but will vary somewhat from lawyer to lawyer.  Unlike the script of the meeting, informal activities are not placed in the minutes.  However, informal discussion of corporate matters should be reported.  Examples of minutes of shareholders' and directors' meetings are included below:

**EXAMPLE—Minutes of Directors' Meeting**

FUN CITY MARKETING, INC.

SPECIAL MEETING OF THE BOARD OF DIRECTORS
MAY 26, 19___

A special meeting of the Board of Directors of Fun City Marketing, Inc. was held at the offices of the corporation, located at 1700 Market Street, Philadelphia, Pennsylvania, on May 26, 19___, at 10:00 A.M.

The following directors were present:

Joan Smith          William Jones
James Green          George Gray
Richard Thomas

being all of the directors of the said corporation.

Joan Smith, the Chairperson of the meeting, announced that a quorum of the directors was present, and that the meeting was ready to proceed with its business.

James Green, acting as Secretary of the meeting, presented a Waiver of Notice [49] to the meeting that had been signed by all directors.  The Chairperson directed that a copy of the signed waiver of notice be affixed to the minutes of this meeting.

---

**48.**  See Section VI of this Chapter for a discussion of minutes.

**49.**  See Section V.C.1 of this Chapter for a sample of this type of form.

Upon motion duly made, seconded and unanimously passed, the reading of the minutes of the last meeting of the board was waived and the minutes were deemed approved.

There were no reports of officers or committees scheduled to be given at the meeting. Instead, the Chairperson informed the directors that Roger Kent, the President of the Company, had resigned as of May 15, 19___. The Chairperson then suggested that the board consider nominations for the office of President of the corporation. After discussion, the name of James Green was placed in nomination. No other names being proposed, the Chairperson declared that nominations be closed and a ballot taken. The Chairperson announced the result of the balloting to be four votes in favor of Mr. Green's election and none opposed, Mr. Green not having voted. Mr. Green thereupon accepted the office to which he was elected.

The Secretary announced that there was no unfinished business pending. The Chairperson asked if there was any new business to be brought before the board. As there was no new business, and no further business to be conducted, the meeting was, on motion duly made, seconded and unanimously carried, adjourned.

/s/James Green [50]

_____

Secretary of the Meeting

Attest:

/s/Joan Smith [51]

_____

Chairperson

**EXAMPLE—Minutes of Annual Shareholders' Meeting**

FUN CITY MARKETING, INC.

ANNUAL MEETING OF SHAREHOLDERS
MAY 26, 19___

**Time and Place [52]**

The annual meeting of the shareholders of Fun City Marketing, Inc. was held at its principal office at 1700 Mar-

---

**50.** Often the only person to sign the minutes will be the Secretary without a cosigner.

**51.** The "/s/" that you often see is the method of conforming a document to an executed (signed) document to indicate that, while it is not a manually

signed document, it is a true and correct copy of the executed document.

**52.** The centered headings are for the convenience of the student only and do not constitute a part of the minutes.

ket Street, Philadelphia, Pennsylvania, on May 26, 19＿, at 10:00 A.M., pursuant to notice given by the Secretary.

### Chairperson and Secretary

Pursuant to the by-laws, Ms. Joan Smith, Chairperson of the Board of Directors of the Corporation, presided over the meeting and Mr. James Green, Secretary of the Corporation acted as Secretary of the meeting.

### Shareholders List

The Chairperson announced that the transfer books and the stock books of the Corporation, together with a full, true, and complete list in alphabetical order of all the shareholders entitled to vote at the ensuing election, with the residence of each, and the number of shares held by each (which list has been on file at the office of the Corporation continuously since May 15, 19＿),[53] were before the meeting and would remain open for inspection during elections.

### Quorum

Upon the Chairperson's request, the Secretary reported that of the 225,000 shares of the Corporation's common stock entitled to vote at the meeting, the holders of 150,000 shares were present in person and the holders of 50,000 shares were represented by valid proxies.

Thereupon the Chairperson announced that holders of stock in excess of the amount necessary to constitute a quorum were present in person or represented by proxy.

The proxies presented were ordered to be filed with the Secretary of the meeting.

### Notice of Meeting

The Secretary presented an affidavit, duly certified by himself as Secretary of the Corporation, to the effect that notice of the meeting had been mailed to each shareholder entitled to such notice, addressed to such shareholder at his address set forth on the shareholder ledger, postage prepaid, as required by the by-laws of the Corporation. The affidavit was approved and ordered attached to the minutes of this meeting.

Upon motion duly made and seconded, Messrs. Able, Baker and Charley (none of whom were candidates for the office of director),[54] were duly appointed Judges of Election pursuant to the by-laws, and their oaths as such Judges, duly subscribed by them, were handed to the Secretary.

---

53. Why is this necessary? See Section II.A.5 of this Chapter.

54. Can a candidate for director be a judge of election ?

## Minutes of Prior Meeting

The Secretary then presented the minutes of the most recent meeting of stockholders which had been held on May 15, 19__. The minutes were read and approved.[55]

Thereupon the Chairperson presented to the meeting the following papers and documents, all of which were laid upon the table and were publicly declared by the Chairperson to be open for inspection by any shareholder:

1. The minutes of the Board of Directors, covering all purchases, contracts, contributions, compensations, acts, proceedings, elections, and appointments by the Board of Directors, since the annual meeting held on May 15, 19__.

2. The 19__ annual report, a copy of which had been mailed to every shareholder of record as of the record date.

## Ratification of Past Actions

Upon motion duly made and seconded, the following resolution was unanimously adopted:

RESOLVED, that all purchases, contracts, contributions, compensations, acts, proceedings, elections, and appointments by the Board of Directors since the Annual Meeting of Shareholders of the corporation on May 15, 19__, and all matters referred to in the Annual Report to Shareholders for the fiscal year ended March 31, 19__, are hereby approved, ratified, confirmed and adopted.[56]

## Election of Directors

The meeting then proceeded to the election of five directors constituting the entire board of directors, to hold office until the next annual meeting of shareholders and until their successors shall be elected and shall qualify.

The Chairperson reported that the following named individuals had been nominated by management in accordance with the by-laws:

| | |
|---|---|
| Joan Smith | William Jones |
| James Green | George Gray |

Richard Thomas

There were no other nominations.

Upon motion duly made, seconded, and unanimously carried, the nominations were closed.

**55.** Often the Chairperson will entertain a motion to dispense with the reading of minutes to expedite the meeting.

**56.** Does this resolution exonerate directors and officers from any future challenges for wrongdoing in the prior year by a complaining shareholder? If the shareholder had personally voted for the resolution?

Mr. John Doe then asked that a ballot be taken upon the foregoing nominations, and on motion duly seconded, it was so ordered.[57]

The Chairperson, before declaring the polls open, asked if there were any other nominations. Hearing none, she thereupon declared the polls open at 10:45 o'clock A.M., and stated that they would remain open for fifteen minutes for the receipt of ballots upon the nominations made.

At 11:00 o'clock A.M., the Chairperson stated that the polls had now been open for fifteen minutes, and she inquired whether there were any shareholders who had not voted and who desired to vote. As no one requested further opportunity to vote, the polls were then declared closed.

The Judges of Election thereupon inspected the proxies, counted the ballots, and submitted their report. Upon motion duly made and seconded, the report of the Judges of Election was unanimously approved, and the Secretary was directed to file the original report.

The Chairperson thereupon declared that Ms. Smith and Messrs. Green, Thomas, Gray and Jones had been duly elected directors of the Corporation, to serve until the next annual meeting, and until their successors shall be elected and shall qualify.

### Documents To Be Attached To Meeting Minutes

The Secretary was directed by the Chairperson to insert copies of the following in the Corporation's minute book:

1. Notice of meeting and the affidavit stating that the notice had been deposited in the mail.

2. Form of proxy.

3. Certificate of the Secretary as to the regularity of the powers of attorney and the number of shares represented by proxies.

4. Judges' oath and report.

### Adjournment

No other business coming before the meeting, it was, on motion duly made and seconded, adjourned.

/s/James Green
_____

Secretary of the Meeting

Attest:

/s/Joan Smith
_____

Chairperson [58]

---

57. Often a ballot will not be required by the by-laws or will be dispensed with on motion.

58. See footnote 50.

## VII.  MINUTE BOOKS

Minutes of shareholders' and directors' meetings and written consents of shareholders and directors are normally kept in a minute book.  Because the minute book serves as a record of the "legal" history of the corporation and the actions taken by the directors and shareholders, it is typical to include the following in a minute book:

A.  Certificate of Incorporation and Articles of Incorporation.

B.  All Certificates of Amendment and Articles of Amendment.

C.  Bylaws and all bylaw amendments.

D.  Fictitious name filings.

E.  Certificate of authority to do business in a foreign state.

F.  Certificates of Merger and Articles of Merger.

G.  Duplicate originals of any other filings with the state required by corporate law (such as Annual Reports in some states, such as New Jersey).

H.  Proof of all publications required by state corporate law.

I.  All minutes of shareholders' and directors' meetings, all written consents and all notices and waiver of notices of meetings.

As in the case of certain matters acted upon at the organization meeting, there are many instances when the board of directors will approve an agreement or instrument "in the form presented to this meeting".  When this occurs, it is important to include within the minute book a copy of the document, such as a lease, purchase agreement, etc., actually presented to the meeting.  In some cases, only a draft of the document will be available for approval at the meeting. In such a case, that draft should be attached.  The document should also be marked to indicate the meeting at which it was presented. Otherwise, a person reading the minute book will be unable to determine what document was approved, an unfortunate situation which could create a question as to whether the execution of a specific form of agreement was in fact authorized by the board of directors.

Chapter Eight

# CORPORATE EQUITY AND DEBT SECURITIES

## I. INTRODUCTION

Chapter Eight is intended to introduce the vocabulary and principal characteristics of debt and equity securities. With such background knowledge, a lawyer's assistant will be better able to perform a variety of tasks, including preparing minutes, reviewing articles of incorporation, arranging for transfers of stock with transfer agents and registrars, obtaining information from loan agreements, assisting in the registration of securities for public sale, and in preparing closing binders. In contrast to drafting minutes or forming a new corporation where the student is expected to master all aspects of the course materials and develop substantial competence in performing tasks, the student is not expected to develop the expertise to create all of the terms of complicated debt or equity securities.

This Chapter provides a comprehensive description of the principal types of securities which a corporation may issue. Corporate securities fall into two categories: (a) securities which evidence a person's ownership interest in a corporation and (b) securities which evidence the corporation's obligation to pay money to another person. The former type is referred to as "equity" securities and the latter is referred to as "debt" securities. Each of these types of securities will be discussed in detail.

## II. EQUITY SECURITIES

### A. CLASS AND SERIES

State corporate laws permit the creation of various types of equity securities. To begin with, the basic unit of equity securities is called a "share", which is defined under the MBCA to mean "the units into which the proprietary interests in a corporation are divided".[1] Statutes do not limit a corporation to issuing one type of shares. Some states differentiate by "classes" and others subdivide classes into a further category of "series". Other states do not make a clear distinction of this nature. The statute of the specific state of incorporation must be reviewed for the permitted characterization of shares. The MBCA is an example of one type of statute that provides that a corporation is permitted to divide its shares into one or more classes as set forth below. Section 15 of the MBCA is the provision authorizing different classes of shares.

1. MBCA, Section 2(d).

In addition to the right granted by the MBCA to create "classes" of stock, Section 16 of the MBCA is an example of a statute that permits certain classes of stock to be further divided into "series" which may vary from other series of the same class only in certain characteristics, and in all other respects must be identical to other series in the same class.

Other statutes may not be as rigid in limiting the characteristics of shares as to which different series of a specific class may differ from each other. Still other corporate statutes may not even contemplate a series subdivision of classes.

## B. CERTIFICATES

Equity securities are always tangibly represented by "certificates". Certificates are pieces of paper *evidencing* shares; they are not the shares of the corporation itself which cannot tangibly be separated out of the mass of corporate assets. Remember that a share is an undivided interest in the corporation; a certificate is merely the physical evidence of a share. Section 23 of the MBCA has language similar to other state statutes describing some of the features of a certificate.

### QUESTIONS

What does Section 23 of the MBCA do to prevent the officers from being required to execute all certificates manually? What alternative does the corporation have to listing all rights of all classes on the certificate?

**EXAMPLE:**  A sample of a certificate is as follows:

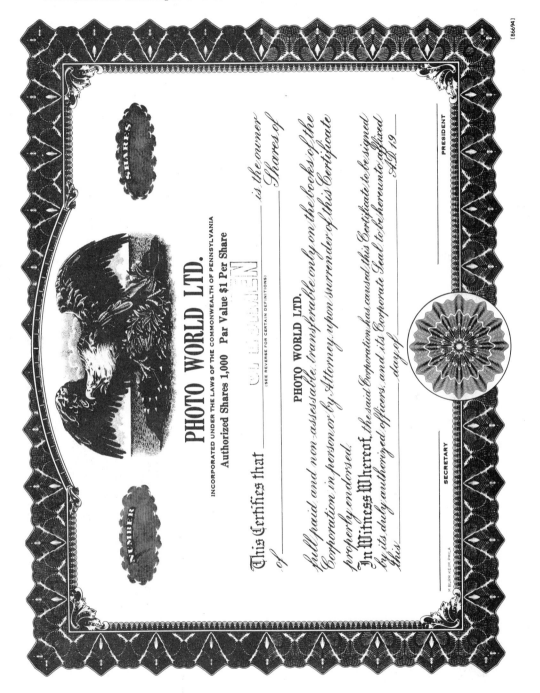

The following abbreviations, when used in the inscription on the face of this certificate, shall be construed as though they were written out in full according to applicable laws or regulations:

TEN COM—as tenants in common
TEN ENT —as tenants by the entireties          UNIF GIFT MIN ACT—.............Custodian.............under
JT TEN —as joint tenants with right of survivorship          (Cust)          (Minor)
     and not as tenants in common          Uniform Gifts to Minors Act..............
                                                            (State)
          Additional abbreviations may also be used though not in the above list.

*For Value Received,_____ hereby sell, assign and transfer unto*

PLEASE INSERT SOCIAL SECURITY OR OTHER
IDENTIFYING NUMBER OF ASSIGNEE

*Shares represented by the within Certificate, and do hereby irrevocably constitute and appoint _____ Attorney to transfer the said Shares on the books of the within named Corporation with full power of substitution in the premises. Dated _____ 19___*

*In presence of*

NOTICE: THE SIGNATURE OF THIS ASSIGNMENT MUST CORRESPOND WITH THE NAME AS WRITTEN UPON THE FACE OF THE CERTIFICATE, IN EVERY PARTICULAR, WITHOUT ALTERATION OR ENLARGEMENT, OR ANY CHANGE WHATEVER.

[B6695]

It should be noted that the statutory language would differ in a state where there was no specific designation of series as part of a class and that merely viewed *any* difference in characteristics of shares as a separate class or category. For most purposes, the difference is one of semantics.

If state law (such as the MBCA example) permits, most corporations that have more than one class of stock authorized do not set forth on their certificates a full statement of the relative rights and preferences of all authorized classes of stock, the variations between series of each class of stock and the authority of the board of directors to fix and determine the relative rights and preferences of additional series of stock. This is because of the considerable expense of printing certificates with all of the terms spelled out in full, and the need to reprint certificates if any change in preferred stock terms occurs. Instead, the following is an example of the type of statement which will normally appear on all certificates representing all classes of stock of the corporation where state law permits:

> "The Corporation shall furnish to any shareholder of the corporation, upon request and without charge, a full statement of (a) the designations, preferences, limitations, and relative rights of the Common Stock and Preferred Stock that the Corporation is authorized to issue, (b) the variations in the relative rights and preferences between series of the Preferred Stock as the same have been fixed and determined and (c) the authority of the board of directors to fix and determine the relative rights and preferences of subsequent series of Preferred Stock."

It should be observed that the specific language of the foregoing statement would be used where appropriate, that is, where there were two classes authorized—Common Stock and Preferred Stock—and where the Board of Directors was permitted by its articles of incorporation to divide the Preferred Stock into series and determine the relative rights and preferences of each series. As is always the case, the paralegal must review the state statute, the articles and by-laws of the specific corporation to determine the appropriate language to use in a specific case. Forms are only guides and examples to aid generally. Be sure to make forms fit the case at hand—don't try to make the case at hand fit forms!

### PROBLEM

**Using the general form of statement set forth above, draft language for a corporation which has Class A Common Stock, Class B Common Stock and Preferred Stock where the board of directors has no authority to authorize series of Preferred Stock.**

## C. PAR VALUE AND NO PAR VALUE STOCK

All shares of stock are either par value stock or no par value stock.

Whether par value or no par value is used by a corporation in a specific case depends on a variety of factors: what the state law permits, how state taxes are imposed differently on the two types and other factors. One of the most important factors is the predilection of the lawyer for whom the paralegal is creating the corporation. In summary, there is no set procedure about whether par value or no par value is used; in one case one type may be used and the other in another case.

If the stock is to be par value stock, then it is important to note the amount per share of the par value. The significance of par value depends upon state corporate law and may be approached by considering certain sections of the MBCA, which is only one example.

### 1. Issuance of Stock

"Shares having a par value may be issued for such consideration expressed in dollars, not less than the par value thereof, as shall be fixed from time to time by the board of directors.

"Shares without par value may be issued for such consideration expressed in dollars as may be fixed from time to time by the board of directors . . ."

Section 18, MBCA.

The par value [2] of shares places a bottom limit on the consideration which a corporation must receive for each share of stock. For

---

2. "Par value" is a legal term of art for the minimum amount that may legally be paid for shares of stock with par value. It is not the "intrinsic" value, "market" value or any other value of the shares. It is simply the legal minimum that must be paid for shares to be validly issued. "No par value" stock has no legal minimum which must be paid for the shares ex-

this reason, the par value should be nominal, e.g., $.10 or $1.00, so that there is no problem that insufficient consideration will be paid for the shares.

## 2.  Corporate Distributions

As will be discussed in Section II.F.3 of this Chapter, the law restricts the amount of assets which a corporation may distribute to its shareholders.  One of the significant limitations is that a corporation cannot pay a dividend which is from the par value it has received for the sale of its stock.  The idea is to protect creditors of the corporation from unwarranted and excessive distributions to shareholders with the possibility of stripping the corporation of assets needed to pay debts.

### D.  WHAT SHARES MAY BE SOLD?

In order for a corporation to issue any shares of stock, the shares must be "authorized".  Section 15 of the MBCA provides that a corporation has the authority to issue the number of shares stated in its articles of incorporation.  As you saw in Chapter Two (in Section IV), the articles of incorporation always specify the number of shares which the corporation may issue.

When shares have been issued (that is, sold by proper corporate action to a shareholder and the required consideration is received by the corporation) and are held by someone *other* than the corporation (and, therefore, outstanding), these shares are referred to as being "issued" and "outstanding".  The reason for this dual description is that a corporation may, subsequent to the issuance of shares, reacquire these same shares (see Section 6, MBCA).  In that case, when the shares are held by the corporation itself, they become "treasury shares" and are deemed to be "issued" but *not* "outstanding".  See Section 2(h), MBCA.  A corporation may resell treasury shares and, when sold, such shares will once again become "outstanding".  Treasury shares are not voted and do not share in dividends or other corporate distributions, due to the fact that they are not "outstanding".

### QUESTIONS

**Are treasury shares treated as an asset?  If treasury shares are cancelled, are a corporation's net assets changed?**

The distinction between "authorized" but "unissued" shares, on the one hand, and "treasury shares" on the other, is relevant because

cept that amount determined by the board of directors.  There is no magic about the amount of par value.  Ordi-narily where shares have par value, it is one cent, ten cents, or one dollar, that is, a small amount.  Why ?

a corporation may not issue "authorized" and "unissued" shares for a consideration which is less than the par value. Treasury shares, however, may be disposed of for a consideration that is fixed by the board of directors, even if that consideration is less than the par value of the shares. See Section 18, MBCA.[3]

## E. CONCEPT OF "FULLY PAID AND NONASSESSABLE"

Corporate statutes normally define the term fully paid and nonassessable in a manner similar to the following: "When payment of a consideration for which the shares are to be issued shall have been received by the corporation, such shares shall be deemed to be fully paid and nonassessable". Section 19, MBCA. Most corporate laws impose certain liabilities upon shareholders unless the shares which have been issued to them are "fully paid and nonassessable". (See, e. g., Section 25, MBCA; Section 609, Pennsylvania Business Corporation Law.) These liabilities may include assessment for unpaid amounts on subscription agreements against the holder of the stock.[4] All stock certificates represent that the shares which they evidence are fully paid and nonassessable. It is unclear whether a good faith purchaser for value[5] of such shares would be liable if such shares were not really fully paid and nonassessable.

Since "limited liability" for shareholders is one of the purposes of incorporation,[6] it is important for the lawyer and paralegal to know what is required in order to achieve limited liability.

An analysis of these statutes indicates that a four-stop factual review is necessary to determine when shares are fully paid and nonassessable.

## 1. What Was the Consideration for the Shares?

Since the board of directors establishes the consideration (the value received for the shares) to be paid for shares, the first step is to determine what consideration was fixed by the board of directors

---

3. The reason is that even though the treasury shares are not outstanding, they have been issued; therefore, par value was paid for them when they were first issued. Accordingly, they may be resold for less than par inasmuch as par has already been paid in for such shares. Can treasury shares with a par value of $1.00 be sold by a corporation for $.50 a share? Can authorized but unissued shares with a par value of $1.00 be sold for $.50?

4. See Section II.D of Chapter Two for an example of subscription agreements.

5. A "good faith purchaser for value" is a person that may be protected by the law in certain circumstances where such person might otherwise be liable. Generally "good faith" means that the person bought the stock (or other asset) without any knowledge or reason to know of any problems with respect to the title to the stock, e. g., that it is not fully paid and nonassessable or subject to other offsets. This concept of protecting an innocent purchaser has application in other areas of law, such as title to real estate.

6. See discussion in Chapter One.

for the shares which have been issued. Normally, this is done by an examination of the minutes of directors' meetings.[7]

## 2.  Was the Consideration Legally Adequate?

For the purpose of deciding whether the shares are fully paid and nonassessable, it is irrelevant that the directors might have sold the shares for more. The legally relevant question is whether the amount of consideration for shares (other than treasury shares) is less than the par value per share.[8] The Articles of Incorporation must be reviewed to determine the required consideration. (See, e. g., Section 18, MBCA.)

## 3.  Was the Consideration Received?

A review must be made to see if the consideration specified by the board of directors has been paid for the shares. Normally, this involves examining the books and records of the corporation to find out what has in fact been received by the corporation.

### QUESTIONS

What books and records would disclose this fact? Would the minute book or stock book disclose this? How about financial records?

## 4.  What Type of Consideration Was Received?

State law also establishes the type of consideration which is acceptable for the issuance of shares, such as the following MBCA requirements:

> "The consideration for the issuance of shares may be paid, in whole or in part, in cash, in other property, tangible or intangible, or in labor or services actually performed for the corporation . . . Neither promissory notes nor future services shall constitute payment or part payment for the issuance of shares of a corporation."

Section 19, MBCA.

### QUESTIONS

Under the MBCA, could shares of stock be issued for a patent? For a promissory note of the prospective shareholder?

If the board of directors authorized the issuance of shares for a legally unacceptable type of consideration, even if the consideration were paid to the corporation, the shares might not be deemed to be fully paid and nonassessable. It should be noted that most courts have interpreted the prohibition against promissory notes to mean only the promissory note issued by the person buying the shares. If the person buying the shares gives the corporation a promissory note made by another, it is deemed to be payment, because such a note is "property" (an asset) of the person buying the shares.

---

7.  See discussion of minutes in Section II.A.10 of Chapter Seven.

8.  See footnote 2 for a definition of "par value".

## F.  COMMON STOCK

In passing, Chapter Two mentioned the existence of several types of stock.[9]  Common stock is the most usual type of equity security. Common stock may be defined as that class of stock which is created when the articles of incorporation provide for a class of stock without any special features.  In such case, state corporate law will describe the characteristics of common stock.  A review of the relevant sections of the MBCA will indicate what a model statute defines these characteristics to be.

### 1.  Voting Rights

Section 33 of the MBCA sets forth the voting rights of holders of common stock.  Note that the MBCA permits the articles to exclude voting rights where there is more than one class of common stock.

### QUESTION

If a certificate for 100 shares of X corporation has been issued to A for only a portion of the total purchase price for such shares, can A have full voting rights with respect to such shares under the MBCA?

When it comes to voting for the election of directors, some states such as Pennsylvania provide for cumulative voting unless the articles of incorporation provide otherwise while other states only have cumulative voting if the articles specifically include it.[10]

### 2.  Pre-emptive Rights

When a shareholder has pre-emptive rights, he has the right to purchase a pro-rata share of a new issue of common stock, or securities convertible into common stock, which the corporation proposes to issue.[11]  Such rights are no longer in vogue because management desires flexibility to issue shares without first offering them to other shareholders.  For example, many times management desires to issue shares in exchange for consideration other than cash, e. g., property or stock of another company.  Could management do this if pre-emptive rights exist?  In recent years, most state laws have denied shareholders pre-emptive rights unless the articles of incorporation specifically provide otherwise.

### 3.  Dividend Rights

Corporate laws generally give the board of directors the power to declare and pay dividends which are distributions to shareholders

---

9.  See Section IV.F of Chapter Two.

10.  See Section IV.H.2 of Chapter Two for a discussion of cumulative voting.

11.  See Section IV.H.1 of Chapter Two for a discussion of pre-emptive rights.

of cash, property or stock out of earnings of the corporation such as the following:

> "The Board of Directors of a corporation may, from time to time, declare and the corporation may pay dividends in cash, property or its own shares."
>
> Section 45, MBCA.

There is no requirement that the board of directors ever declare dividends. Even if the Board wanted to declare a dividend, there are two restrictions on the right of common stockholders to receive dividends:

(a) Preferred stockholders [12] may have priority if dividends are paid. The effect of this priority is that no dividends may be paid on common stock until preferred stockholders have received all dividends to which they are entitled.

(b) In order to protect creditors who may not be able to collect a corporation's debts from its shareholders because of the corporate characteristics of limited liability, dividends may not be paid if the payment would make the corporation insolvent or would deplete the corporation's net worth below a certain minimum level.[13]

### 4. Liquidation Rights

A corporation that desires to liquidate (wind up its affairs and distribute remaining assets) is required by state law to pay, or adequately provide first, for the payment of, all liabilities and obligations then outstanding and to distribute the remainder of its assets, either in cash or in kind, among its shareholders according to their respective rights and interests. See Section 87 of the MBCA.

When the only class of stock outstanding is common stock, the holders will share in the remainder of the corporation's assets in proportion to their relative ownership of the corporation's common stock. If there is outstanding any preferred stock which has priority in liquidation, then the holders of common stock will not receive any payments in the corporate liquidation until the rights of the preferred stockholders have been satisfied.

### 5. Obligations of Common Stockholders

Section 25 of the MBCA succinctly states the only basis for shareholder liability to the corporation or its creditors:

> "A holder of or subscriber to shares of a corporation shall be under no obligation to the corporation or its creditors with respect to such shares other than the obligation to pay to the corporation the full consideration for which such shares were issued or to be issued."

---

12. See Section II.H of this Chapter for a discussion of preferred stock.

13. Section II.G.2 of this Chapter discusses dividends.

Once a shareholder has paid the agreed price for the shares, there is generally no further financial responsibility of any sort. This statement, however, requires one slight qualification.

A few states still have a provision in their corporate law which makes some or all shareholders liable for certain wages due to employees. For example, Section 630 of the New York Business Corporation Law imposes such an obligation on the ten largest shareholders of a corporation, unless the shares are "publicly held", i.e., held by a large number of shareholders as designated in the statute.

## G. DIFFERENT CLASSES OF COMMON STOCK

Some corporations have two classes of common stock, which may vary in one or more of the following respects:

### 1. Voting Rights

One reason for the existence of two classes of common stock is to insure certain persons that they will be in control of a corporation even though they do not own a majority of the outstanding common stock.

#### QUESTION

What corporate document would create two classes of common stock?

The persons in control may own voting common stock while other shareholders own non-voting common stock. In such a case, the holders of non-voting common stock will not be entitled to vote in any matter which requires shareholder approval (e.g., election of directors, merger or consolidation), unless state law otherwise requires such a vote. Another way of accomplishing the same result is to have one class of common stock with a greater number of votes per share than the other class. In either event, persons who control a small fraction of the total number of outstanding shares of common stock will have control of the corporation.

Normally, a corporation creates two classes of common stock with different voting rights when the shareholders wish to preserve their control but recognize the need to issue a large number of shares in the future to "outsiders" (e.g., in a public offering).

#### QUESTION

Why would a corporation have a need to issue a large number of shares?

The "insiders" in such a case are issued voting common stock, and the corporation is then in a position to issue non-voting or common stock with lesser voting power to new shareholders.

The two classes of common stock will be provided for and described in the articles of incorporation. Typical provisions, as they might appear in the articles, follow:

**EXAMPLE 1**—Two classes, one voting, one non-voting

"The Corporation shall have an authorized capital of 1,000,000 shares, divided into 200,000 shares of Class A Common Stock, par value $1.00 per share, and 800,000 shares of Class B Common Stock, par value $1.00 per share. Shares of Class A Common Stock and Class B Common Stock shall be identical in all respects except that the holders of Class A Common Stock shall be entitled to vote on all matters submitted to a vote of shareholders and holders of Class B Common Stock shall not be entitled to vote on any matter submitted to a vote of shareholders."

**EXAMPLE 2**—Two classes, one entitled to one vote per share, one entitled to 15 votes per share

"The Corporation shall have an authorized capital of 1,000,000 shares of Class A Common Stock, par value $.01 per share, and 100,000 shares of Class B Common Stock, par value $.01 per share. Shares of Class A Common Stock and Class B Common Stock shall be identical in all respects except that the holders of Class A Common Stock shall be entitled to one vote per share and the holders of Class B Common Stock shall be entitled to fifteen votes per share on all matters submitted to a vote of shareholders."

It should be noted again that, while the articles of incorporation may deprive the holders of any class of stock of all voting rights, state law requires that such persons be entitled to vote on certain matters.[14]

## 2. Dividend Rights

Two classes of common stock may differ in their priority with respect to dividends. Normally, such an arrangement is described in the articles in a manner similar to the following:

"The Corporation may not declare and pay a dividend in cash or property on shares of Class B Common Stock without declaring and paying an equal dividend on shares of Class A Common Stock. The corporation may declare and pay a dividend on shares of the Class A Common Stock without declaring and paying any dividend on shares of the Class B Common Stock."

In such a situation, the Class B Common Stock will usually be owned by the persons in control of the corporation while the Class A Common Stock will be publicly-held. The holders of Class A Common Stock are assured that if any dividends are paid, they will at least receive the same amount per share as the holders of Class B Common Stock, and it is possible that they may receive more. The holders of Class B Common Stock (i.e., the persons in control of the

---

14. See Section II.H.4 of this Chapter.

corporation) may be more interested in paying dividends to the Class A stockholders in order to increase the value of the Class A Stock than they are in receiving dividends themselves. This interest in the value of Class A Stock is seldom altruistic. The Class B Common Stock is usually convertible into Class A Common Stock. After helping to create a higher market price for Class A Stock, the Class B shareholder will convert the stock to Class A.

### 3. Conversion

Often, the class of common stock with the lesser rights (i. e., without voting rights or with a lower priority in the payment of dividends) will be convertible, either immediately or at some future date, on a share-for-share basis into the other class of common stock. In the case of classes of common stock which differ as to voting rights, provisions to convert the non-voting common stock into voting common stock may reflect the judgment that in the long run it is inappropriate to deprive shareholders of voting rights. In the case of classes of common stock with different dividend rights, the holders of the class with the lesser dividend rights (who are normally the persons in control of the corporation) will normally want the right to convert into the publicly-held common stock with the superior dividend rights so that their shares may be made more attractive to potential buyers and therefore command a higher purchase price when sold.

When conversion on a share-for-share basis from one class of common stock to another class of common stock is permitted, it is necessary to provide in the articles that no changes by way of a stock dividend [15] or stock split [16] may occur with respect to one class of common stock without the same changes being made to the other class of common stock. This is commonly called an "anti-dilution" provision because it prevents a class from having its interest reduced by such events.

An example of articles of incorporation which provide for two classes of common stock and for the right of conversion from one class to the other is set forth below:

### EXAMPLE—Capital Stock Description (Two Classes of Common Stock) Excerpted from Articles of Incorporation

"Any holder of Class B Common Stock may, at his or her option, convert all or any part of such Class B Common Stock into Class A Common Stock at the rate of one (1) share of Class A

---

15. A distribution of additional stock by a corporation rather than money. It involves a transfer of accumulated profits to capital stock by giving shareholders additional stock.

16. An increase in outstanding shares by dividing shares into a greater number of shares, usually by an amendment to the articles. The result is that each shareholder holds more shares but with a proportionately reduced value per share.

Common Stock for each share of Class B Common Stock, upon presentation and surrender to the Corporation at its principal office, or to any agency maintained for the transfer of Class B Common Stock, of the certificates for such Class B Common Stock so to be converted, duly endorsed for transfer; and thereupon the holders of such Class B Common Stock shall be entitled to receive in exchange therefor, a certificate or certificates for fully paid and nonassessable shares of Class A Common Stock. The Class B Common Stock shall be deemed to have been converted and the person converting the same to have become a holder of record of Class A Common Stock for the purpose of receiving dividends and for all other purposes whatsoever, as of the date when the certificate or certificates for such Class B Common Stock are presented and surrendered to the Corporation as aforesaid, provided, however, that no share of Class B Stock surrendered for conversion after the date of declaration of and before or on the record date for a dividend on Class A Common Stock shall be converted into Class A Common Stock during such period.

"The Corporation shall, so long as any of the Class B Common Stock is outstanding, reserve and keep available out of its authorized and unissued Class A Common Stock, solely for the purpose of effecting the conversion of the Class B Common Stock, such number of shares of Class A Common Stock as shall from time to time be sufficient to effect the conversion of all shares of the Class B Common Stock then outstanding. The Corporation shall, from time to time, if necessary, amend its Articles of Incorporation to increase its authorized capital stock and take such other action as may be necessary to permit the issuance from time to time of the shares of Class A Common Stock as fully paid and nonassessable shares, upon the conversion of the Class B Common Stock as herein provided."

## H.   PREFERRED STOCK

"Preferred stock"[17] is a generic term used to describe any class of stock which has a priority vis a vis common stock with respect to the assets of the corporation. There is no such thing as a typical type of preferred stock, and the only effective limit on the types of preferred stock which may be created is the imagination of lawyers and their corporate clients.

The characteristics of preferred stock are found in the corporation's articles of incorporation. Section 15 of the MBCA specifically states that a corporation may issue shares of preferred or special classes "when so provided in its articles of incorporation". Unfortunately this is somewhat misleading. If a corporation never intends to have more than two classes of stock outstanding—a common stock and a preferred stock—and does not intend to have series of preferred stock, then the articles of incorporation will contain all of the

---

17.  Preferred stock was mentioned in
Section II of this Chapter.

provisions governing both classes of stock. In recent years, however, companies have found it desirable to be able to issue different types of preferred stock (i. e., different "series"). Why? Modern state statutes have permitted corporations to issue these series of preferred stock without amending the articles of incorporation each time a new series of preferred stock was to be issued by resolution of the board of directors. A full discussion of this will be set forth below under "Creation of Preferred Stock".[18]

A description of some customary provisions which may be found in preferred stock follows.

## 1. Dividends

As discussed previously in connection with common stock,[19] a corporation is never under an obligation to pay dividends. A dividend is only paid by the corporation after the board of directors has declared the dividend and there are sufficient assets, as determined by state law, available for the payment. These legal limitations on available assets apply not only to dividends on common stock but also to dividends on preferred stock.

Although preferred stockholders do not have a "right" to require the corporation to pay a dividend, normally they are entitled to receive a dividend in a specified amount and at specified times before any dividends are paid by the corporation on any class of stock "junior" to the preferred stock. Common stock is "junior" to preferred stock in most cases insofar as the payment of dividends is concerned.

### QUESTION

Can one class of preferred stock be "junior" to another class?

The priority to dividends may either be "cumulative" or "non-cumulative". If it is cumulative, the corporation must pay to the preferred stockholders all dividends specified in the terms of the preferred stock from the date the dividends begin to cumulate through to the current dividend before it pays any dividends on junior classes of stock.

### QUESTIONS

Could a corporation have two classes of common stock, one with a preference only as to dividends rather than a class of preferred stock and a class of common stock? Is there really any difference between the two types of classes other than their names?

The terms of the preferred stock may provide, for example, that the payment of dividends shall be at a rate of $1.00 per share, per annum, payable quarterly, that such dividends shall be paid prior to the

18. Section II.I of this Chapter.          19. Section II.F.3 of this Chapter.

payment of any dividend on shares of common stock, and that such shares are cumulative from the date of issue. If this class of preferred stock has been outstanding for three years and no dividends have been paid on the stock (called a "dividend arrearage"), then the corporation must pay the preferred stockholders a dividend of $3.00 (covering the period during which the shares were outstanding) before it can pay any dividend to the common stockholders. For each additional year that no dividends are paid on the preferred stock, another $1.00 would cumulate to be paid before any dividends may be paid on the common stock.

### QUESTIONS

Can the preferred stock ever get more than $1.00 per share dividend per year? Must such a payment be provided for in the articles?

If the preferred stockholders were not entitled to cumulative dividends, then the corporation would only be required to pay them a dividend of $.25 per share for the then current quarter-year period prior to the payment of any dividends on the outstanding shares of common stock.

It is usual for preferred stock to contain the following dividend terms:

(1) specified annual rate,

(2) specified time of payment,

(3) the first payment date,

(4) if the dividends are cumulative, when the accumulation begins, and

(5) specification that no dividends may be paid on the common stock (other than dividends payable in common stock rather than cash or other property [20]) unless all dividends due to preferred stockholders have been paid.

### SAMPLE PROVISION:

"Each share of Preferred Stock shall entitle the holder of record thereof to receive, out of funds legally available therefor, when and as declared by the Board of Directors, dividends in cash at the annual rate of $1.00 per share, which shall be payable in equal quarterly installments on the first day of January, April, July and October of each year, beginning with July 1, 19—. Cash dividends on each share of Preferred Stock shall be cumulative, whether or not earned and whether or not surplus would be available therefor, and shall commence to accrue and accumulate from the first dividend payment date following the issuance thereof, such accumulation to include, if not paid, the full quarterly dividend payable on

20. These are stock dividends. See footnote 15 of this Chapter.

such first dividend payment date. Such cash dividends shall be declared and set apart or paid before any dividends (other than dividends payable in shares of Common Stock) shall be paid on the Common Stock."

An analysis of the terms in the sample provision follows:

(1) A beginning date for dividend payment: July 1, 19___. This is desirable so that it is clear what date dividend arrearages commence if the corporation fails to pay a dividend to the preferred stockholders.

(2) It provides, as is normally the case, that dividends are cumulative even if, as a matter of state law, the corporation is not legally permitted to pay dividends.

(3) In determining the amount of accrued but unpaid dividends, the dividend payable on the first payment date is a full quarterly dividend, no matter how soon before such date the preferred stock was issued. If the sample provision provided for the accumulation of dividends from the date of issue, then the corporation would not be in arrears if, on the first dividend payment date following issuance, it paid to the preferred stockholders a portion of the regular quarterly dividend pro rated on the basis of the number of days of the quarter during which the stock was outstanding.

### QUESTION

**If the first quarterly dividend date is April 1, 1977, and the stock is issued March 1, 1977, what payment would a preferred shareholder be entitled to receive if no provision is made for a full payment for the first dividend?**

(4) Since a dividend in common stock to existing common stockholders does not deplete the corporation of any assets [21] or impose any additional obligations on the corporation, a stock dividend is permitted even if the corporation is in default in the payment of dividends on preferred stock.

The dividend preference is meaningful for three reasons. First, a corporation will generally be considered to be in poor financial shape if it fails to pay preferred stock dividends, and the board of directors, to avoid this impression, will normally want to keep these dividends current. Second, if the board of directors wants to declare dividends to common stockholders, dividends must not be in arrears on cumulative preferred stock. Third, the value of the preferred stock (and the common stock) may be severely depressed by passing up dividends.[22]

21. Why are assets not depleted by such a dividend? See footnote 15 of this Chapter.

22. The depressed price may result from reluctance of investors to invest in stock of a company unwilling or unable to meet its preferred stock dividends.

## 2. Liquidation Rights

Preferred stock provisions will also indicate what rights, if any, the preferred stockholders have upon the liquidation or dissolution [23] of the corporation. While the holders of preferred stock are not guaranteed that they will receive anything upon the liquidation of the corporation (as is true of any investor in the corporation), they are normally given the right to receive a specified amount (if available for distribution), plus any dividends which have accrued but have not been paid, prior to any payments to holders of junior stock.

### SAMPLE PROVISION:

"In the event of any dissolution, liquidation or winding up of the affairs of the corporation, and after payment or provision for the payment of the debts and other liabilities of the corporation has been made, the holders of the Preferred Stock shall be entitled to receive, out of the net assets of the corporation, $10.00 per share, plus an amount per share equal to accrued but unpaid dividends, whether or not earned or declared, on each such share up to the date fixed for distribution and no more before any distribution shall be made to the holders of the Common Stock. If the net assets of the corporation are not sufficient to pay such amounts in full, holders of all shares of Preferred Stock shall participate ratably in the distribution of assets in proportion to the full amounts to which they are entitled."

The foregoing provision is reasonably self explanatory.

### QUESTIONS

If there were 1,000,000 shares of the above preferred stock outstanding, how much would preferred shareholders receive upon liquidation? How much would be received for each preferred share if only $7,000,000 were available for distribution on liquidation to holders of preferred stock?

It should be noted that it is important to spell out in such a provision that the holder of preferred stock is entitled to a certain dollar amount "and no more". Otherwise, a question might arise as to whether the holders of preferred stock were entitled, after receiving a specified amount, to participate with the holders of common stock in any remaining assets of the corporation.

### QUESTION

Is there ever a "liquidation price" established for common stock?

## 3. Redemption Rights

A corporation does not, unless it is specifically spelled out in the terms of a class of stock, have the right of redemption, i.e. the right

23. Dissolution is the formal termination of corporate existence, whereas liquidation may wind up the business without formal dissolution, e. g., where the shareholders wish to keep the name for possible future use.

to require the holders of such stock to sell all or any part of their shares to the corporation. Redemption provisions are present frequently with respect to a preferred stock.

## QUESTIONS

**Why would the corporation ever want to redeem preferred stock? Is common stock redeemable?**

A redemption provision must establish the terms of the forced sale by the preferred stockholders and the procedures which must be followed by the corporation when it invokes its redemption right. In some instances, the redemption terms may be the most complicated of the preferred stock provisions. A sample provision is set forth below. The sample provision, which is less complex than many provisions may be, might typically be found in the terms of a preferred stock which has been issued to one or two persons.

**SAMPLE PROVISION**—Simple notice of redemption; specification of method of payment and effect:

"Shares of Preferred Stock are subject to redemption by the corporation, at the option of its board of directors, in whole or in part, at any time and from time to time, upon 30 days prior written notice to the registered holders thereof, at the addresses of such holders as the same appears on the corporation's records, at the price of $10.00 per share, plus an amount equal to the accrued and unpaid dividends thereon to the date of said redemption. In case of the redemption of a part only of the shares of Preferred Stock at the time outstanding, the corporation may select by lot, or in such other equitable manner as the board of directors may determine, the shares of Preferred Stock so to be redeemed. If such notice of redemption shall have been duly given and if, on or before the redemption date specified in such notice, the funds necessary for such redemption shall have been set apart, so as to be and to continue to be available therefor, then, notwithstanding that any shares of Preferred Stock called for redemption shall not have been surrendered for cancellation, such shares of Preferred Stock shall no longer be deemed outstanding; and all rights of the holders of such shares of Preferred Stock so called for a redemption shall forthwith on such redemption date cease and terminate, except only the right of the holders thereof to receive the redemption price as specified above."

In analyzing the sample provision, the following considerations should be noted:

(a) The corporation has the right to redeem all or any part of the preferred stock at any time. The determination of when to cause the redemption and the number of shares to be covered is in the sole discretion of the board of directors.

(b) In order to redeem stock, it is necessary for the corporation to give notice to all preferred stockholders who are affected. The notice must be given at least 30 days prior to the date set for redemption and must specify the redemption date. If less than all of the shares of preferred stock are being redeemed, the notice must also contain a statement of the number of shares of preferred stock being redeemed from each holder.

(c) The amount payable upon redemption has two components: a fixed dollar amount and an amount equal to all accrued and unpaid dividends on the shares of preferred stock being redeemed.

(d) In order to protect the preferred stockholders, the corporation is required to set aside funds sufficient to pay the redemption price for all shares called for redemption. If the corporation fails to do this, then the redemption is not effective, and the shares of preferred stock called for redemption will still be deemed outstanding.

(e) The corporation will pay the redemption price only when the stock certificates representing the preferred stock are surrendered to the corporation for cancellation. There is no time limit on the surrender of the certificates. However, any preferred stockholder will be penalized if his shares have been called and he does not act promptly, because the redemption price does not include any interest from the proposed date of redemption to the date of payment.

### QUESTION

If there is a dividend arrearage of $3.00 per share on a cumulative preferred stock and the redemption price is $10.00 per share, what does the holder of such preferred stock receive upon redemption?

Most state corporate laws focus on two aspects of the redemption of stock. First, there will be some limitations on the right of the corporation to redeem stock based upon the corporation's capital and surplus,[24] such as the following Pennsylvania provision:

"In the case of shares which are subject to redemption, [a business corporation shall not redeem such shares except] to the extent of the aggregate of (i) its stated capital represented by such shares and (ii) its unrestricted capital surplus and if such stated capital

---

**24.** Surplus is the excess of net assets of a corporation over its stated capital (the aggregate of the par value of shares having par value plus the consideration received by a corporation for shares without par value). Generally speaking, surplus equals the sum of profits earned by a corporation over its lifetime that have not been distributed to shareholders.

surplus are insufficient, to the extent, with respect to the deficiency, of its unrestricted and unreserved earned surplus."

Section 701(B)(2), PBCL

The purpose of the limitations are to prevent redemptions of stock where the corporation may not have adequate "cushion" of assets to pay creditors.

Secondly, state law may require a statement to be filed with the appropriate state agency with respect to the redemption of shares of stock, such as Section 67 of the MBCA.

## QUESTIONS

**Is common stock required to be cancelled upon redemption? In a state adopting a provision like the above MBCA provision, could a corporation hold preferred stock as "treasury stock" for reissuance?**

A sample statement of cancellation appears below:

**EXAMPLE:**

Filing fee: $_____

### STATEMENT OF
### CANCELLATION OF REDEEMABLE SHARES
### OF

_____

To the Secretary of State
of the State of _____:

Pursuant to the provisions of Section 67 of the _____ Business Corporation Act, the undersigned corporation submits the following statement of cancellation by redemption or purchase of redeemable shares of the corporation:

FIRST: The name of the corporation is _____

_____.

SECOND: The number of redeemable shares of the corporation cancelled through redemption or purchase is _____, itemized as follows:

| **Class** | **Series** | **Number of Shares** |
|---|---|---|

THIRD: The aggregate number of issued shares of the corporation after giving effect to such cancellation is _____, itemized as follows:

| **Class** | **Series** | **Number of Shares** |
|---|---|---|

FOURTH: The amount of the stated capital of the corporation after giving effect to such cancellation is $_____.

FIFTH: The number of shares which the corporation has authority to issue after giving effect to such cancellation is _____, itemized as follows:

**Class**              **Series**              **Number of Shares**

Dated _____, 19__.

_____  (Note 1)

By _____  ⎤

    Its _____ President                  ⎬ (Note 2)

and _____

    Its _____ Secretary              ⎦

(Add Verification Form A)

Notes: 1. Exact corporate name of corporation making the statement.

       2. Signatures and titles of officers signing for the corporation.

## 4. Voting Rights

If there was no provision in the terms of preferred stock dealing with voting rights, a state law similar to the MBCA would grant to the preferred stockholders the same voting rights as the holders of common stock:

> "Each outstanding share, regardless of class, shall be entitled to one vote on each matter submitted to a vote at a meeting of shareholders, except as may be otherwise provided in the articles of incorporation."

Section 33, MBCA.

Even when the holders of preferred stock are specifically denied general voting rights in the articles of incorporation, the articles may grant them the right to vote, as a class, on certain types of proposed actions such as:

(a) the creation of another class of stock ranking prior to or on a parity with the preferred stock as to dividends or liquidation,

(b) an increase in the authorized number of shares of preferred stock,

(c) any change in the preferences and special rights of the outstanding preferred stock,

(d) any other action which would adversely affect the rights of the holders of preferred stock.

Any of these proposed actions may be omitted from the articles in a specific case.

## QUESTION

**Would a grant of voting rights to preferred stock by the by-laws be effective under Section 33 of the MBCA?**

Even if the terms of a preferred stock did not grant to the holders special voting rights in connection with certain corporate actions, state law would grant comparable rights, irrespective of what was set forth in a corporation's articles of incorporation.[25]

## QUESTIONS

**Why do some corporate statutes grant voting rights to holders of preferred stock in connection with amendment to the articles of incorporation even if the articles deny such preferred stock all voting rights? Which prevails in such a case: the statute which grants the preferred voting rights or the articles of incorporation which denies such rights?**

When an applicable provision of state law covers the subject of voting rights accorded holders of preferred stock, the natural question is why the matter should be covered in the terms of the preferred stock. The answer to this is that the terms of the preferred stock may provide greater protection to the preferred stockholders by establishing greater voting rights than the statute accords holders of preferred stock.

## QUESTION

**Why would management ever want to give greater voting rights to holders of preferred stock than that provided by law?**

In addition, the terms may provide for the relative rights between two or more series of the same preferred stock. Still another reason for including voting terms is that state law can change without any ability of the corporation or holders of preferred stock to control the change, while the terms of a preferred stock can be changed only by a majority of preferred stockholders.

Holders of preferred stock are often granted the right to elect a specified number of directors if certain conditions should occur. Under most circumstances, preferred stockholders do not vote in the election of directors, or, if they do, their votes may be counted with the common stock in the election, and in the latter case they do not vote separately as a class. Therefore, they may not have an effective voice in the management of the corporation. This lack of control is critical when a corporation has failed to pay dividends on preferred

25. For example, see Section 60 of the MBCA.

stock for a period of time, for this failure indicates either unprofitable operations or a decision by the board of directors not to pay dividends. Under such conditions, the terms of the preferred stock normally grant the right to the holders of preferred stock to elect a specified number of directors for as long as the failure to pay dividends continues. Such rights would appear in the place where the preferred stock is authorized (either the articles or the authorizing resolution of the board of directors).

**SAMPLE PROVISION**—Voting rights for preferred stock when dividends are in arrears:

"If and whenever, and as often as, dividends on any Preference Shares [26] shall be in arrears in an aggregate amount of at least $10.00 per share, the holders of Preference Shares shall have the additional right, voting separately as a class (without losing any other voting rights), at each meeting of shareholders thereafter held for the election of a Board of Directors, to elect two of the total number of Directors to be elected at such meeting. Such additional right shall continue in the Preference Shares until such time as all accumulated dividends on Preference Shares have been paid or declared and set aside for payment, whereupon such right shall cease until such time, if any, as such right shall again accrue as hereinabove provided. In the event of any vacancy occurring in the case of the two Directors elected by the Preference Shares voting as a class as aforesaid, unless (at the time when such vacancy shall have occurred as aforesaid) all accumulated dividends on Preference Shares shall have been paid or declared and set aside for payment, a special meeting of the holders of Preference Shares shall be called promptly to fill any such vacancy, which meeting shall be within thirty (30) days after such call, and at a place and upon notice as provided for the holding of meetings of shareholders, except that no such special meeting shall be required to be called if any such vacancy shall occur less than ninety (90) days before the date fixed for the annual meeting of shareholders. As to each meeting held as aforesaid while the Preference Shares have the right, voting separately as a class, to vote for the election of the two Directors, or to fill any vacancy, a majority of the outstanding Preference Shares shall be required to constitute a quorum for the election of such Directors or to fill any such vacancy at any such meeting. The Directors so elected shall serve until the next annual meeting or until their successors shall be elected and shall qualify; provided, however, whenever, during the term of office of such Directors all accumulated dividends shall have been paid or declared and set apart for payment, the term of office of such Directors shall forthwith terminate."

The above provision says that the holders of the class of Preference Stock can elect two directors when dividends are in arrears.

---

26. Sometimes preferred stock may be referred to as "preference stock", merely as a different name.

## QUESTIONS

What does it provide if a vacancy occurs in one of the two directorships elected by the holders of the Preference Stock? What happens to the Directors elected by holders of the Preference Stock if the dividend arrearages are eliminated?

The special voting rights which arise when preferred dividends are in arrears may be granted irrespective of any general voting rights the preferred shareholders may have under state law. The sample provision set forth above clearly reflects the fact that such voting rights are in addition to any other voting rights.

If the terms of a preferred stock grant special voting rights in the election of directors, there may be a provision included which requires a special meeting at which the holders of preferred stock may exercise these rights.

### 5. Sinking Fund

Under the terms of the typical preferred stock, the shares will remain outstanding until the corporation's liquidation or dissolution, unless the corporation decides to exercise its right to redeem all or any part of the preferred stock. Holders of preferred stock have no assurance that they will ever be able to have a fund for any payments from the corporation.

Prospective purchasers of preferred stock sometimes require as a condition to such purchase, that a "sinking fund" provision be included within the terms of the proposed preferred stock. Basically, a sinking fund provision states that the corporation shall, out of funds available according to state corporate law, and after all cumulative dividends have been paid, either (i) redeem a specified number of shares of preferred stock each year or (ii) place each year a specified sum of money in a separate account, out of the control of the corporation (such as a separate trust account where the corporation is not the trustee) to be used only for retiring the preferred stock at a specified date. Unless the specified number of shares have been redeemed or the required sum set aside, no dividends or other distributions (other than stock dividends payable in common stock) may be declared or paid on any shares of common stock and no shares of common stock may be purchased or otherwise acquired by the corporation. This provision grants the preferred stockholders some assurance that payments will be made to them periodically to repurchase their stock so long as the corporation has sufficient assets available.[27]

**SAMPLE PROVISION**—Sinking fund provision; credit against sinking fund for other preferred stock purchases:

"Out of any funds of the corporation legally available therefor after cumulative dividends in full on all outstanding shares of Pre-

---

27. See, e. g., Section 6, MBCA.

ferred Stock for all quarterly dividends periods up to and including the then current dividend period have been paid or declared and a sum set apart for payment, and before any dividends or other distributions may be paid or declared and set apart for payment in respect of any shares of Common Stock or any shares of Common Stock may be purchased or otherwise acquired for consideration, the corporation shall set aside, as and for a sinking fund for the Preferred Stock, on the twentieth day of February, May, August and November, beginning November 20, 19—, the sum or sums sufficient to redeem on or before the next March 1, June 1, September 1, and December 1, respectively, 2000 shares of Preferred Stock at $10.00 per share plus an amount equal to all accrued and unpaid dividends, whether or not declared or earned, provided that the amount to be so set aside need never exceed the amount sufficient to redeem at such price plus such dividends all shares of Preferred Stock then outstanding. Sums so set aside for the sinking fund shall be applied to the redemption of Preferred Stock."

## QUESTIONS

What amount of money does the above provision require to be set aside per year for the sinking fund? How much must be set aside if only 1,000 shares of preferred stock are left outstanding?

As the above example indicates, the sinking fund operates as a means of forced redemption and ties in with the redemption provisions of the preferred stock terms.

### 6.  Conversion Rights

A holder of preferred stock who has "conversion rights" is able to exchange preferred stock for common stock of the same corporation at a specified exchange rate. Convertible preferred stock permits the holders to enjoy the protection of having a "senior" security, that is, one entitled to preference as to dividends and on liquidation or dissolution, while still being able to benefit from any increase in the market value of the corporation's common stock. Such right is often called an "equity kicker" because the preferred has the additional possibility of increase in value as the price of the common stock goes up. Investors are usually willing to pay more for a preferred stock with such a "kicker".

The advantage of having convertible preferred stock can best be appreciated by examining the factors which contribute to the value of preferred stock without any conversion rights. The value of such a preferred stock will be determined largely by the size and profitability of the issuing corporation (because a profitable corporation is more likely to pay the dividend on preferred stock), the preferred stock's liquidation and redemption prices, the existence of a sinking fund and, most importantly, its fixed dividend rate. Anyone purchasing a straight preferred stock has, as the most immediate concern, the amount of the dividend which is payable on each preferred share. If the annual dividend per share is $1.00, then a prospective purchaser has to decide how many dollars to pay in order to justify investment in a preferred stock yielding a dividend of that amount. If the purchaser expected a 10% return on such an investment, then he would be willing to pay $10.00 a share for the preferred stock.

### QUESTION

**How much would such an investor be willing to pay for such a preferred stock if the investor required a return of 5%?**

A prospective purchaser would, as indicated above, also consider the liquidation price and redemption price. The liquidation price, however, is only of major significance if the corporation intends or is likely to liquidate in the near future. This is not a normal occurrence because a corporation only liquidates at the termination of its business activities. Therefore, the liquidation price normally has little effect on the price of the stock. The redemption price is only relevant if the board of directors is likely to decide to redeem outstanding preferred stock. Since redemptions are again not a normal occurrence in the absence of a schedule of redemption in the terms of the preferred stock, the redemption price will also not have a significant effect upon the value of the preferred stock.

As the value of preferred stock is dependent primarily upon a fixed dividend rate and the ability of the corporation to continue to make dividend payments, the value is not likely to change much, if at all, if the corporation is able to meet the dividend adequately when it becomes more profitable. The only change in value (assuming the corporation has continued to pay the required dividends) that is likely to take place results from a change in the collective judgment of investors regarding a satisfactory rate of return on preferred stocks, e. g., a desire to earn 10% rather than 5%.

When preferred stock is convertible into common stock, however, a new factor is introduced into the valuation of the preferred stock. If, for example, one share of preferred stock is convertible into one share of common stock, and if the preferred stock pays dividends at an annual rate of $1.00 per share, it is unlikely that the value of the preferred stock will be affected when the market price of the common stock is, for example, $5.00 per share if investors demand a rate of return for such preferred stocks of 10%. Why? At such time, it would not make economic sense for the holder of preferred stock, who could sell that preferred stock for $10.00 per share (assuming investors are willing to accept a 10% return on such preferred stocks), to convert it into a security which has a market value of only $5.00 per share. If, however, the common stock of the company had a market value of $30.00 per share, then a holder of preferred stock would be able to realize $30.00 for each share of preferred stock by converting it to common stock. Under such circumstances, the preferred stock would no longer have a price primarily established by the relation to the dividend rate but instead would have a price established almost exclusively as a result of its ability to be converted into common stock. The market value for the preferred stock at such a level will then fluctuate almost directly in relation to the market value of the common stock.

## PROBLEM

If a preferred stock has a dividend rate of $2.50 per year and the investor demands a return of 8% what would be the likely market price of such preferred stock? Assume that such preferred stock is convertible into common stock on the basis of one share of preferred stock for each two shares of common receivable on conversion. If the market price of the common stock is $12.00 per share, what is the likely price of the preferred stock if the required rate of return is 8%? If the required rate of return is 10%? What if the required rate of return is 8% and the price of the common stock is $18.00 per share? $20.00 per share?

## QUESTIONS

If a preferred stock has both a redemption feature and a conversion feature, can the call for redemption of the convertible preferred force holders to convert into common stock? What relation between the preferred stock redemption price and common stock market price is likely to force conversions? Should the right to convert terminate with the notice of redemption of the convertible preferred stock?

The principal components which may be found in the conversion terms of a convertible preferred stock are set forth below. These components will appear in the articles of incorporation if the preferred stock is authorized in the articles.

## QUESTION

Where would they appear if the board of directors have the power to authorize the series?

(a) *Conversion Rate*

The terms of the preferred stock will specify the number of shares of common stock into which each share of preferred stock is convertible.

## SAMPLE PROVISION:

"Shares of Preferred Stock may be converted at any time or from time to time into shares of Common Stock at the rate of two (2) shares of Common Stock for each share of Preferred Stock, such conversion rate to be subject to adjustment as hereinafter provided."

### (b) *Method of Conversion*

Preferred stock terms will usually set forth the specific procedure which must be followed by the holder of preferred stock in order to convert into common stock.

**SAMPLE PROVISION**—Effective date of conversion; effect of subscription rights of Preferred Stock:

"Any holder of shares of Preferred Stock who elects to convert them shall surrender the certificate therefor at the principal office of the Corporation, with the form of written notice on such certificate endorsed to reflect his election to convert them. The conversion privilege shall be deemed to have been exercised and the shares of Common Stock issuable upon such conversion shall be deemed to have been issued, upon the date the Corporation receives for conversion the certificate representing such shares with the requirements for conversion satisfied, except that as to any shares of Preferred Stock which are surrendered for conversion on a date which is less than five business days preceding the date fixed for the determination of holders of Common Stock entitled to receive rights to subscribe for or to purchase shares of Common Stock or other securities of the Corporation convertible into Common Stock, the conversion privilege shall have been deemed to have been exercised on the business day next succeeding the date fixed for such determination. Each person entitled to receive the Common Stock issuable upon such conversion shall from the same date be treated as the record holder of such Common Stock, and the person who surrenders such shares for conversion shall on that date cease to be treated as the record holder of the shares surrendered."

Such provisions establish the date on which the conversion becomes effective, contain language which delays the effective date if certificates are not surrendered to the corporation a specified number of days before the record date [28] fixed to determine the common stockholders entitled to receive subscription rights. As the name implies, subscription rights are rights granted to shareholders to purchase the corporation's common stock at a specified price during a specified period of time. Such rights are valuable because the purchase price is normally below the then current market price for the common stock in order to encourage the shareholders to exercise the right. The corporation can then raise a substantial portion of the money it desires from a new stock issuance from among its existing shareholders and reduce the selling effort to outsiders. The reason for the delay in the effective date of conversion is to permit the corporation to know, before the record date, exactly how many shares of common stock will be outstanding as of the record date.

---

28. The record date is the specific date set by the board of directors to' determine the name and number of record shareholders entitled to the right.

### (c) *Treatment of Fractions*

Normally, corporations do not issue fractional shares of common stock because of the inconvenience and expense involved. If, in connection with a conversion of a preferred stock into common stock, the holder of preferred stock would otherwise be entitled to a fractional share, a procedure is usually established to pay the converting shareholder an appropriate cash value for the fractional share.

In cases of corporations which do not have a public market (and, therefore, an easily ascertainable market value) for the shares of their common stock, appropriate provision must be made to value one share of common stock for the purpose of determining the value of the fractional share. One way around the problem is to give the board of directors the responsibility of determining the fair value of one share of common stock.

### (d) *Adjustments to Conversion Rates*

Perhaps the most difficult terms in any convertible preferred stock have to do with the method of adjusting the conversion rate in the event of certain actions by a corporation. These are called "antidilution" provisions because they preserve the value of the preferred stock in certain events, such as a stock dividend, stock split, reverse stock split or other change in capitalization.[29]

These provisions are very complex and may take an infinite number of forms. It is rare that a paralegal would be asked to draft a complex antidilution provision from scratch. Such provisions would appear in the articles if that is the place where the preferred stock is authorized or in the resolutions of the board of directors if it has the power to authorize series preferred stock provisions.

### (e) *Documenting Changes in Conversion Rights*

In order that the interested parties know of a change in the conversion rate of a preferred stock and the events which gave rise to the change, the board of directors is normally required to give notice to all preferred stockholders and the applicable transfer agents who effect transfers of the preferred and common stock on the books of the corporation.

**SAMPLE PROVISION:**

"Whenever the conversion rate is required to be adjusted, (i) the Corporation shall file a certificate setting forth such adjusted conversion rate and the facts upon which the adjustment is based with the Transfer Agents for the Preferred Stock and Common Stock and thereafter (until further adjusted), the adjusted conversion rate shall be as set forth in such certificate, and (ii) the Corporation shall mail notice of such adjusted conversion rate to each holder of shares of Preferred Stock."

---

**29.** See Chapter Eleven for a discussion of such changes.

If there were no transfer agents, the provision could be simplified by ignoring the notice to transfer agent.

### (f) *Reservation of Adequate Number of Shares of Common Stock*

When a corporation has outstanding a convertible preferred stock, the corporation must have available at all times a sufficient number of shares of authorized stock to permit conversion of all outstanding shares. Typically, a corporation undertakes to reserve by a resolution of its board of directors an adequate number of shares, from its authorized and unissued shares of common stock or treasury stock.

### QUESTION

As a review, what is the difference between "authorized but unissued" stock and "treasury" stock?

### SAMPLE PROVISION:

"So long as any shares of the convertible Preferred Stock remain outstanding, and the holders thereof have the right to convert them into shares of Common Stock, the corporation shall reserve from the authorized and unissued shares of its Common Stock a sufficient number of shares to provide for such conversion."

## I. CREATION OF PREFERRED STOCK

As briefly discussed above, the articles of incorporation may contain all provisions regarding preferred stock. However, if a "series" of preferred is allowed by corporate law and is authorized in the articles of incorporation, amendment of the articles may not be necessary for authorizing a new preferred stock.[30]

For states that have adopted statutes similar to the MBCA, Section 16 permits shares of any class of preferred stock to be divided into series.

Section 16 additionally permits the articles of incorporation to authorize the board of directors to fix the relative rights and preferences of all series into which any class of preferred stock may be divided.

If a corporation in a MBCA-type state is willing to have different types of preferred stock that differ in only the above-mentioned ways, it can, by having the appropriate provisions in its articles of incorporation, enjoy the flexibility of having different series of preferred stock issuable by action of its board of directors alone.

### QUESTIONS

Why is such flexibility useful? What is the alternative method for establishing preferred stock?

Before discussing the specific terms of a class of preferred stock which may be divided into series by action of the board of directors,

---

30. See Section II.H of this Chapter.

we should review the difference between a "class" of stock and a "series" of a class of stock.   (This discussion is *only* true for states which have adopted a scheme similar to the MBCA as to series and classes of preferred stock.)   Section 15 of the MBCA permits "shares" to be divided into classes.

### QUESTION

**What kinds of classes are there?**

Section 15 also permits classes of preferred stock or special classes to have terms which are different from common stock in the areas of dividends, assets distributed upon liquidation, redemption and conversion.   In contrast, Section 16 of the MBCA requires that the holders of different series of stock within the same class are on a parity with each other except in certain areas.   The differences between the series of the same class, therefore, primarily are differences either in numbers (e. g., the dividend rate) or in certain characteristics which do not affect their relative rights to the assets of the corporation (e. g., voting rights and conversion rights).

While the MBCA establishes reasonably precise differences between "classes" and "series" of stock, and limits the ways in which "series" of stock may vary, certain state laws permit the corporation greater latitude in creating series of stock.   For example, under Section 151 of the Delaware General Corporation Law, the following provides in part:

> "(a) Every corporation may issue one or more classes of stock or one or more series of stock within any class thereof, any or all of which classes may be of stock with par value or stock without par value and which classes or series may have such voting powers, full or limited, or no voting powers, and such designations, preferences and relative, participating, optional or other special rights, and qualifications, limitations or restrictions thereof, as shall be stated and expressed in the certificate of incorporation or of any amendment thereto, or in the resolution or resolutions providing for the issue of such stock adopted by the board of directors pursuant to authority expressly vested in it by the provisions of its certificate of incorporation.   The power to increase or decrease or otherwise adjust the capital stock as provided in this chapter shall apply to all or any such classes of stock."

From the standpoint of statutory construction, Delaware law has minimized the differences between "classes" and "series" of stock. In effect, different series of the same class of stock must be identical only in their par value or lack of par value.

### QUESTIONS

**Why does Delaware have this scheme rather than that of the MBCA?   Who benefits most from the broad Delaware-type provision?**

## 1. Board of Directors' Resolutions

When the articles of incorporation grant authority to the Board of Directors to establish a series of preferred stock, the Board must adopt resolutions, if it proposes to issue the stock, setting forth the terms of the series as in the following example:

"RESOLVED, that this Company hereby establishes 50,000 shares of its authorized Preferred Stock, par value $1.00 per share, as a series of such Preferred Stock which shall be designated as the '7% Convertible Preferred Stock'."

"RESOLVED, that the terms of the 7% Convertible Preferred Stock in the respects in which the shares of such series may vary from the shares of other series of the Preferred Stock shall be as follows:

*[Terms of Series]*

"RESOLVED, that the President or any Vice-President and the Secretary or any Assistant Secretary of this Company be and each of them hereby is authorized and empowered to execute in the name of and on behalf of this Company a statement setting forth the terms of the 7% Convertible Preferred Stock in the form presented to this meeting, which form is hereby approved, with such changes therein, if any, as may be approved by the officers of this Company executing same, as conclusively evidenced by their execution thereof; and that the proper officers of this Company be and each of them hereby is authorized and empowered to file said statement with the office of the Secretary of State of the State of New York, to pay such taxes and fees and to take any such other action as may be necessary or desirable, in the opinion of any one of such officers, to cause the foregoing terms of the 7% Convertible Preferred Stock to become validly established and fixed under applicable law."

A sample form of the statement required to be filed in a state utilizing the MBCA format in order to fix the terms of a series of preferred stock established by the Board of Directors is included below:

## EXAMPLE—Statement of Creation of Series of Preferred Stock (MBCA)

Filing fee: $_____

STATEMENT OF

RESOLUTION ESTABLISHING SERIES OF SHARES

OF

_____

To the Secretary of State
   of the State of _____:

Pursuant to the provisions of Section 16 of the _____ Business Corporation Act, the undersigned corporation submits the following statement for the purpose of establishing and designating a series of shares and fixing and determining the relative rights and preferences thereof:

FIRST: The name of the corporation is _____

_____.

SECOND: The following resolution, establishing and designating a series of shares and fixing and determining the relative rights and preferences thereof, was duly adopted by the board of directors of the corporation on _____, 19__:

[Insert copy of resolution]

Dated _____, 19__.

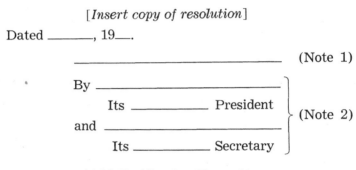

_____ (Note 1)

By _____
    Its _____ President
and _____  } (Note 2)
    Its _____ Secretary

(Add Verification Form A)

Notes: 1. Exact corporate name of corporation making the statement.

2. Signatures and titles of officers signing for the corporation.

## J. TRANSFER AGENTS AND REGISTRARS

A corporation is required by state law to keep a record of the names and addresses of all shareholders and the number and class of shares held by each as in the following MBCA example:

> "Each corporation shall keep at its registered office or principal place of business, or at the office of its transfer agent or registrar, a record of its shareholders, giving the names and addresses of all shareholders and the number and class of the shares held by each."

Section 52, MBCA.

The statute above recognizes that corporations may use transfer agents and registrars (who are normally banks or companies that specialize in the business of acting as transfer agents), to keep records of the shareholders of the corporation, but does not describe their function. Surprisingly, most state corporate laws do not define the duties of transfer agents and registrars.

It is important to recognize one important advantage that a corporation derives by using a transfer agent and registrar. Under many state laws, stock certificates must be manually signed by officers of a corporation unless a transfer agent or registrar is used:

> "The signatures of the president or vice-president and the secretary or assistant secretary upon a certificate may be facsimiles if the certificate is manually signed on behalf of a transfer agent or a registrar, other than the corporation itself or an employee of the corporation."

Section 23, MBCA.

The use of transfer agents and registrars to keep the records of shareholders and account for transfers eliminates the need for officers of a corporation to sign each stock certificate manually. This is very important for corporations with thousands of shareholders, where the new stock certificates are continually being issued as shares of stock are bought and sold on the public markets.

Many companies do not have separate transfer agents and registrars. In these cases, one bank usually performs both functions, by preparing stock certificates and keeping records of the outstanding certificates.

When a corporation has a transfer agent and a registrar, the board of directors must, in its resolutions authorizing the issuance of additional shares of stock, provide for appropriate instructions to the transfer agent and registrar. An example of such resolutions is included below:

**EXAMPLE—Sample Resolutions of the Board of Directors**

### ISSUANCE OF NEW SHARES OF COMMON STOCK INVOLVING AUTHORIZATION TO THE TRANSFER AGENT AND REGISTRAR

RESOLVED, that this Company issue 10,000 shares of Common Stock, par value $1.00 per share, of the Company (the "Common Stock") to John Smith against payment therefor of a price of $10.00 per share, or an aggregate price of $100,000, payable in cash; that, upon the receipt of said aggregate price of $100,000, the First National Bank, as Transfer Agent for the Common Stock, be and hereby is authorized and directed to countersign for original issue, and to deliver to John Smith when registered by The Trust Company, Registrar for the Common Stock, one certificate for 10,000 additional shares of Common Stock registered in the name of John Smith; and that The Trust Company, as Registrar for the Common Stock, be and hereby is authorized and directed to register and countersign, when presented to it for such purpose by the Transfer Agent, the certificate for said additional 10,000 shares of Common Stock.

RESOLVED, that the President, any Vice President, the Secretary or the Treasurer of this Company be and each of them hereby is authorized and empowered to give such instructions to the Transfer Agent and Registrar of the Common Stock and to take such other action as any one of them may deem necessary or desirable to effect the issuance and delivery of the 10,000 shares of Common Stock to John Smith, against payment therefor, in accordance with the foregoing resolution.

RESOLVED, that the Board of Directors of this Company declares that the 10,000 additional shares of Common Stock, when issued, sold, paid for and delivered in accordance with the foregoing resolutions shall be fully paid and non-assessable shares of the Common Stock of this Company.

## III.   DEBT SECURITIES

### A.   INTRODUCTION

A person is a creditor of a corporation when the corporation owes money (generally because of a loan, but possibly as a result of the sale of property to the corporation or the performance of services for the corporation on credit).  The corporation's debt is usually evidenced by some written instrument,[31] which is referred to as a "debt security".  Debt can also exist without a formal document, such as an account payable for goods purchased by a corporation.  A security is represented by a writing, however.

In contrast to equity securities, the holder of debt securities will have no right to (1) participate in the control of the corporation by electing directors, (2) receive all or a portion of the corporation's surplus or profits, or (3) share in its assets upon any dissolution (except to the extent of any unpaid portion of said debt).  Instead, the holder of debt securities will have the right to receive money from the corporation at stipulated times, together (generally) with interest.  "Interest" is merely the charge which the corporation pays for the use of the money.  The corporation, at the request of the debtor and to further assure repayment of the debt, often undertakes certain additional obligations in the operation of its business when it issues debt securities.  These obligations are usually part of the written agreement or "deal" with the corporation's creditors.  The terms may be set forth in the debt security itself or in a separate document.  Such obligations may act to prohibit or limit dividends, other debt, change in business operations, expansion and other matters.  The obligations do not arise out of state law or the provisions of the articles of incorporation but out of the agreement of the debtor corporation

---

31.   A formal written document.

and its creditor. However, they may be very restricting on a corporation and its management and severely limit certain types of corporate actions in order to increase the likelihood of repayment of the debt.

In the remaining portion of this Section, some of the more common types of debt securities will be discussed. The variations in debt securities are almost limitless, and it is the ingenuity of the parties and their relative bargaining positions rather than any statute which will determine their rights.

## B. TYPES OF DEBT SECURITIES

### 1. Simple Note

A "note" represents the simplest form of debt security. It will contain at least the following elements:

(a) A statement of the amount of the debt, referred to as the "principal" or the "principal amount".

(b) A promise by the corporation to pay the principal to a specific person or bearer [32] at a certain time or times and in certain amounts, and at a certain place.

(c) A promise to pay interest at certain times, rates, and in certain amounts, and at a certain place, or a statement that no interest is to be paid.

(d) Signature of the obligor (the person making the note).

(e) Date of issuance.

A "demand note" is distinguished from other types of simple notes in that the time that the principal is to be paid by the corporation is not stated. Instead, the holder of the demand note has the right to require the payment of the principal of the note at any time after making "demand" for payment.

**EXAMPLES:**

**Simple Note:**

"$1,000,000          NOTE          July 1, 19__

"Jones Corporation, a Delaware corporation, herein called the 'Corporation', hereby promises to pay to the order of Sam Smith the sum of $1,000,000 on December 31, 19__, and to pay interest thereon from the date hereof at the rate of 9% per annum, payable monthly commencing on the first day of the month next following the month in which this Note is dated. The principal and interest shall be payable

32. A "bearer" is one in possession of the note who presents the note for payment.

when due at the principal office of Sam Smith in San Francisco, California.

> Jones Corporation
>
> By: _____
>
>    Samuel Jones, President" [33]

**Demand Note:**

"$250,000    NOTE    July 1, 19__

"Jones Corporation, a Delaware corporation, herein called the 'Corporation', hereby promises to pay to the order of Tammy Katman the sum of $250,000 upon demand made in writing to the Corporation at its principal office in Philadelphia, Pennsylvania, plus interest thereon from July 1, 19__ to the date of payment at the rate of 7% per annum.

> Jones Corporation
>
> By: _____
>
>    Samuel Jones, President"

The above demand note is different from the simple note in that it provides for the payment of interest at the time the principal of the note is paid.

### PROBLEM

Draft a promissory note payable to Jessica Amy Smith issued on January 15, 197– to X Corporation with interest at 8.5% per annum payable quarterly. The amount is $150,000, and Henry Johnson is President of X Corporation. The note is due on January 15, 198–. Ms. Smith lives in Cherry Hill, New Jersey.

The following form sets forth a note which is more complicated and has additional characteristics:

**EXAMPLE:**

$30,000.00         _____, 19__

### NOTE

FOR VALUE RECEIVED, Macro Electric Vehicle Corporation, a Delaware corporation (hereinafter called "Maker"), promises to pay to the order of _____ (hereinafter called "Holder"), the principal sum of Thirty Thousand Dollars ($30,000) in lawful money of the United States of America, together with interest calculated at the following rates per annum on the outstanding principal balance from time to time.

---

33. Note the form of signature of a corporation. The corporate name is given with a line for the executing officer.

1. During the period commencing with the date of this Note and terminating one (1) year from said date, at one-half of one percent ($\frac{1}{2}$ of 1%) in excess of the "prime rate" (as hereinafter defined) in effect on the date of this Note:

2. During the period commencing one (1) year and one (1) day from the date of this Note and terminating two (2) years from the date of this Note, at one percent (1%) in excess of the "prime rate" in effect one (1) year and one (1) day from the date of this Note;

3. During the period commencing two (2) years and one (1) day from the date of this Note and terminating three (3) years from the date of this Note, at one and one-half ($1\frac{1}{2}$%) percent in excess of the "prime rate" in effect two (2) years and one (1) day from the date of this Note.

"Prime rate" is herein defined as the average interest rate charged by the following New York City banks for short term unsecured loans to their most credit-worthy borrowers: Chase Manhattan Bank; First National City Bank; Chemical Bank.

Interest shall be paid on the first day of each month after the date hereof until the principal amount hereof is paid in full.

The unpaid principal balance of this Note, together with accrued interest thereon, shall be paid in full three (3) years from the date of this Note.

All or any portion (in multiples of $10,000 only) of the outstanding principal balance of this Note from time to time may be paid on any interest payment date without penalty; provided, however, that said payment must be accompanied by the interest payment due on said date. All payments of principal and/or interest hereunder shall be first applied to unpaid interest which has accrued to the date of said payment and then to the unpaid principal.

Both the unpaid principal and accrued interest of this Note shall bear interest at the rate of 12% per annum after the date when due.

Upon the occurrence of any "Event of Default" (as hereinafter defined), Holder shall have the right, after seven (7) days written notice to the Maker, to declare the unpaid balance of the principal, together with the accrued interest thereon, due and owing, anything herein to the contrary notwithstanding, and payment of said principal sum and interest may be collected at once, provided that prior to the expiration of the said seven (7) days, the Maker shall not have cured all Events of Default set forth in Holder's notice to Maker.

"Event of Default" is herein defined as any one or more of the following:

1. Failure to make any payment of principal or interest hereunder after the same shall have become due and payable;

2. The filing of any petition or the commencement of any proceedings against Maker, if consented to or acquiesced in by Maker or not dismissed within thirty (30) days, (a) under any Chapter of the Bankruptcy Act, as amended, (b) for the appointment of a receiver (c) seeking other relief under any bankruptcy, reorganization, insolvency, dissolution or liquidation statute of the Federal or any state government.

3. The institution by Maker of a general assignment for the benefit of Maker's creditors.

4. The suspension of Maker's business or the commission of any act by Maker which can reasonably be construed as a business failure.

The Maker hereby empowers the prothonotary, clerk or any attorney of any court of record within the United States or elsewhere to appear for the Maker and, with or without one or more declarations filed, to confess a judgment or judgments against the Maker in favor of the holder hereof as of any term for the unpaid balance of principal and interest hereof with costs of suit and an attorney's commission of 5% for collection, with release of all errors and without stay of execution, and inquisition and extension upon any levy on real estate is hereby waived and condemnation agreed to, and the exemption of all property from levy and sale on any execution thereon, and exemption of wages from attachment, are also hereby expressly waived, and no benefit of exemption shall be claimed under or by virtue of any exemption law now in force or which may hereafter be enacted.[34]

MACRO ELECTRIC VEHICLE CORPORATION

Attest: _____    By: _____

An analysis of the foregoing note follows:

(a) *Interest Rate Tied to "Prime Rate"*

The "prime rate" of interest is that rate of interest charged by banks to their most credit-worthy borrowers for short-term unse-

---

**34.** This paragraph, which is typically referred to as a confession of judgment clause, is taken from a note used in a transaction in Pennsylvania. Each state's law must be followed in drafting a provision for use in that state. Many states do not allow use of such a provision. Does your state?

cured debts. This rate will vary over time and, in the opinion of most businesspersons, represents a reasonable index of prevailing interest rates. However, the rate varies from bank to bank, and, as set forth above, the prime rate of a specific bank or banks should be designated.

### (b) Rights Upon Default

Notes will often contain provisions which specify when the obligor is in default and the remedies available to the holder of the note in the event of default. One such remedy may be the right of the holder to "confess judgment" against the obligor. A confession of judgment clause in the note, where permitted, allows a court procedure pursuant to which the holder of the note, without obtaining the obligor's consent or approval, may obtain an immediate judgment from a court against the obligor and enforce the judgment by levy and execution on the obligor's property in accordance with state law. However, many states prohibit its use absolutely and even in those states where the procedure is permitted, it has been severely reduced in effectiveness in recent years on constitutional grounds. Care must be taken to review the current law in the specific state to ascertain its applicability.

### 2. Secured Debt

The note described above is an "unsecured debt" of the corporation. In such a case the creditor only has a claim against the general assets of the corporation. The holder has no special rights to any particular asset of the corporation. If there is a default on a debt and the holder of a debt security has the right to require the sale of a designated asset and to use the proceeds of such sale to pay the corporation's debt to the holder, then the debt is considered "secured".

### (a) Mortgage

Where the asset securing the debt is an interest in land and/or buildings or real estate improvements, the instrument which grants these rights is referred to as a "mortgage" and the debtor corporation is called a "mortgagor". The mortgage does not create the debt itself but rather grants certain rights to the creditor that is the holder of the mortgage, the "mortgagee", in the event of a default in the underlying debt obligation. The note secured by the mortgage is designated a mortgage note. The mortgage note will refer to the mortgaged real estate and the mortgage and will normally impose certain obligations upon the mortgagor to protect and preserve the assets which secure the note. The mortgage note usually requires the mortgagor among other things, to keep the mortgaged property adequately insured, to maintain the property in good order and condition and to pay all taxes due respecting the mortgaged property.

A person who holds a corporate debt which is secured by a mortgage wants to be certain that no one else will be able to obtain any rights to the mortgaged property that are superior to or on a parity with his rights. Obviously, the mortgage would not provide good security for the debt if the corporation could sell or transfer the property to someone else and if as a result of the transfer, the property was no longer securing the debt owed by the corporation. Such a result can occur if the party to whom the property was transferred did not have notice of the existence of the mortgage. State laws provide a procedure by which mortgages are to be "recorded", thereby providing a public record which notifies all other parties of the secured interest of the lender. Anyone who desires to purchase the property must check the public records to ascertain the state of the title to the real estate. No transfer of the property subject to such notice can cut off the lender's interest in the security. It should be noted that the subject of mortgages is generally within the field of "real estate" law and is not covered by state corporate statutes.

### (b) *Security Agreements*

Every state in the United States (except Louisiana) has adopted the Uniform Commercial Code. The Code, while "uniform", varies in each state in many respects. Article 9 of the Code establishes a procedure by which individuals and corporations may secure debts with "personal property". Personal property is a catch-all phrase that encompasses all non-real estate assets, whether tangible or intangible. Personal property includes machinery, equipment, inventory, raw materials and furniture (tangible assets) as well as accounts receivable and contract rights (intangible assets).

In order for a creditor to secure a corporate debt with designated personal property, and thereby acquire a "security interest" in the property, Article 9 requires that a "security agreement" exist. The security agreement must be in writing and be signed by both the debtor and the secured party. It must also contain certain minimum information in order to be valid, including a list of the assets which secured the debt, generally called the "collateral". In addition, at the very least, it must contain language granting the security interest. It usually goes much beyond the minimum requirements. The following example is a sample agreement granting the security interest and protecting the rights of the "secured party" in the assets securing the debt.

**EXAMPLE:**

### SECURITY AGREEMENT

SECURITY AGREEMENT made this 1st day of July, 19___, between XYZ CORPORATION, 1700 Market Street,

Philadelphia, Pennsylvania, a Pennsylvania corporation ("DEBTOR"), and THE ABC INSURANCE COMPANY, Five Penn Center, Philadelphia, Pennsylvania, a Pennsylvania corporation ("SECURED PARTY"):

## WITNESSETH:

On this date SECURED PARTY will lend to DEBTOR $1,000,000 with interest, all as provided in and evidenced by a Note ("Note") of even date herewith, in the face amount of One Million Dollars ($1,000,000).

NOW, THEREFORE, to induce the SECURED PARTY to lend the sum of $1,000,000 to DEBTOR, DEBTOR and SECURED PARTY, intending to be legally bound hereby, agree as follows:

1. DEBTOR hereby grants to SECURED PARTY a security interest in and mortgages to SECURED PARTY all of the interest of DEBTOR in the property described in Exhibit A hereto, wherever said property may from time to time be located, together with all parts, accessories, attachments and equipment at any time installed therein or affixed thereto and all accessories thereto and additions and replacements thereof, including any after-acquired property of the type described in Exhibit A and all proceeds and products of the foregoing (collectively referred to as the "Collateral"):

2. This security interest is given as security for the repayment of the aforementioned loan in accordance with the terms of the Note. DEBTOR, for itself and any subsequent owner, will at DEBTOR'S expense execute and deliver for filing all financing and other statements and take or join with SECURED PARTY in taking any other action requested by SECURED PARTY to perfect and continue perfected SECURED PARTY'S secured interest throughout the term of the Note.

3. All of the covenants and agreements in the Note to be performed by DEBTOR thereunder are incorporated herein by reference, and all of the remedies provided for herein may be exercised concurrently with the remedies provided for in the Note.

4. Until default DEBTOR shall be entitled to possession, use and enjoyment of the Collateral. A default under the Note shall also constitute a default to this Agreement. Under such circumstances SECURED PARTY may exercise all rights and remedies of a SECURED PARTY under the Uniform Commercial Code of Pennsylvania.

IN WITNESS WHEREOF, the parties have executed this Agreement as of the day and year first above written.

THE ABC INSURANCE       XYZ CORPORATION
COMPANY

By: /s/ George Green       By: /s/ Leonard Low

_____     _____
     Vice President            President
Attest:                    Attest:
    /s/ William White         /s/ Eileen Ajax

_____     _____
      Secretary            Secretary

Article 9 also requires the filing and recording of "financing statements" as a public record to all persons of the existence of the security interest. This is similar to the recording of a mortgage as discussed above. The filing of a financing statement is called "perfection" of the security interest. It gives the secured party added assurance of prevailing over competing creditors for the collateral. A standard type of financing statement used in many states follows:

### EXAMPLE—Financing Statement

| This FINANCING STATEMENT is presented to a Filing Officer for filing pursuant to the Uniform Commercial Code. | | No. of Additional Sheets Presented: | Maturity Date 3. (optional): |
|---|---|---|---|
| 1. Debtor(s) (Last Name First and Address(es): | 2. Secured Party(ies): Name(s) and Address(es): | | 4. For Filing Officer: Date, Time, No.-Filing Office |
| XYZ Corporation 1700 Market Street Philadelphia, PA | The ABC Insurance Company Five Penn Center Philadelphia, PA | | |

5. This Financing Statement covers the following types (or items) of property:

All property on Exhibit A attached hereto.

6. Assignee(s) of Secured Party and Address(es)

☒ Proceeds — _____     ☐ Products of the Collateral are also covered.

7. ☐ The described crops are growing or to be grown on: *
    ☐ The described goods are or are to be affixed to: *
    * (Describe Real Estate Below).

8. Describe Real Estate Here:

9. Name(s) of Record Owner(s):

| No. & Street | Town or City | County | | Section | Block | Lot |
|---|---|---|---|---|---|---|

10. This statement is filed without the debtor's signature to perfect a security interest in collateral (check appropriate box)

    ☐ already subject to a security interest in another jurisdiction when it was brought into this state, or
    ☐ which is proceeds of the original collateral described above in which a security interest was perfected:

XYZ CORPORATION                 ABC INSURANCE COMPANY

_____     _____
By _____                     By _____
Leonard Low, Signature(s) of Debtor(s) President    George   Signature(s) of Secured Party(ies)
    (1) FILING OFFICER COPY - NUMERICAL          Green, Vice President
      FORM DSCB:UCC-1 (Rev. 8-72)—Approved by Department of State of the Commonwealth of Pa.

[B6697]

A financing statement has, at the minimum, the following requirements:

1. Name and address of debtor
2. Name and address of secured party
3. Designation of collateral covered
4. Signature of debtor
5. Signature of secured party.

Note that some states only permit the official state-approved financing statements to be filed or charge a higher fee for nonapproved forms. In all cases a paralegal must ascertain the state filing requirements before preparing the forms. The proper offices for filing against a specific debtor must be carefully ascertained in every case.

### QUESTION

**Where is a financing statement properly filed in your state?**

As in the area of mortgages, security interests are not covered in state corporate statutes. The Uniform Commercial Code, although found among a state's statutes, is not within the corporate statutes.

### 3. Trust Indenture

The debt securities discussed in the preceding sections involve only two parties: the corporation which is the debtor, and the person to whom the corporation is obligated and who may have the advantage of a mortgage or security agreement covering certain real or personal property of the corporation. In many instances, however, there is a third party—a trustee—which acts on behalf of several individual holders of a debt security. A trustee is usually a bank.

When a corporation proposes to issue a debt security, whether secured or unsecured, to more than one person, it may decide (or by law be required) to designate one person, the trustee, to act on behalf of all holders of the debt security in case of default by the corporation. This avoids the necessity to deal with many individual creditors in the event of a default. The corporation will execute a trust indenture with a trustee prior to the issuance of debt securities. The trust indenture will contain all of the terms and conditions of the securities, and, pursuant to its terms, the corporation will be permitted to issue bonds or debentures. (Normally, the phrase "bonds" is used to describe secured debt and the phrase "debentures" is used to describe unsecured debt.) In certain instances, where the debt is a large amount to be held by many persons, the use of a trustee is required by the Federal Trust Indenture Act of 1939. A trust indenture will normally contain complex provisions designating the trustee and its responsibilities, the form of the debt instrument, the events of default, certain obligations of the corporation as to its operation and the mortgage or security interest, if any.

## C.   COMMON PROVISIONS IN DEBT SECURITIES

In the remaining parts of this Section, certain of the more common substantive provisions of debt securities will be discussed. These provisions, for the most part, are the counterpart for debt securities of provisions found in equity securities. The only new concept which is introduced is "subordination". In simple terms, subordination is an agreement by the holders of one type of debt security that they will not be entitled to receive any interest or principal from the corporation if the corporation has not paid one or more other types of debt securities or if the holders of another type of security have not been paid in full. In effect, the subordination of debt establishes relative priorities between various debt securities of a corporation.

## QUESTION

**Why would the holders of debt securities ever agree to be subordinate to another type of indebtedness?**

## 1.   Redemption

Most holders of debt securities are unwilling to permit the corporation to redeem debt before its maturity date. The reason for this is that the holder of the debt security desires some minimum period of time during which the holder can expect to receive the bargained-for interest on the debt security even if interest rates have declined and the corporation would be able to borrow money at lower interest rates. Therefore, debt securities often provide for a period of time after the issuance of the debt during which no redemption can take place. After this period has elapsed, the corporation may redeem the debt but in many cases will have to pay a premium. The premium usually declines as the maturity date of the debt approaches. The rationale of such an arrangement, once again, is to assure the holders of the debt security that they will receive the anticipated interest for a certain period of time. This is accomplished by discouraging the corporation from redeeming the debt with money borrowed at a lower interest cost if interest rates should decline.

## SAMPLE PROVISION—Redemption at premium

"This note and the notes of this issue are subject to redemption by the Corporation, at the option of its Board of Directors, in whole or in part, at any time after July 1, 1985 and from time to time thereafter and until maturity, upon thirty (30) days prior written notice to the registered holder at the address of such holder as the same appears on the Corporation's records, at the following redemption prices (expressed in percentages of the principal amount), together in each case with accrued interest to the date fixed for redemption:

| Time | Percentage of Principal Amount |
|---|---|
| July 1, 1985 to June 30, 1986 | 106% |
| July 1, 1986 to June 30, 1987 | 105% |
| July 1, 1987 to June 30, 1988 | 104% |
| July 1, 1988 to June 30, 1989 | 103% |
| July 1, 1989 to June 30, 1990 | 102% |
| July 1, 1990 to June 30, 1991 | 101% |
| July 1, 1991 to maturity | 100% |

"In case of the redemption of a part only of the notes of this issue at the time outstanding, the Corporation may select by lot, or in such other equitable manner as the Board of Directors may determine, the notes so to be redeemed. The Board of Directors shall have full power and authority, subject to the limitations and provisions herein contained, to prescribe the manner in which, and the terms and conditions upon which, the notes shall be redeemed from time to time. If such notice of redemption shall have been duly given, and if, on or before the redemption date specified in such notice, the funds necessary for such redemption shall have been set apart so as to be and continue to be available therefor, then, notwithstanding that any notes called for redemption shall not have been surrendered for cancellation, the notes shall no longer be deemed outstanding; the right to receive interest thereon shall cease to accrue from and after the date of redemption so fixed; and all rights with respect to such notes so called for redemption shall forthwith on such redemption date cease and terminate, except only the right of the holders thereof to receive the redemption price therefor, together with accrued interest to the date fixed for redemption."

## PROBLEM

If a corporation has the above provision in its debt security, what price must it pay if the security is to be called in its entirety as of August 1, 1988 and $10,000,000 is outstanding?

## 2. Sinking Fund

A sinking fund provision in a debt security is designed to minimize the burden on the corporation of paying the entire principal amount of the debt at maturity by providing for a regular procedure for retiring part of the debt periodically before maturity or setting aside money in a separate account outside of the control of the corporation for the purpose only of retiring the debt.[35] The holders of the debt security are likely to favor such a provision because the lessened burden to the corporation will increase the likelihood of repayment.

---

35. See Section II.H.5 of this Chapter for a discussion of sinking funds with respect to preferred stock.

## QUESTION

Why might the holders dislike such a provision? (Hint: See the immediately preceding subsection relating to redemption.)

Sinking fund provisions may be very complex when the debt has been issued under a trust indenture because of the role of the trustee.

### 3. Conversion

Corporate debt securities are frequently convertible into equity securities.[36] It is designed to be an "equity kicker" to make the security more attractive to prospective purchasers. The terms of the conversion and the mechanics for carrying it out must be set forth in detail. The form should be similar to those for preferred stock with respect to "antidilution provisions".[37]

### 4. Subordination

When holders of a debt security agree to "subordinate" that debt to other debt which the corporation may then or at some future time have outstanding, they are agreeing to permit the holders of other debt securities to have a prior right to the corporation's assets in the event that the superior debt is not paid. The following is a sample of a relatively simple form of subordination provision. Note how carefully the terms are defined and spelled out.

### SAMPLE PROVISION:

"The notes of this issue are subordinate and junior in right to payment, as to principal only, to any and all indebtedness which is now due or which in the future may become due by the Corporation, hereinafter called 'Senior Debt',[38] except to the extent that any such indebtedness is evidenced by notes of this issue. The holder of this note, by acceptance hereof, agrees to such subordination and junior right to payment, and, in furtherance thereof also agrees: (1) that, in the event of liquidation of the Corporation, in dissolution (voluntary or involuntary), bankruptcy, any other insolvency proceedings, or otherwise, not to receive any amount on account of the principal of this note unless and until all Senior Debt is first paid in full, and the holder hereof agrees to and does hereby assign all claims against and rights to share in the assets of the Corporation in any such liquidation, arising from the principal of this note, pro rata to holders of the Senior Debt, to the extent necessary to assure payment in full of all Senior Debt prior to

36. See Section II.H.6 for a discussion of conversion with respect to preferred stock.

37. See Section II.H.6 of this Chapter.

38. Note again the importance of using a shorthand definition for a complicated term or concept.

any payment in such liquidation of any of the principal hereof; and (2) if, at the maturity of this note, the Corporation is in default with respect to any Senior Debt, the maturity of this note shall be extended without notice until such time as there shall be no default by the Corporation with respect to any Senior Debt; and (3) that, in the event the holder of this note obtains a judgment for the principal hereof, not to enforce collection of such judgment while Senior Debt is in existence, and to make on or insert in the record of such judgment the fact that such judgment is subordinate and junior in right to payment to Senior Debt as herein defined. The foregoing agreements are expressly and solely for the benefit of holders of Senior Debt and nothing herein shall impair the obligation of the Corporation to the holder hereof under the terms hereof."

## QUESTION

**Why is it extremely advantageous to the corporation to have some of its debts subordinated?**

In deciding whether the purchase of senior debt securities is a good investment, a purchaser can basically ignore the amount of subordinated debt outstanding because the senior debt must be paid in full before the subordinated debt receives any payments or principal. For that reason, however, the subordinated debt itself is less attractive to investors. Subordinated debt is usually salable only if the debt security has some other feature which compensates for its inherent disadvantage (e.g., higher interest rate, conversion feature, favorable redemption terms). It may be purchased by an existing shareholder of the corporation who wants to supply the corporation with additional cash without adversely affecting the corporation's ability to borrow money from other sources. Such a shareholder would, at the same time, perhaps want to have rights to the corporation's assets which are superior to that of a common stockholder. By making the shareholder a lender, even on a subordinated basis with respect to the new injection of money, the corporation makes the shareholder prior in right of payment to shareholders.

## QUESTIONS

**Is the shareholder's status as a shareholder affected with respect to the money already invested as a shareholder by becoming a subordinated lender? How?**

It should be noted that, with the agreement of the lender, debt may be subordinated after its creation. That situation may occur where the corporation is in a period of financial hardship and cannot fully repay the original debt. The holders of the debt securities might believe that with further borrowed capital, the corporation would have a chance to recover. Accordingly, they may be willing to subordinate their right of repayment to the new borrowing.

## QUESTIONS

Can a debt security be subordinate to some debt and superior to other debt? Who must agree to such an arrangement if it is possible to create it?

## Chapter Nine

## EMPLOYMENT AGREEMENTS

---

### Introduction

Since lawyers are often called upon to prepare employment contracts for their clients, and since there are common elements in most of these contracts, it is natural to expect that lawyers' assistants may be expected to prepare initial drafts of employment contracts. Chapter Nine is intended to provide the necessary training for this purpose. It is also designed to further refine the drafting skills of a lawyer's assistant and to introduce the lawyer's assistant to the typical format of legal agreements.

## I. GENERAL CONSIDERATIONS

### A. PURPOSE

The purpose of an employment agreement is rather obvious—to set forth in writing the terms on which an employment relationship is entered into, and the rights, duties and obligations of the employer and employee. While the terms of an employment agreement may vary substantially from one agreement to another depending upon the nature of the job, the duration of the agreement, the amount of compensation involved and numerous other factors, every well-drafted employment agreement will contain provisions dealing with the basic components of the employment relationship. These basic components are listed below and will be individually discussed and analyzed.

### B. EMPLOYMENT RELATIONSHIPS WITHOUT WRITTEN AGREEMENTS

The vast majority of employment relationships are never documented by written agreements. Employees performing relatively routine services who do not have special skills which would make replacement difficult normally perform without an employment agreement. The employment relationship of such employees is governed in accordance with compensation provisions and other rules and regulations developed by the employer and applicable federal and state laws establishing wage and hour requirements and requirements as to working conditions systematically applied to the class of employee involved. The rights of employees who are members of an organized union are normally governed exclusively by the union agreement. It is unusual for such an employee to have an individual employment agreement.

223

## C. GENERAL BENEFITS AND BURDENS OF WRITTEN EMPLOYMENT AGREEMENTS

Written employment agreements are commonly entered into with persons who occupy key managerial and executive positions, salesmen, research and development personnel engaged in projects which may be entitled to legal protection (such as patent, copyright or trade secret protection) and other employees bringing special skills to their jobs. However, even with respect to these types of employees, many employers strongly resist or, as a matter of policy, refuse, to enter into written employment agreements. This attitude is based on the fact that in many cases an employment agreement establishes legal rights and security for the employee without providing comparable benefit to the employer.

Fundamentally, an employee, upon entering into an employment agreement, makes a commitment to render certain services for a certain period of time, and the employer, in return, commits itself to pay the agreed compensation and provide other benefits during that period. If the employee comes to dislike the employment, either because of the rate of compensation, the co-workers, or the opportunity to get a better job, the employee can simply leave the employment, and as a practical matter, incur no liability to the employer by the decision to leave. While an employment agreement may extend for a specified period of time (e. g., three years), the employer has no legal right to force an employee to remain in its employ for such period; all that can happen if an employee leaves is for the employer to terminate the benefits payable to the employee under the contract. The reason that an employer cannot require an employee to perform as agreed is that such a requirement would be involuntary servitude in violation of federal and state constitutions.

On the other hand, the employer cannot terminate the employment of an employee who is under contract, without remaining financially liable to the employee, unless the employer can demonstrate, as an objective factual matter, that the employee has failed to perform the duties under the agreement or has otherwise violated a provision of the agreement. If no oral or written agreement existed, an employment relationship could be terminated by the employer at will, without legal consequences or continuing financial responsibility to the employee. Absent union provisions, employment with the ability of the employer to terminate at will is the situation existing in the vast majority of employment relationships.

### QUESTION

If an employee does not have a written employment contract but was hired on the understanding that the employee would be compensated "at $200,000 per annum", is such employee assured of at least one year of employment?

The principal legal obligations incurred by an employee in signing an employment agreement are to perform as required by the agreement and to comply with the "restrictive covenant" (one of the basic components of employment agreements, to be separately discussed below). A restrictive covenant exists where an employment agreement provides that if the employee terminates the employment in violation of the agreement, or upon the termination of employment through expiration of the agreement itself, the employee will be legally barred for a period of time thereafter from engaging in activities competitive to the business activities of the employer. Such a restrictive covenant is intended to prevent an employee from breaking the relationship for the employee's own economic self-interest to the detriment of the employer or to use business secrets or customer lists obtained during the employment. However, there are legal and practical considerations which limit the effectiveness of restrictive covenants in many employment agreements.

## D. GENERAL STATEMENT OF BASIC COMPONENTS AND STRUCTURE OF EMPLOYMENT AGREEMENTS

The basic components of an employment agreement are as follows:

1. Mutual agreement to employ and to perform duties.

2. Capacity and duties to be performed by employee.

3. Term of employment and termination.

4. Compensation and other economic benefits to employee.

   (a) Basic compensation

   (b) Incentive compensation

   (c) Other benefits

   (d) Expense reimbursement

5. Restrictive covenants, trade secret protective clauses and related provisions.

Each of these basic components of an employment agreement will be separately analyzed. Depending upon the general complexity of the agreement, the nature of the employment and other considerations, one of the basic components listed above may not appear as a single section or paragraph of an agreement, but, rather, may be covered in numerous different sections or paragraphs. Alternatively, a single section or paragraph of an employment agreement may deal with certain aspects of two or more of such basic components. The structure of an employment agreement will become evident from the form provisions and form agreements contained in these materials.

## II. ANALYSIS OF BASIC COMPONENTS OF EMPLOYMENT AGREEMENTS

### A. MUTUAL AGREEMENT TO EMPLOY AND PERFORM DUTIES

#### 1. Form Provision

The following clause is a typical example of this normally short and simple provision, which commonly is the initial provision of the employment agreement:

"Company hereby employs Employee as its sales manager, and Employee hereby accepts said employment, subject to all of the terms and conditions of this agreement."

#### 2. Discussion

This provision is intended to do nothing more than express the basic undertaking of each party to the other. It has legal significance because, as a general rule, an agreement must contain obligations or benefits running to or from both parties in order to be binding. It has become a matter of common practice to have such a general expression of mutual obligation at the outset of any agreement, whether employment or otherwise.[1]

### B. CAPACITY AND DUTIES

#### 1. Form Provisions

The following are two typical examples of employment agreement provisions setting forth the capacity and duties of the employee:

#### EXAMPLE—Form 1

"(a) Employee is employed as the executive officer of Corporation in charge of production, and to assist the chief executive officer of Corporation in the operation and management of the business and affairs of Corporation, subject to the supervision and direction of Corporation's Board of Directors, and to perform such other technical, managerial and executive functions and services for Corporaton as Employee may from time to time be requested to perform by the President or the Board of Directors of Corporation.

"(b) During the period of employment hereunder, Employee agrees to devote Employee's time, energy, skill and best efforts to promote the business and affairs of Corporation, and to perform faithfully to the fullest extent of Employee's ability all the duties

---

1. Look at the form agreements at the end of this Chapter for variations on this type of provision.

which relate to Employee's position as may be requested of Employee by Corporation's Board of Directors or President. Employee agrees that during the original term of this agreement and any renewal terms, Employee will not be employed by, participate or engage in, or be a part of in any manner, directly or indirectly, the affairs of any other business enterprise or occupation which would interfere with the performance of Employee's full time duties hereunder."

### EXAMPLE—Form 2

"Employee shall serve as a salesperson in the territory comprised of the states of Pennsylvania, New Jersey and Delaware (herein called the 'Territory'). Employee agrees to devote Employee's entire time, energy, skill and attention to the sale of products fabricated or sold by Employer, to the exclusion of all other business interests, and in that connection to solicit orders actively for the sale of said products of Employer, to generally promote the business and affairs of Employer, and to perform such other duties as may from time to time be assigned to Employee by the officers of Employer. Employee shall travel throughout the Territory, and give it thorough coverage in accordance, and in compliance, with instructions and directions from Employer, which shall include the time or times when Employee shall travel in the aforesaid Territory and the duration of the trips. Employee shall submit periodic itineraries, reports and other data, as required, in accordance with Employer's sales program."

## 2. Discussion

### (a) *General*

While the above examples state the employee's duties in rather summary fashion, they are typical of provisions on the subject included in agreements with executives, high level supervisory personnel and sales personnel. When an employee's work is more specialized or unique, the agreement is more likely to detail the specific function. Such a detailed description is sometimes included even in common employment situations.[2] The provisions dealing with capacity and duties are of great legal importance. In the event an employee asserts a claim based on an alleged improper termination of employment, the employer's defense will usually be that the employee failed to carry out the prescribed duties. Note carefully that, as is true of form utilization in all cases, a paralegal must modify forms to fit the matter at hand, not try to make the matter at hand fit an available form. Moreover, agreements are not drafted in a vacuum; they have a point of view and perspective. If a paralegal is drafting an employment agreement for the employer, it shall look far different than if

---

**2.** See, for example, paragraph 1 of Form Agreement 1 and paragraph 2 of Form Agreement 2 at the end of this Chapter.

the paralegal were drafting it for the employee in the same transaction.[3]

### (b) *Principal Elements*

### (i) Breadth of Coverage

Regardless of the extent to which duties are specifically designated, it is desirable from the employer's point of view to have "catch-all" language which provides that the employee shall perform such other duties as may be requested by higher ranking officers of the company or the company's board of directors. From the employee's point of view, it is important that the agreement at least indicate that the other duties which may be requested shall be "reasonable" and be related to the principal duties which are to be performed. The form provisions above are favorable to the employer in that they do not clearly specify such limitations. While a court interpreting these provisions might conclude, in the event of a dispute, that such limitations are implicit, the employee would have been well-advised to ask for express language, and the employer would not be likely to refuse such a request.

### (ii) Time Commitment

It is important to the employer that the capacity and duties provision state that the employee's commitment is a full-time one, if that is in fact the understanding. When dealing with executives, it is not unusual for the employee to insist that the agreement specify that the employee shall, nevertheless, be permitted to have investments in other companies, to serve on boards of directors of other non-competing companies, to. participate in civic and charitable organizations or other similar activities.[4]

### (iii) Title of Employee

An employee is often quite concerned about a title. Although it may be contemplated that an executive will be the president or vice president of the employer, the employment agreement should, from the employer's point of view, designate the employee's capacity as that of chief executive or as a senior executive rather than as president or vice president. This is because corporate officers, as a matter of law, are elected in each year by the company's board of directors, and the corporation cannot properly make a contractual commitment on a subject which the directors have the right and obligation to determine.[5]

---

3. In this connection consider the difference in detail of job description that would be drafted from an employer perspective rather than an employee perspective. Which side (employer or employee) is more likely to desire a very detailed description of the job?

4. See, for example, paragraphs 2(c) and 8 of Form Agreement 2.

5. The provisions of paragraphs 2(a), 7(b) and 8 of Form Agreement 2 recognize that the employee has no contractual right to be elected an officer but gives the employee certain termi-

### (iv) Other

Depending upon the nature of the employment, the capacity and duties provisions may specify the place of employment,[6] may have particular provisions as to hours, may specify the amount of vacation to which the employee is entitled,[7] may put maximums on the portion of time that the employee can be required to travel, or deal with any number of other particulars.[8]

### (c) *Restrictions on Employee's Authority*

In establishing the capacity and duties of an employee, the employment agreement will in some instances set forth specific limitations on the employee's authority. For example, the following provision or some comparable language commonly appears in an agreement with a salesperson:[9]

> "Employee's authority to act for Employer is limited strictly to the solicitation of orders, and all orders received as a result of Employee's solicitation shall be subject to acceptance or rejection by Employer at its principal office in Philadelphia, Pennsylvania. Employer may refuse or reject, either in whole or in part, any order received as a result of Employee's solicitations, and may cancel any such order, either in whole or in part, after acceptance. Employee agrees in all respects to observe the rules and regulations of Employer as to price, terms and other conditions of sale, and Employee shall have no power to authorize returns or offer special prices, terms or conditions unless special written instructions are given to Employee by Employer."

Another express limitation might specify a dollar ceiling on the size of contracts which the employee is permitted to enter into on behalf of the company without prior approval by a higher officer or the company's board of directors, for example, a limit on the dollar amount of raw materials which may be ordered by a production manager. The purposes of such provisions are two-fold: (a) to make clear to the employee the limits of authority, and (b) to provide support to the employer in justifying that it is not "doing business" within a particular state even if one of its salesperson-employees is soliciting sales or performing certain other functions in that jurisdiction.[10]

nation rights if not so elected. Such provisions are rare and represent good provisions from the employee's perspective.

6. See paragraphs 1 and 3 of Form Agreement 3.

7. See paragraph 2(b) of Form Agreement 2.

8. Again, the detail as to which particulars are covered depends on the item,

which side is being represented, and the results of negotiations.

9. See also Form 2 under Section II.B.-1 of this Chapter.

10. Certain burdens are assumed by a corporation which is "doing business" in a state other than its state of incorporation and must, therefore, qualify to do business in such state. Under Section 106 of the MBCA, a foreign corporation is not deemed to be

## PROBLEM

Which of the following is the better provision in an employment contract from the employer's standpoint? Why?

Alternative 1.

"Employee will carry out such business activities as may be requested by the Board of Directors from time to time during the term of this Agreement."

Alternative 2.

"Employee will perform as a sales executive and in such other sales supervisory positions as may be requested by the Board of Directors from time to time during the term of this Agreement."

## C. TERM OF EMPLOYMENT; TERMINATION

### 1. Form Provision

The following is a typical provision setting forth the duration of the obligations of the parties under an employment agreement:

"This agreement shall be for a term of three (3) years, commencing on the date hereof, and thereafter shall automatically be renewed from year to year, unless either party shall give notice to the other no less than ninety (90) days prior to the end of the initial term or of any renewal term of such party's intention to terminate the agreement at the end of said term."

### 2. Discussion

(a) *General*

In the absence of an employment agreement, the employment relationship is terminable at the will of either party. If a written employment agreement does not specify the term of the agreement, the agreement is assumed to be for a term which is reasonable in the light of the circumstances. That doctrine leaves so much uncertainty that it is basic to every employment agreement that a term be specified.

## QUESTIONS

Does an employer guarantee that an employee will stay in the employ for the specified term by execution of an employment agreement? Does the employee guarantee employment for that period of time? Which party benefits more?

transacting business within the state so as to require qualification, if all it does is solicit or procure orders "where such orders require acceptance without this state before becoming binding contracts." A restriction of the type found in the preceding form will support the position that a corporation need not qualify as a foreign corporation and thereby subject itself to additional regulatory and tax burdens.

If, as in the above form provision, renewals of the employment term are automatically assumed, a notice period must be specified to provide for the mechanics of termination of the agreement by either party. The notice period is not necessarily the same for both parties although it usually is. The appropriate length of the notice period varies depending upon the nature of the employment, with more specialized and unique employees properly calling for longer notice periods because of the difficulty of finding suitable employment and/or replacement.[11]

Employment agreements sometimes do not have automatic renewal provisions, but are simply for a specified term. In such a case, neither party has an obligation to continue the employment relationship after the term has expired or to notify the other party of termination.

#### (b) Termination

Many employment agreements do not have any express provisions dealing with what acts or omissions provide justification for the other party to terminate the agreement. However, it is implicit in every employment agreement that if one party breaches or fails to perform the agreement, the other party has the right to terminate without further liability or obligation. As indicated in the discussion of capacity and duties, a dispute about whether termination by the employer was proper will usually turn on whether or not the employee properly performed, which is an inherently factual matter that frequently cannot be adequately dealt with by written standards in an agreement, no matter how well drafted. Some agreements do spell out specific grounds for termination, such as the employee's being convicted of a crime, committing an act involving moral turpitude or being adjudicated a bankrupt.[12]

In the case of executives, continuation of employment is sometimes made dependent on the attainment of certain sales increases or profit levels, although it is more common to set lower fixed compensation levels and provide for bonuses or another form of incentive compensation based on sales or profit targets. Disability which causes an inability of the employee to work for more than a specified period of time and death are other reasons for termination.[13]

---

11. The mechanics of form and place of notice are dealt with by a notice provision which is one of the routine provisions near the end of every employment agreement. See, for example, paragraph 7 of Form Agreement 1, paragraph 9 of Form Agreement 2, paragraph 14 of Form Agreement 3 and paragraph 10 of Form Agreement 4.

12. See, for example, paragraph 7(c) of Form Agreement 2.

13. See the sample clause under Section II.D.3 of this Chapter, which provides for termination after a specified period of disability.

Special drafting becomes necessary when an employment agreement provides for incentive compensation. For example, if the agreement gives the employee the right to a bonus of 5% of the employer's profits for a given year, the agreement should set forth what happens if employment is terminated during the course of that year.[14]

## D. COMPENSATION

The compensation arrangements in an employment agreement can range from a simple straight salary or straight commission arrangement to a complex combination of various incentive compensation arrangements, fringe benefits and expense allowances coupled with a salary. The discussion of compensation arrangements will, therefore, be divided into several subsections dealing with these matters.

### 1. Basic Compensation

(a) *Form Provisions*

The following are two typical examples of employment agreement provisions setting forth basic compensation arrangements, the first establishing a straight salary arrangement and the second a straight commission arrangement, with a "draw":

**EXAMPLE—Form 1**

"Corporation shall pay to Employee, as basic compensation for all services rendered by Employee during the employment hereunder, a salary at the rate of $20,000 per annum, payable in such weekly, bi-weekly or monthly installments as shall be in accordance with Corporation's prevailing payroll arrangements."

**EXAMPLE—Form 2**

"As sole compensation for Employee's services as a sales person, Employer shall (subject to the withholding provisions of all applicable federal, state and local employment taxes) pay Employee the commissions hereinafter set forth on all orders which are obtained by Employee and filled by Employer, for which full payment is received. In the event of returns by, or credits or allowances to any customer, Employee's commission account will be charged for any commissions previously credited or paid pertaining to such merchandise or account.

"The commission on merchandise sold at regular prices will be paid at the rate of 5% of net sales of Employer from orders obtained by Employee. The commission paid on merchandise sold below regular wholesale price (or with special terms and/or conditions) will be 2% of net sales of Employer based on orders obtained by Employee, except if otherwise specified by Employer

14. See the sample forms under Section II.D.2 of this Chapter.

prior to such offering of merchandise (Employee shall be authorized to solicit orders below regular wholesale price or with special terms and/or conditions only when expressly permitted to do so by Employer). Furthermore, no commission shall be paid with respect to merchandise sold 33⅓% or more below regular wholesale price, except as otherwise specified by Employer prior to such offering of merchandise.

"Employer agrees that Employee shall have the right to make a weekly draw of $200 against future commissions, such drawings to be deemed on account of, or advances against commissions to be earned by Employee and to be charged and deducted from commissions earned as and when such commissions shall be payable to Employee.

"Employer agrees to furnish Employee with a copy of all invoices covering any goods shipped into Employee's territory and to furnish Employee with a statement on or before the 25th day of each month covering the amount of sales represented by such shipments for the previous month and the amount of commission due Employee, which amount shall be paid at the time said statement is delivered."

### (b) *Discussion*

### (i) Salary

Form 1 above provides for a straight salary and is simple and self-explanatory. The provision indicates the amount of compensation and the frequency with which the compensation is to be paid. Straight salary provisions will sometimes have escalation arrangements, for example, a salary of $20,000 during the first year, $22,000 the second year and so forth, or a rate of escalation based upon a certain percentage of the initial year's compensation.[15] The presence of a fixed compensation amount or schedule does not, of course, prevent the parties from agreeing to a change in salary arrangements during the term of the agreement, by an amendment to the agreement.[16]

### (ii) Commission

Form 2 above sets forth a complex commission arrangement involving numerous issues, such as which sales are included, at what point in the course of processing a customer's order for goods the commission on that order has been earned, varying commission rates on sales at different prices, and the right of the salesman to make draws against commission. It is critical, however, to spell out all of

---

15. See paragraph 3 of Form Agreement 1.

16. Language in an agreement such as that of the last clause of paragraph 4 of Form Agreement 4 stating that compensation is subject to adjustments which may be mutually agreed upon, is often desired by employees, but has no legal effect. In the absence of an actual amendment to the agreement which must be agreed upon, the specified compensation amount remains applicable, without the employee's having any right to adjustments.

these aspects with clarity so that there is no ambiguity in the provision. Without attempting to illustrate all the possible variations on each of these issues, it is sufficient to point out that each of the issues can be resolved in numerous ways. For example, the commission clause above states that the commission on a particular order is earned only at such time as full payment therefor has been received from the customer. It is probably more common (particularly in a seasonal or special order business in which goods may not be shipped, billed or paid for for several months after an order is placed) for a commission to be earned at the time that the goods are shipped, with a subsequent charge against the employee's commission account if the customer fails to pay. In some cases, the commission is earned regardless of payment and the risk of uncollectibility is borne by the employer.

### (iii) Effect of General Legal Principles When Agreement is Silent

The commission provision in Form 2 above may be considered deficient in at least one respect. It establishes the right of the employee to make a weekly "draw" which is an advance against future commissions earned. This means that commission payments are reduced by the amount previously drawn by the employee, but the clause does not spell out what the result will be if the salesman does not earn an amount equal to or greater than what he has "drawn". In some states, the law on this point is that the "draw" is a minimum compensation to which the employee is entitled regardless of commissions earned. In other states, the employer would have the right to recover from the employee the amount by which the draw exceeded commissions earned. Since the laws of different states vary on this point, and since the law in many other states is unclear, it is important to recognize this problem at the time the agreement is being prepared and deal with it expressly in the agreement when it is feasible to do so. If disputes or questions arise in the course of the employment relationship, the lawyer will be called upon to interpret the agreement for his client, and the lawyer's task will be simplified to the extent that the point in issue is covered by clear language in the agreement, rather than by general principles of law which may not be well-defined and will, in any event, require time-consuming and expensive research.

It must be noted that a client will sometimes prefer that an agreement be silent on a certain point, rather than raise a sensitive issue, even at the risk of weakening the client's legal position if a dispute arises. In the case of the "draw" provision, for example, most employers would probably be very hesitant to present an agreement to an employee that states that the employee may be obligated to repay certain amounts previously paid to him. It is the responsibility of the paralegal to highlight the issue to the lawyer for presentation to the client, so that the lawyer may advise the client of the implications of the silence of the agreement on the issue. In the absence of clear law on the subject in the jurisdiction involved, unless there is persuasive evidence that the agreement was thoroughly negotiated, an issue on which the agreement is silent is likely to be resolved in favor of the employee.

## QUESTION

* **Why do you suppose that this is the case?**

## 2. Incentive Compensation

### (a) *General*

The concept underlying any incentive compensation arrangement is that all or some portion of the employee's compensation should be dependent upon the success of the employer's efforts. The theory is, of course, that the employee will strive to make the employer successful when the employee will directly share in this success. There are an almost unlimited number of possible forms which an incentive compensation arrangement may take. There may be payments in cash or in stock of the employer corporation, payments based on the sales or profits of the corporation or the market value of the corporation's stock, payments which are made currently or payments which are deferred for a short period or until retirement. The incentive compensation may be based upon the performance of an entire company, or upon the performance of a particular subsidiary or division of a company or even the company's success with respect to a particular product.

The paralegal will ordinarily not frame the incentive compensation arrangement. However, understanding of the possibilities is necessary so that the paralegal can draft a provision that has been negotiated.

The basic idea of incentive compensation usually is to have the arrangement relate to the employee's functions. Therefore, a person who is a sales manager is likely to have an incentive compensation arrangement based on the company's sales, or increases in sales over what they were before the manager joined the company. If the employee is a sales manager for a particular territory, a sales-based incentive compensation arrangement would normally relate to sales performance in that territory. In the case of an executive whose duties are not principally in the sales area, the arrangement would be more likely to be based upon the company's profits or profit increases.

Because of the wide variety of incentive compensation arrangements, the discussion will be divided into several sub-categories.

### (b) *Cash Incentive Compensation*

### (i) Form Provisions

As mentioned above, the basis and method of computing incentive compensation can have any number of variations. The following are two typical examples of incentive compensation arrangements, the first being based upon the net income of the division of the employing company for which the employee works, and the second being based upon increases in the sales revenues of the employing company over sales revenues for the previous year:

### EXAMPLE—Form 1

"In addition to the fixed salary specified above, Employee shall be entitled to a bonus, as follows:

"(a) For each of the first two years of employment under this Agreement, five percent (5%) of the net income of the Fletcher Division during each fiscal year of the Company.

"(b) For each year of employment under the Agreement thereafter, two and one-half percent (2½%) of the net income of the Fletcher Division during each fiscal year of the Company.

"Said bonus shall be payable within thirty (30) days following the receipt by Company and Employee of the statement of profit and loss for the fiscal year prepared by Company's independent certified public accountants. For the purposes of this paragraph:

"(i) The "net income" of the Fletcher Division shall be determined by the Company's independent certified public accountants in accordance with generally accepted accounting principles consistently applied (except for adjustments expressly specified in the subsequent subparagraph of this paragraph), based upon the separate records and books of account maintained for the Fletcher Division, and said determination shall be conclusive and binding on the parties to this Agreement;

"(ii) No charge against the income of the Fletcher Division shall be made for any federal or state taxes paid or payable by Company which are determined or measured by the amount of the income of Company or of the Fletcher Division;

"(iii) Gains or losses resulting from the disposition of assets other than inventory and any other extraordinary gains or losses shall be excluded from the computation of the net income of Company and the Fletcher Division;

"(iv) All transactions between the Fletcher Division and other divisions of the Company or between the Fletcher Division and the parent corporation of the Company or other subsidiaries of said parent corporation shall be at the going rates then in effect for those transactions, in accordance with overall policies established by the parent corporation of the Company;

"(v) For any period less than a full fiscal year of Corporation during which Employee is employed hereunder, the portion of the Fletcher Division's net income with respect to which Employee shall be entitled to a bonus shall be the Fletcher's Division's net income for that portion of the fiscal year during which the Employee was employed."

**EXAMPLE—Form 2**

"(i) In addition to the fixed salary above, Employee shall be entitled to incentive compensation, to be paid within ninety (90) days after the end of the fiscal year in question, computed by multiplying the amount by which the "Adjusted Net Sales" (as hereinafter defined) of Employer for said year exceed Employer's "Net Sales" (as hereinafter defined) for the fiscal year immediately prior to said year, by the applicable percentage set forth in subparagraph (ii) hereof.

"(ii) For the purposes of the preceding subparagraph hereof, the percentages applicable to the amount by which the Adjusted Net Sales of Employer during the fiscal year in question exceeds the Net Sales of Employer for the immediately preceding fiscal year are as follows:

| | |
|---|---|
| Up to $250,000 of excess net sales | ½% |
| More than $250,000 and up to $500,000 of excess net sales | ¾% |
| More than $500,000 of excess net sales | 1% |

"(iii) For the purpose of this Agreement, "Net Sales" shall mean the gross sales of Employer, less all returns, allowances, credits and discounts, as set forth on the income statement prepared by Employer's independent accountants for the fiscal year in question. For the purpose of this Agreement "Adjusted Net Sales" shall mean Net Sales, reduced by the portion of Net Sales revenues attributable to increases in average unit prices over the average unit prices of the previous year, it being the understanding of the parties that Employee's incentive compensation is to be based upon increases in the number of units sold rather than increases in Net Sales revenues arising from price increases.

"(iv) If Employee ceases to be employed hereunder on a date other than the last day of the fiscal year of Employer, then Employee shall be entitled to a portion of the incentive compensation which would have been payable to Employee if Employee had been employed throughout said fiscal year, determined by computing the full amount of incentive compensation which would have been payable and multiplying said amount by a fraction, the numerator of which shall be the number of working days of said fiscal year during which Employee was employed, and the denominator of which shall be the total number of working days in that fiscal year."

### (ii) Discussion

Every well-drafted cash incentive compensation provision should deal with each of the issues discussed below:

### (a) Frequency and Specific Time of Payment

Each of the form provisions above provides for a single annual incentive compensation payment. This arrangement has the advantage of requiring computations only once per year, and also facilitates reliance upon the accountants engaged by the employer for making the computations, since most companies have annual financial statements prepared by independent accountants.   There are other forms of incentive compensation arrangements which provide for monthly, quarterly or semi-annual payments, particularly when the incentive compensation represents a substantial portion of the employee's overall compensation.   In such cases, it is common to provide that the first payment to be made after the end of the company's fiscal year will be adjusted if the payments made during the year aggregate an amount different from what would have been paid based on a single payment made on the basis of the company's performance throughout the year.   The need for such a provision arises from the fact that many accounting determinations which may significantly affect the company's financial results (for example, the taking of inventory by a physical count on last day of the fiscal year) are made accurately only once a year, with estimates being made in the interim.

In addition to the matter of frequency of payments, the specific time of payment should also be set forth.   With annual payments, it is normal to specify a date which can reasonably be expected to be an early date after the completion of the financial statements by the accountants.   The first form provision expressly ties in with the annual financial statements by stating that the payment date is to be thirty days after receipt of the financial statements by the company.   The second form provision specifies a payment date ninety days after the end of the fiscal year.   This date is intended to tie in with the company's yearly financial statements, but the provision leaves itself open to the possibility that the financial statements may be delayed beyond the payment date.

### (b)  Who Makes Determinations

Both of the above form provisions spell out that the independent accountants engaged by the company shall make the determinations which establish the amount of the incentive compensation.   When the company engages independent accountants to certify that the statements that they have prepared are true and correct, without qualification (so-called "certified" or "audited" statements), it is customary to have their determinations be conclusive on all parties.   Reliance on accountants' computations is common even when "certified" statements are not being prepared, but since the accountant is engaged and paid by the employer, there may be some risk to the employee of an unfavorable determination in such circumstances, and the risk may be still greater if the determinations are being made by a company officer.   In such circumstances the employee may be wise to insist that the provision merely state that net income or net sales shall be determined in accordance with generally accepted accounting principles, consistently applied, leaving it open for assertion with respect to any particular computation that in fact the computation was not in accordance with a consistent application of such principles.

### (c) Accounting Questions and Definitions

Regardless of who is making the determinations, it is always necessary to consider whether there should be any variations from generally accepted accounting principles for purposes of computing incentive compensation. In Form 1 there are several express deviations from the general definition of net income. The theory behind these definitions is simply that unusual occurrences in the company's operation should be disregarded for purposes of determining compensation of an employee who has no control over nor anything to do with such occurrences. Note that such exclusions can favor or disfavor the employee depending upon whether the unusual transaction was beneficial or disadvantageous to the company.

It will be necessary to define certain terms in order that the accounting provisions as well as other terms are well-drafted. The general form used by lawyers to define terms in agreements, including parties, concepts, places and the like, is to define the term and place the defined term in quotations. Look at the first paragraph in Form Agreement 1 setting forth the parties, and notice the method of defining "Employer" and "Employee". The terms "Employer" and "Employee" (as well as other defined terms) are capitalized to indicate that for purposes of the agreement they are proper nouns. The importance of defining terms at the earliest possible point in the agreement is that the person drafting the agreement then has a shorthand, precise method of utilizing the term later in the agreement. If "Net Sales" or "Adjusted Net Sales" were not defined terms, the person drafting would repeatedly have to restate the concept. In doing so, variations and errors would creep into the term, as well as unnecessary repetition of the concept and great lengthening of the agreement.

As illustrated by both of the above form provisions, the definitions for accounting terms frequently involve simply making it clear that generally accepted accounting principles will be applicable except for specific inclusions or exclusions which might not be taken into account in accordance with generally accepted accounting principles. However, just as it is true that general legal principles are sometimes uncertain, so it is true with respect to generally accepted accounting principles. Therefore, when the parties have in mind a clear idea of what the method of computation is to be, it is generally worthwhile to set that forth even though it may be that the same result would be reached by the accountants in applying generally accepted accounting principles.[17] When a payment is to be based on "profits" or "in-

---

17. See, for example, the definition of "Net Sales" in the Form 2 above.

come", it is always important to make clear whether the reference is to profits or income before or after income taxes.[18]

If the incentive bonus depends upon the performance of a subsidiary or a division of a corporation, then it is important to deal with those transactions between a parent corporation and its subsidiary or between the corporation and its division [19] which might affect the performance result.[20]  In addition, it would be prudent to indicate that some part or none, as the parties may agree, of the parent corporation's overhead is to be included as a charge against net income for the purpose of calculating the incentive bonus.

Form 2 illustrates an incentive compensation arrangement based on changes in sales from one year to the next.  In such circumstances, it is particularly important for the paralegal to focus on elements which could cause changes with which the employee has nothing to do and no control and which should, therefore, be eliminated in making the comparative computations.[21]

### (d)  Termination During Fiscal Period

The possibility of termination of employment during a period with respect to which incentive compensation is being earned must be dealt with expressly in the agreement since, in the absence of an express provision there are numerous possible methods of determining what, if any, compensation has been earned by the employee for the partial period of employment.  The two form provisions illustrate two of the possibilities.  In Form 1 compensation is computed upon the company's performance during the portion of the year in which the employee worked.  Form 2 provision takes into account the performance of the company throughout the fiscal period and makes the payment a pro rata portion of what would have been paid if employment had continued throughout the period.

While at first glance these two provisions may seem essentially the same, they may well not be, and they present different problems. When the employer is in a business which is seasonal, e. g., sales of toys which are concentrated at the end of the calendar year, if the approach of making the incentive compensation payment based upon the period of actual employment is used, the employee may do very well or very poorly.  The performance would depend upon whether

---

18. See, for example, subparagraph (ii) of the Form 1 above.

19. A division differs from a subsidiary in that a division is merely part of the corporation's operations which is segregated for corporate and financial purposes by product, location, function or some other logical basis of differentiation.  A subsidiary is a separate corporation, all or a portion of the stock of which is owned by another corporation called its "parent".

20. See subparagraph (iv) of the Form 1 above.

21. The distinction between "Net Sales" and "Adjusted Net Sales" in subparagraph (ii) of the Form 2 illustrates a method of making this elimination.

the portion of the year in which the employee worked has the high yield portion or the low yield portion. This is a contrast to what the employee would have received on the basis of a prorated portion of an entire year's performance. Proration based upon the entire year's performance has the definite advantage of eliminating the need for making special mid-year computations. It also carries with it the necessity that the payment be deferred until the end of the year, although the employment may have been terminated a substantial time prior to the end of the year. Proration also means that the compensation received by the employee will be affected favorably or unfavorably by the performance of a successor during the balance of the year.

Incentive compensation provisions sometimes specify no adjustment for short periods—that is, that no incentive compensation will be paid unless the employee remains in the employ throughout the entire period in question. If this is the desired result, it should be expressly stated because of the likelihood that an ambiguity in the agreement will be resolved in favor of the employee.

This discussion points up the importance of covering all issues. The parties, at the time of entering into an employment agreement, would be unlikely to consider this issue and in most cases would accept almost any provision dealing with this subject. Yet, in the event of termination, this issue is almost certain to arise and will be disputed if not dealt with clearly in the agreement. One of the principal purposes of an employment agreement is to eliminate the possibility of such disputes.

(c) *Stock Options*

(i) Discussion

It has been common to provide employee incentive compensation by giving employees an ownership interest in the company, through the issuance to the employee of shares of stock or rights to purchase shares of stock of the company. The theory of such an incentive arrangement is that if, through the employee's efforts, the company's profits improve, the improvement is likely to be reflected in an increase in the value of the company's stock and, therefore, an increase in the value of the stock or stock rights which an employee has.

A stock option is simply a right to purchase stock during a certain period of time at a certain purchase price, regardless of the market price of the stock at the time the option is exercised. The option may be granted at the present market value of the stock or above or below present market value. The option is or becomes valuable when the market value of the employer's stock is higher than the purchase price specified in the employee's option. If the market value is not higher the employee will probably not exercise his option as there is no obligation or incentive to do so.

### (ii) Form Provision

The grant of stock options to an employee may or may not be a part of that employee's employment agreement. The following is a typical example of an employment agreement provision covering the right of an employee to receive stock options:

> "Corporation, by action of its Board of Directors at the next regularly scheduled meeting of the Board of Directors, shall grant to Employee an option exercisable at any time or times within five years after the date on which said option is granted, to purchase from Corporation up to a total of 10,000 shares of its Common Stock at a purchase price per share equal to the greater of $1.00 or the fair market value of Corporation's Common Stock on the date of grant. The option to be granted hereunder shall be evidenced by an instrument in writing containing all of the terms and conditions which are included in the form Stock Option Agreement which was approved by the Board of Directors of the Corporation."

### QUESTIONS

**What if the Board of Directors does not grant the option as required? Is it obligated to do so?**

### (iii) Economic Comparison

The essence of a stock option is the grant of a right to the employee to purchase a specified number of shares at a specified purchase price per share during a specified period of time. A stock option is similar to a cash incentive payment arrangement in that its worth is likely to depend on the success of the employer. However, it differs from a cash arrangement in a number of ways.

First, the market value of the stock, and hence the value of the option, may increase or decrease based on general market fluctuations, regardless of the success of the employer. Second, the benefit to the employee is usually not immediate because the right to exercise the option may be deferred until a future date and, in any event, will produce "spendable" income only after the option has been exercised and the stock has been sold. Third, there are restrictions on the exercise and sale or transfer of the stock purchasable under the option both to satisfy the requirements of the Federal and state securities acts and to permit treatment of any gain at more favorable capital gains tax rates. Because of these restrictions, the benefits which may be derived from the option may disappear before the stock can be sold.

## 3. Other Benefits

(a) *Form Provision*

The following are typical examples of provisions providing other employee benefits (often referred to as "fringe benefits"):

### EXAMPLE—Form 1

"Throughout the term of Employee's employment hereunder, Employee shall be entitled to participate in Employer's Profit Sharing Plan, Pension Plan, Group Insurance Plan, and Long Term Disability Protection Insurance Plan, and such other employee benefit plans as may hereafter be instituted by Employer, in the same manner and to the same extent as may from time to time be provided for other employees of Employer who are department heads."

### EXAMPLE—Form 2

"Employee shall be entitled to the benefits of the Company's accident and sickness policy and disability income plan underwritten by Provident Life and Accident Insurance Company. Benefits payable are $1,100/month lifetime for accident and $1,100/month for sickness disability to age sixty-five. Employee shall be entitled to receive the following life insurance coverage with benefits payable to beneficiaries designated by Employee:

| | |
|---|---|
| Group life | –$40,000 upon death |
| | 80,000 upon accidental death |
| Key person life [22] | – 75,000 upon death, provided that |
| | Employee is insurable at |
| | regular rates |
| Travel group policy | – 60,000 upon accidental death." |

(b) *Discussion*

(i) General

The provision of Form 1 is simple and is applicable when the employer has well-established employee benefit arrangements. Normally, in such cases, the employer will have a brochure describing the benefits which will be furnished to the employee. Since these benefits may change from time to time, due to the employer's switching from one group insurance plan to another, or discontinuing certain plans or because of cancellation of a plan by the insurer, the language "as may from time to time be provided" in Form 1 is important to the employer in order to avoid being held responsible to an employee for benefits described in the brochure which may not exist at the time that the employee becomes entitled to such benefits.

The Form 2 provision illustrates benefits which, at least with respect to the life insurance arrangements, may not be part of an over-

---

22. "Key person" insurance is a separate policy specifically on the life of a valuable individual employee as contrasted with "group life" which is for all employees or all employees of a specific class.

all plan but rather represent insurance coverage for a particular employee, with greater or lesser coverage, or no such coverage, being provided to other employees.

### (ii) Pension and Profit Sharing Plans

Pension and profit sharing plans represent the most common form of deferred compensation—that is, compensation which vests in the employee during his years of service with the employer, but the receipt of which is deferred until retirement. There is nothing to prohibit an employer and an employee from entering into an agreement which would provide that for each year of employment a specified sum will be "earned" which will be payable to the employee or his heirs upon retirement or death. However, such arrangements are normally entered into as part of an overall plan applicable to a class of employees, because certain tax advantages can be obtained through adoption of such plans. Furthermore, the Employee Retirement Income Security Act of 1974 ("ERISA") imposes many restrictions on employers with respect to such plans. Such plans must meet certain technical requirements in order to achieve the desired tax advantages.

From the employee's point of view, language such as that in Form 1 above covering "such other employee benefit plans as may hereafter be instituted by employer" is particularly important in employment situations with a young, growing company which may not have adopted significant benefit arrangements at the time that employment commences but which is likely to institute such plans with the passage of time. Even without such language, however, the employee will automatically get the benefit of any tax-qualified profit sharing plan or pension plan adopted by the employer for any employees of the same general class or level, since such plans must be implemented on a non-discriminatory basis—that is, on a basis which gives large classes of employees equal rights to participate.[23]

### (iii) Disability

Both of the above form provisions include insured disability benefit plans. When such insured plans have not been implemented by the employer, the employment agreement will frequently establish certain arrangements respecting disability, the following provision being typical:

> "If Employee should become unable to perform Employee's duties hereunder, because of partial or total disability or incapacity due to illness, accident, or other cause, Corporation shall continue Employee's salary at the full rate set forth in this agreement for a period of six months. If Employee is still unable to perform the du-

---

23. ERISA and income tax regulations require such non-discrimination.

> ties hereunder at the end of said six month period, Corporation shall have the right at any time thereafter to terminate Employee's employment upon ten (10) days' written notice to Employee, in which event Corporation shall have no further liability or obligation under this Agreement."

Needless to say, such a contractual provision is no substitute for long term insured disability protection.

### QUESTIONS

**Would an employee desire the foregoing sample provision? What changes might be reasonable to request in such a provision?**

### (iv) Automobile

Certain executive and sales positions normally carry with them the use by the employee of a company car. A typical clause is as follows:

> "During Employee's employment hereunder, Company will provide Employee with an automobile having a manufacturer's suggested retail price of not less than $7,000.00, for Employee's use in connection with the performance of duties hereunder, and Employee shall be entitled to a new automobile of such value every two years during such employment."

### QUESTION

**What problems from an employee's point of view can result from the foregoing method of determining the automobile to be supplied?**

Frequently, the contract provision on this subject will simply provide for a "suitable automobile" and will not specify the frequency with which the employee will be entitled to a new automobile.[24] If such issues can be readily resolved at the outset, however, it is desirable to do so in order to avoid possible disagreements at a subsequent date.[25]

### 4. Expense Reimbursement

### (a) *Form Provision*

A typical general provision for reimbursement of expenses is as follows:

> "During Employee's employment hereunder, Employer will reimburse Employee for all ordinary and necessary business expenses incurred by Employee in connection with the business of Employer. Such payment shall be made by Employer upon submission by Employee of vouchers itemizing such expenses in a form satisfactory to Employer."

24. See paragraph 6 of Form Agreement 4.

25. See paragraph 11 of Form Agreement 3 for the treatment of a related issue.

(b) *Discussion*

(i) General

The words "ordinary and necessary" are quite important from the employer's point of view. An employer would normally expect that any expenses incurred by an employee which are reimbursable under the employment agreement would be deductible by the employer on its tax return. From a tax point of view, only business expenses which are "ordinary and necessary", as that term is defined in the Internal Revenue Code and the regulations thereunder and in judicial decisions interpreting the term, are properly deductible.

The employee may desire that this provision make clear that the reimbursable expenses include expenses for entertainment, automobile, travel and other items, to avoid any implication to the contrary. In some instances, an employee is granted an expense allowance permitting expenditures up to a specified amount of dollars monthly or annually without the requirement to make any specific accounting. When the employee is to bear certain of the expenses, which is often the case with territorial sales personnel, it is advisable that the employer so specify in the agreement, to avoid a contrary implication.[26]

(ii) Moving Expenses

Under certain circumstances of employment, there may be particular provisions covering moving expenses or allowances. For example, when an employee is moving from one geographical area to another, moving expenses are frequently reimbursed by the employer, pursuant to a clause such as the following:

> "Company agrees to reimburse employee for the reasonable moving expenses (up to a maximum of $2,500) incurred by him in moving his family residence from Chicago, Illinois, to the San Francisco, California, area."

Internal Revenue Service provisions may limit the amount an employer will be willing to pay for moving expenses because of limitations on deductibility of moving expenses as "ordinary and necessary" business expenses.[27]

(iii) Product Allowances or Discounts

When the employer is in the business of producing consumer goods, the employee may contract for the right to select, free of charge, or at a specified discount, up to a certain dollar amount of such goods during each year. An example of such a clause follows:

> "Employee shall be entitled to select, free of charge, clothing manufactured by Employer to the extent of five hundred dollars

---

26. See, for example, paragraph 10 of Form Agreement 3.

27. See the preceding subsection for a discussion of "ordinary and necessary" business expenses.

($500.00) per annum, said amount being based upon Employer's regular wholesale prices less ten per cent (10%) thereof."

## E. RESTRICTIVE COVENANTS, TRADE SECRET PROTECTIVE CLAUSES AND RELATED PROVISIONS

### 1. General Considerations

As stated in the introductory portion of these materials, the provisions of an employment agreement falling within this category are those which represent the most significant advantage to be derived by the employer from an employment agreement. Although the variety of such clauses have much in common and are frequently dealt with in a single section of an employment agreement, various provisions within this category differ greatly in their importance, legal enforceability and legal effect as compared to the legal effect which would flow if the employment agreement did not contain such a clause. Therefore, various types of provisions coming within the general category of employer protection and employee restriction will be discussed separately.

### 2. Trade Secrets Protective Provisions

#### (a) *Form Provisions*

The following is a typical example of a clause designed to protect the employer from the employee's appropriation of trade secrets:

> "Employee covenants and agrees that Employee will not, during the term of employment or thereafter, for any reason or purpose whatsoever, use for personal benefit, or disclose, communicate or divulge to, or use for the benefit, direct or indirect, of any person, firm, association or corporation other than Corporation,[28] any information as to business methods, business policies, systems, procedures, techniques, computer programs, research or development projects or results thereof, trade secrets, inventions, knowledge and processes used or developed by Corporation, any forms, names and addresses of customers or clients, data on or relating to past, present or prospective customers or clients or any other information relating to or dealing with the business operations or activities of Corporation, made known to Employee or learned or acquired by Employee while in the employ of Corporation."

#### (b) *Discussion*

#### (i) Underlying Legal Principles

Even in the absence of an employment agreement or a provision such as the form provision above, employers are generally entitled to

---

**28.** Note the differentiation in this clause of *the* Corporation (a capitalized defined term) and *a* corporation in general (with a lower case "c").

protection against the appropriation by an employee or former employee of "trade secrets". A basic legal dictionary definition of a trade secret may be "a plan or process, tool, mechanism or compound known only to its owner and those of its employees to whom it is necessary to disclose it". The basic notion is that a process, technique or method developed by an employer or by its employees during the course of employment is, in effect, "property" of the employer and, therefore, the employer is entitled to be protected from having the employee learn or become acquainted with the "trade secret" and thereafter use it for the employee's own economic interests or those of another employer.

Although the law provides protection for trade secrets, such protection is not freely given by the courts. Just as copyright or patent rights are available only if the party desiring to assert these rights can establish that the subject matter is in fact worthy of protection, the same concepts are applicable in the trade secrets area.

### (ii) Analysis of Contract Provision

Inclusion of a clause such as the form provision above serves several purposes for the employer. First, the specification of particular items which, by implication, are acknowledged by the employee as deserving of protection, increases the likelihood that such items will be given legal protection, whereas they might not be given such protection under general legal trade secrets principles. Therefore, it is important to the employer that, in addition to having the clause include broad language such as "trade secrets, inventions, knowledge and processes", the clause specify other particular details of knowledge which are to be protected. The form provision above was drafted for a computer software business which creates specific computer programs for individual customers for a fee. Obviously the particular form of the provision will vary depending upon the nature of the business and the employment.

The inclusion of such a provision may also have an inhibiting effect on an employee who might otherwise not be fully aware that there are general legal principles which prohibit appropriation of trade secrets learned during employment. This is the kind of area where the very presence of a well-drafted, comprehensive clause may deter the employee from doing something and may encourage a court to afford protection where it otherwise might not.

The above provision also seeks to protect information as to customers of the employer. While this kind of information is not within the basic definition of a "trade secret", it has often been afforded legal protection by the courts in certain instances, and in many businesses it represents the principal information which the employer would seek to protect from competitors.

## 3. Restrictive Covenants (Non-Competition Agreements)

(a) *Form Provision*

The following are typical examples of clauses which are intended to bar an employee from competing with the employer:

### EXAMPLE—Form 1

"Employee covenants and agrees that Employee will not, during the term of the employment hereunder and for a period of two years after the termination or expiration of the employment hereunder, for any reason whatsoever, within the continental United States, directly or indirectly engage in any activities relating to evaluation and selection of computer equipment and software, conversion of computer programs and information files from one computer system to another, or in any other activities or operations carried on by Corporation at any time during the period of employment by Corporation, or planned or contemplated by Corporation at the time of termination of Employee's employment by Corporation. The term 'engage in' shall include, but shall not be limited to, activities, whether direct or indirect, as proprietor, partner, stockholder, principal, agent, employee or consultant."

### EXAMPLE—Form 2

"In order to insure to Company the effective enjoyment of the property, assets and business of Fletcher Packaging, Employee agrees that Employee will not engage in any business other than that of Company during Employee's employment under this Agreement, and that for a period of three (3) years after the termination of employment hereunder, regardless of the reason for such termination, Employee will not, within the states of California, Illinois, New Jersey, New York and Pennsylvania engage in the manufacture or sale of products the same as, similar to, or in general competition with, products manufactured or sold by Company. The term 'engage in' shall include, but shall not be limited to, activities, whether direct or indirect, as proprietor, partner, stockholder, principal, agent, employee, consultant or lender."

(b) *Discussion*

(i) Underlying Legal Principles

As stated previously, there are significant legal and practical limitations on the use of restrictive covenants in employment agreements. State laws vary substantially with regard to the circumstances under which a restrictive covenant in an employment agreement will be enforced by a court. Unlike the trade secrets area, a covenant against competition will never be implied—that is, an employee will never be presumed to have agreed not to compete upon termination of employment in the absence of a specific provision in the employment agreement. Furthermore, all courts have a strong presumption against enforcement of such provisions because of a fundamental resistance to impairing an individual's ability to earn a living in the type of employment to which he is accustomed. Therefore, these covenants must be carefully drawn, reasonable and limited in order to be enforced. In some instances, a court will refuse to enforce an employment agreement regardless of how well drawn and how severely limited the restriction is.

### (ii) Length of Time

A restrictive covenant would probably never be enforced by a court of law if the provision attempted to restrict the employee from engaging in a competitive activity forever. There is no clear maximum period which is permissible. One often-used rule of thumb is that the period after termination of employment during which the employee is restricted can never be longer than the initial term of the employment agreement. The acceptable length of a restriction will vary depending upon numerous circumstances. For example, a court would probably be more likely to find a two year restriction on a sales person to be too long even though the same court might enforce a three year restriction against an employee who, through the employment, acquired a great deal of specialized technological information developed by the employer. What is reasonable as to time depends generally on the nature of the employment and the length of the employment agreement.

### (iii) Territorial Limit of Restriction

The smaller the geographical area in which the restriction is applicable, the more likely it is that the restriction will be enforced. A clause restricting a sales person from selling products competitive with those of the former employer in geographic areas in which the employer did not sell, or outside of the scope of the employee's sales territory (even though within the employer's market area), would probably be unenforceable. On the other hand, with respect to an executive or technical employee, a national restriction might well be enforced if the employer's actual or potential market were nationwide, or the nature of the business was such that competition would be equally injurious whether generated by a business across the street from the employer or across the country. What is reasonable depends on the scope of the employee's activities and the employer's business.

### (iv) Correlation with Trade Secrets Protection

Restrictive covenants are more likely to be enforced in accordance with their terms when the nature of the employment is such that there is a high probability that competitive activity would be likely to carry with it the appropriation of the employer's trade secrets. In certain businesses, it would be very difficult, if not impossible, for an employer to prove the appropriation of a trade secret. In the area of computer software, for example, where certain mechanical changes in systems design or programming could make it most difficult to identify the materials as being the same as those developed by the employer, a restrictive covenant becomes, as a practical matter, the only effective means of protecting the information from appropriation.

(v)  Circumstances Which Give Rise to Implementation of Restriction

Both of the form provisions above provide that the restriction shall become applicable upon termination of the employment regardless of the reason for such termination. This is desirable from the employer's point of view, except that it increases the risk of the provision's being deemed unenforceable by a court sympathetic to an employee whose job was terminated by the employer. From the employee's point of view, it is wise to provide that the restriction is applicable only if the employment is terminated by the employee or by reason of the employee's breach of the agreement.[29]

## QUESTION

**Who would determine that the termination was a result of the employee's breach or employer's breach?**

(vi)  The Meaning of Unenforceability

Some courts take the position that if any aspect of the restriction (whether time, area or restricted activity) is deemed unduly broad, it will be held totally unenforceable so that the employee will not be subject to any restrictions. In other cases, courts have decided that the provision will be enforced but for a lesser period in a more limited territory or for a less broad activity than that prescribed in the agreement. Some employment agreements contain a provision such as the following:

> "If any of the provisions of subparagraphs (a) or (b) are held to be in any respect an unreasonable restriction upon Employee, then the court so holding may reduce the territory to which the provisions pertain, and/or the period of time in which they operate, or effect any other change, to the extent necessary to render the provisions enforceable by said court."

In certain states, however, this kind of provision has been treated as an invitation to the court to restrict the non-competition clause or hold it entirely unenforceable.

29. See, for example, paragraph 8 of
Form Agreement 2.

## QUESTION

**Is a court required to follow such a provision?**

(vii) Procedural Provisions

The following is a typical example of a provision which would be included as part of the section of an employment agreement which sets forth trade secrets and restrictive covenants:

> "Employee acknowledges that the restrictions contained in this paragraph 9, in view of the nature of the business in which Corporation is engaged, are reasonable and necessary to protect the legitimate interests of Corporation. Employee understands and agrees that the remedies at law for a violation of any of the covenants or provisions of this paragraph 9 will be inadequate, that such violations will cause irreparable injury within a short period of time, and that Corporation shall be entitled to preliminary injunctive relief and other injunctive relief against any such violation. Such injunctive relief shall be in addition to, and in no way in limitation of, any and all other remedies Corporation shall have in law and equity for the enforcement of those covenants and provisions. In the event of any violations or breaches of subparagraph (b) of this paragraph 9, the covenants therein contained shall remain in force during a period of two years subsequent to the termination of the conduct constituting a breach or violation."

Usually, it will be more important to an employer to stop an employee from breaching a restrictive covenant through the obtaining of a court injunction than it will be to obtain money damages from the employee for the breach. As courts are generally reluctant to provide injunctive relief to require an individual to act in a specific manner, the foregoing provision is included in order to help establish the right of the employer to obtain an injunction against the competitor's employment of the employee.

## QUESTION

**Could an employer obtain an injunction against an employee to require the employee to work for the employer as the employee agreed to do?**

(viii) Restrictions When Agreement is Related to Acquisition of a Business

A restrictive covenant is more likely to be enforced when the employment agreement is part of the acquisition of a business. The usual circumstances of this are that the principal shareholder of a business who also acted as one of its principal operating executives, negotiates, in connection with the sale of the business to another person or corporation, for an employment agreement. Because the acquiring company which will become the employer or the parent company of the employer has made a significant investment which will be threatened if a key employee enters into competition, the court is more likely to enforce a restrictive covenant in such situation. (Restrictive covenants connected with an acquisition are enforceable even if there is no employment agreement, as part of the agreement respecting the purchase of the business, although those covenants also must contain territorial and time limitations.) It is to the employer's advantage to make it clear in the agreement that the employment agreement was entered into in connection with an acquisition. This can be done by a recital at the beginning of the agreement and it is also done by including language, at the outset of the restrictive covenant provisions, such as "In order to insure to employer the effective enjoyment of the property, assets and business of the ABC Company of which employee was a principal stockholder and operating executive prior to its acquisition by employer . . ." [30]

### (ix) Other Drafting Considerations

Form 1 under this Section III.E demonstrates an attempt to describe specifically particular activities of the company in which the employee is to be prohibited from engaging. This is important in circumstances in which the nature of the employer's business activities are not well known or common. When the business of the employer is essentially the production and sale of easily definable products, language such as that in Form 2 of this Section III.E is adequate. From the employer's point of view the "catch-all" language such as "or in any other activities or operations . . ." in Form 1 above is, of course, important. From the employee's point of view, it would be wise to resist the "planned or contemplated by corporation" language of that provision or require some more specific definition.

Notwithstanding that broad language in restrictive covenants threatens the enforceability of the entire covenant, employers will sometimes want broadly drafted provisions. The theory is that, as discussed above in connection with trade secret provisions, the presence of the clause will deter the employee from competing because the employee (and a prospective successor employer) cannot be any more certain that the clause will not be enforced than the employer can be certain that the clause will be enforced.

### 4. Patent and Copyright Provisions

In employment situations in which the employee may be doing original research or experimentation, or otherwise has technical skills such as may lead to the creation or development of something which is protected by law, the employer will want to obtain the rights to any such creative product of the employee. The following is an elaborate clause respecting this subject matter:

"Employee covenants and agrees that any and all writings, inventions, improvements, processes, systems, procedures, techniques

---

30. See, for example, Form 2 under this Section III.E.

and/or computer programs which Employee may make, conceive, discover or develop, either solely or jointly with any other person or persons, at any time during the term of this agreement and any renewal hereof, whether during working hours or at any other time, whether at the request or upon the suggestion of Corporation or otherwise, which relate to or are useful in connection with the business now or hereafter carried on or contemplated by Corporation, including developments or expansions of its present fields of operations, shall be and hereby are the sole and exclusive property of Corporation. Employee shall make full disclosure to Corporation of all such writings, inventions, improvements, processes, systems, procedures, techniques and computer programs, and shall do all such acts and execute, acknowledge and deliver all such instruments in writing as may be necessary to vest in Corporation the absolute title thereto. Employee further covenants and agrees to write and prepare all specifications and procedures and to aid and assist Corporation in all other ways in order that Corporation properly can prepare and present all applications for copyright or Letters Patent thereof, can secure such copyright or Letters Patent wherever possible, as well as reissues, renewals, and extensions thereof, and can obtain the record title to such copyright or patents so that Corporation shall be the sole and absolute owner thereof in all countries in which it may desire to have copyright or patent protection. It is understood and agreed that Employee shall not be entitled to any additional or special compensation or reimbursement in regard to any and all such writings, inventions, improvements, processes, systems, procedures, techniques and computer programs."

The above provision is, of course, quite broad and favorable to the employer. Depending upon the circumstances involved, it may be totally unacceptable to the employee or acceptable only with significant limitations.[31]

### 5.  Inclusion or Exclusion of Restrictive Covenants and Related Provisions in Employment Agreements

Although restrictive covenants and the other types of provisions discussed in this section represent a significant element of the employment relationship, many employment agreements, even though involving high level employees and substantial amounts of compensation, do not include restrictive covenants, trade secrets, patent or copyright provisions.[32] The principal reasons for the absence of a restrictive covenant are that the employer is not concerned about the risk of competition, the employer regards a restrictive covenant as basically unfair, or the employee has some bargaining power and is totally unwilling to accept such a restriction, or a combination of

31. See Paragraph 9 of Form Agreement 4 for an example of the structure and coverage of a full employment agreement section dealing with this area.

32. See, for example, Form Agreement 1.

these factors is present. In connection with the preparation of any material employment agreement, the lawyer representing the employer must discuss fully with his client whether or not such a restriction is to be included and communicate to the drafting paralegal the results of such discussion. The importance of the covenant will vary depending upon the nature of the employer's business and the job to be performed by the employee. Similarly, many high level employment situations do not involve trade secret exposure, nor the likelihood of production of materials which may be patented or become subject to copyright so that provisions relating to those matters are unnecessary. Restrictive covenants are included in many agreements in which trade secrets clauses and patent and copyright provisions are not included.

## III. THE CORPORATION AS A PARTY TO THE EMPLOYMENT AGREEMENT

In order for the corporation to become a party to the employment agreement or any other important agreement, the Board of Directors must authorize the entry into the agreement by the corporation and the officers authorized to execute the agreement on its behalf.[33] A form of resolution authorizing such an agreement might be as follows:

"RESOLVED, that this Corporation enter into an employment agreement (the 'Employment Agreement') between this Corporation and John Albert ('Albert') pursuant to which this Corporation shall employ Albert as Sales Manager on the terms and subject to the conditions of the Employment Agreement attached hereto, made a part hereof and incorporated herein by reference; and

"RESOLVED, that any officer or officers of this Corporation be and each of them is hereby authorized and empowered to execute the Employment Agreement, expend any monies and do any and all acts and things necessary or appropriate to effectuate the purposes of the foregoing resolution."

Note that these resolutions call for a copy of the employment agreement to be attached to the resolutions and placed in the minute book. The authorized officers may execute the agreement on the corporation's behalf.

### Employment Agreement Examples

The following pages contain four forms of employment agreements which include some of the form provisions previously set forth in these materials or alternative provisions. These form agreements illustrate the overall form and structure of employment agreements, and include those standard provisions which are a part of nearly all

---

33. See Chapter Seven for a general discussion of the role of directors and meetings of directors.

employment agreements and many other written agreements. The standard provisions, sometimes referred to as "boiler-plate", are essentially self-explanatory. To assist the student, comments have been added to the end of Form Agreement 1.

Following the form agreements is a checklist for paralegals to consider in making a draft of employment agreements.

## PROBLEM

**Utilizing Form Agreement 1 as a format, prepare the following employment agreement:**

1.  Employer: XYZ Corp., a Nevada corporation

2.  Employee: Hugh Horning

3.  Duties: Sales manager for employer's magazine "Flirtation"

4.  Term: One year commencing October 15, 1980—automatic renewal from year to year unless either party gives other 90 days written notice of termination

5.  Compensation: $52,000 per year plus 5% of gross revenues of "Flirtation" for year in question

6.  Additional Benefits: Same as other supervisory personnel of employer

7.  Reimbursement of Expenses: Employer will reimburse for necessary expenses of employee incurred on business of employer—employee must submit receipts for reimbursement

8.  Automobile: Employer to provide new car for use of employee in carrying out of duties

## NOTE

**Do not fail to add additional necessary provisions. If information provided is inadequate, describe what additional information is needed or your assumptions.**

## EXAMPLE—Form Agreement 1

**Special Features:**

  **A.** Employee's duties are set forth in detail in a schedule attached to, and made part of, the agreement (paragraph 1—Schedule A).

  **B.** The employer is a non-technical business enterprise (clothing manufacturer), and the employee will perform non-technical services (sales manager). There is no restrictive covenant or trade secret or patent or copyright protection clause. The employer has relied, by implication, on general trade secrets principles for protection of customer information.

**C.** There is a significant cash incentive compensation arrangement (paragraph 3).

(Numbers in brackets refer to paragraph numbers in the comments at the end of this Form.)

## EMPLOYMENT AGREEMENT

[1]

AGREEMENT made this 12th day of July, 1977 by and between XYZ, Inc., a Pennsylvania corporation ("Employer") and John Albert ("Employee").

[2]

### WITNESSETH:

WHEREAS, Employer and Employee desire to enter into an employment agreement on the terms and conditions hereinafter set forth.

[3]

NOW, THEREFORE, in consideration of the premises and the mutual agreements hereinafter set forth, the parties hereto, intending to be legally bound, hereby agree as follows:

[4]

1. *Capacity and Duties.* Employer hereby employs Employee and Employee hereby accepts employment by Employer as Sales Manager of Employer. In his capacity as Sales Manager, Employee shall carry out all of the functions set forth on Schedule A hereto and such other sales and sales supervisory activities as may be reasonably requested from time to time during the term of this Agreement by the officers of Employer. Employee agrees that throughout the term of his employment hereunder he will devote his entire time, energy, skill and best efforts to the promotion of sales of Employer's products, and to promote generally the business and affairs of Employer, to the exclusion of all other business interests, and that he will perform faithfully and to the fullest extent of his ability all of his duties hereunder.

[5]

2. *Term.* The initial term of this Agreement shall be one year, which shall be deemed to have commenced on March 1, 1977. Thereafter, this Agreement shall remain in full force and effect so long as Employee is employed as Employer's Sales Manager, until terminated by Employer or

Employee, with either party having the right to terminate this Agreement after the initial one year term by written notice to the other party given not less than sixty (60) days prior to the specified termination date.

3. *Compensation.* (a) *Compensation During Initial Period.* By reason of the fact that the fiscal year of Employer ends on November 30, the initial period of employment for purposes of this paragraph 3 shall be the period from July 12, 1977 through November 30, 1977 (the "Initial Period"). Employer shall pay to Employee as full compensation for all services rendered by Employee in any capacity during the Initial Period:

(i) A fixed salary at the rate of $30,000 per annum, payable in such weekly, bi-weekly or monthly installments as may be agreed upon between Employer and Employee, said salary to aggregate $12,500 during the Initial Period of employment provided that this agreement remains in effect throughout said Initial Period; plus

[6]

(ii) Incentive compensation, to be paid within ninety (90) days after November 30, 1977, computed by multiplying the amount by which the Adjusted Net Sales (as hereinafter defined) of Employer for Employer's fiscal year ending November 30, 1977 exceed $7,700,000, [which amount represents the Net Sales (as hereinafter defined) of Employer during its fiscal year ended November 30, 1976] by the applicable percentage set forth in subparagraph (iii) below.

(iii) For the purposes of subparagraph (ii) above and subparagraph 3(b) hereof, the percentages applicable to the amount by which the Adjusted Net Sales of Employer during the fiscal year in question exceeds the Net Sales of Employer for the immediately preceding fiscal year (herein called "Excess Net Sales") are as follows:

| | |
|---|---|
| Up to $250,000 of Excess Net Sales | ½% |
| More than $250,000 up to $500,000 of Excess Net Sales | ¾% |
| More than $500,000 of Excess Net Sales | 1% |

(iv) For the purpose of this Agreement, "Net Sales" shall mean the gross sales of Employer, less all returns, allowances, credits and discounts, as set forth on the income statement prepared by Employer's independent accountants for the fiscal year in question. For the purpose of this Agreement, "Adjusted Net Sales" shall mean Net Sales, reduced by the portion of Net Sales revenues attributable to increases in average unit prices over the average unit prices of the previous year, it being the understanding of the parties that Employee's incentive compensation is to be based upon increases in the number of units sold rather than increases in Net Sales revenues arising from price increases.

(b) *Compensation After Initial Period.* After the Initial Period, Employer shall pay to Employee as full compensation for all services rendered by Employee in any capacity during the term of this Agreement:

(i) A fixed annual salary equal to one hundred five per cent (105%) of the fixed salary payable for the immediately preceding fiscal year, provided that Employer's Adjusted Net Sales for the immediately preceding fiscal year were equal to or greater than Employer's Net Sales for the fiscal year prior to the immediately preceding fiscal year. If the aforesaid proviso has not been satisfied, then Employee's fixed annual salary shall be at the same rate as Employee's fixed annual salary for the immediately preceding fiscal year. For the purposes of this provision, Employee shall be deemed to have been paid a fixed salary of $30,000 for Employer's fiscal year ending November 30, 1977.

(ii) Incentive compensation, to be paid within ninety (90) days after the end of the fiscal year in question, computed by multiplying the Excess Net Sales by the applicable percentage set forth in subparagraph 3(a)(iii) hereof.

(iii) If Employee ceases to be employed hereunder on a date other than the last day of the fiscal year of Employer, then Employee shall be entitled to a portion of the incentive compensation which would have been payable to him if he had been employed throughout said fiscal year, determined by computing the full amount of incentive compensation which would have been payable and multiplying said amount by a fraction, the numerator of which shall be the number of working days of said fiscal year during which Employee was employed, and the denominator of which shall be the total number of working days in that fiscal year.

[7]

4. *Additional Benefits.* Throughout the term of his employment hereunder, Employee shall be entitled to par-

ticipate in Employer's Profit Sharing Plan, Pension Plan, Group Insurance Plan and Long Term Disability Protection Insurance Plan, and such other employee benefit plans as may hereafter be instituted by Employer, in the same manner and to the same extent as may from time to time be provided for other employees of Employer who are department heads.

5. *Reimbursement of Expenses.* During Employee's employment hereunder, Employer will reimburse Employee for all ordinary and necessary business expenses incurred by him in connection with the business of Employer. Such payment shall be made by Employer upon submission by Employee of vouchers itemizing such expenses in a form satisfactory to Employer.

6. *Clothing Allowance.* Employee shall be entitled to select, free of charge, clothing manufactured by Employer to the extent of five hundred dollars ($500.00) per annum, said amount being based upon Employer's regular wholesale prices less ten per cent (10%) thereof.

[8]

7. *Miscellaneous Provisions.* (a) Any notices pursuant to this Agreement shall be validly given or served if in writing and delivered personally or sent by registered or certified mail, postage prepaid, to the following addresses:

> If to Employer: XYZ, Inc.
> 255 Main Street
> Wilmington, Delaware

> If to Employee: John Albert
> 14 Blossom Court
> Cherry Hill, N. J.   08003

[9]

(b) The waiver by either party of a breach or violation of any provision of this Agreement shall not operate or be construed as a waiver of any subsequent breach or violation thereof.

[10]

(c) This writing represents the entire Agreement and understanding of the parties with respect to the subject matter hereof; it may not be altered or amended except by an Agreement in writing.

[11]

(d) This Agreement has been made in and its validity, performance and effect shall be determined in accordance with the laws of the Commonwealth of Pennsylvania.

[12]

(e) The headings of paragraphs in this Agreement
are for convenience only; they form no part of this Agreement and shall not affect its interpretation.

[13]

IN WITNESS WHEREOF, the parties have executed
this Agreement under seal on the day and year first above
written.

[14]

XYZ, Inc.

[*Corporate Seal*]     By: /s/George Hallan

_____

George Hallan, President

Attest: /s/Mary Tolan

_____

Mary Tolan, Secretary

/s/Jill Moyer          /s/John Albert

_____     _____

Witness                John Albert

**Comments on Form Agreement 1**

(1) The first paragraph sets forth the parties, defines them with
a proper noun in quotation marks and recites the date of the Agreement. This is standard not only for employment agreements but virtually every type of agreement.

(2) The "Witnesseth" section gives the background of the
Agreement. Note Form Agreement 3, which actually calls the paragraph "Background of Agreement". It may be a simple sentence or
an elaborate series of sentences commencing with the term "Whereas" or may simply be a narrative paragraph as in Form Agreement 3.
It is present in virtually every type of agreement. It serves the function of stating the purposes of the agreement to aid a court in interpreting the agreement if that becomes necessary. Form Agreements
2 and 3 do not contain such a paragraph, but it is much better to include it to spell out the purposes of the agreement. Whether the
paragraph utilizes "whereas" clauses and is called "Background of
Agreement" or headed by "Witnesseth" (the much older form) is a

matter of personal preference of the person drafting the agreement and practice, not a matter of legal significance. The paralegal should determine what is the preferred form of the lawyer for whom the agreement is being drafted.

(3) The "Now, therefore" clause is present in all agreements to recite the mutual consideration to make the agreement binding. It, too, may vary slightly according to the preference of the person drafting the agreement.

(4) Note that paragraph 1 leaves the Employee no room for other business involvements. Contrast paragraph 2(c) of Form Agreement 2.

(5) Note the definition of Initial Period to specify clearly what term is being discussed. If no incentive compensation were paid to the Employee, the compensation section could end for the Initial Period with subparagraph (i).

(6) Note particularly in paragraph 3 the method of referring to terms such as "Net Sales" which are to be defined after having been earlier stated. The definition of such terms prevents the necessity of repeating the concept they define, possibly in a different or erroneous manner. It also shortens the agreement greatly. Other comments regarding this paragraph are contained in Section II.D.1 and II.D.2 of this Chapter.

(7) Paragraphs 4, 5 and 6 have been discussed under Section II.-D.3.

(8) It is critical that the agreement provide for notices to be in writing, registered or certified mail, return receipt requested, so that all parties are certain notices have been delivered. Often the attorneys for each side are required to receive a copy of all notices to assure early information to such attorneys. See, for example, paragraph 9 of Form Agreement 2. Review the Agreement to determine what circumstances could require a notice under the Agreement. This is a standard boiler plate clause in every type of agreement.

(9) This is a standard clause in all types of agreements indicating that a waiver one time by a party of a breach does not act as a waiver of any later breach.

(10) Although many courts may not enforce this provision, it is useful to encourage the parties to reduce changes to writing. This is a standard clause in every type of agreement.

(11) The parties can select the state law which will be applied to construe the agreement. Courts usually enforce the provision if the state has any logical relationship to the agreement of the parties, e. g., the place of incorporation of a party, residence of a party, place of business of a party or place where the agreement is to be performed. It is a standard clause in all types of agreements. Here it is at least the state of incorporation of the Employer. Note that

New Jersey (as the residence of the Employee) or Delaware (as the place of business of the Employer) might have been logically chosen as well. Ordinarily the person drafting the agreement picks the applicable state law that which that person has the most familiarity. It may be a matter of negotiation between the parties.

(12) This provision is intended to aid in construction by a court to show that the paragraphs themselves are the critical factors, not the headings. It is a standard clause in most agreements.

(13) This is the standard closing phrase for agreements in general.

(14) Note the method of having a corporation execute an agreement. Contrast this with execution by the individual. While often included, the corporate seal is not a necessity to make the agreement binding on the Employer. The authorizing resolutions (see Section III of this Chapter above) and execution by duly authorized officers bind the corporation. The witness similarly is not a necessity.

**EXAMPLE—Form Agreement 2**

**Special Features:**

    **A.** Employee is to be chief executive officer. The issue of the employee's election as President and director is covered as it relates to *capacity and duties* (paragraph 2(a)), *term of agreement* (paragraph 7(b)) and applicability of *restrictive covenant* (paragraph 8).

    **B.** The applicability of the restrictive covenant depends upon who terminates or breaches the agreement (paragraph 8).

    **C.** Termination provisions for employee if employee is not elected president, chief executive officer and a director, and for employer under certain other circumstances (paragraph 7).

### EMPLOYMENT AGREEMENT

This Agreement made as of this _____ day of May, 1977, by and between ABC, Inc., a Delaware corporation (the "Company"), and Tami Zandra, of Deerfield, Illinois ("Employee").

### WITNESSETH:

1. *Employment.* The Company hereby agrees to employ Employee and Employee hereby accepts employment by the Company for the period and upon the terms and conditions hereinafter set forth.

2. *Capacity and Duties.* (a) Employee shall be employed by the Company exclusively in an executive capacity and Employee shall have such authority and shall perform such key executive duties and responsibilities as may from time to time reasonably (in view of the expectation of the parties referred to in the next sentence) be specified by the Board of Directors of the Company with respect to the Company and its affiliates. It is the present expectation of the parties that Employee will be elected and re-elected during the entire term of this Agreement to serve as President and chief executive officer of the Company and as director of the Company and, if elected, Employee agrees to serve in such capacities without any compensation in addition to that herein provided. Employee acknowledges that neither the Company nor its Board of Directors is legally obligated to elect or re-elect Employee as President or chief executive officer of the Company.

(b) During the terms of this Agreement, Employee shall devote her full business time and her best efforts to the performance of her duties hereunder, and shall not be employed by, participate or engage in, or be a part of, in any manner, the management or operation of any business enterprise other than the Company and its affiliates. Employee shall be entitled to at least four weeks vacation with pay during each calendar year during the term hereof.

(c) Notwithstanding the foregoing, Employee shall be entitled to have investments in other business enterprises provided, however, that she shall not have any investment or financial interest in any business enterprise which conducts business activities competitive with any business activities conducted by the Company now or at any time during the term of Employee's employment hereunder (other than an investment of no more than 5% of any class of equity securities of a company whose securities are traded on a national securities exchange).

3. *Compensation.* Employee's basic compensation shall be at the rate of not less than $36,000 per year, plus such bonuses and additional compensation as the Board of Directors of the Company may, in its discretion, determine. Such basic compensation shall be paid to Employee in equal installments not less frequently than monthly. Employee shall be entitled to participate fully in and to receive the benefit of (on a basis no less favorable to Employee than that available to any other executive employee of the Company) all plans and benefit programs made available to any executive employee of the Company.

4. *Expenses.* Employee is authorized to incur reasonable expenses for promoting the business of the Company and in carrying out her duties hereunder, including without limitation, expenses for entertainment, automobile, travel and similar items. The Company shall reimburse Employee for all such ordinary and necessary expenses upon the presentation by Employee from time to time of an itemized account of such expenditures. Employee shall present such an itemized account not less frequently than monthly. In addition, Company agrees to reimburse Employee for the reasonable moving expenses incurred by her in moving her family's residence from Illinois to the Phoenix area.

5. *Additional Benefits.* Employee shall be entitled to the benefits of the Company's accident and sickness policy and disability income plan underwritten by Provident Life and Accident Insurance Company. Benefits payable are $1,100/month lifetime for accident and $1,100/month for sickness disability to age sixty-five (65).

6. *Insurance.* Employee shall be entitled to receive the following life insurance coverage with benefits payable to beneficiaries designated by Employee:

| | |
|---|---|
| Group life | —$40,000 upon death 80,000 upon accidental death |
| Key person life | — 75,000 upon death, provided that Employee is insurable at regular rates |
| Travel group policy | — 60,000 upon accidental death |

7. *Term of Agreement; Termination.* (a) The term of this Agreement shall be two (2) years commencing on the date hereof, and thereafter shall continue from year to year unless and until either party shall give notice to the other at least 180 days prior to the end of the original or then current renewal term of her or its intention to terminate at the end of said term.

(b) Notwithstanding the provisions of subparagraph (a) above, in the event that Employee shall not be elected President and chief executive officer and a director of the Company within thirty (30) days after the date of this Agreement, or if at any time during the initial two-year term of this Agreement Employee shall be removed as President or chief executive officer or director of the Company or shall not be re-elected as President and chief executive officer and director of the Company, Employee shall have the right to terminate her employment hereunder at her convenience, and, provided that as of the date of such removal or failure to re-elect, Employee shall not have breached or otherwise failed to perform in accordance with this Agreement, such termination shall be considered a termination by reason of a breach of this Agreement by the Company.

(c) Notwithstanding the provisions of subparagraph (a) above, the Company shall have the right to terminate the employment under this Agreement, without further liability or obligation hereunder in the event that Employee (i) is adjudicated a bankrupt, (ii) is convicted of a felony involving moral turpitude, (iii) dies (but in such event the applicable benefits set forth in paragraph 6 above shall be effective), or (iv) becomes disabled such that she has been unable to perform her duties hereunder for ninety (90) days during any year of this Agreement or for any period of ninety (90) consecutive days (but in such event the applicable benefits set forth in paragraph 5 hereof shall be effective).

8. *Restrictions on Competition.* Employee covenants and agrees that: (a) during the initial term and any renewal terms of her employment hereunder and, (b) if but only if this Agreement is terminated by Employee (as hereinafter defined) during the initial term or any renewal term hereof, for a period of two (2) years after the termination of her employment hereunder, she shall not directly or indirectly engage in any business activities within the continental United States, the same as, similar to or in competition with business activities carried on by Company during the period of Employee's employment by Company, or in the definitive planning stages at the time of termination of Employee's employment. The term "engage in" shall include, without being limited to, activities as proprietor, partner, stockholder, principal, agent, employee or consultant. However, nothing contained in this paragraph 8 shall prevent Employee from having investments of the types permitted in subparagraph 2(c) hereof. For the purposes of this paragraph 8, a termination of employment by Employee shall be deemed to have occurred only if Employee shall cease to be employed by Company pursuant to notice of election by Employee to terminate at the end of the initial term or any renewal term hereof, or if Employee shall fail to perform in accordance with this Agreement, or if Company shall terminate employment by reason of a breach of this Agreement by Employee.

If the employment is not terminated by Employee as defined in this paragraph 8 during the initial or any renewal term hereof, or if the Agreement is breached by Company, the restrictions on competition imposed by this paragraph 8 shall not apply.

9. *Miscellaneous Provisions.* (a) Any notices pursuant to this Agreement shall be validly given or served if in writing and delivered personally or sent by registered or certified mail, postage prepaid, to the following addresses:

If to Company:    ABC, Inc.
                   2401 First Avenue
                   Phoenix, Arizona   85003

Attention:       President

with a copy to   Hiram Lawyer, Esq.
                   1801 First Avenue
                   Phoenix, Arizona   85003

If to Employee:   Ms. Tami Zandra
                   101 Second Lane
                   Deerfield, Illinois   60619

with a copy to   Jane Wilson, Esq.
                   1213 North Square
                   Deerfield, Illinois   60619

or to such other addresses as either party may hereafter designate to the other in writing.

(b) If any provision of this Agreement shall be or become illegal or unenforceable in whole or in part for any reason whatsoever, the remaining provisions shall nevertheless be deemed valid, binding and subsisting.[34]

(c) The waiver by either party of a breach or violation of any provision of this Agreement shall not operate or be construed as a waiver of any subsequent breach or violation thereof.

(d) This writing represents the entire agreement and understanding of the parties with respect to the subject matter hereof; it may not be altered or amended except by an agreement in writing.

(e) This Agreement has been made in and its validity, performance and effect shall be determined in accordance with the laws of the State of Arizona.

(f) The headings of paragraphs in this Agreement are for convenience only; they form no part of this Agreement and shall not affect its interpretation.

---

34. This type of provision is called a "severability clause" and is a boiler plate provision for many agreements. It tells a court that, notwithstanding the fact that a provision such as the restrictive covenant is unenforceable, the remainder of the agreement shall be effective. Consider what this provision might do if a fundamental element of the agreement is unenforceable.

IN WITNESS WHEREOF, and intending to be legally bound, the parties have executed this Agreement under seal on the day and year first above written.

[*Corporate Seal*]　　　　ABC, Inc.

By: /s/Henry George

_____

President

Attest: /s/John Henry

_____

Secretary

/s/Tami Zandra　·　　　　[*Seal*]

_____

Tami Zandra

### EXAMPLE—Form Agreement 3

**Special Features:**

A. This agreement is a relatively sophisticated agreement designed to be used by employer as a form agreement for a class of sales personnel. The agreement provides blanks for variables such as territory (paragraph 1), special customers (house accounts) in particular territories (paragraph 8), and commission rates and draw rates (paragraphs 9 and 10).

B. Commissions do not necessarily go to the employee responsible for the sales territory (paragraphs 7 and 8).

### EMPLOYMENT AGREEMENT

This AGREEMENT entered into this _____ day of _____, 19__, by and between _____, New York, New York, hereinafter referred to as EMPLOYER, and _____ hereinafter referred to as EMPLOYEE.

In consideration of the mutual covenants herein contained, the parties hereto agree as follows:

1. EMPLOYER agrees to employ EMPLOYEE, and EMPLOYEE accepts employment as traveling representative of EMPLOYER in the following Territory:



2. EMPLOYEE agrees to devote his entire time, energy, skill and attention to the sale of products manufactured by or for EMPLOYER or sold by EMPLOYER (the "Prod-

ucts"), and in that connection to actively solicit orders for the sale of the Products to retail stores. EMPLOYEE agrees not to accept or engage in any other employment or undertaking during the term of this agreement.

3. EMPLOYEE is to travel throughout the Territory, and give it thorough coverage in accordance, and in compliance with instructions and directions from EMPLOYER, which shall include the time or times when EMPLOYEE shall travel in the aforesaid Territory and the duration of the trips. EMPLOYEE is to submit periodic itineraries and call reports, and other data, as required, in accordance with EMPLOYER'S sales control program.

4. EMPLOYEE'S authority to act for EMPLOYER is limited strictly to the solicitations of orders, and all orders received as a result of EMPLOYEE'S solicitations shall be subject to acceptance or rejection by EMPLOYER at its principal office in New York, New York. EMPLOYER may refuse or reject, either in whole or in part, any order received as a result of EMPLOYEE'S solicitation, and may cancel any such order, either in whole or in part, after acceptance. EMPLOYER further may consent to the cancellation of any order, either in whole or in part, either before or after shipment, or may accept returns and grant such credits or allowances as it deems proper. EMPLOYEE agrees in all respects to observe the rules and regulations of EMPLOYER as to price, terms and other conditions of sale, and he shall have no power to authorize returns or offer special prices, terms or conditions unless written instructions are given to him by EMPLOYER, in which event EMPLOYEE shall be so empowered only with respect to the particular circumstances covered by such instructions.

5. All samples delivered by EMPLOYER to EMPLOYEE shall at all times remain the property of EMPLOYER, and EMPLOYEE agrees that he will keep, maintain and preserve them in good condition. EMPLOYER shall have the right at any time to direct the sale of any such samples, and all samples sold by EMPLOYEE pursuant to EMPLOYER'S instructions shall be credited to EMPLOYEE'S account in full satisfaction of any charge made upon delivery of such samples to EMPLOYEE. All samples not sold by EMPLOYEE shall be returned in good condition to EMPLOYER at any time upon EMPLOYER'S request or upon termination of this Agreement. Notwithstanding any provisions to the contrary contained herein, EMPLOYEE shall reimburse EMPLOYER for the then prevailing wholesale price of any samples lost, stolen, destroyed, damaged or

misplaced while in the possession or control of EMPLOYEE. At EMPLOYER'S request, EMPLOYEE shall use his best efforts to obtain, and shall pay the premiums for, casualty insurance covering samples while in EMPLOYEE'S possession or control.

6. Except as provided in paragraph 7 or 8 of this agreement, EMPLOYEE shall be credited with commission on all shipments made on orders received after the date of this Agreement to men's retail clothing stores in his Territory, as specified in paragraph 1, and likewise will be charged with commission on all returns by and allowances to such accounts, during the term of this Agreement. It is understood that sales to customers other than men's retail clothing stores shall not be considered part of this Agreement, and no commission shall be paid on such sales except where specifically agreed in writing.

7. In the event that EMPLOYEE obtains an initial order from a new customer who requires that merchandise be delivered into an area which is not part of the Territory of EMPLOYEE, EMPLOYEE shall nevertheless receive the commission on the initial order received from such customer. On any subsequent orders from such customer the commission on merchandise shipped into territories other than the Territory of EMPLOYEE shall be credited to the account of the employee into whose territory such merchandise is shipped; provided, however, that in any case, EMPLOYER shall have the right to apportion commissions among EMPLOYEE and other employees in the event shipments are made into more than one employee's territory as a result of a single order, or if for any other reason, in EMPLOYER'S sole determination, considerations of fairness require it to make the apportionment.

8. EMPLOYEE shall not be entitled to receive or be credited with commissions on account of shipments made to those customers in his Territory which are designated as house accounts on Exhibit "A" to this Agreement attached hereto and hereby made part hereof. EMPLOYER shall have the right from time to time to designate additional customers in EMPLOYEE'S Territory as house accounts by giving thirty (30) days' prior written notice to EMPLOYEE. With respect to customers which may hereafter be designated as house accounts, it is intended that EMPLOYER shall make such designation only as to customers or potential customers whose business is not actively being solicited by EMPLOYEE, or who have not placed any orders with EMPLOYEE for the Products during the immediately

preceding two years or whose orders are primarily the result of the sales effort of EMPLOYER or other employees, rather than EMPLOYEE.

9. As sole compensation for EMPLOYEE'S services, EMPLOYER shall (subject to the withholding provisions of all applicable federal, state and local employment taxes) pay EMPLOYEE the commissions hereinafter set forth on all orders which shall be filled by EMPLOYER and for which full payment is received. In the event of returns by, or credits or allowances to any customer, or in the event of non-payment, EMPLOYEE'S commission account will be charged for any commissions previously credited or paid pertaining to such merchandise or accounts.

The commission on merchandise sold at regular prices will be paid on the following basis (less returns, credits and allowances):

The commission paid on merchandise sold below regular wholesale price (when such merchandise is available) or with special terms and/or conditions will be two per cent (2%) of net sales, except if otherwise specified by EMPLOYER prior to such offering of merchandise. Furthermore, no commission shall be paid with respect to merchandise sold $33\frac{1}{3}\%$ or more below regular wholesale price, except if otherwise specified by EMPLOYER prior to such offering of merchandise.

10. If EMPLOYER shall agree to make periodic advances to EMPLOYEE, such advances are to be on account of, or advances against, commission to be earned by EMPLOYEE, and said advances shall be charged and deducted from commission as and when such commission shall be payable to EMPLOYEE.

The EMPLOYER agrees to furnish EMPLOYEE with a copy of all invoices covering any goods shipped into the above described territory and to furnish EMPLOYEE with a statement on or before the 25th of each month covering the amount of sales represented by such shipments for the previous month and the amount of commission due EMPLOYEE, which shall be paid at the time the statement is rendered.

EMPLOYEE shall bear all of his traveling and other out-of-pocket expenses incurred in connection with the employment hereunder, and the same shall not be reimbursable to him by EMPLOYER.

11. EMPLOYEE shall maintain liability insurance on each automobile used by him in the course of his employment hereunder at least in the amount of $100,000 for injury to any one person and $300,000 for injuries to all persons in any one occurrence, and property damage insurance at least in the amount of $50,000. EMPLOYER shall be named as an insured on such policy or policies so long as this Agreement shall be in effect, and EMPLOYEE shall deliver to EMPLOYER a certificate of insurance naming EMPLOYER as an insured within ten (10) days from the date hereof, which certificate shall provide that the coverage to which such certificate relates shall be non-cancellable for a period of ten (10) days after notice to EMPLOYER. EMPLOYEE agrees that he will use no vehicle in the course of his employment hereunder which is not covered by such insurance, and the use of any such uninsured vehicle shall be grounds for immediate termination of this agreement.

12. EMPLOYER will make every effort to fill orders solicited by EMPLOYEE and make shipment thereon. It is understood, however, that EMPLOYER'S performance of and deliveries on any order are subject to delays or failure due to fires, floods, storms and abnormal weather conditions, wars, riots, civil commotions, strikes, lockouts, shortages of or delays in receiving materials, credit restrictions, governmental regulations or other causes or conditions beyond the EMPLOYER'S reasonable control, and in the event any of the foregoing occur, EMPLOYER may cancel any order or extend the time for delivery of any undelivered portion.

13. This agreement may be terminated in any of the following circumstances:

(a) Upon the sixty-sixth birthday of EMPLOYEE, or upon his death, this agreement will automatically terminate unless other arrangements in writing have been made at least sixty (60) days prior to the date of such occurrence.

(b) In the event of EMPLOYEE'S inability to perform his duties by reason of illness, incapacity, or any other cause which shall continue for a period in excess of six (6) weeks, or the discontinuance of operations by the EMPLOYER, EMPLOYER shall have the right to terminate this agreement by ten (10) days written notice to EMPLOYEE.

(c) Either party shall have the right to terminate this agreement at any time upon thirty (30) days prior written notice.[35]

---

35. Note that this agreement is, in effect, a thirty day agreement by this provision.

In the event of termination of this agreement, EMPLOYER shall continue to pay EMPLOYEE the commission above provided on all shipments made into EMPLOYEE'S Territory pursuant to orders received prior to the date of termination, subject to any charges outstanding against EMPLOYEE'S commission, and provided that EMPLOYER has received full payment for the merchandise shipped.

14. All notices required or permitted to be given under this agreement shall be in writing sent by first class mail, addressed if directed to EMPLOYEE to:


and if directed to EMPLOYER, at _____, New York, New York, Attention: _____ or to such other address as each party may hereafter notify the other in writing.

15. This Agreement shall be governed by and construed in accordance with the laws of the State of New York and shall be binding upon and inure to the benefit of the parties hereto and their respective heirs, personal representatives, successors and assigns.

IN WITNESS WHEREOF, EMPLOYEE has fixed his hand and seal and EMPLOYER has caused this Agreement to be executed by a duly authorized person the day and year first above written.

_____ [*Seal*] [36]

Witness

_____

By: _____

**EXAMPLE—Form Agreement 4**

**Special Features:**

This agreement is for an employer engaged in a technical business activity. The employee is performing technical and creative services. There is a rather elaborate set of provisions dealing with restrictive covenants and other forms of employer protection (paragraph 9).

### EMPLOYMENT AGREEMENT

AGREEMENT made this _____ day of _____, 19__, by and between _____ ("Corporation") and _____ ("Employee").

---

36. The term "Seal" is often added to a signature line to make the document a sealed instrument which, in many states, is enforceable even without consideration.

### BACKGROUND OF AGREEMENT:

Employee has served Corporation as Vice President since the commencement of Corporation's business operations in December, 1977. Corporation and Employee now desire to enter into an Employment Agreement on the terms and conditions hereinafter set forth.

NOW, THEREFORE, in consideration of the premises and the mutual covenants herein contained, the parties hereto, intending to be legally bound, hereby agree as follows:

1. *Employment Term.* Corporation hereby employs Employee and Employee hereby accepts said employment, subject to all the terms and conditions of this Agreement. This Agreement shall be for a term of three (3) years, commencing on the date hereof, and thereafter shall automatically be renewed from year to year unless either party shall give notice to the other no less than ninety (90) days prior to the end of the initial term or any renewal term of his or its intention to terminate the Agreement at the end of said term.

2. *Capacity.* Employee is employed as a technical director of Corporation, and to assist the chief executive officer of Corporation in the operation and management of the business and affairs of Corporation, subject to the supervision and direction of Corporation's Board of Directors, and to perform such other technical, managerial and executive functions and services for Corporation as he may from time to time be requested to perform by the President or the Board of Directors.

3. *Duties.* During the period of his employment hereunder, Employee agrees to devote his time, energy, skill and best efforts to promote the business and affairs of Corporation, and to perform faithfully to the fullest extent of his ability all the duties which relate to his position as an executive and a technical director of Corporation as may be requested of him by Corporation's Board of Directors or President. Employee agrees that during the original term of this Agreement and any renewal term he will not be employed by, participate or engage in, or be a part of in any manner, directly or indirectly, the affairs of any other business enterprise or occupation which would interfere with the performance of his full time duties hereunder.

4. *Compensation.* Corporation shall pay to Employee, as compensation for all services rendered by Employee during his employment hereunder, a salary at the rate of $40,000

per annum, payable in bi-weekly installments, subject to such revisions as Corporation's Board of Directors and Employee may, from time to time, approve and agree upon.

5. *Reimbursement of Expenses.* During Employee's employment hereunder, Corporation will reimburse Employee for all ordinary and necessary business expenses incurred by him in connection with the business of Corporation. Such payments shall be made by Corporation upon submission by Employee of vouchers itemizing such expenses in a form satisfactory to Corporation.

6. *Automobile.* During Employee's employment hereunder, Corporation will provide Employee with a suitable automobile selected by Corporation for his use in connection with the performance of his duties hereunder.

7. *Other Benefits.* Corporation shall, during the period of Employee's employment hereunder, maintain in effect such hospitalization, medical, group life and other insurance coverage and such other benefits as Corporation presently has in effect with respect to Employee or hereafter during the term of Employee's employment hereunder provides to its executive personnel.

8. *Disability.* If Employee should become unable to perform his duties hereunder, because of partial or total disability or incapacity due to illness, accident, or other cause, Corporation shall continue Employee's salary at the full rate set forth in this Agreement for a period of six (6) months. If Employee is still unable to perform his duties hereunder at the end of said six (6) month period, Corporation shall have the right at any time thereafter to terminate Employee's employment, in which event Corporation shall have no further liability or obligation under this Agreement.

9. *Trade Secrets, Noncompetition, etc.* (a) Employee covenants and agrees that he will not, during the term of his employment or thereafter, for any reason or purpose whatsoever, use for his personal benefit, or disclose, communicate or divulge to, or use for the benefit, direct or indirect, of any person, firm, association or corporation other than Corporation, any information as to business methods, business policies, systems, procedures, techniques, computer programs, research or development projects or results thereof, trade secrets, inventions, knowledge and processes used or developed by Corporation, any forms, names and addresses of customers or clients, data on or relating to past, present or prospective customers or clients or any other information relating to or dealing with the business operations or ac-

tivities of Corporation, made known to Employee or learned or acquired by Employee while in the employ of Corporation.

(b) Employee covenants and agrees that he will not, during the term of his employment hereunder and for a period of two (2) years after the termination or expiration of his employment hereunder for any reason whatsoever, within the continental United States, directly or indirectly engage in any activities relating to evaluation and selection of computer equipment and software, conversion of computer programs and information files from one computer system to another, or in any other activities or operations carried on by Corporation at any time during the period of his employment by Corporation, or planned or contemplated by Corporation at the time of termination of his employment by Corporation. The term "engage in" shall include, but shall not be limited to, activities, whether direct or indirect, as proprietor, partner, stockholder, principal, agent, employee or consultant.

(c) Employee covenants and agrees that any and all writings, inventions, improvements, processes, systems, procedures, techniques and/or computer programs which he may make, conceive, discover or develop, either solely or jointly with any other person or persons, at any time during the term of this Agreement and any renewal hereof, whether during working hours or at any other time, whether at the request or upon the suggestion of Corporation or otherwise, which relate to or are useful in connection with the business now or hereafter carried on or contemplated by Corporation, including developments or expansions of its present fields of operations, shall be and hereby are the sole and exclusive property of Corporation. Employee shall make full disclosure to Corporation of all such writings, inventions, improvements, processes, systems, procedures, techniques and computer programs, and shall do all such acts and execute, acknowledge and deliver all such instruments in writing as may be necessary to vest in Corporation the absolute title thereto. Employee further covenants and agrees to write and prepare all specifications and procedures and to aid and assist Corporation in all other ways in order that Corporation properly can prepare and present all applications for copyright or Letters Patent thereof, can secure such copyright or Letters Patent wherever possible, as well as reissues, renewals, and extensions thereof, and can obtain the record title to such copyright or patents so that Corporation shall be the sole and absolute owner thereof in all countries in which it may desire to have copyright or patent protection. It is understood and agreed that Employee shall not be entitled to any additional or special compensation or reimbursement in regard to any and all such writings, inventions, improvements, processes, systems, procedures, techniques and computer programs.

(d) Employee covenants and agrees that he will, upon termination of his employment with Corporation for any reason whatsoever, deliver to Corporation any and all records, forms, contracts, lists of names or other customer data and any other articles or papers which have come into his possession by reason of his employment with Corporation or which he holds for Corporation, irrespective of whether or not any of said items were prepared by him, and he shall not retain memoranda or copies of any of said items.

(e) Employee acknowledges that the restrictions contained in this paragraph 9, in view of the nature of the business in which Corporation is engaged, are reasonable and necessary to protect the legitimate interests of Corporation. Employee understands and agrees that the remedies at law for his violation of any of the covenants or provisions of this paragraph 9 will be inadequate, that such violations will cause irreparable injury within a short period of time, and that Corporation shall be entitled to preliminary injunctive relief and other injunctive relief against any such violation. Such injunctive relief shall be in addition to, and in no way in limitation of, any and all other remedies Corporation shall have in law and equity for the enforcement of those covenants and provisions. In the event of any violations or breaches of subparagraph (b) of this paragraph 9, the covenants therein contained shall remain in force during a period of two years subsequent to the termination of the conduct constituting a breach or violation.

(f) Employee covenants and agrees that even though his employment by Corporation may be terminated, he will at any time, either before or after such termination, cooperate with Corporation in the prosecution or defense of any litigation relating to Corporation's activities during the course of his employment or in connection with any copyright or patent rights of Corporation, at Corporation's expense.

10. *Miscellaneous Provisions.* (a) Any notices pursuant to this Agreement shall be validly given or served if

in writing and delivered personally or sent by registered or certified mail, postage prepaid, to the following addresses:

If to Corporation:


If to Employee:

or to such other addresses as either party may hereafter designate to the other in writing.

(b) If any provision of this Agreement shall be or become illegal or unenforceable in whole or in part for any reason whatsoever, the remaining provisions shall nevertheless be deemed valid, binding and subsisting.

(c) The waiver by either party of a breach or violation of any provisions of this Agreement shall not operate or be construed as a waiver of any subsequent breach or violation thereof.

(d) This writing represents the entire agreement and understanding of the parties with respect to the subject matter hereof; it may not be altered or amended except by an agreement in writing.

(e) This Agreement has been made in and its validity, performance and effect shall be determined in accordance with the laws of the Commonwealth of Pennsylvania.

(f) The headings of paragraphs in this Agreement are for convenience only; they form no part of this Agreement and shall not affect its interpretation.

IN WITNESS WHEREOF, the parties have executed this agreement under seal on the day and year first above written.

By: _____

[*Corporate Seal*]                    Attest: _____

_____         _____ [*Seal*]

Witness

## Checklist of Information Required for Drafting Employment Agreement

1. Name and address (for notices) of employer

2. Name and address (for notices) of employee

3. Term of Agreement and date of commencement of term

**Checklist of Information Required for Drafting Employment Agreement**—Continued

4. Capacity and Duties of Employee

   (a) Nature of duties and functions

   (b) Title

   (c) Territory—if a salesman

   (d) Full-time or part-time

   (e) Limitations on outside activity

   (f) Limitations on authority—salesmen, particularly

   (g) Provision for vacation

   (h) Persons to whom employee reports

5. Compensation

   (a) Straight salary—escalation provisions

   (b) Commission—which sales is it based upon—any variations in rate—provisions for drawing account

   (c) Incentive compensation

   (d) Stock Options

   (e) Stock Bonus

   (f) Fringe benefits

       (i) Car

       (ii) Coverage under insurance or health and accident plans

       (iii) Pension or Profit Sharing Plans

   (g) Expense account

6. Special provisions for termination

   (a) Disability provisions

   (b) Breach of Agreement

7. Restrictive covenants

   (a) Length of time

   (b) Geographical area

   (c) Description of restricted activity

8. Need for trade secrets or patent protection clause

Chapter Ten

# SHAREHOLDERS' AGREEMENTS

## I. INTRODUCTION

Shareholders' agreements are very common for closely-held corporations. Since these agreements fall into certain patterns, the preparation of the initial draft of this type of agreement can be delegated to a lawyer's assistant. Moreover, the basic drafting techniques applicable to such agreements are relevant to many other types of agreements as well.

The term "Shareholders' Agreement" is susceptible of many meanings, but usually it refers to a written agreement entered into among two or more shareholders of a corporation that has a small number of shareholders (which corporation may or may not be a "close corporation" as that term is defined under state corporate laws [1]). A shareholders' agreement contains restrictions on the transferability of shares of stock in the corporation by the parties during their lifetimes and also restricts the transferability of a deceased party's shares upon death. Frequently all shareholders of the corporation are parties to such an agreement, and the corporation itself is generally a party as well. Such agreements are sometimes referred to as "Buy-Out Agreements," "Buy-Sell Agreements," "Stock Purchase Agreements" or "Shareholders' Restrictive Agreements."

Shareholders' agreements are most frequently executed upon or shortly following incorporation of a business, upon an issuance or transfer of stock to a shareholder or group of shareholders, when a shareholder is retiring from the business and the purchase of such shareholder's interest is being negotiated, or when there has been some disagreement among the shareholders which is resolved by, or avoided for the future by, a shareholders' agreement.

In the case of corporations whose stock is held by a few persons, the shareholders are often also the directors and officers of the corporation and work together intimately in the business; they frequently are members of the same family; their livelihoods often depend largely on the profits of the corporate business; and their shares are not readily saleable because of the absence of a public market for the shares and because the benefits of stock ownership are often realized indirectly, e. g., in the form of the salary received as an officer or employee of the corporation. To this extent, a closely-held business corporation is very much like a partnership.

1. See Chapter Five for a discussion of statutory close corporations.

It is often of utmost importance to a shareholder of a closely-held corporation to have some control over who the co-shareholders are, just as a partner in a partnership must have some say as to who the partners are. Moreover, the person becoming a part of a closely-held corporation should not be easily able to terminate the "corporate marriage" which would cause great uncertainty for the remaining shareholders. If co-shareholders in a closely-held corporation are looked upon as partners, it is not surprising to find the existence of agreements which severely limit the right of a shareholder to transfer shares during lifetime and thereby prevent the former co-shareholders from being surprised by a new partner. Such agreements also govern the disposition of shares upon death and thereby protect the surviving co-shareholders from having a widow or widower or personal representative as their new partner. The typical shareholders' agreement, therefore, provides that a shareholder may not dispose of shares during lifetime without first offering them to the corporation and/or the co-shareholders, and provides that upon the death of a shareholder the corporation or the surviving shareholders can, or must, purchase the deceased shareholder's shares. Shareholders' agreements also frequently contain, as do partnership agreements, provisions respecting the manner in which certain aspects of the business are to be managed. The provisions normally found in shareholders' agreements are discussed in detail in the following sections of this Chapter.

## II. PROVISIONS RESTRICTING TRANSFER OF SHARES DURING LIFETIME

### A. GENERAL CONSIDERATIONS

#### 1. Whose Interests Are to Be Protected?

Under the laws of most states, the holder or holders of a majority of the outstanding shares of voting stock of a corporation have virtually absolute control over corporate decisions. This is true as a practical matter even with respect to corporations which grant shareholders cumulative voting in the election of directors.[2] Consequently, a majority block of shares, carrying with it corporate control, is much more readily saleable than a minority block of shares. A minority shareholder who is suddenly confronted with a new incompatible majority shareholder is in a very poor position. The minority shareholder may be dismissed as an officer and employee of the corporation and may not receive any dividends on the shares of stock. The minority stock interest, for all practical purposes, may become virtually worthless. A minority shareholder, therefore, generally has much to gain by restrictions on the transfer of stock by all shareholders during lifetime. From the standpoint of majority share-

---

**2.** See the discussion of cumulative voting in Chapter Two.

holders, difficulties can be created by a troublesome minority shareholder who, with cumulative voting, may be able to be elected a director of the corporation, or who, even without being a director, may initiate lawsuits and otherwise harass existing directors and officers. For these reasons, majority shareholders frequently desire restrictions as much as do minority shareholders.

### 2.    Should All Shareholders Be Party to the Agreement?

There is no absolute answer to this question. The situation determines the result. Although in most cases all shareholders are party to a shareholders' agreement, this is not invariable. Sometimes one or more shareholders may simply refuse to sign the agreement. The remainder must then decide whether to have an agreement absent the refusing shareholder. Sometimes one or more shareholders are not invited to sign the agreement. For example, in instances where the shareholders fall into two or more ascertainable groups, such as different family groups, an agreement may be limited to those shareholders falling within a particular group.

### 3.    Should the Corporation Be Party to the Agreement?

When all of the shareholders are party to a shareholders' agreement, the corporation is almost always without exception an additional party to the agreement. Where all shareholders are not a party, however, as a matter of preference the remaining shareholders may wish the corporation not to be a party.

In most cases, however, the agreement will contain provisions granting certain rights and imposing certain obligations on the corporation, thus requiring the corporation to be a party in order to bind the corporation to the obligations set forth in the agreement. For example, the entire effort to preserve the percentage stock interest of a minority shareholder could be completely thwarted if the corporation were free to issue new shares, whether to certain existing shareholders or to third parties. Absent the corporation's agreement not to do so, the corporation could issue such shares upon the authorization of a majority of the Board of Directors of the corporation. Moreover, the agreement of the corporation is required to prevent it from honoring transfers in violation of the agreement. Shareholders' agreements also frequently require the corporation to purchase shares under certain circumstances, and the corporation's written agreement to do so is therefore necessary.

### B.    ABSOLUTE RESTRICTIONS ON TRANSFERABILITY

The considerations which suggest the use of a shareholders' agreement often, if carried to their logical extreme, lead to the conclusion that an absolute prohibition on any lifetime transfers of stock by shareholders of a corporation would be the most desirable alternative. Such a restriction, if embodied in a shareholders' agreement, would most likely be unenforceable by court action because of the established legal principle that "unreasonable" restraints on transfers of property of a person are not permitted. The examples of restrictions on transferability which follow represent, under most, if not all state laws, reasonable restrictions on transferability and are used, in effect, to achieve a result which cannot be achieved directly by an absolute prohibition on transferability.

## C. RIGHT OF FIRST REFUSAL TO PURCHASE SHARES UPON A PROPOSED TRANSFER

Faced with the dilemma of desiring to restrict a person's right to sell the person's stock in a closely-held corporation, but unable to impose an absolute restriction on such a transfer, a paralegal or lawyer drafting shareholders' agreements normally provides that any shareholder who wants to transfer stock and who has received a valid offer (often described as a "bona fide offer" [3]) for such stock must offer the stock first to the corporation or to all or some of the co-shareholders. This requirement is often referred to, from the perspective of the shareholders or corporation who may purchase the stock of a shareholder before it is sold to an outsider, as a "right of first refusal": the right to decide whether to buy or refuse to buy the stock before the stock can be sold to anyone else. This section of the Chapter will analyze different varieties of the "right of first refusal".

### 1. Corporation's Right of First Refusal

Shareholders' agreements may provide that if a shareholder receives a bona fide offer to purchase such shareholder's shares, the offer cannot be accepted until the shares are first offered to the corporation; if the corporation does not exercise its option to purchase such shares within a stipulated time, the shares may be sold to the bona fide offeror. Most agreements provide that the bona fide offer must cover all, and not less than all, of the offeree's shares. Some agreements also provide that a bona fide offeror, who actually purchases such shares, must take the purchased shares subject to the restrictions contained in the shareholders' agreement as though the offeror were an original signatory to the agreement. Generally, the corporation is required to exercise its option in full or not at all, since as a practical matter a prospective purchaser will not make a bona fide offer for shares without knowing how many shares will be available for purchase if the offer is accepted.[4]

3. A bona fide offer is often described as an offer in writing by a person who is ready, willing and able to buy and who has no external constraint to buy. Such a person may be hard to find for the purchase of stock of a closely-held corporation. Why?

4. For an example, see the sample provisions following subparagraph 2 below. The terms (e. g., the price, etc.) on which shares may be purchased by the corporation are discussed in Section IV of this Chapter.

## 2. Shareholders' Right of First Refusal

A right of first refusal of the remaining shareholders to purchase the shares of a shareholder who desires to sell shares pursuant to a bona fide offer is sometimes found in lieu of, and sometimes found in addition to, the corporation's right of first refusal. In most instances, the shareholders' right of first refusal is in addition to the corporation's right; that is, the agreement will provide that if the corporation fails to exercise its right of first refusal, the shares as to which the corporation has not exercised its option are then offered to the other shareholders, generally pro rata in accordance with their holdings. This type of provision is often difficult to draft, since it should cover the eventuality of the exercise by some shareholders and non-exercise by others. In such a case it is generally desirable to provide for a further right of first refusal to the exercising shareholders to purchase the shares not taken by the nonexercising group.[5] Again, as pointed out with respect to a corporation's right of first refusal, it is generally provided that if less than all of the offered shares are taken (whether by the corporation or the other shareholders or both), none of the options are deemed to have been exercised and the selling shareholder is free to sell the shares to the bona fide offeror.[6]

The most desirable format usually is to provide a right of first refusal to the corporation followed by a right of first refusal to the remaining shareholders.[7] From the viewpoint of the remaining shareholders, it is usually best to have the corporation purchase the shares of a selling shareholder. This is true because the remaining shareholders, if they are the purchasers, might have to obtain the funds to purchase the shares by borrowing, thus incurring interest expense, or by taking money out of the corporation as taxable dividends or taxable salary. However, there may be situations where the corporation is legally unable to purchase all or any of the shares, as for example, when such a purchase would impair capital.[8] In that case the shareholders should have the right to purchase any shares the corporation does not purchase. A sample form of provision of this nature is set forth in paragraphs A–3 to A–6 of Form Agreement 2 of this Chapter.[9]

5. See, for example, paragraph A–5 of Form Agreement 2 to this Chapter.

6. An example is contained in paragraph A–6 of Form Agreement 2.

7. This format is followed in paragraph 2 of Form Agreement 1 and paragraph A of Form Agreement 2.

8. See, e. g., Section 6, MBCA.

9. Note that paragraph A–6 requires that a bona fide offeror who purchases must buy within a specified period of time after expiration of the options and will be subject to the restrictions in the Agreement.

## D.  MANDATORY PURCHASES ("PUTS") AND/OR SALES ("CALLS")

### 1.  Mandatory Purchases by the Corporation or Shareholders from a Selling Shareholder

As noted above, the shares in a closely-held corporation are not readily saleable, and this is particularly true of minority interests.[10] Shareholders' agreements sometimes provide, therefore, that if a shareholder desires to dispose of shares in the corporation, the shareholder may compel the corporation and/or the other shareholders to buy the shares at a stipulated price, so as not to be "locked in" forever into the investment.  The right of one person to be able to compel another to purchase an asset at a specified price is often called a "put".  This sort of provision is most frequently given to certain shareholders, usually minority shareholders, and not to others.  This right of a shareholder to "put" the stock to the corporation and/or the other shareholders is rarely exercisable at will by a shareholder, but rather is exercisable only upon the occurrence of a specified event or events, e. g., termination of employment with the corporation due to retirement, disability or discharge.  The right is sometimes given to a majority shareholder in cases where a majority shareholder uses control to have the corporation issue stock or sells some stock to new shareholders, in effect "junior partners".  The understanding is that the new shareholders will be required to take over the entire business by purchasing the stock of the majority shareholder whenever the "senior partner" wants to retire.[11]

**SAMPLE PROVISION:**

Clark, at any time and from time to time after his 65th birthday, may notify the Company and other Stockholders in writing of his desire to sell some or all of his shares of Stock in the Company. Upon the Company's receipt of such a notice, the Company shall have the option, exercisable for a thirty (30) day period from the date of receipt of such a notice, to purchase from Clark all or any part of the stock offered for sale by his notice at the price and upon the terms set forth in Paragraph D–1. The option shall be exercised by the Company's giving written notice of its election to purchase to Clark and to the other Stockholders. If the Company shall decide not to purchase all of the shares of Stock set forth in Clark's notice, it shall give written notice of that fact to the other Stockholders within said thirty (30) day period. Should the Company fail to give any notice as provided in this paragraph, it shall be presumed conclusively that the Company has decided not to purchase any shares of Stock offered for sale by Clark. If the Company has not purchased all of the shares of

---

10.  See Section I of this Chapter.

11.  For a discussion of an analogous problem, see Section II.D.3 on manda-

tory purchases by the corporation and/or shareholders of a deceased shareholder's interest.

Stock set forth in Clark's notice, the other Stockholders shall be obligated to purchase from Clark all of the Stock offered by him and not purchased by the Company. Each such Stockholder shall purchase such proportionate part of Clark's Stock which he has offered for sale but which has not been purchased by the Company as the number of shares of Stock in the Company owned by such Stockholder bears to the total number of shares of Stock owned by all Stockholders other than Clark. Purchases shall be at the price and upon the terms set forth in Paragraph D–1.

The sample provision above provides the corporation with an option to purchase the selling shareholder's stock, but requires the other shareholders to purchase the stock in the event that the corporation fails to exercise its option. The person drafting this provision probably realized that there might be circumstances when the corporation would be unable, as a matter of state law [12] to purchase its own stock and it would therefore be inappropriate to impose the obligation solely upon the corporation. The value of the mandatory put depends upon the ability of the other shareholders to purchase any stock offered for sale.

### 2. Mandatory Sales by a Shareholder to the Corporation or Other Shareholders

Shareholders' agreements sometimes give the corporation or some of its shareholders the right to compel certain shareholders to sell their shares to the corporation or to the other shareholders. This right to "call" shares is almost always exercisable against particular shareholders who are parties to the agreement, not all shareholders. As with the case of "puts" discussed in the previous paragraph, a call is rarely exercisable by the corporation or shareholders at will, but rather is exercisable only upon the occurrence of a specified event or events, most commonly termination of employment with the corporation due to retirement, disability or discharge. The provision is most often used to protect existing shareholders against the possibility that new shareholders who are also new employees may not "work out", and there is frequently a time limit upon its exercise. The theory underlying this device in such a case is that the new employee, if he or she proves to be capable, should have an equity interest in the business; therefore, the employee is allowed to purchase a stock interest at the inception of employment. If the employee does not work out, however, and is discharged or quits within a certain number of months or years, the employee can be compelled to sell back the shares, frequently at their original purchase price. The following provision is typical of such arrangements:

### SAMPLE PROVISION:

"In the event that Smith's employment with the Company is terminated on or prior to December 31, 19—, due to her discharge by

12. See footnote 8 of this Chapter.

the Company with or without cause or by her voluntarily leaving the Company (but not due to her death or serious illness which incapacitates her from performing her duties to the Company for a period of three consecutive months or longer), the Company shall have the option, exercisable by notice in writing to Smith given within 30 days of such termination of employment, to purchase from Smith all of her shares of Stock in the Company at a purchase price of $1.00 per share. Upon the receipt of said notice, Smith shall sell all of her shares of Stock to the Company in accordance with the following terms. Such purchase price shall be paid in full by the Company at settlement, in cash or by certified check, at the executive offices of the Company, on the date and at the hour fixed by the Company in its written notice to Smith, such time to be no later than on the 45th day following such termination of employment."

## QUESTION

Why does the option not occur if Smith dies or is disabled? Could it be present in such situations?

### 3. Mandatory Purchase and Sale

The two preceding sections described unilateral rights, or options, exercisable generally upon the occurrence of specified events. Specified events frequently trigger bilateral obligations, however. For example, there may be an obligation of the corporation to purchase and the concurrent obligation of the shareholder to sell such shareholder's shares upon retirement, disability or discharge. Because of the similarity in the reason for puts, calls and mandatory purchases and sales (particularly in the context of termination of employment) to the reason for the purchase of shares of a deceased shareholder upon death, agreements sometimes lump together retirement, disability and discharge with death in a single section of the shareholders' agreement. More commonly, however, purchases on death are treated separately in light of the fact that the purchase price is frequently different (generally higher) with respect to such purchases and the payment terms are frequently different (generally payable sooner).[13] Moreover, purchase prices frequently differ, even where death is not involved, depending upon the event giving rise to the purchase. The purchase price to a disabled shareholder-employee, for example, will generally be higher than the purchase price to a discharged shareholder-employee.[14]

---

13. This is true particularly when funded by life insurance as discussed in Section III. Consider the reasons for differences in price and terms of payment under different circumstances.

14. Why would such a disparity in price exist? Consider in your answer the main purpose of shareholders' agreements—discouraging transfers.

**SAMPLE PROVISION:**

"Upon the termination of Green's employment with the Company for whatever reason other than death, the Company shall purchase from Green and Green shall sell to the Company all of his shares of Stock in the Company at a purchase price of $1.00 per share. Such purchase price shall be paid in full by the Company at settlement, in cash or by certified check, at the executive offices of the Company, on the date and at the hour fixed by the Company in a written notice to Green, such time to be no later than on the 45th day following such termination of employment."

## E.  SPECIAL RESTRICTIONS FOR TWO OR MORE GROUPS OF SHAREHOLDERS

In some instances, the shareholders of a corporation fall into two or more ascertainable groups, such as family groups.  For example, where the shares of the corporation are owned in part by members of the Smith family and in part by members of the Jones family, particularly when the two families have equal or nearly equal interests, it is often necessary to preserve the balance of power and relative percentage ownership of the two families.  If one of the Smiths wants to sell shares, the other Smiths will not want the corporation to have a right of first refusal, since a purchase by the corporation will result in a proportionately smaller ownership in the corporation by the Smith family in relation to the combined stock interest of the Jones family.  Indeed, control of the corporation could shift from the Smith family to the Jones family in such a case.  Nor would the Smith family want all of the shareholders to have the right of first refusal pro rata, since that also could lead to the same adverse result.  This is illustrated in the following two examples:

**EXAMPLE 1**—Corporation purchases John Smith's shares

| Shareholder | Shares Outstanding Before Purchase | Shares Outstanding After Purchase |
|---|---|---|
| John Smith | 200 | None |
| Helen Smith | 300 | 300 |
| Bill Smith | 50 | 50 |
| Dan Jones | 200 | 200 |
| Pauline Jones | 100 | 100 |
| Dick Jones | 150 | 150 |
| | 1,000 | 800 |

**EXAMPLE 2**—Remaining Shareholders purchase, pro rata, John Smith's shares

| Shareholder | Shares Outstanding Before Purchase | Shares Outstanding After Purchase |
|---|---|---|
| John Smith | 200 | None |
| Helen Smith | 300 | 375 |
| Bill Smith | 50 | 62.5 |
| Dan Jones | 200 | 250 |
| Pauline Jones | 100 | 125 |
| Dick Jones | 150 | 187.5 |
| | 1,000 | 1,000 |

In each of the above examples, the Smith family controlled 55% of the outstanding shares of the corporation before the purchase, whereas in each case after the purchase it would control only 43.75% of the outstanding shares. Accordingly, shareholders' agreements in this situation generally define the groups involved and provide the members of each group the initial right of first refusal to purchase the shares of a group member who proposes to transfer shares or who had died. Where a group does not exercise its right of first refusal in full, the corporation and/or the other group will usually have a right of first refusal before shares can be sold to an outsider. See paragraphs A–5 to A–7 of Form Agreement 3 of this Chapter.

## III.   DISPOSITION OF SHARES OF A DECEASED SHAREHOLDER UPON DEATH

### A.   GENERAL CONSIDERATIONS

**1.   Whose Interests Are to Be Protected?**

As a general rule, the beneficiaries receiving the stock of a deceased shareholder upon the death of the shareholder are more likely to be favored than the surviving shareholders. (In the same way, the interests of the older shareholders are more likely to be protected than the interest of the younger shareholders and the interests of the minority shareholders are more likely to be protected than the interests of the majority shareholders.) The reason for protecting the beneficiaries of a deceased shareholder is that shares in a closely-held corporation rarely pay dividends and rarely prove saleable. The stock can constitute a virtually worthless asset in an estate, although it was the deceased shareholders' principal asset during lifetime because the decedent was drawing a salary from the corporation. If the beneficiaries of the stock of a deceased shareholder are minority shareholders, then, by virtue of their lack of control, they are not in a position to direct the flow of cash out of the corporation in the form of dividends or other distributions.

## B. OPTION OR OBLIGATION TO PURCHASE AND TO SELL

Shareholders' agreements frequently provide that upon the death of a shareholder, the corporation is obligated to purchase, and the personal representatives [15] of the deceased shareholder are obligated to sell, the shares of the deceased shareholder. A minority shareholder, particularly one more advanced in age, should generally insist that the corporation be obligated to purchase all shares owned by such shareholder upon death, so that the beneficiaries will have cash rather than noncash-producing shares of stock. In light of the obligation of the corporation to purchase, the majority shareholder will generally insist that the personal representatives of the deceased shareholder be obligated to sell the shares to the corporation, rather than have an option to do so.

**SAMPLE PROVISION:**

Upon the death of a Stockholder, the Company shall purchase from the personal representatives of the deceased Stockholder, and the personal representatives of the deceased Stockholder shall sell to the Company, all of the shares of Stock in the Company owned by the deceased Stockholder, at the price and upon the terms set forth in Paragraph D–2, and the surviving Stockholders shall adopt such resolutions and take such action as may be required by law to authorize such purchase at such time.

If the purchase price to be paid to the personal representatives of the deceased Stockholder is in excess of the then existing aggregate of capital surplus and earned surplus of the Company, each of the surviving Stockholders shall be obligated to make a contribution in cash to the capital of the Company, five (5) or more days prior to the settlement date set forth in Paragraph D–2, in an amount equal to that proportion of the amount by which the purchase price exceeds the aggregate of capital surplus and earned surplus as the number of shares of Stock in the Company owned by such surviving Stockholder bears to the number of shares of Stock in the Company owned by all of the surviving Stockholders.

Shareholders' agreements frequently obligate the surviving shareholders to purchase the deceased shareholder's shares in the event that the corporation cannot, or does not, purchase the shares. In some cases the corporation has no obligation to purchase the

---

15. The personal representative is the individual who administers the estate of a decedent or carries out the will of the decedent.

shares and the obligation falls directly on the surviving shareholders. There are situations, moreover, in which there is no mandatory purchase or sale, but where the corporation and/or the surviving shareholders have the option to purchase the deceased shareholder's shares, or, conversely, agreements in which the personal representatives of the deceased shareholder have an option to compel the corporation and/or the surviving shareholders to purchase. An example of a corporation's option clause follows:

**SAMPLE PROVISION:**

> Upon the death of Clark, and for a period of 30 days thereafter, the Company shall have the option, exercisable by notice in writing to Clark's personal representatives and to the Smith Group Stockholders, to purchase all or a part of the shares of Stock in the Company owned by Clark at the time of his death, at the price and upon the terms set forth in Paragraph D–2 hereof.

## C.  INSURANCE FUNDING BY CORPORATION AND/OR BY SURVIVING SHAREHOLDERS

A corporation or surviving shareholders obligated to purchase a deceased shareholder's shares may be obligated to make a substantial payment for such shares without any certainty that, at the time, they will be in a sufficiently liquid cash position to make the payment. Many corporations with millions of dollars of assets are, from time to time, very short of cash, for example, as a result of their current assets being tied up primarily in inventory or receivables. As a safeguard against the difficulties occasioned by such a situation, a corporation may carry life insurance on the lives of its shareholders—most commonly on the lives of its principal shareholders—in order to provide the cash with which to purchase the deceased shareholder's interest in the corporation.[16] Similarly, shareholders may carry insurance on the lives of their co-shareholders for the same purpose. Shareholders' agreements in such situations sometimes provide for an affirmative obligation of the corporation or shareholders to carry such insurance.

**SAMPLE PROVISION:**

> The Company shall promptly obtain and maintain in force for the duration of this Agreement, as owner and as beneficiary, a policy of life insurance insuring the life of each Stockholder for $50,000. The parties acknowledge that the principal purpose for such life insurance is to fund the purchase by the Company of the Stock of a deceased Stockholder; accordingly, the Company shall, as and when appro-

---

16. Consider the impact of the possibility of funding a purchase through life insurance on the question raised by footnote 14 of this Chapter.

priate, increase the amount of life insurance on the life of each Stockholder so as to be reasonably certain of having sufficient net proceeds from such policies to redeem completely a deceased Stockholder's interest in accordance with the terms of this Agreement. Any proceeds from such life insurance policies received by the Company shall be held by the Company in trust for the purposes of this Agreement. The Company shall pay all premiums on such life insurance policies, and it shall be a provision of each of such policies that each Stockholder shall be notified by the insurance company, before the expiration of any grace period, of the failure of the Company to pay the necessary premiums.

## QUESTIONS

What is the problem of insurance funding where there is an old shareholder and a young shareholder? Where one shareholder has high blood pressure?

## IV.  THE PURCHASE PRICE

### A.  GENERAL CONSIDERATIONS

Where shares of stock of a shareholder (whether during lifetime or upon death), are to be purchased by the corporation and/or the other shareholders, the interest of the shareholder disposing of shares is generally to receive the highest possible purchase price immediately in cash, while the interest of the purchaser is to have a lower purchase price which is payable over a long period of time at the lowest interest rate that can be negotiated. The problem with an immediate cash payment in full is that it is often unrealistic to expect a substantial cash payment on short notice. This is particularly true in the case of lifetime purchases which cannot be funded by life insurance. On the other hand, there are several problems with providing for payment over time. In the first place, circumstances may occur between the time the payments begin and the time they are scheduled to be completed which make payment in full impossible. An example of this is the insolvency of the purchaser. Second, there is always a danger that the purchaser may refuse to pay, even though able to, for any number of reasons. Third, the interest rate provided in a shareholders' agreement, if fixed, may be fixed at a level bearing a relationship to prevailing interest rates at the time the agreement is executed. Yet many years, possibly decades later, when payments are to be made, interest rates may be materially higher (or lower) than the rates prevailing at the time the agreement was executed. As a consequence, the recipient of the purchase price (who might be able to invest the cash proceeds at a 10% return if received immediately) may be locked into a mandatory investment which yields only 5%. The problem caused by fluctuating interest rates can be ameliorated, if the parties agree, by tying the interest rate in the agreement to the prevailing "prime rate." [17]   Such a provision, however is uncommon in shareholder agreements.

## B.   MATCHING OFFERS

When the corporation or remaining shareholders have a right of first refusal with respect to a proposed transfer of stock by a shareholder to a bona fide offeror, it is common to provide that the corporation or remaining shareholders may purchase such shares at the price and upon the terms contained in the bona fide offer, thus involving no economic prejudice to the selling shareholder.   Alternatively, the agreement might provide that the purchase price shall be the same as that contained in the bona fide offer, but that the terms of payment may be, at the option of the corporation or other shareholders, either the terms contained in the bona fide offer or alternative terms (generally payment over a long period of time at a low interest rate).   Agreements frequently provide, however, that the corporation or shareholders have a right to buy at the lesser of two or more alternative prices, one of which is the bona fide offer price.   What is finally agreed upon is a decision of the shareholder.   Each shareholder, however, in executing the agreement, must consider that any shareholder, including himself or herself, in the future may be either buyer or seller.

A formula price may be used, such as the lesser of the bona fide offer or book value.   This kind of formula, particularly where the book value or other stipulated measure is materially less than the bona fide offer, obviously discourages proposed transfers.

**SAMPLE PROVISION:**

Settlement for the purchase by the Company or by a Stockholder of shares of Stock in the Company pursuant to the options granted in Paragraph A–6 shall be made within sixty (60) days from the date of exercise of the option.   At the option of the purchaser, the purchase price per share and the terms of payment shall be either (a) the price per share contained in the bona fide offer referred to in Paragraph A–3, payable upon the terms contained in said bona fide offer, or (b) the Book Value per share, payable in twenty (20) equal quarterly installments of principal, the first of which is to be paid at settlement, with interest on the unpaid balance of the purchase price at the rate of 6% per annum, payable quarterly when payments of principal are due.

17.   See Section III.B of Chapter Eight
for a definition of "prime rate".

## C.   AGREED VALUES

An occasional, though generally undesirable, provision with respect to price, applicable with respect to both lifetime transfers and dispositions upon death, is to fix a specified dollar purchase price, such as $10.00 per share.  This is not usually selected as a pricing method as an economic matter since such a price, while perhaps realistic at the time the agreement is entered into, could lead to a undesirable result when applied many years later to an actual transfer.

**SAMPLE PROVISION:**

> Settlement for the purchase by the Company or by a Stockholder of shares of Stock in the Company pursuant to the options granted in Paragraph A–6 shall be made within sixty (60) days from the date of exercise of the option.  The purchase price shall be $10.00 per share, payable in full, by cash or certified check, at settlement.

## D.   ADJUSTABLE AGREED VALUES

In order to eliminate the inequity of a fixed agreed value as discussed in the preceding paragraph, an agreed value can be designated at the time of execution of the agreement with a provision that the shareholders and corporation must redetermine the agreed value on an annual or other periodic basis in order to maintain the agreed value, as adjusted, at a realistic level.  Such provisions generally require complete unanimity in order to modify the agreed value, although, of course, it is possible to provide for some percentage vote, majority or greater, to control.  As the value of the shares increases, the motivation of the younger shareholders is generally to keep the price low, while the motivation of the older shareholders is generally to set the agreed value high.  Why?  As a result of this conflict, or any other conflict, shareholders under such a procedure are frequently unable to reach agreement with respect to adjusting the agreed value.  For that reason, it is desirable in using such a format to provide for the eventuality of failure, whether by neglect, or by disagreement, of the parties to adjust the agreed value periodically.[18]  The common manner of doing this is to provide that if an agreed value is not readjusted for a period of two consecutive years (or some other shorter or longer period), the agreed value shall be deemed to be the last established agreed value plus or minus some formula value.  See the following sample.  As is always true, the sample is only one variation.  The parties may create many other alternatives.

18.  A form of agreement for periodically adjusting agreed values is attached as Schedule A to Form Agreement 3.

**SAMPLE PROVISION:**

The Agreed Value per share of the Stock of the Company is hereby determined to be as set forth on Schedule A hereto. On January 31 and on July 31 of each year, the Stockholders shall redetermine in writing the Agreed Value of the Stock for purposes of this Agreement and shall record such agreed redetermination of Agreed Value on a Schedule substantially in the form of Schedule A hereto. A redetermination of Agreed Value shall be effective only if agreed to unanimously in writing by all the Stockholders. Should the parties fail to redetermine the Agreed Value for a period of 12 consecutive months, then the Agreed Value per share shall, subsequent to the expiration of such 12-month period and until a redetermination of Agreed Value by the Stockholders, be the last determined Agreed Value per share, plus or minus the aggregate of the net income or loss (on a consolidated basis with subsidiaries, if any), after federal and other income and other taxes, less the aggregate of dividends paid on the Company's capital stock, from the beginning of the Company's last fiscal year in which there occurred a determination of Agreed Value until the close of the fiscal year last preceding the time in question, divided by the total number of shares of common stock of the Company then outstanding. The aggregate of the net income or loss shall be as computed by the Company's regularly engaged public accountants in accordance with generally accepted accounting principles and practices applied on a basis consistent with that of preceding years, whose determination shall be binding and conclusive upon the parties.

## QUESTION

If it is possible to get regular redetermination of agreed values, do you believe it to be a good basis for determining the purchase price?

## E.   FORMULA PRICES

### 1.   Book Value or Appraisal Value

Shareholders' agreements will frequently provide that the purchase price applicable to lifetime and/or death transfers is the book value of the shares purchased. Although the definition of "book value" in these agreements can become quite complicated, book value per share is essentially determined by dividing the net assets (gross assets less liabilities) of the corporation by the number of outstanding shares of stock of the corporation. Under this formula, the purchase price will increase as the corporation's net assets increase, and will correspondingly decrease upon a decrease in net assets. A book value formula is frequently not a realistic measure of the worth of shares of stock, and must be used carefully. It is a mechanistic approach to valuation depending on accounting principles. For example, in a highly profitable service business, such as a law firm or an accounting firm which is incorporated, a corporation may have negligible assets (i. e., desks, chairs, typewriters and telephones) and yet produce several hundred thousand dollars or more of income each year, all of which is withdrawn from the corporation in the form of salaries. In such a situation, the book value of a 40% interest in the corporation may be measured in hundreds of dollars, while the actual worth of a 40% interest may as an economic matter be properly measured in tens or even hundreds of thousands of dollars because of the earnings potential of the business. However, book value is an objective measure and may have a real relation to value where the corporation is a manufacturing company with much inventory and assets in machinery, equipment and accounts receivable. Many times book values will be used even where it may not be the best pricing method because of its ease of application.

## SAMPLE PROVISION:

The "Book Value" per share of the Company's Stock shall be equal to the net assets of the Company (on a consolidated basis with subsidiaries, if any [19]) on the date in question divided by the number of shares of Common Stock of the Company outstanding on such date, as determined by the Company's regularly engaged independent public accountants in accordance with generally accepted accounting principles and practices applied on a basis consistent with prior years. For purposes of Paragraph D–1 hereof, the Book Value shall be determined as of the close of the fiscal year preceding exercise of the option pursuant to Paragraph A–4 or A–5 hereof, unless such option is exercised more than 100 days following the close of such fiscal year, in which case the Book Value shall be determined as of the end of the month preceding the month in which the option was exercised.

In certain circumstances, particularly where a corporation's assets are for the most part real estate holdings, fair market value—as distinguished from book value—is a satisfactory measure of the corporation's value. Book value is not a satisfactory measure of asset value due to depreciation of buildings and other improvements on the financial books of the corporation. Depreciation decreases the book value of the real estate even though, as an economic fact, the fair market value of the real estate may be appreciating in value. In

---

19. A "consolidated basis" means combination of the financial statements of the Company and its subsidiaries in computing Book Value.

such circumstances, a shareholders' agreement might provide for the purchase price to be based on fair market value, with the asset value to be determined by a disinterested appraiser. In such event the appraiser should be named, preferably with an alternate if the first choice is unavailable.

## QUESTIONS

What are the advantages of an appraiser? What are its disadvantages?

## SAMPLE PROVISION:

The Book Value per share of the Company's Stock shall be equal to the net assets of the Company (on a consolidated basis with subsidiaries, if any) on the date in question divided by the number of shares of Common Stock of the Company outstanding on such date, as determined by the Company's regularly engaged independent public accountants in accordance with generally accepted accounting principles and practices applied on a basis consistent with prior years, except with respect to the valuation of the Company's consolidated real estate assets and improvements thereon. With respect to such real estate assets and improvements, they shall be valued at fair market value in lieu of the value, net of depreciation, at which they are reflected on the books of the Company or a subsidiary. The fair market value shall be determined by unanimous agreement among the purchasers and sellers involved; in the event they are not able to unanimously agree upon a valuation within thirty (30) days of the event giving rise to the exercise of the options, the valuation shall be made by an appraiser acceptable to all of the purchasers and sellers, whose appraisal shall be conclusive and binding upon the purchasers and sellers; in the event that the purchasers and sellers are not able to unanimously agree upon an appraiser within thirty (30) days of the event giving rise to the exercise of the options, the valuation shall be made by a disinterested appraiser designated by the American Arbitration Association in New York, New York, whose determination shall be conclusive and binding upon the purchasers and sellers.[20]

20. The American Arbitration Association is a group of lawyers and other private persons who stand willing to serve as arbitrators of disputes between parties in order to avoid the necessity of litigation in court with its attendant delay and expense. Many types of agreements will call for arbitration of disputes for this purpose. See paragraph 12 of Form Agreement 1 as an example. If an arbitration clause is provided, the party drafting the agreement should be careful to designate a location for the arbitration which is convenient to its side. After all, there will be costs of travel, legal fees and other expenses with an arbitration, just as there is

## 2. Earnings Multiples

A formula that is often used to fix the purchase price for both lifetime and death transfers is the so-called "earnings multiple" formula, which provides in effect that the value of the corporation for purposes of determining the purchase price for a number of shares is determined by multiplying the net income of the corporation by a fixed number, such as three times earnings or ten times earnings. The multiple is a number that must be selected by the shareholders because the number is totally a subjective amount. The net income may be the net income in the preceding fiscal year or the average of several preceding fiscal years. The following is one form of such a provision.

### QUESTION

What difficulties can you perceive in utilizing an earnings multiple?

### SAMPLE PROVISION:

The aggregate "fair market value" of the Company's Stock for purposes of Paragraph D–1 is hereby stipulated and agreed to be five (5) times the aggregate net income, if any (on a consolidated basis with subsidiaries, if any), for the two (2) full fiscal years of the Company last preceding the time in question, but without reducing such income or increasing such loss in either year by virtue of any dividends paid in such years on the Company's Stock; provided, however, that in no event shall the fair market value of the Company's Stock for purposes of Paragraph D–1 be less than $1.00 per share. The aggregate net income or loss for the two (2) fiscal years in question shall be determined by the Company's regularly engaged independent public accountants in accordance with generally accepted accounting principles and practices applied on a basis consistent with prior years.

## 3. Other

Special situations frequently make the more traditional purchase price fixing methods inapplicable. For example, in a closely-held corporation where one particular shareholder is the person primarily responsible for the success of the corporation and is a person without whom the corporation will have difficulty remaining in business, it may be appropriate to provide for different purchase prices for different shareholders.

with litigation, although the expenses are usually less in an arbitration. Sometimes different types of arbitration provisions are utilized, for example, as in paragraph J of Form Agreement 3. Are there any circumstances under which an agreement should not contain an arbitration clause?

Another special situation can exist where the success of the business is determined primarily by the existence of an important contract which produces the major share of the corporation's income. In such a situation, it is judicious to provide one method for determining the purchase price with respect to a transaction taking place while that contract is still in force, and a different method of determining the price if that contract has been terminated and no equivalent contract or contracts obtained. These examples are only samples of many possible alternatives for pricing the shares.

## F. TERMS OF PAYMENT

### 1. Cash and/or Notes

As mentioned earlier, it is frequently impractical, particularly in the case of lifetime transfers, to provide for a prompt lump sum cash payment for the purchase of shares. It is therefore common to provide for an extended payment over a period of years, with either a fixed interest rate or a variable interest rate. Frequently cash and notes are used in combination, that is, there is provision for an initial cash payment with the balance to be paid over a period of time. Where the entire purchase price is not to be paid immediately, it is not always necessary to provide for notes. The agreement itself may contain the obligation of the purchaser to pay the purchase price over time, and the obligation is as binding as it would be if the obligation was represented by notes.

### SAMPLE PROVISION:

At settlement, the stock certificate or stock certificates representing the shares being sold shall be delivered by the seller to the purchaser or purchasers, duly endorsed for transfer, with the necessary documentary and transfer tax stamps, if any, affixed by the seller. The unpaid balance of the purchase price payable by each purchaser shall be represented by such purchaser's promissory note in negotiable form, payable to the order of the seller, dated the date of settlement and providing for an interest rate of 6% per annum. It is hereby agreed that upon any default in payment under the note, whether of an installment of principal or of interest, the full amount due under the note shall accelerate and become immediately due and payable, and the note shall contain a provision providing as aforesaid.

### QUESTION

What does the provision for acceleration of the unpaid balance of a note do for the holder of a note?

Where payments over time are contemplated, it is frequently advisable, whether or not notes are used, to have the spouse of the obligor join in the agreement and in any notes delivered at a closing, so that upon a default in payment of the obligation, joint property owned by both husband and wife can be reached by an execution on their property.

## QUESTION

**What property may be reached by a creditor if the debtor, but not the spouse, signs the note?**

## 2.  Security Devices

Where payments over a period of time are contemplated, it is customary to provide for some sort of collateral or security to protect the selling shareholder.  If there is no security, a default in one of the installment payments leaves the selling shareholder with only the option of filing a lawsuit, which might take several years, in order to obtain payment.

One security device used to protect the selling shareholders is a "confession of judgment" note which will in some cases substantially expedite litigation.  Confession of judgment authorizes any attorney, even the attorney for the holder of the note, to enter judgment against the obligor.  The use of the "confession of judgment" is limited to those states where the procedure is permitted.  This device has become severely limited by courts in recent years even in those states where it is permitted.

## QUESTION

**Is it permitted in your state?**

Another type of security device is to require the obligor to give to the obligee a mortgage on real property, or to deposit marketable securities or other property.

Still another means of securing the debt is to provide that the actual shares of the corporation being purchased are to be pledged as collateral security pending payment in full of the purchase price, and that upon default in such payment, the shares are to be returned to the seller.  A sample provision follows, but, as is always the case, it is advisable to ascertain whether the lawyer for whom the paralegal is working has a model rather than the sample.  These provisions can be quite complex and are seldom completely satisfactory since they may prove unfair to one shareholder or another if a default should occur.  For example, in the sample provision below, the selling shareholder may receive all of the stock back in the event of a default even though a great portion of the purchase price has been paid.  This could be corrected, perhaps, by providing a sliding scale of stock that could be retained by the selling shareholder on default based upon the percentage of payments that have been made.

## QUESTION

**What problem arises from such a sliding scale?**

**SAMPLE PROVISION:**

Whenever a Shareholder or the Company purchases shares of Stock pursuant to the rights or obligations contained in this agreement, such purchaser (unless the purchaser shall have paid the entire purchase price in cash) shall, following the delivery of said Stock, endorse the new certificates of Stock issued and deliver the same in pledge to Selling Shareholder or the Selling Shareholder's designated agent (herein called the "Holder") as collateral security for payment of the unpaid purchase price.  The Holder shall hold the collateral only as security for the sole benefit of the Selling Shareholder until the entire purchase price has been paid. If the balance of the purchase price is paid while the Stock is held in pledge, the Holder shall deliver the Stock to the purchaser.  While the Stock is held in pledge as collateral security, the purchaser shall be entitled to all voting rights and all dividends with respect thereto so long as the purchaser is not in default in its obligations to the Selling Shareholder.  If the purchaser is in default then the Holder shall deliver the Stock to the Selling Shareholder who shall have the option of retaining the Stock in full payment of the debt or of selling the Stock in a commercially reasonable manner (without first offering the Stock to the Shareholders or the Company pursuant to the terms of this Agreement) and applying the proceeds towards the unpaid balance of the purchase price.  Any proceeds in excess of the unpaid balance shall be sent forthwith to the purchaser. The Selling Shareholder shall exercise this option by notifying the purchaser in writing within fifteen (15) days after receipt of the Stock.  A failure to notify the purchaser within this time period shall be deemed to be an election by the Selling Shareholder to retain the Stock in full payment of the balance of the debt.

The Holder shall release the Stock only upon receipt of a written notice from the Selling Shareholder, with a copy to the other party or parties, that an event has occurred which warrants the release of the Stock.  In the event of a dispute concerning the Stock, the Holder may request an arbitration of the dispute in accordance with the provisions of paragraph 15 of this Agreement.  The Holder shall be liable only for willful misconduct or bad faith in the performance of its duties.

## V. PROVISIONS RESPECTING MANAGEMENT

### A. GENERAL CONSIDERATIONS

### 1. Whose Interests Are to Be Protected?

An interest in a closely-held corporation is frequently the principal asset of the shareholder as well as the principal source, through salary or dividends, of income. Whether the holder of a majority or minority interest, the shareholder is vitally interested in the management and growth of the business operated by the corporation and can be entirely dependent upon distributions from the corporation for a livelihood. Particularly in a corporation where there are a small number of shareholders, all of whom actively participate in the business, it is not uncommon to find salaries fixed in the same or a similar proportion to the respective stock interests of the shareholders. The motivation to take cash out of the business by way of salary rather than by way of dividends is obvious; salaries are deductible by the corporation for tax purposes, while dividends are not.[21]

The majority shareholders control the business of the corporation, including hiring, firing and the fixing of salaries (subject to employment contracts). The majority shareholders are thus in a position, should disagreements arise between them and the minority shareholders, to revise the salary structure to the detriment of the minority shareholders. The minority shareholders may realize partial protection against this abuse through the device of long-term employment contracts. Employment contracts, however, generally provide for a stipulated dollar amount of salary and do not protect against majority shareholder-employees taking considerable increases in their salaries which are disproportionately greater than the other shareholders' salaries. It is quite difficult to structure employment contracts to protect against this possibility. Moreover, there are certain material transactions in which corporations may become involved in which a minority shareholder is vitally interested but is powerless to control, such as liquidation and dissolution of the corporation, merger of the corporation, change in the nature of the business of the corporation, sale of substantially all of the assets of the corporation, composition of the Board of Directors of the corporation and other matters. Although a 49% stockholder has, as a practical matter, virtually the same economic stake in a corporation as a 51% shareholder, the former is virtually powerless while the latter is in virtually complete control.[22]

21. See Chapter Eleven for a discussion of "double taxation". Proposals have constantly been put forth in the United States Congress to eliminate the difference, but as yet they have not been enacted.

22. For sample provisions with respect to management, see generally Section G of Form Agreement 2.

## B.   CONCENTRATION OF VOTING POWER:  VOTING TRUSTS

In order to give minority shareholders a voice in the management of the corporation, shareholders' agreements sometimes provide for greater than majority vote—in some cases unanimity—of the shareholders in order for the corporation to take certain action. Matters requiring this greater percentage or unanimity might include a liquidation and dissolution, merger, etc., as listed above.  Such a device, however, is not always a complete solution.  For example, a corporation with several shareholders, no one of whom is in control when acting alone, can experience inter-shareholder "deals" whereby a group of shareholders may make alliances with certain other shareholders to the detriment of excluded shareholders.  In order to avoid inter-shareholder politics, some or all shareholders may select one or more shareholders, or even nonshareholders to give them sole voting authority with respect to the shares of the corporation.  The legal device used to accomplish this is the voting trust, which is generally provided for by statute and which generally has a legally limited term.[23]  During the term of the voting trust, the shares of stock deposited in trust are actually registered in the names of the voting trustees.  As a result only the designated voting trustees have a right to vote the shares of the corporation which are deposited with them in trust.  The statutory prescription for a particular state must be carefully reviewed for implementation of a voting trust.[24]

## C.   DILUTION OF STOCK INTERESTS

Shares of stock of a corporation are generally issuable, as a matter of corporate law, at the times, in the amounts and at the prices (so long as the prices equal or exceed any par value) determined from time to time by the board of directors acting by majority vote, and may be issued for money, property or services rendered.[25]  It is of utmost importance to a minority shareholder, in order to preserve his or her percentage interest in the corporation, to have limits imposed on the board with respect to the issuance of additional shares of capital stock.  Most frequently, shareholders' agreements prohibit the issuance of any additional shares of capital stock without the agreement of all of the shareholders.  Where this restriction is unacceptable to the majority shareholders, a common substitute is a provision, sometimes effectuated by an actual amendment to the corporation's articles of incorporation, granting "preemptive rights" to the shareholders.[26]

---

23.  Section 34 of the MBCA and Section 511 of the Pennsylvania Business Corporation Law limits a voting trust to ten years; Section 218 of the Delaware General Corporation Law similarly limits the period to ten years. Why do you believe time limits are placed on the life of voting trusts?

24.  See Section 34 of the MBCA.

25.  See Chapter Eight, Section II.E.

26.  See Chapter Two, Section III.H.1 for a discussion of preemptive rights.

### D.   COVENANTS NOT TO COMPETE

Although generally, and more appropriately, the subject is covered in employment contracts,[27] shareholders' agreements sometimes contain provisions prohibiting shareholders from engaging in business competitive with that of the corporation.  Such restrictions, when included, invariably embrace the period of time the shareholder is employed by the corporation, the period of time the shareholder remains as a shareholder even if not employed by the corporation, and also some period of time following the termination of the shareholder's stock interests and/or employment.  The importance and scope of a covenant not to compete depends generally on the collective estimate by the shareholders of the threat to the corporation which a particular shareholder would pose as a competitor, and thus covenants not to compete are not always uniform in their applicability to all shareholders.

**SAMPLE PROVISION:**

Each Stockholder hereby agrees that he or she will not, for so long as he or she owns, directly or indirectly, any shares of the Stock of the Company and for a period of two (2) years after having disposed of the last remaining interest in any of the Stock of the Company, engage in, be financially interested in or be employed by any business in the states of New York, Pennsylvania and New Jersey which is competitive with the Company or any of its subsidiaries. The term "engage in" as used in the preceding sentence shall include, but shall not be limited to, activities, whether direct or indirect, as proprietor, partner, stockholder, principal, agent, employee or consultant.  Each Stockholder acknowledges that the restrictions contained in this paragraph, in light of the nature of Company's industry, are reasonable and necessary to protect the Company's legitimate interests, and that a violation thereof would result in irreparable injury to the Company and thus to its Stockholders. Each Stockholder acknowledges that, in the event of a violation of any such restrictions the Company and/or the remaining Stockholders shall be entitled to preliminary and permanent injunctive relief as well as an equitable accounting of all of such defaulting Stockholder's income, gain or benefits arising out of such violation (which rights shall be cumulative and in addition to any other rights or remedies to which the Company and/or the Stockholders may be entitled).  In the event of a violation, the two-year period re

---

**27.**  See Chapter Nine generally for a discussion of covenants not to compete.

ferred to above shall be extended by an amount of time equal to the time during which such violations took place.[28]

## VI.  MISCELLANEOUS

### A.  MULTIPLE CLASS OF SHARES

The simplest form of capital structure for a corporation is to have a single class of common stock.  Many corporations, however, have more complicated capital structures, in which several classes of stock might exist, some of which are preferred and some of which are common, some of which are voting and some of which are non-voting, some of which are convertible and some of which are not, etc.[29]  In such cases, the shareholders' agreement must be drafted with particular care to achieve the intended result.  For example, the shareholders' agreement might only apply to dispositions of voting common stock, since the transfer by a shareholder of nonvoting preferred stock is likely to have less impact on the corporation or its shareholders.

### B.  BANKRUPTCY OR INSOLVENCY OF A SHAREHOLDER

It is usually advisable to provide in shareholders' agreements that upon the threatened bankruptcy or insolvency of a shareholder, the corporation and/or the other shareholders have a right to purchase the shares of such shareholder.  If there is no such right, and the shareholder in fact becomes insolvent or bankrupt, the remaining shareholders might suddenly find as their new partner a trustee in bankruptcy.  A trustee in bankruptcy is under a fiduciary obligation to conserve the assets of the bankrupt under the trustee's jurisdiction, and is therefore under an obligation to supervise very closely the conduct of the business of the corporation in a manner which may prove inconvenient or burdensome to the other shareholders.  It should be noted that the following provision is desirable and should be included if there is any possibility to avoid having the shares controlled by the trustee, but it may not be enforceable against the trustee in certain circumstances.

**SAMPLE PROVISION:**

In the event that any Stockholder shall be adjudicated a bankrupt or make an assignment for the benefit of creditors, or bankruptcy, insolvency, reorganization, arrangement, debt adjustment, liquidation or receivership proceedings in which such Stockholder is alleged to be insolvent or unable to pay his or her debts as they mature are instituted by or against such Stockholder and, if instituted against

28.  See also paragraph 8 of Form Agreement 1.

29.  See the discussion generally in Chapter Eight relative to different classes of securities of a corporation.

such Stockholder, such Stockholder shall consent thereto or admit in writing the material allegations of the petitions filed in said proceedings or said proceedings shall remain undismissed for sixty (60) days, or the Stock of such Stockholder in the Company is attached, or any judgment is obtained in any legal or equitable proceeding against such Stockholder and the sale of his or her Stock in the Company is contemplated or threatened under legal process as a result of such judgment, or any execution process is issued against such Stockholder by which the Stock in the Company may be sold either voluntarily or involuntarily, then the Company shall have the option to buy forthwith such Stockholder's Stock in the Company. The purchase shall be at the price and upon the terms set forth in Paragraph D–2 hereof.

## C.   INTER–FAMILY TRANSFERS

Notwithstanding the general purpose of shareholders' agreements to avoid the disposition of shares, it is not uncommon to find in shareholders' agreements the right of a shareholder to transfer during lifetime a portion of the shares to members of the immediate family or trusts for the benefit of members of the immediate family. This right is frequently granted in order to facilitate estate planning by shareholders who wish to make gifts during their lifetime of property which is likely to appreciate in the future, in order to avoid having those assets included in their estate upon their death. The shareholders' agreement will generally provide, in such cases, that the transferees must take such shares subject to all of the restrictions contained in the shareholders' agreement.

Shareholders' agreements also frequently provide that when shares of a shareholder are divided among family members, the family members must act as a unit with respect to any proposed sales. For example, if a shareholder transfers some shares to a spouse, some to a son and some to a daughter, the shares owned by the entire family group must be the subject of a bona fide offer to purchase before the shares can be transferred or offered to the corporation pursuant to a right of first refusal.

With respect to death, shareholders' agreements frequently discriminate between the death of one of the transferees and the death of the initial shareholder. If the initial shareholder dies, the transferees, as well as the personal representatives of the decedent, must comply with the death provisions with regard to the decedent's shares; in the event of the death of one of the transferees while the initial shareholder is still living, the personal representatives of that transferee are obligated to resell the shares to the initial shareholder.[30]

30.  For sample provisions, see paragraphs A–7, B–1, B–2, B–3 and C–2 of Form Agreement 2.

## D.　TERM OF AGREEMENT

A shareholders' agreement usually remains in effect until all but the last surviving shareholder has died, unless lifetime transfers or various other intervening circumstances, such as a public offering of the corporation's stock, lead the shareholders to terminate the agreement prematurely.　Some agreements do, however, expire by their terms after a fixed period of time or upon the occurrence of a specified event such as the death of a certain shareholder or a public offering of securities of the corporation:

**SAMPLE PROVISION:**

> Unless terminated sooner by unanimous agreement in writing of the Company and the Stockholders then living, this Agreement shall terminate on the earlier of the following dates: (1) ten (10) years from the date hereof or (2) upon the repurchase of the shares of Stock of the next to the last of the Stockholders upon his death pursuant to Section K of this Agreement.
>
> Notwithstanding anything to the contrary contained in this Agreement, in the event that all of the Stockholders die within sixty (60) days of each other, then the provisions of this Agreement shall be of no further legal force and effect, and this Agreement shall terminate in all respects. Any and all transfers, payments or other action made or taken with respect to the sale of Stock of the Company during said sixty (60) day period, except transfers to family transferees, shall be rescinded by the parties or their respective personal representatives.[31]

## E.　AUTHORIZATION OF AGREEMENT

Where a corporation is a party to a shareholders' agreement, it is advisable to have the agreement formally approved by the board of directors and shareholders of the corporation.　Where a corporation is a party to the agreement as a shareholder of the subject corporation (rather than the subject corporation itself), approval by the board of directors alone is sufficient.　The precise language of the authorizing resolution should be determined in light of the applicable state law, but a form of resolution might be as follows:

**EXAMPLE:**

> "RESOLVED, that this Board of Directors hereby authorizes, empowers and directs the proper officers of this corporation to execute and deliver, and thereafter to perform, on behalf of this cor-

31.　What is the purpose of sample provision H–2?

poration, a certain agreement among this corporation and John Smith, John Brown and Jean Jones, providing, *inter alia,* for the purchase of shares of stock of this corporation by this corporation under certain circumstances, a copy of which agreement is attached hereto and incorporated herein by reference."

It is also generally considered prudent, because one does not know when courts will hold otherwise, to insert language along the following lines at the very end of a shareholders' agreement following the signatures of the shareholders and the corporation. It is a waiver of any rights of a non-shareholder spouse to object to the agreement and its provisions.

"Each of the undersigned hereby acknowledges that he or she has read and approves the foregoing Agreement dated January 12, 19___, by and among Thomas Brown, Alice Brown, Joseph Brown and Brown Company, Inc., and each of the undersigned, intending to be legally bound hereby, covenants and agrees to be bound by its restrictions, terms and conditions in the event he or she should acquire, by virtue of death or otherwise, any interest in any shares of stock of Brown Company, Inc., now owned by his or her spouse or hereafter acquired by such spouse.

_____[*Seal*]
Mary Brown
_____[*Seal*]
Harold Brown
_____[*Seal*]"
Ruth Brown

## F.  "BOILER PLATE" CLAUSES

"Boiler plate clauses" for a certain type of agreement are those clauses which are generally found in substantially identical language in all agreements of that type. Many of the boiler plate clauses in shareholders' agreements are found in many other agreements as well. The subject matter of the various boiler plate clauses in shareholders' agreements follows:

(1) As required by the Uniform Commercial Code,[32] the face of the stock certificates representing the shares within the scope of the agreement must be prominently marked with a legend indicating the restrictions on transfer to place prospective transferees on notice of the existence of restrictions; [33]

(2) Neither the shareholders nor the company may assign, transfer, pledge or otherwise encumber or dispose of any of their rights or obligations under the agreement; [34]

32. See Section III.B of Chapter Eight for a description of the Uniform Commercial Code.

33. See, for example, paragraph 11 of Form Agreement 1 and paragraph I of Form Agreements 2 and 3.

34. See paragraph J of Form Agreements 2 and 3.

(3) Specific enforcement is an available remedy for breach of the agreement; [35]

(4) The agreement may not be modified or amended other than by an agreement in writing; [36]

(5) The agreement is binding upon the parties and their respective personal representatives, successors and assigns; [37]

(6) All notices must be in writing and sent to the addresses specified in the agreement; [38]

(7) Paragraph headings are for convenience only and do not form a part of the agreement; [39] and

(8) The law of a particular jurisdiction controls the interpretation and enforceability of the agreement.[40]

Samples of these provisions may be found in the Form Agreements which follow. In order to understand more general rules of drafting agreements, see the comments to Form Agreement 1 of Chapter Nine. Many of the considerations discussed therein are equally applicable to shareholders' agreements.

A checklist of considerations in drafting shareholders' agreements is included at the end of this Chapter. It should be reviewed and retained for future reference.

## PROBLEMS FOR REVIEW

Smitty Corp. has an authorized capital of 100 shares of common stock, par value $1.00 per share. John Smith owns 70 shares and Harry Smith, his younger brother, owns 30 shares. In discussing a shareholders' agreement, John Smith, the dominant brother, rejects the concept of a right of first refusal based upon a bona fide written offer. John says that it is impossible to negotiate for a bona fide written offer, when the offeror knows that after expending the time and expense, including legal

---

35. See paragraph J of Form Agreements 2 and 3.

36. For example, see paragraph K of Form Agreements 2 and 3. However, some courts may not enforce this provision in view of statutes such as the Statute of Frauds, which has been enacted in many states. The Statute of Frauds defines what agreements must be in writing in order to be enforceable. In view of this, why would we put this provision in the agreement? What benefit does it have if it is enforceable?

37. See paragraph L of Form Agreements 2 and 3. Would the agreement be binding upon such persons without such a provision?

38. See paragraph M of Form Agreements 2 and 3. What purpose does the paragraph serve? Is a notice effective if it is oral and not in writing?

39. See paragraph N of Form Agreements 2 and 3. For whose benefit is this provision included? Why is it important to include such a provision?

40. See paragraph O of Form Agreements 2 and 3. See also the comments to Form Agreement 1 in Chapter Nine relating to Employment Agreements.

fees, of investigating the corporation and preparing an offer, the shares will be bought out by the other shareholder at a stipulated low value. It is John's view, therefore, that if either shareholder desires to sell his interest, he should first offer all of his shares at book value to the other shareholder; if the other shareholder does not purchase them, the offering shareholder is then free to find a buyer at the same or a higher price at any time during the ensuing year. Harry agrees with this approach. John also feels that insofar as it was he that built up the business, he should have the right to buy out Harry at book value at any time he pleases. Harry agrees with this proposition, but points out a problem. Suppose John learns of a buyer who is willing to pay a considerable amount of money for all of the stock of the company. John might be tempted to exercise his right to purchase Harry's shares at book value, and then turn around and sell all of the stock to the prospective purchaser at a much higher price. John agrees that he should not have that right, and that if he should reach any agreement to sell substantially all of the stock of the Company within a year following the exercise of his call on Harry's shares, that Harry should have the option to return the price paid to him by John in exchange for 30% (i. e., his former interest) of the consideration received by John upon the subsequent sale. Both brothers are satisfied with the foregoing, and you are asked to prepare the sections relating to restrictions on transfer of stock during lifetime in accordance with the foregoing. In drafting the section, you can refer to book value without defining it, on the assumption that it is defined elsewhere in the agreement. Any problems that you anticipate in drafting should be pointed out in your answer.

## EXAMPLE—Form Agreement 1

### Special Features:

    **A.**     Straightforward agreement for Company with only two shareholders. Spouses join as parties. Transfers to spouses permitted.

    **B.**     Price to be determined yearly and then adjusted based upon changes in book value.

    **C.**     Short form of a covenant not to compete, specific performance provision and arbitration provision.

### SHAREHOLDERS RESTRICTIVE AGREEMENT

AGREEMENT made this 1st day of January, 19__ by and between Albert Able and Benjamin Baker (hereinafter referred to individually as "Shareholder" and jointly as "Shareholders"), Alice A. Able and Betty B. Baker (the respective spouses of the Shareholders and hereinafter referred to individually as "Spouse" and jointly as "Spouses"), and AB corporation (hereinafter referred to as the "Company").

WITNESSETH:

The Company is a Pennsylvania corporation having an authorized capitalization of 100,000 shares of Common Stock, par value $10.00 per share (the "Stock"), 40,000 shares of which are issued and outstanding. Each Shareholder now owns 20,000 shares of the Stock.

Shareholders desire to impose certain restrictions on their right to transfer Stock and otherwise to establish certain rights between themselves.

NOW, THEREFORE, in consideration of the mutual covenants contained herein, the parties hereto, each intending to be legally bound hereby, agree as follows:

1. *Restriction on Transfer.* (a) Shareholders shall not sell, assign, transfer, give, donate, pledge, deposit, alien, or otherwise encumber or dispose of any Stock now or hereafter held by them, except as permitted by this Agreement and in accordance with its terms.

(b) The Company shall not cause or permit the transfer of any shares of the Stock to be made on its books unless the transfer is permitted by this Agreement and has been made in accordance with its terms.

2. *Inter Vivos Sale.*[41] (a) If either Shareholder shall receive a bona fide written offer for the purchase of all, but not less than all, of the Stock owned by him which such Shareholder desires to accept (hereinafter referred to as the "Selling Shareholder"), the Company and the other Shareholder shall have options, as hereinafter described, to purchase all of the Stock of the Selling Shareholder.

(b) The option price for all Stock owned by Selling Shareholder shall be the higher of (1) the price contained in such bona fide written offer, or (2) $10.00 per share, as adjusted pursuant to Paragraph 5.

(c) The Selling Shareholder shall give the Company and the other Shareholder written notice of the receipt by him of the above mentioned offer, together with a copy of said offer and a statement as to the identity of the real party in interest making the offer. The Company shall have a period of twenty (20) days from the receipt of such written notice to exercise in writing its option to purchase all of the Stock owned by the Selling Shareholder.

---

41. The term "inter vivos" means between the living.

(d) If the Company does not exercise its option in full, the other Shareholder shall have a period of ten (10) additional days beyond the twenty-day period mentioned in Paragraph 2(c) to exercise in writing his option to purchase any of the Stock owned by the Selling Shareholder not theretofore purchased by the Company.

(e) If the Company and the other Shareholder fail to exercise the options herein granted in full, the Selling Shareholder may accept the offer referred to in Paragraph 2(a) and, pursuant thereto, may dispose of all of his Stock free and clear of all the restrictions, terms and conditions of this Agreement.[42] However, if such offer made to Selling Shareholder is not accepted by him within thirty (30) days after the expiration of the options herein granted to the Company and to the other Shareholder, and the closing of said sale is not held within thirty (30) days thereafter or in accordance with the terms of the offer, whichever is the earlier, the Selling Shareholder may not thereafter transfer any of his Stock in the Company without again complying with the provisions of this Paragraph 2.

3. *Sale Associated with Legal Proceedings Against Any Shareholder.* (a) In the event that (1) voluntary proceedings by, or involuntary proceedings against, any Shareholder are commenced under any provision of any federal or state act relating to bankruptcy or insolvency, or (2) the Stock of any Shareholder is attached or garnished, or (3) any judgment is obtained in any legal or equitable proceeding against any Shareholder and the sale of his Stock is contemplated or threatened under legal process as a result of such judgment, or (4) any execution process is issued against any Shareholder or against his Stock or (5) any other form of legal proceedings or process is threatened or commenced, by which the Stock of any Shareholder may be sold either voluntarily or involuntarily, then the Company, and, alternatively, the other Shareholder, are hereby granted options, as hereinafter described, to purchase from such Shareholder, or his successor in interest, as the case may be, all, but not less than all, of the Stock owned by such Shareholder prior to such event. The price to be paid shall be $10.00 per share, as adjusted pursuant to Paragraph 5, for each share of such Shareholder's Stock.

(b) The Company shall have a period of forty (40) days from the date on which it receives actual notice of the event which gives rise to such option to exercise in writing its option.

---

**42.** Contrast this provision with paragraph A–6 of Form Agreement 2. What considerations go into the selection of one of these approaches?

(c) In the event the Company does not exercise its option in full, the other Shareholder shall have a period of twenty (20) additional days beyond the forty-day period mentioned in Paragraph 3(b) to exercise in writing his option.

4. *Death of a Shareholder.* Upon the death of either Shareholder (hereinafter called the "Deceased Shareholder") [43], the other Shareholder shall purchase, and the Deceased Shareholder's estate shall sell all, but not less than all, of the Stock which had been owned by the Deceased Shareholder at the time of his death at a price of $10.00 per share, as adjusted pursuant to Paragraph 5, for all of the Deceased Shareholder's Stock.

5. *Adjustment of Purchase Price.* After October 31st and on or before December 15th of each year following execution of this Agreement, the Shareholders shall redetermine the prices to be paid pursuant to Paragraphs 2, 3 and 4 in a writing signed by the Shareholders. Each such determination of the purchase price shall prevail until a new purchase price shall have been determined, except that it shall be adjusted to the extent of the increase or decrease in the "Book Value" (as hereinafter defined) of the shares of Stock from October 31st of the year in which a determination was last made to the end of the month in which a Shareholder receives an offer to purchase his Stock, an event specified in Paragraph 3 occurs, or a Shareholder dies, as the case may be. Shareholders shall cause the most current written determination to be attached to the copy of this Agreement kept on file at the Company's registered office. Until the first redetermination hereunder is made, the prices specified in Paragraphs 2, 3 and 4 of this Agreement shall, for purposes of this paragraph, be deemed to have been determined as October 31, 19__.

6. *Terms and Conditions of Sale.* (a) In the event of a sale of Stock to the Company or either Shareholder pursuant to Paragraph 2 hereof, twenty-five percent (25%) of the total purchase price shall be paid in cash or by certified check at closing and the balance by the delivery of a negotiable note providing for payment of the balance in twenty-four (24) equal, successive monthly installments, with the first such installment due one (1) month after the date of the closing. The note shall bear interest at the rate of six per cent (6%) per annum, shall provide for acceleration of the remaining balance in the event of default, and shall give

---

43. Notice how creating the defined term "Deceased Shareholder" simplifies and shortens the agreement where the concept is needed later on.

the maker the right to prepay all or any part of the remaining balance without penalty, any such prepayment of less than all of the remaining balance to be applied to the payments last becoming due.

(b) In the event of a sale of stock to the Company or either Shareholder pursuant to Paragraph 3 hereof, the total purchase price shall be paid by the delivery of a negotiable note, containing the provisions set forth in Paragraph 6(a) hereof, except that the note shall be payable in sixty (60) equal, successive monthly installments.[44]

(c) In the event of a sale of Stock pursuant to Paragraph 4 hereof, the purchase price shall be paid in cash or by certified check at closing.

(d) Closing shall be held at such time and place as may be mutually agreed by the parties to the transaction, but in default of such agreement, closing shall take place at the offices of the Company at 2:00 p. m. on the 60th day after the date of exercise of the option if the sale is pursuant to Paragraph 2 or 3, or on the 10th day after the receipt of the life insurance proceeds or the 90th day after the death of Deceased Shareholder, whichever is later, if the sale is pursuant to Paragraph 4; provided, however, that if such day is a Saturday, Sunday, or legal holiday in the Commonwealth of Pennsylvania the closing shall take place at such time and place on the next business day.

(e) At closing, the Stock being sold shall be delivered to the purchaser properly endorsed for transfer and with all necessary transfer tax stamps affixed, if any, and if the sale is pursuant to Paragraph 4, with all necessary evidence of the authority of the persons completing the sale on behalf of the Deceased Shareholder's estate.

7. *Determination of Book Value.* "Book Value" per share shall be determined by the Company's regularly employed certified public accountant in accordance with generally accepted accounting principles, applied on a basis consistent with that of the preceding year, as of the applicable date for which such determination is to be made, and such determination shall be conclusive and binding upon all of the parties affected by it. No value for goodwill, firm name or any other intangible shall be included in Book Value, nor shall any independent appraisal or valuation of the Company's assets be made.

44. What is the basis for the different payment terms for a purchase under paragraph 3 as contrasted to paragraph 2? Under paragraph 4 as contrasted to paragraphs 2 and 3?

8. *Covenant Not to Compete.* No Shareholder, so long as he holds any Stock and for a period of three (3) years thereafter, shall engage, as principal, partner, agent, employee, shareholder, director, officer, or in any other manner or capacity, or have any financial interest, in any business which is competitive to that of the Company.

9. *Specific Performance.* The parties agree that any violation of this Agreement (other than a default in the payment of money), cannot be compensated for by damages, and any aggrieved party shall have the right, and is hereby granted the privilege, of obtaining specific performance of this Agreement in any court of competent jurisdiction in the event of any breach hereunder.

10. *Transfers Between Shareholders and to Spouses.* Notwithstanding anything else in this Agreement to the contrary, each Shareholder may transfer all or any part of his Stock to the other Shareholder or to his Spouse or the Spouse of the other Shareholder. If any Stock is transferred to a Spouse, such Stock shall, for all purposes of this Agreement, be deemed to be owned by the Shareholder and shall be subject to purchase by the Company or other Shareholder pursuant to Paragraphs 2, 3 and 4 as if owned by the Shareholder.

11. *Stock Certificates to be Marked with Legend.* The face of all certificates of stock now or hereafter issued by the Company shall be marked with the following legend:

"This certificate of stock and the shares represented thereby are held subject to the terms, covenants and conditions of a certain agreement among this company and its then shareholders, dated January 1, 19___, and all amendments thereto, and may not be transferred except in accordance with the terms and provisions thereof."

12. *Arbitration.* In the event of any dispute whatsoever arising as to the interpretation of any provision of this Agreement or arising as to the rights, duties or obligations of any of the parties hereto in connection with any provision of this Agreement, such dispute shall be submitted to arbitration in accordance with the rules then obtaining of the American Arbitration Association in Philadelphia, Pennsylvania, and any decision made in accordance with such rules shall be binding on all parties in interest.

13. *Notices.* (a) All notices required or permitted to be given to any of the Shareholders pursuant to any of the terms hereof shall be sent by registered or certified mail,

return receipt requested, postage prepaid, addressed to the following addresses of the Shareholders:

| Albert Able | | Harold Lawyer, Esq. |
| 1 Main Street | with a copy to | 3 Bay Street |
| Philadelphia, Pa. | | Philadelphia, Pa. |
| | | |
| Benjamin Baker | | Joan Barrister, Esq. |
| 2 Second Street | with a copy to | 14 Sage Place |
| Philadelphia, Pa. | | Philadelphia, Pa. |

(b) All notices required or permitted to be given to the Company pursuant to any of the terms hereof shall be sent by registered or certified mail, return receipt requested, postage prepaid, addressed to the Company at 2600 Market Street, Philadelphia, Pennsylvania.

(c) All notices required or permitted to be given to the personal representative or heirs of a Deceased Shareholder pursuant to any of the terms hereof shall be given by registered or certified mail, return receipt requested, addressed to the last address of the Deceased Shareholder appearing on the records of the Company, or to such address as may have been supplied in writing and received by the Company from the personal representative of said Deceased Shareholder.

(d) Either of the Shareholders or the Company may change his or its address for notice purposes by notice given to the other parties hereto in accordance with the provisions of this paragraph.

14. *Joinder of Spouses.* The Spouses of the Shareholders have joined in this Agreement for the purpose of acknowledging that they have full knowledge of its contents and that they approve the prices which are agreed upon herein, and approve specifically the provisions of Paragraph 5, providing for redetermination of the prices by future action of the Shareholders, and the provisions of Paragraph 10, providing for the treatment of any Stock transferred to a Spouse as if it were still owned by the Shareholder, including purchase by the Company or other Shareholder pursuant to Paragraphs 2, 3 and 4.

15. *General.* (a) The masculine pronoun, wherever used herein, shall be construed to include the feminine and the neuter where appropriate. The singular form, wherever used herein, shall be construed to include the plural, where appropriate.

(b) All rights, obligations, duties, restrictions and qualifications herein provided for shall inure to and be binding upon the parties hereto, and each of their heirs, personal representatives, successors and assigns, and upon all Shareholders of the Company whether they become such by the exercise or any rights or options hereunder or by transfer pursuant to or contrary to the terms of this Agreement.

(c) In computing a number of days for any purpose of this Agreement, all days shall be counted including Saturdays, Sundays and holidays.

(d) The headings of paragraphs in this Agreement are for convenience only; they form no part of this Agreement and shall not affect its interpretation.

(e) This writing represents the entire agreement and understanding of the parties with respect to the subject matter hereof; it may not be altered or amended except by an agreement in writing.

(f) In the event that any provision hereof shall be unenforceable, the agreement shall continue in full force and effect and construed as if such unenforceable provision had never been contained herein.

(g) This agreement shall be governed by and construed in accordance with the laws of the Commonwealth of Pennsylvania.

IN WITNESS WHEREOF, Company has caused this Agreement to be executed by its President and its corporate seal affixed, duly attested by its Secretary, and Shareholders and Spouses have hereunto set their hands and seals, the date and year first above written.

AB CORPORATION

Attest:

_____          By: _____
Secretary                                          President

SHAREHOLDERS AND SPOUSES
_____ [Seal]
Albert Able
_____ [Seal]
Alice A. Able
_____ [Seal]
Benjamin Baker
_____ [Seal]
Betty B. Baker

**EXAMPLE—Form Agreement 2**

**Special Features:**

**A.** Three equal shareholders. Transfers permitted to spouse, adult children and trusts for their benefit, who must agree in writing to be bound by agreement and to grant irrevocable proxy to transferor shareholder.

**B.** Mandatory purchase upon death.

**C.** Purchase price to be price in offer, the agreed value or book value.

**D.** Life insurance provision.

**E.** Management provisions.

**F.** Agreement terminates upon the occurrence of one of several specified events.

**G.** If all shareholders die within short time of each other, all transfers are rescinded.

AGREEMENT made this 31st day of July, 19___, by and among THOMAS BROWN, ALAN BROWN and JOSEPH BROWN (hereinafter referred to collectively as "Stockholders" and individually as "Stockholder") and BROWN COMPANY, INC., a Delaware corporation (hereinafter referred to as the "Company"),

### WITNESSETH:

The Company is a Delaware corporation having an authorized capitalization of 500,000 shares of Common Stock, par value $.10 per share; and

WHEREAS, there are presently outstanding 75,000 shares of Common Stock, of which each Stockholder owns 25,000 shares; and

WHEREAS, the Stockholders and the Company wish to enter into an agreement respecting limitations on the transfer of shares of stock in the Company, respecting disposition of such shares upon the death of a Stockholder, and certain other matters;

NOW, THEREFORE, in consideration of the premises and the mutual covenants, conditions and agreements herein contained, the parties hereto, each intending to be legally bound hereby, agree as follows:

### A.  Restrictions on Transfer of Stock

**A–1.** No Stockholder will sell, assign, transfer, give, donate, pledge or otherwise encumber or dispose of any of the shares of common stock (the "Stock") in the Company now owned or hereafter acquired by him, except as permitted by this Agreement and in accordance with its terms.

**A–2.** The Company, by its execution of this Agreement, agrees that it will not cause or permit the transfer of any common stock to be made on its books except in accordance with the terms of this Agreement. The Company further agrees not to issue any common stock, whether by original issue or in connection with the sale of common stock now or hereafter held in the Company's treasury.

**A–3.** If any Stockholder receives a bona fide written offer to purchase all of his shares of Stock in the Company which offer he desires to accept (said offeree hereinafter sometimes referred to as "Selling Stockholder"), he may transfer such Stock to the bona fide offeror as hereinafter provided only if he complies with the provisions of Paragraphs A–4 and A–5.

**A–4.** Within five (5) days after receiving such a bona fide offer, which he desires to accept, the Selling Stockholder shall notify the Company and each of the other Stockholders in writing of the receipt thereof, together with a copy of such offer, and of his desire to accept the offer. The Company shall have the option, exercisable within thirty (30) days of receipt of such notice, to purchase from the Selling Stockholder all or any part of the shares of Stock in the Company owned by him at the price and upon the terms set forth in Paragraph D–1 hereof; provided, however, that the option to purchase less than all of the shares of Stock owned by the Selling Stockholder shall not be effective unless the other Stockholders purchase the shares of stock of the Selling Stockholder not purchased by the Company. The Company shall exercise its option by giving written notice of its election to the Selling Stockholder and to each of the other Stockholders, specifying the number of shares of Stock, if less than all, the Company has elected to purchase from the Selling Stockholder. If the Company does not notify the Selling Stockholder or the other Stockholders of its election to purchase shares of stock of the Selling Stockholder within said 30-day period, it shall be deemed to have not exercised its purchase option.

**A–5.** If the Company has elected to purchase none or less than all of the shares of Stock of the Selling Stockholder, the other Stockholders shall have the option to purchase the shares of Stock of the Selling Stockholder not purchased by the Company (the "Remaining Stock") in such proportions as may be agreed upon between them. The exercise of such option shall be reflected in a written notice signed by all of the other Stockholders and delivered to the Selling Stockholder and the Company within ten (10) days after the end of the above-mentioned 30-day period. If an agreement among the other Stockholders cannot be reached, then each Stockholder shall have the right, by giving written notice thereof to the Company and all other Stockholders, including the Selling Stockholder, during the next 10-day period, to purchase all or any part of that proportion of the Remaining Stock as the number of shares of Stock owned by him bears to the total number of shares of Stock owned by all of the Stockholders other than the Selling Stockholder. If the other Stockholders elect to purchase less than all of the Remaining Stock, then the Stockholder who elected to purchase the maximum number permissible pursuant to the preceding sentence shall have the further right, by giving written notice thereof to the Company and all other Stockholders, including the Selling Stockholder, during the next 10-day period to purchase the shares of Stock of the Selling Stockholder not theretofore purchased. Shares purchased pursuant to this Paragraph A–5 will be at the price and on the terms set forth in Paragraph D–1.

**A–6.** If the Company and the other Stockholders do not elect to purchase all of the Stock of the Selling Stockholder pursuant to Paragraphs A–4 and A–5, above, no elections to purchase a portion of such Stock shall be effective and the Selling Stockholder shall have the right to sell all, but not less than all, of the shares of Stock covered by the bona fide offer on the terms set forth in such bona fide offer, provided that such sale shall be consummated and the shares of Stock transferred to the offeror within thirty (30) days after expiration of the options granted in Paragraph A–5, and provided further that such purchaser shall agree in writing, prior to such transfer, with the Company and the other then living Stockholders, to be bound by all of the terms and provisions of this Agreement as though such purchaser were an original signatory hereto.

**A–7.** Notwithstanding anything foregoing in this Section A, each Stockholder shall have the right to sell or make gifts of up to forty percent (40%) of his Stock in the aggregate to his wife, his adult children or trusts for the sole benefit of his wife, his children and their issue (said wife, children and trusts hereinafter collectively referred to as "Family Transferees"); provided, however, that shares of Stock owned by a Family Transferee shall, during the lifetime of the Stockholder transferor, be deemed to be shares of stock owned by such Stockholder transferor for purposes of Paragraphs A–3 through A–6; and provided further, that a Family Transferee may not, during the lifetime of the Stockholder transferor, sell, assign, transfer, give, donate, pledge or otherwise encumber or dispose of any shares of Stock in the Company owned by such Family Transferee except (a) to the Stockholder transferor or (b) together with all Stock owned by the Stockholder transferor and by all other of such Stockholder's Family Transferees, pursuant to Paragraphs A–3 through A–6. Prior to any transfer of shares of Stock to a Family Transferee, said Family Transferee shall (a) agree in writing with the Company and the then living Stockholders to be bound by all of the terms and provisions of this Agreement relating to Family Transferees, and (b) grant to the Stockholder transferor an irrevocable proxy for the lifetime of the Stockholder transferor, satisfactory in form and substance to the Company's counsel as constituting a "proxy coupled with an interest," which irrevocable proxy such Stockholder transferor hereby agrees in advance he will not surrender or release during his lifetime.[45]

## B.  Dispositions Upon Death

**B–1.**  Upon the death of a Stockholder, the Company shall purchase from the personal representatives of the deceased Stockholder and from all Family Transferees of such deceased Stockholder, and the personal representatives of the deceased Stockholder and all Family Transferees of such deceased Stockholder shall sell to the Company, all of the shares of Stock in the Company owned by the deceased Stockholder and his Family Transferees, at the price and upon the terms set forth in Paragraph D–2, and the surviving Stockholders and their Family Transferees shall adopt such resolutions and take such action as may be required by law to authorize such purchase at such time.

**B–2.**  If the purchase price to be paid to the personal representatives of the deceased Stockholder and the Family Transferees of the deceased Stockholder is in excess of the then existing aggregate of capital surplus and earned surplus of the Company, each of the surviving Stockholders and their Family Transferees shall be obligated to make a contribution in cash to the capital of the Company, five (5) or more days prior to the settlement date set forth in Paragraph D–2, in an amount equal to that proportion of the amount by which the purchase price exceeds the aggregate of capital surplus and earned surplus which the number of shares of Stock in the Company owned by such surviving Stockholder or Family Transferee bears to the number of shares of Stock in the Company owned by all of the surviv-

45. For a description generally of proxies, see Chapter Seven, Section II.A.6. A "proxy coupled with an interest" is, contrary to the general rule, not revocable. An "interest" is a relationship between the granter and recipient of the proxy, such as debtor-creditor or donor-donee, which may render the proxy irrevocable. Is such a proxy irrevocable forever?

ing Stockholders and their Family Transferees. Should any Family Transferee of a surviving Stockholder fail to make the required capital contribution as aforesaid, such Stockholder shall forthwith make such contribution on behalf of the defaulting Family Transferee.

**B–3.** Upon the death of a Family Transferee, the Stockholder transferor shall, unless the shares of Stock owned by such deceased Family Transferee are bequeathed outright or pass by intestacy to such Stockholder or to one or more of his existing Family Transferees, purchase from the personal representatives of the deceased Family Transferee, and the personal representatives of the deceased Family Transferee shall sell to such Stockholder, all of the shares of Stock in the Company owned by such deceased Family Transferee. Such purchase shall be made within thirty (30) days of the death of the Family Transferee and shall be at a price of $1.00 per share, payable in cash or by certified check at settlement, unless some other price and/or terms have been previously agreed to between such Stockholder and the deceased Family Transferee or some other price is agreed to between such Stockholder and the personal representatives of the deceased Family Transferee within the aforesaid thirty-day period.

## C. Further Option

**C–1.** In the event that any Stockholder shall be adjudicated a bankrupt or make an assignment for the benefit of creditors, or bankruptcy, insolvency, reorganization, arrangement, debt adjustment, liquidation or receivership proceedings in which such Stockholder is alleged to be insolvent or unable to pay his debts as they mature are instituted by or against such Stockholder and, if instituted against such Stockholder, such Stockholder shall consent thereto or admit in writing the material allegations of the petitions filed in said proceedings or said proceedings shall remain undismissed for sixty (60) days, or the Stock of such Stockholder in the Company is attached, or any judgment is obtained in any legal or equitable proceeding against such Stockholder and the sale of his Stock in the Company is contemplated or threatened under legal process as a result of such judgment, or any execution process is issued against such Stockholder or against his Stock in the Company, or any other form of legal proceeding or process is instituted by which the Stock of such Stockholder in the Company may be sold either voluntarily or involuntarily, then the Company shall have the option to buy forthwith such Stockholder's Stock in the Company. The purchase shall be at the price and upon the terms set forth in Paragraph D–2 hereof.

**C–2.** In the event of financial difficulties, as described in Paragraph C–1, of a Family Transferee, the Stockholder transferor shall forthwith, upon notice of such financial difficulties, purchase all of such Family Transferee's Stock in the Company for cash or by certified check at the Agreed Value per share. Upon his failure to do so within twenty (20) days of learning of such Family Transferee's financial difficulties as described in Paragraph C–1, the Company shall have the option to purchase all of such Family Transferee's stock in the Company, at the price and upon the terms set forth in Paragraph D–2.

### D. Purchase Price and Terms

**D–1.** Settlement for the purchase by the Company or by a Stockholder of shares of Stock in the Company pursuant to the options granted in Paragraphs A–4 and A–5, respectively, shall be made within sixty (60) days from the date of exercise of the option. At the option of the purchaser, the purchase price per share and the terms of payment shall be either (a) the price per share contained in the bona fide offer referred to in Paragraph A–3, payable upon the terms contained in said bona fide offer, or (b) the "Agreed Value" (as hereinafter defined) per share, payable in cash or by certified check at settlement, or (c) the "Book Value" (as hereinafter defined) per share payable in cash or by certified check at settlement.

**D–2.** Settlement for the purchase by the Company of shares of Stock in the Company pursuant to the obligations set forth in Sections B and C hereof shall be within sixty (60) days from the date of death of the deceased Stockholder with regard to Section B, or within sixty (60) days of the exercise of the option with regard to Section C. The purchase price per share shall be the higher of the Agreed Value per share or the Book Value per share with regard to Section B and the lesser of the Agreed Value per share or the Book Value per share with regard to Section C, payable with regard to Section B in cash or by certified check at settlement and payable with regard to Section C (i) twenty-five percent (25%) in cash or by certified check at settlement and (ii) seventy-five percent (75%) by note of the purchaser, bearing interest at the rate of six percent (6%) per annum, payable six (6) months from the date of settlement.

**D–3.** At settlement, the stock certificate or stock certificates representing the shares being sold shall be delivered by the seller to the purchaser or purchasers, duly endorsed for transfer, with the necessary documentary and transfer tax stamps, if any, affixed by the seller.

**D–4.** All settlements for the purchases and sales of shares of Stock shall, unless otherwise agreed to by all of the purchasers and sellers, be held at the principal executive offices of the Company during regular business hours. The precise date and hour of settlement shall be fixed by the purchaser or purchasers (within the time limits allowed by the provisions of this Agreement) by notice in writing to the seller or sellers given at least five (5) days in advance of the date specified. In the event that more than one purchaser is involved in a settlement and the purchasers cannot agree on a precise time of settlement, the precise time of settlement shall be fixed by the President of the Company by five (5) days' written notice to the purchasers and sellers.

### E. Agreed Value and Book Value

**E–1.** The "Agreed Value" of the Stock of the Company is hereby determined to be $1.00 per share, which determination shall remain in effect for a period of six (6) months from the date hereof. The parties may, from time to time, unanimously redetermine in writing the Agreed Value per share of the Stock, and each such written redetermination shall remain in effect for a period of six (6) months from the date of such written redetermination. There shall be no Agreed Value for the Stock at times more than twelve (12) months remote from a written determination of Agreed Value. No Family Transferee shall participate in the determinations of Agreed Value, but all Family Transferees shall be bound by such determinations thereof.

**E–2.** The "Book Value" per share of the Company's Stock shall be equal to the net assets of the Company (on a consolidated basis with subsidiaries, if any) on the date in question divided by the number of shares of Common Stock of the Company outstanding on such date, as determined by the Company's regularly engaged independent public accountants in accordance with generally accepted accounting principles and practices applied on a basis consistent with prior years. For purposes of Paragraph D–1 hereof, the Book Value shall be determined as of the close of the fiscal year preceding exercise of the option pursuant to Paragraph A–4 or A–5 hereof, unless such option is exercised more than 100 days following the close of such fiscal year, in which case the Book Value shall be determined as of the end of the month preceding the month in which the option was exercised. For purposes of Paragraph D–2 hereof the Book Value shall be determined as of the close of the fiscal year preceding the date of death (with respect to Section B) or the date of exercise of the option (with respect to Section C), unless such date of death or exercise of option is more than 100 days following the close of such fiscal year, in which case the Book Value shall be determined as of the end of the month preceding the date of death (with respect to Section B) or the date of exercise of the option (with respect to Section C).

### F. Insurance

The Company shall promptly obtain and maintain in force for the duration of this Agreement, as owner and as beneficiary, a policy of life insurance insuring the life of each Stockholder for $50,000. The parties acknowledge that the principal purpose for such life insurance is to fund the purchase by the Company of the Stock of a deceased Stockholder; accordingly, the Company shall, as and when appropriate, increase the amount of life insurance on the life of each Stockholder so as to be reasonably certain of having sufficient net proceeds from such policies to redeem completely a deceased Stockholder's interest in accordance with the terms of this Agreement. Any proceeds from such life insurance policies received by the Company shall be held by Company in trust for the purposes of this Agreement. The Company shall pay all premiums on such life insurance policies, and it shall be a provision of each of such policies that each Stockholder shall be notified by the insurance company, before the expiration of any grace period, of the failure of the Company to pay the necessary premiums.

### G. Certain Provisions with Regard to Management of the Company

G–1. The Stockholders agree that promptly following execution of this Agreement they shall:

(a) Elect Thomas Brown, Alan Brown and Joseph Brown to the Board of Directors of the Company; a transferee of shares pursuant to Paragraph A–6 shall not, by virtue of acquiring the stock interest of a Stockholder, be entitled to election to the Board of Directors of the Company.

**(b)** Use their best efforts to cause the following persons to be elected, so long as they are Stockholders, as the only officers of the Company:

| | |
|---|---|
| President | — Thomas Brown |
| Sales Vice President | — Alan Brown |
| Manufacturing Vice President | — Joseph Brown |
| Treasurer | — Thomas Brown |
| Secretary | — Joseph Brown |

**(c)** Use their best efforts [46] to cause the following officers
to receive the following annual compensation:

| | |
|---|---|
| President | — $30,000 |
| Sales Vice President | — $22,500 |
| Manufacturing Vice President | — $20,000 |
| Treasurer | — None |
| Secretary | — None |

**(d)** Adopt by-laws containing provisions to effect the provisions of Paragraph G–2 hereof, and a provision fixing the size of the Board of Directors at three (3) members.

**G–2.** The Stockholders agree that throughout the term of this Agreement, except with the unanimous consent in writing of the then living Stockholders who are not disqualified from voting pursuant to Paragraph G–3:

**(a)** The Company shall not merge, consolidate, liquidate, dissolve, sell all or substantially all of its assets out of the ordinary course of business, amend its Articles of Incorporation, incur any debt on which payment is due beyond one (1) year, incur any debt in excess of $50,000 or declare or pay dividends.

**(b)** Neither Thomas Brown, Alan Brown nor Joseph Brown will be removed from the Board of Directors while a Stockholder.

**(c)** The Company shall not remove from office the officers of the Company set forth in Paragraph G–1(b) hereof.

**(d)** The compensation of the officers of the Company shall not be changed, unless the ratios established in Paragraph G–1(c) are maintained, in which latter case

---

**46.** Note the difference in terminology between subparagraph (a) and (b) and (c). The Stockholders cannot agree to vote on matters within the province of the Directors. Directors are fiduciaries and have obligations not to fetter their ability to act. See Chapter Seven, Section II.B.6.

such compensation may be changed by vote of a majority of the Board of Directors.

(e) The by-laws of the Company will not be amended.

(f) The Company will not exercise any of its options pursuant to Sections A or C of this Agreement.

**G–3.** A Selling Stockholder pursuant to Section A, and his Family Transferees, shall not be entitled to vote, as stockholders or directors of the Company, on the question whether the Company should exercise its option pursuant to Paragraph A–4. A Stockholder whose shares of Stock of the Company may be purchased pursuant to Section C, and his Family Transferees, may not vote, as stockholders or directors of the Company, on the question whether the Company should exercise its option pursuant to Paragraph C–1.

## H. Term of Agreement

**H–1.** Unless terminated sooner by unanimous agreement in writing of the Company and the Stockholders then living, this Agreement shall terminate on the earlier of the following dates: (1) ten (10) years from the date hereof, (2) upon the death of the next to the last of the Stockholders, or (3) upon the receipt by the Company of the proceeds from a public distribution of securities of the Company.

**H–2.** Notwithstanding anything to the contrary contained in this Agreement, in the event that all of the Stockholders die within sixty (60) days of each other, then the provisions of this Agreement shall be of no further force and effect, and this Agreement shall terminate in all respects. Any and all transfers, payments or other action made or taken with respect to the sale of Stock of the Company during said sixty-day period, except transfers to Family Transferees, shall be rescinded by the parties or their respective personal representatives.[47]

## I. Stock Certificates to be Marked with Legend

All certificates of Stock now or hereafter issued by the Company shall be marked with the following legend:

"This certificate of stock and the shares represented hereby may not be transferred except in accordance with the provisions of a certain agreement dated July 31, 19___, and all amendments thereto, a

---

47. This provision is to prevent the undue burden of requiring payments for two purchases within a very short period of time.

copy of which Agreement and any amendment thereto is on file at the principal office of the Company."

## J.   Rights, Obligations and Remedies

Neither any Stockholder nor the Company may assign, transfer, pledge or otherwise encumber or dispose of any of his or its rights or obligations or both under this Agreement.  The rights and obligations under this Agreement and the remedies to enforce them, are joint and several as to each of the parties hereto, with each party being completely free to enforce any or all rights of obligations under this Agreement against any other party with or without the concurrence or joinder of any other party hereto.  The shares of capital stock of the Company are unique, and the damages which might result to any of the parties by breach of this Agreement by a party or parties or their personal representatives, successors, or assigns are difficult to determine, and therefore, in addition to all of the other remedies which may be available under applicable law, any party hereto shall have the right to equitable relief, including without limitation, the right to enforce specifically the terms of this Agreement by obtaining injunctive relief against any violation hereof, or otherwise.

## K.   Amendment, Modification, Termination

This Agreement may be amended, modified or terminated at any time or times by mutual agreement in writing executed by the Company and signed by all the Stockholders then living.  No such amendment, modification or termination, however, shall affect the right of any person to receive, or the obligation of any person to pay, on the terms and conditions of this Agreement, the purchase price for Stock sold pursuant to this Agreement prior to such amendment, modification or termination, or the right or obligation of any person to sell or purchase stock on the terms and conditions of this Agreement, if such purchase or sale is to occur hereunder immediately upon the death of a Stockholder and that Stockholder has in fact died prior to such amendment, modification or termination.

## L.   Representatives, Successors and Assigns

This Agreement shall be binding upon and inure to the benefit of the respective parties hereto, and their personal representatives, successors and assigns, including a Family Transferee of Stock of the Company pursuant to Paragraph A–6.

## M. Notices

Notices, requests, demands and other communications relating to this Agreement and the transactions contemplated herein shall be in writing and shall be deemed to have been duly given or made if mailed by United States registered or certified mail, postage prepaid, return receipt requested, addressed as follows:

(a) If to Brown Company, Inc.:

Attention: Thomas Brown, President
[NOTE: If Thomas Brown is the person directing the communication to the Company, then the communication shall be addressed to the Company to the attention of "Alan Brown, Vice President."]

(b) If to Thomas Brown:

(c) If to Alan Brown:

(d) If to Joseph Brown:

(e) Any addressee may designate a different address to which communications are to be sent, by giving notice of such change of address in conformity with the provisions of this paragraph for giving of notice. All communications shall be deemed to have been given as of the date mailed in accordance herewith.

## N. Headings and Miscellaneous

The paragraph headings in this Agreement are for convenience only; they form no part of this Agreement and shall not affect its interpretation. Words used herein, regardless of the number and gender specifically used, shall be deemed and construed to include any other number, singular or plural, and any other gender, masculine, feminine, or neuter, as the context requires. No indulgences extended by any party hereto to any other party shall be construed as a waiver of any breach on the part of such other party, nor shall any waiver of one breach be construed as a waiver of any rights or remedies with respect to any subsequent breach. This Agreement may be executed in any number of counterparts, each of which when so executed and delivered shall be deemed an original, and it shall not be necessary, in making proof of this Agreement, to produce or account for more than one counterpart.

## O. Controlling Law

This Agreement shall be governed by and construed in accordance with the laws of the Commonwealth of Pennsylvania.

### P.  Severability

In the event that any provision hereof shall be unenforceable, the Agreement shall continue in full force and effect and be construed as if such unenforceable provision had never been contained herein.

IN WITNESS WHEREOF, the parties hereto have executed this Agreement the day and year first above written.

Attest:                    BROWN COMPANY, INC.

By: _____ [*Seal*]

_____ [*Seal*]          President

Secretary

_____ [*Seal*]

Thomas Brown

_____ [*Seal*]

Alan Brown

_____ [*Seal*]

Joseph Brown

[*Corporate Seal*]

Each of the undersigned hereby acknowledges that she has read and approves the foregoing Agreement dated July 31, 19__, by and among Thomas Brown, Alan Brown, Joseph Brown and Brown Company, Inc., and each of the undersigned, intending to be legally bound hereby, hereby covenants and agrees to be bound by its restrictions, terms and conditions in the event she should acquire, by virtue of the death of her husband or otherwise, any interest in any shares of stock of Brown Company, Inc., now owned by her husband or hereafter acquired by him.

_____ [*Seal*]

Mary Brown

_____ [*Seal*]

Alice Brown

_____ [*Seal*]

Ruth Brown

### EXAMPLE—Form Agreement 3

**Special Features:**

    **A.**  One individual and a "group" of related shareholders. Individual has a "put" to the group. Each group member has an option as to any shares being offered by another group member.

    **B.**  Purchase price will depend upon who is the selling shareholder.

    **C.**  Prepayment permitted. Payments to individual are guaranteed pro-rata by group members.

**D.** Non-competition provision.

**E.** Insurance provision. Insurance can be purchased if selling shareholder is covered and sells all stock owned by such shareholder.

**F.** Long arbitration provision with arbitrators selected by each of parties to dispute.

**G.** Voting restricted on certain matters such as the Company's exercise of an option.

AGREEMENT made this 21st day of July, 19— by and among JOHN SMITH, HELEN SMITH and BILL SMITH (hereinafter sometimes referred to collectively as the "Smith Group"), and DAN JONES (hereinafter sometimes referred to as "Jones") (Jones and the members of the Smith Group are hereinafter sometimes referred to collectively as "Stockholders" and individually as "Stockholder"), and SMIJO CORP., a New York corporation (hereinafter referred to as the "Company").

### BACKGROUND OF AGREEMENT

The Company is a New York corporation having an authorized capitalization of 5,000 shares of common stock, par value $10 per share, of which 1,000 shares are issued and outstanding and owned as follows:

| Stockholder | No. of Shares |
|---|---|
| John Smith | 200 |
| Helen Smith | 300 |
| Bill Smith | 50 |
| Dan Jones | 450 |
| | 1,000 |

The Stockholders and the Company wish to enter into an agreement respecting limitations on the transfer of shares of stock in the Company, respecting disposition of such shares upon the death of a Stockholder, and certain other matters;

NOW, THEREFORE, in consideration of the premises and the mutual covenants, conditions and agreements herein contained, the parties hereto, each intending to be legally bound hereby, agree as follows:

#### A. Restrictions on Transfer of Stock

**A–1.** No Stockholder will sell, assign, transfer, give, donate, pledge or otherwise encumber or dispose of any shares of common stock in the Company now owned or hereafter acquired (the "Stock"), except as permitted by this Agreement and in accordance with its terms.

**A-2.** The Company, by its execution of this Agreement, agrees that it will not cause or permit the transfer of any common stock to be made on its books except in accordance with the terms of this Agreement. The Company further agrees not to issue any common stock, whether by original issue, or in connection with the sale of common stock now or hereafter held in the Company's treasury, or in connection with any transfer, except in accordance with the terms of this Agreement.

**A-3.** If Jones desires to dispose of any of his Stock during his lifetime, he shall make an offer in writing to the Company to sell such shares of his Stock to the Company, and shall at the same time deliver a copy of such written offer to each of the then living Smith Group Stockholders. Upon the Company's receipt of such notice, the Company shall have the option, exercisable for a 30-day period, to purchase from Jones all or, at the Company's option, a part of the Stock owned by Jones which is being offered for sale, at the price and upon the terms set forth in Paragraph D-1. The option shall be exercised by the Company's giving written notice of its election to do so to Jones and to the then living Smith Group Stockholders.

**A-4.** If the Company shall decide not to exercise in full its option to purchase, it shall give written notice of that fact to Jones and to the then living Smith Group Stockholders within the said 30-day period. Should the Company fail to give notice within the said 30-day period of its election to exercise the option as provided in Paragraph A-3, it shall be presumed conclusively that the Company has decided not to exercise the option. If, within the said 30-day period, the Company has not exercised in full the option or has decided not to exercise in full its option, as herein provided, the then living Smith Group Stockholders shall be obligated to purchase from Jones all of the Stock in the Company offered by him and not purchased by the Company pursuant to its option. Each then living Smith Group Stockholder shall purchase such proportionate part of Jones' Stock not purchased by the Company pursuant to its option which the number of shares of Stock in the Company owned by such Smith Group Stockholder bears to the total number of shares of Stock owned by all Smith Group Stockholders. Purchases shall be at the price and upon the terms set forth in Paragraph D-1.

**A-5.** If any Smith Group Stockholder receives a bona fide written offer to purchase all shares of Stock in the Company, which offer such Smith Group Stockholder desires to accept (said offeree hereinafter sometimes referred to as "Selling Stockholder"), the Selling Stockholder may transfer such Stock to the bona fide offeror as hereinafter provided only after compliance with the following provisions of this Section A.

**A–6.** Within five (5) days after receiving such a bona fide written offer, the Selling Stockholder shall notify each of the other then living Smith Group Stockholders and Jones, if then living, of the desire to accept the offer, and shall deliver to each of such Stockholders together with such notice, a copy of such offer. Upon receipt by the other Smith Group Stockholders of such notice, the other Smith Group Stockholders shall have the option to purchase from the Selling Stockholder, in such proportions as may be agreed upon between them, all of the shares of Stock in the Company owned by the Selling Stockholder at the price and upon the terms set forth in Paragraph D–1 hereof. The exercise of such option shall be reflected in a written notice signed by all of the other Smith Group Stockholders and delivered to the Selling Stockholder and to Jones within twenty (20) days after receipt of the above mentioned notice. If an agreement among the other Smith Group Stockholders cannot be reached, then each of the other Smith Group Stockholders shall have the option, exercisable by written notice to the Selling Stockholder and to Jones within twenty (20) days after the end of the above-mentioned 20-day period, to purchase such proportionate part of the Selling Stockholder's Stock which the number of shares of Stock in the Company owned by such purchasing Stockholder bears to the total number of shares of such Stock owned by all Smith Group Stockholders entitled to exercise the option.

In the event that one or more Smith Group Stockholders entitled to exercise an option pursuant to this Paragraph A–6 does not exercise his option, the Selling Stockholder shall immediately notify the purchasing Stockholder or Stockholders of such fact, and each purchasing Stockholder shall thereupon have a further 10-day period in which to agree to purchase that proportion of the Selling Stockholder's Stock not taken up by the exercise of the option mentioned in this Paragraph A–6 which the number of shares owned by such purchasing Stockholder bears to the total number of shares owned by all Stockholders who exercised in the first instance their option first mentioned in this Paragraph A–6.

In the event the balance of Selling Stockholder's Stock is not sold as aforesaid, the Selling Stockholder shall immediately notify Jones, if then living, of such fact and of the number of shares not covered by the options exercised to such time by the Smith Group Stockholders, and such notice shall constitute an option to Jones, exercisable by Jones within ten (10) days of receipt of such notice, to elect to purchase the balance of the shares not covered by the options exercised to such time, at the price and upon the terms set forth in Paragraph D–1 hereof. In the event the balance of Selling Stockholder's Stock is not sold as aforesaid, all of the options exercised pursuant to this Paragraph A–6 shall be deemed not to have been exercised.

**A–7.** If the options contained in Paragraph A–6 are not exercised for purchase of all of the Selling Stockholder's Stock offered for sale, then none of such options shall be deemed to have been exercised, and the Selling Stockholder shall have the right to sell all, but not less than all, of the shares of Stock, free of restrictions, covered by the bona fide offer on the terms set forth in such bona fide offer, provided that such sale shall be consummated and the shares of Stock transferred to the offeror within thirty (30) days after expiration of the option granted to Jones in Paragraph A–6.

**A–8.** Notwithstanding the provisions of Paragraphs A–3 and A–4 hereof, the Smith Group Stockholders shall not be obligated to purchase Jones' Stock pursuant to Paragraph A–4 if, within twenty (20) days from the expiration of the 30-day period referred to in Paragraphs A–3 and A–4 hereof, (1) the Board of Directors and stockholders of the Company adopt and do not thereafter rescind a resolution providing for the prompt liquidation and dissolution of the Company, and (2) Jones and his nominees are offered and are allowed to retain at least fifty percent (50%) representation on the Board of Directors of the Company until completion of dissolution.

## B.  Dispositions Upon Death

**B–1.** Upon the death of Jones, and for a period of thirty (30) days thereafter, the Company shall have the option, exercisable by notice in writing to Jones' personal representatives and to the then living Smith Group Stockholders, to purchase all or a part of the shares of Stock in the Company owned by Jones at the time of his death, at the price and upon the terms set forth in Paragraph D–2 hereof.

**B–2.** If the Company shall not exercise in full its option to purchase or shall decide not to do so, it shall notify the then living Smith Group Stockholders and Jones' personal representatives of that fact, and of the amount of the Stock as to which the Company has not exercised its option, within the said 30-day period. Should the Company fail to give any notice as aforesaid within the said 30-day period, it shall be presumed conclusively that the Company has decided not to exercise its option. Upon receipt of such notice or upon failure of the Company to give such notice, the then living Smith Group Stockholders shall be obligated to purchase, and Jones' personal representatives shall be obliged to sell, all of the Stock in the Company owned by Jones at the time of his death which is not purchased by the Company pursuant to its option under Paragraph B–1 hereof.

**B–3.** Each of the then living Smith Group Stockholders shall be obligated to purchase and shall purchase such proportionate part of Jones' Stock which the number of shares of Stock in the Company owned by such purchasing Stockholder bears to the total number of shares of such Stock owned by all then living Smith Group Stockholders. The purchase shall be at the price and upon the terms set forth in Paragraph D–2.

**B–4.** Upon the death of a Smith Group Stockholder, the surviving Smith Group Stockholders shall be obligated to purchase, and the personal representatives of the deceased Stockholder shall be obliged to sell, all of the Stock in the Company owned by the deceased Smith Group Stockholder at the time of death.

**B–5.** Each of the surviving Smith Group Stockholders shall be obligated to purchase such proportionate part of the deceased Stockholder's Stock which the number of shares of Stock in the Company owned by such purchasing stockholder bears to the total number of shares of such Stock owned by all surviving Smith Group Stockholders. The purchase shall be at the price and upon the terms set forth in Paragraph D–2.

**B–6.** Notwithstanding the provisions of Paragraphs B–2 and B–3 hereof, the surviving Stockholders upon the death of Jones shall not be obligated to purchase the Stock owned by Jones at the time of his death if, within sixty (60) days following the death of Jones, (1) the Board of Directors and stockholders of the Company adopt and do not thereafter rescind a resolution providing for the prompt liquidation and dissolution of the Company, (2) the Company, within thirty (30) days of the adoption of such resolution, makes a distribution of $100,000 to Jones' personal representatives in partial liquidation, and (3) the personal representatives of Jones are offered and are allowed to retain at least fifty percent (50%) representation on the Board of Directors of the Company until completion of dissolution.

### C.   Further Option

In the event that any Stockholder shall be adjudicated a bankrupt or make an assignment for the benefit of creditors, or bankruptcy, insolvency, reorganization, arrangement, debt adjustment, liquidation or receivership proceedings in which such Stockholder is alleged to be insolvent or unable to pay debts as they mature are instituted by or against such Stockholder and, if instituted against such Stockholder, such Stockholder shall consent thereto or admit in writing the material allegations of the petitions filed in said proceedings or said proceedings shall remain undismissed for sixty (60) days, or the Stock of such Stockholder in the Company is attached, or any judgment is obtained in any legal or equitable proceeding against such Stockholder and the sale of the Stock of such Stockholder in the Company is contemplated or threatened under legal process as a result of such judgment, or any execution process is issued against such Stockholder or against the Stock of such Stockholder in the Company, or any other form of legal proceeding or process is instituted by which the Stock of such Stockholder in the Company may be sold either voluntarily or involuntarily, then the Company shall have the option to buy forthwith such Stockholder's Stock in the Company. The purchase shall be at the price and upon the terms set forth in Paragraph D–2 hereof.

### D.   Purchase Price and Terms

**D–1.**   Settlement for the purchase by the Company or by a Stockholder of shares of Stock in the Company pursuant to Paragraph A–3 and/or A–4 hereof shall be made within sixty (60) days from the date of exercise of the option (if all of Jones' Stock being offered for sale is purchased pursuant to Paragraph A–3) or from the date of the partial exercise of the option or the expiration of the option, as the case may be (if all or a part of Jones' Stock being offered for sale is purchased pursuant to Paragraph A–4). The purchase price per share shall be the "Agreed Value" (as hereinafter defined) per share, payable in twenty (20) equal quarterly installments of principal, the first of which is to be paid at settlement. The unpaid balance of the purchase price shall bear interest at the rate of six percent (6%) per annum, payable quarterly when payments of principal are due.

Settlement for the purchase by the Company or by a Stockholder of shares of Stock in the Company pursuant to the options granted in Paragraph A–6 shall be made within sixty (60) days from the date of exercise of the option. At the option of the purchaser, the purchase price per share and the terms of payment shall be either (a) the price per share contained in the bona fide offer referred to in Paragraph A–5, payable upon the terms contained in said bona fide offer, or (b) the "Agreed Value" per share, payable in twenty (20) equal quarterly installments of principal, the first of which is to be paid at settlement, with interest on the unpaid balance of the purchase price at the rate of six percent (6%) per annum, payable quarterly when payments of principal are due.

**D–2.** Settlement for the purchase by the Company or by a Stockholder of shares of Stock in the Company pursuant to the obligations set forth in Sections B and C hereof shall be within sixty (60) days from the date of death of the deceased Stockholder with regard to Section B, or within sixty (60) days of the exercise of the option with regard to Section C. The purchase price per share shall be the Agreed Value per share. With respect to Section C, the purchase price shall be payable in twenty (20) equal quarterly installments of principal, the first of which is to be made at settlement. With regard to Section B, the purchase price shall be paid as follows: (a) If the Company is purchasing shares of Stock upon the death of Jones, the Company shall pay at settlement the full purchase price or $100,000, whichever is less; the unpaid balance of principal, if any, shall be payable in twenty (20) equal quarterly installments of principal, the first of which is to be paid three (3) months from the date of settlement; (b) If the surviving Stockholders are purchasing shares of Stock upon the death of Jones, they shall, on a pro rata basis, pay at settlement an amount equal to $100,000 reduced by the amount, if any, of the payment to be made at settlement by the Company pursuant to subparagraph (a) immediately above; the unpaid balance of principal, if any, shall be payable in twenty (20) equal quarterly installments of principal, the first of which is to be paid three (3) months from the date of settlement; (c) if the surviving Smith Group Stockholders are purchasing shares of Stock upon the death of a Smith Group Stockholder, the purchase price shall be paid in twenty (20) equal quarterly installments of principal, the first of which is to be paid at settlement. The unpaid balance of the purchase price pursuant to this Paragraph D–2 shall bear interest at the rate of six percent (6%) per annum, payable quarterly when payments of principal are due.

**D–3.** At settlement, the stock certificate or stock certificates representing the shares being sold shall be delivered by the seller to the purchaser or purchasers, duly endorsed for transfer, with the necessary documentary and transfer tax stamps, if any, affixed by the seller.

**D–4.** All settlements for the purchases and sales of shares of Stock shall, unless otherwise agreed to by all of the purchasers and sellers, be held at the principal executive offices of the Company during regular business hours. The precise date and hour of settlement shall be fixed by the purchaser or purchasers (within the time limits allowed by the provisions of this Agreement) by notice in writing to the seller or sellers given at least five (5) days in advance of the date specified. In the event that more than one purchaser is involved in a settlement, the precise time of settlement shall be fixed by the President of the Company by five (5) days' written notice to the purchasers and sellers.

### E. Agreed Value

The "Agreed Value" per share of the Stock of the Company is hereby determined to be as set forth on Schedule A hereto. On January 31 and July 31 or each year, the then living Stockholders shall redetermine in writing the Agreed Value of the Stock for purposes of this Agreement and shall record such agreed redetermination of Agreed Value on a Schedule substantially in the form of Schedule A hereto. A redetermination of Agreed Value shall be effective only if agreed to unanimously in writing by the then living Stockholders. Should the parties fail to redetermine the Agreed Value for a period of twelve (12) consecutive months, then the Agreed Value per share shall, subsequent to the expiration of such 12-month period and until a redetermination of Agreed Value by the Stockholders, be the last determined Agreed Value per share, plus or minus the aggregate of the net income or loss (on a consolidated basis with subsidiaries, if any), after federal and other income and other taxes, less the aggregate of dividends paid on the Company's capital stock, from the beginning of the Company's last fiscal year in which there occurred a determination of Agreed Value until the close of the fiscal year last preceding the time in question, divided by the total number of shares of common stock of the Company then outstanding; provided, however, that in no event shall the Agreed Value be less than $1.00 per share. The aggregate of the net income or

loss shall be as computed by the Company's regularly engaged public accountants in accordance with generally accepted accounting principles and practices applied on a basis
consistent with that of preceding years, whose determination shall be binding and conclusive upon the parties.

### F.  Prepayment; Guarantee; Non-Competition; Allocation; Insurance

**F–1.**  Any amounts payable pursuant to Section D
hereof may be prepaid at any time, in whole or in part,
without premium or penalty.

**F–2.**  The Smith Group Stockholders hereby guarantee to Jones, severally but not jointly, payment by the
Company to Jones of any amounts which might become payable to Jones pursuant to Section D hereof, to the following
extent:  John Smith—36$\frac{4}{11}$%;  Helen Smith—54$\frac{6}{11}$%;  Bill
Smith—9$\frac{1}{11}$%.  The foregoing guarantees shall survive the
deaths of the respective guarantors.[48]

**F–3.**  Each Stockholder hereby agrees that such
Stockholder will not, for so long as such Stockholder owns,
directly or indirectly any shares of the Stock of the Company and for a period of two (2) years after having disposed
of the last remaining interest in any of the Stock of the
Company, engage in, be financially interested in or be employed by any business in the United States which is competitive with the Company or any of its subsidiaries.  The
term "engage in" as used in the preceding sentence shall include, but shall not be limited to, activities, whether direct
or indirect, as proprietor, partner, stockholder, principal,
agent, employee or consultant.  Each Stockholder acknowledges that the restrictions contained in this paragraph, in
light of the nature of Company's industry, are reasonable
and necessary to protect the Company's legitimate interests,
and that a violation thereof would result in irreparable injury to the Company and thus to its Stockholders.  Each
Stockholder acknowledges that, in the event of a violation of
any such restrictions, the Company and/or the remaining
Stockholders shall be entitled to preliminary and permanent
injunctive relief as well as an equitable accounting of all of
such defaulting Stockholder's income, gain or benefits arising out of such violation (which rights shall be cumulative
and in addition to any other rights or remedies to which the
Company and/or the Stockholders may be entitled).  In the

---

48.  Note that the Smith Group Stockholders are only guaranteeing a payment by the Company to a limited extent—the relative percentage in the
Company owned by such Stockholder.

event of a violation, the two-year period referred to above shall be extended by an amount of time equal to the time during which such violations took place.

**F–4.** So long as Jones is a Stockholder, the Company will maintain a policy or policies of life insurance on his life in a face amount of not less then $100,000, and shall not borrow against such policies. Upon the death of Jones, to the extent that the Company rather than the Smith Group Stockholders is purchasing Jones' Stock pursuant to Section B, the net proceeds of such insurance shall be used to make the initial payment by the Company at settlement pursuant to Paragraph D–2 hereof, and any excess shall be used to prepay, in whole or in part, any remaining obligation of the Company pursuant to Paragraph D–2. In the event that Jones sells all of his Stock during his lifetime, he may purchase from the Company the policies of insurance on his life for the cash surrender values of such policies on the date of transfer. Jones' right to purchase such policies shall terminate absolutely if not exercised by Jones within sixty (60) days following the sale of his Stock, and thereafter the Company will cease to be obligated to maintain such insurance.

## G. Voting

**G–1.** Neither Jones (if offering to sell his Stock pursuant to Section A) nor a Selling Stockholder pursuant to Section A hereof shall be entitled to vote as a director of the Company on the question whether the Company should exercise any option pursuant to Section A, nor may Jones vote as a director of the Company on the question whether the Company should liquidate and dissolve pursuant to Paragraph A–8. Neither the personal representatives of a deceased Stockholder nor their nominees may vote as directors of the Company on the question whether the Company should exercise any option, or liquidate and dissolve, pursuant to Section B. A Stockholder whose shares of Stock of the Company may be purchased pursuant to Section C may not vote as a director of the Company on the question whether the Company should exercise its option pursuant to Section C.

**G–2.** In a vote, if any, of Stockholders of the Company on the question whether the Company should exercise an option or liquidate and dissolve pursuant to Section A, exercise an option or liquidate and dissolve pursuant to Section B, or exercise the option pursuant to Section C, the shares of the Selling Stockholder (or Jones, if Jones proposes to sell) with respect to Section A, or of the deceased

Stockholder with respect to Section B, or of the Stockholder whose Stock may be purchased pursuant to Section C, as the case may be, shall be voted in the same manner as the majority of all other votes cast have been voted, and this Agreement shall constitute a proxy coupled with an interest, for so long as this Agreement is in effect, by each Stockholder to the other Stockholders to implement the foregoing.

## H.  Term of Agreement

**H–1.** Unless terminated sooner by unanimous agreement in writing of the Company and the Stockholders then living, this Agreement shall terminate upon the repurchase of the shares of Stock of the next to the last of the Stockholders.

**H–2.** Notwithstanding anything to the contrary contained in this Agreement, in the event that all of the Stockholders die within one hundred twenty (120) days of each other, then the provisions of this Agreement shall be of no further force and effect, and this Agreement shall terminate in all respects. Any and all transfers, payments or other action made or taken with respect to the sale of Stock of the Company during said 120-day period shall be rescinded by the parties or their respective personal representatives.

## I.  Stock Certificates to Be Marked with Legend

All certificates of Stock now or hereafter issued by the Company shall be marked with the following legend:

"This certificate of stock and the shares represented hereby may not be transferred except in accordance with the provisions of a certain agreement dated July 31, 19__, and all amendments thereto, a copy of which agreement and any amendment thereto is on file at the principal office of the Company."

## J.  Rights, Obligations and Remedies

Neither any Stockholder nor the Company may assign, transfer, pledge or otherwise encumber or dispose of any rights or obligations or both under this Agreement. The rights and obligations under this Agreement and the remedies to enforce them are joint and several as to each of the parties hereto, with each party being completely free to enforce any or all rights or obligations under this Agreement against any other party with or without the concurrence or joinder of any other party hereto.

Any and all disputes and controversies arising under or in connection with the terms or provisions of this Agreement, or in connection with or relating to the application or interpretation of any of the terms or provisions hereof, or in respect to anything not herein expressly provided, but germane to the subject matter of this Agreement, which the Smith Group and Jones have been unable to adjust, shall be submitted to arbitration at the request of either Jones or a member of the Smith Group, said arbitration to be conducted in the following manner: Jones and the Smith Group shall each choose one arbitrator, and all matters in dispute shall be referred for decision to said two (2) arbitrators, whose decision shall be final, binding and conclusive upon the parties. If the said two arbitrators shall be unable to agree upon the decision of the disputed matters so referred to them within ten (10) days after referral, then they shall, within the following ten (10) days, jointly select a third arbitrator. The decision of any two (2) of the said three (3) arbitrators shall be final, binding and conclusive upon the parties. If either party shall refuse or neglect to appoint an arbitrator within five (5) days after the other party shall have appointed an arbitrator, and such other party shall have served a written notice upon the first mentioned party requiring such party to make such appointment, then the arbitrator appointed as aforesaid shall, at the request of the appointing party, proceed to hear and determine the matters in contest as if such arbitrator were an arbitrator appointed by both parties for such purpose, and the decision of such arbitrator shall be final, binding and conclusive upon the parties. If the two (2) arbitrators appointed by the parties hereto shall be unable to agree upon a third arbitrator within the time limit above provided, the matter shall be referred to the American Arbitration Association in New York, New York for decision by a panel of three (3) arbitrators under such Association's then current rules and procedures relating to commercial arbitration, and the decision of such Association's panel of arbitrators shall be final, binding and conclusive upon the parties hereto. With respect to expenses incurred in connection with any arbitration hereunder, Jones shall bear the expenses relating to any arbitrator appointed by him, the Smith Group shall bear the expenses of any arbitrator appointed by it, and any expenses in connection with a third arbitrator or in connection with an arbitration referred to the American Arbitration Association shall be borne one-half by Jones and one-half by the Smith Group.

The parties acknowledge that the shares of capital stock of the Company are unique, and the damages which might result to any of the parties by breach of this Agreement by a party or parties or their personal representatives, successors or assigns are difficult to determine, and therefore, in addition to all of the other remedies which may be accorded by the arbitrators, the arbitrators shall have the right to afford equitable relief, including, without limitation, the right to enforce specifically the terms of this Agreement, by enjoining any violation hereof, or otherwise.

### K.   Amendment, Modification, Termination

This Agreement may be amended, modified or terminated at any time or times by mutual agreement in writing executed by the Company and signed by all the Stockholders then living.  No such amendment, modification or termination, however, shall affect the right of any person to receive, or the obligation of any person to pay, on the terms and conditions of this Agreement, the purchase price for Stock sold pursuant to this Agreement prior to such amendment, modification or termination, or the right or obligation of any person to sell or purchase Stock, on the terms and conditions of this Agreement, if such purchase or sale is to occur hereunder immediately upon the death of a Stockholder and that Stockholder has in fact died prior to such amendment, modification or termination.

### L.   Representatives, Successors and Assigns

This Agreement shall be binding upon and inure to the benefit of the respective parties hereto, and their personal representatives, successors, and assigns, except that a transferee of Stock of the Company pursuant to Paragraph A–7 hereof shall not be subject to the terms and provisions of this Agreement and shall not succeed to any of the rights granted to Stockholders pursuant to this Agreement.

### M.   Notices

Notices, requests, demands and other communications relating to this Agreement and the transactions contemplated herein shall be in writing and shall be deemed to have been duly given or made when wired or when deposited in the United States mail, postage prepaid, registered or certified with return receipt requested, addressed as follows:

    (a)   If to the Company:

        Smijo Corp.
        12 E. 3rd Street
        New York, New York    10016

Attention: Dan Jones, President

> [NOTE: If Dan Jones is the person directing the communication to the Company, then the communication shall be addressed to the Company to the attention of John Smith.]

(b) If to Dan Jones:

[*Address*]

(c) If to John Smith:

[*Address*]

(d) If to Helen Smith:

[*Address*]

(e) If to Bill Smith:

[*Address*]

(f) Any addressee may designate a different address to which communications are to be sent, by giving notice of such change of address in conformity with the provisions of this paragraph for giving of notice.

## N.  Headings and Miscellaneous

The paragraph headings in this Agreement are for convenience only; they form no part of this Agreement and shall not affect its interpretation. Words used herein, regardless of the number and gender specifically used, shall be deemed and construed to include any other number, singular or plural, and any other gender, masculine, feminine or neuter, as the context requires. No indulgences extended by any party hereto to any other party shall be construed as a waiver of any breach on the part of such other party, nor shall any waiver of one breach be construed as a waiver of any rights or remedies with respect to any subsequent breach. This Agreement may be executed in any number of counterparts, each of which when so executed and delivered shall be deemed an original, and such counterparts shall, together, constitute and be one and the same instrument. In the event that any provision hereof shall be unenforceable, the Agreement shall continue in force and effect and construed as if such unenforceable provision had never been contained herein.

### O. Controlling Law

This Agreement shall be governed by and construed in accordance with the laws of the State of New York.

IN WITNESS WHEREOF, the parties hereto have executed this Agreement the day and year first above written.

Attest:

                                         SMIJO CORP.

                                         By _____

_____
Secretary                             President
[*Corporate Seal*]

                                  _____ [*Seal*]
                                  Dan Jones
                                  _____ [*Seal*]
                                  John Smith
                                  _____ [*Seal*]
                                  Helen Smith
                                  _____ [*Seal*]
                                  Bill Smith

## SCHEDULE A

### AGREED VALUE OF STOCK

The undersigned shareholders hereby agree that the Agreed Value (as defined in a certain Agreement dated _____, 19__, to which they are all parties) of the common stock of Smijo Corp. is $_____ per share.

                                  _____ [*Seal*]
                                  Dan Jones
                                  _____ [*Seal*]
                                  John Smith
                                  _____ [*Seal*]
                                  Helen Smith
                                  _____ [*Seal*]
                                  Bill Smith

Dated: _____, 19__.

### EXAMPLE—Shareholders' Agreement Checklist

1. Exact name and address of corporation?
2. Is corporation a party to the agreement?
3. Shareholders who are party to the agreement:

   **Name**              **Address**              **No. of Shares**

4. Do the above constitute all of the shareholders of the corporation?

5. Authorized capital of the corporation?

6. Lifetime transfers:

   (a) Are all shareholders treated alike?

   (b) What are conditions to transfers during lifetime?

      (1) Must there first be a bona fide written offer? If not, what conditions?

      (2) Can a shareholder dispose only of all, and not less than all, of the shares owned by such shareholder pursuant to offer or other conditions?

   (c) Does corporation have right of first refusal? At what price and upon what terms?

   (d) Do other shareholders have right of first refusal? If so, do all shareholders have right pro rata or does a particular group of shareholders have the right? At what price and upon what terms?

   (e) Does a third party transferee take shares free of restrictions? If not, does the transferee get the benefits as well as the restrictions which were applicable to the transferor?

   (f) Do any shareholders have the right to "put" their shares to the corporation? To the other shareholders? If so, upon what conditions? At what price and upon what terms?

   (g) Does the corporation or do any shareholders have the right to "call" the shares of any shareholder? If so, upon what conditions? At what price and upon what terms?

   (h) Are inter-family transfers permitted?

   (i) Are inter-shareholder transfers permitted?

   (j) Is there an option to purchase shares of a shareholder in financial jeopardy?

7. Dispositions upon death:

   (a) Are all shareholders treated alike?

   (b) Does corporation have obligation to purchase shares upon death? Option to purchase? Must estate sell? If so, at what price and upon what terms?

   (c) Do surviving shareholders have obligation to purchase shares upon death? Option to purchase? Must estate sell? Do all surviving shareholders participate pro rata, or does a particular group of shareholders participate differently? What price and upon what terms?

   (d) Will there be any insurance funding?

8.  Terms of payment:

    (a)  All cash at settlement?

    (b)  If installment payments:

        (1)  Amounts and payment dates?

        (2)  Any notes?  Wives to sign?  Confession of judgment?  Negotiable?

        (3)  Any collateral security for payment?

        (4)  Interest rate?  Interest payable when?

        (5)  Is prepayment allowed in year of settlement?

9.  Provisions respecting management:

    (a)  Composition of Board of Directors?

    (b)  Designation of Officers?

    (c)  Regulation of Salaries?

    (d)  Limitations on mergers and consolidations?  On liquidation and dissolution?  On sale of assets out of the ordinary course of business?  On amendment of articles or certificate of incorporation?  On amendment of by-laws?  On payment of dividends?  On incurring large or long-term debt?  Other?

    (e)  Non-competition agreement?

    (f)  Right of corporation to issue additional shares?  Pre-emptive rights?

10.  Term of Agreement?

11.  Provision for Subchapter S election?

Chapter Eleven

# CORPORATE DISTRIBUTIONS

## I. INTRODUCTION

Chapter Eleven is designed to expand the ability of a lawyer's assistant to draft resolutions dealing with certain corporate activities and to acquaint the student with a variety of tax considerations and reporting requirements relating to corporate distributions. The Chapter is also designed to familiarize the student with state law restrictions on a corporation's ability to pay dividends or purchase its own shares. Finally, Chapter Eleven is intended to provide a simple introduction to accounting for the student.

A person acquires shares of a corporation's stock to derive economic benefit from the ownership of the stock. This benefit may be achieved in many ways: (a) a shareholder who owns a majority of the voting shares of the corporation may control election of directors who may, in turn, elect the shareholder as an officer of the corporation and pay a salary;[1] (b) if the corporation is profitable, and its net assets increase, a shareholder may be able to sell the shares at a higher price than the amount paid for them and realize a profit on the difference; and (c) a shareholder may benefit if the corporation distributes its cash or property. It is this latter category, corporate distributions, which is the subject matter of his Chapter.

A corporate distribution may be in the form of cash, tangible property, stock of the distributing corporation, stock of another corporation which is owned by the distributing corporation, or other intangible property. The distribution may be of all or a portion of the corporation's property and may, or may not, be distributed in exchange for stock owned by the corporation's shareholders. These different types of corporate distributions have various economic effects on the shareholders and the corporation, and may be treated differently under both corporate laws and Federal and state tax laws. Each principal type of corporate distribution will be discussed in this Chapter.

## II. THE CORPORATE BALANCE SHEET

Before examining the different types of corporate distributions, it is important to see how the assets and liabilities of a corporation are described by the use of a balance sheet. In the course of analyz-

---

1. See Chapter Seven for a discussion of election of shareholders and directors and actions taken by directors.
**QUESTIONS: Can the majority shareholder require the directors to elect** the shareholder as an officer as a condition of the shareholder's voting for them as director? Why or why not? If not, what can the majority shareholder do?

ing a balance sheet, certain terms which are used in state corporate laws will be defined. These terms are important because their function is to establish limits on the amount of assets which a corporation may distribute. State law imposes these limits on corporate distributions in order to protect creditors who, because of the concept of "limited liability," are limited to the assets of the corporation and cannot recover corporate debts from the personal assets of shareholders.[2]

For purposes of this Chapter, our model will be the X Corporation, which is engaged in the manufacture and sale, through retail stores, of house paint. Since X Corporation is engaged in business, it has certain assets. For example, it owns a plant and equipment for manufacturing paint. X Corporation also owns (i) raw materials to make paint, (ii) paint in the process of being manufactured and packaged and (iii) paint which it had manufactured (raw materials, work in process and finished goods are referred to collectively as "inventory"). In addition, the corporation owns the retail stores in which the paint is sold. In order to pay its bills, the X Corporation must have cash, either on hand or deposited in bank accounts. Moreover, if X Corporation sold paint to customers and had to wait for payment, it would have as an asset the amounts owing from these customers ("accounts receivable"). X Corporation will also have some liabilities. For example, it has not paid all of the bills it received from suppliers of raw materials or electric and telephone bills ("accounts payable"). Moreover, it owes money for goods and services for which it has not yet been billed.

A balance sheet is used to describe, in dollar terms, the assets and liabilities of a corporation as of a given point in time. It is sometimes referred to as a "snapshot," as of a specific moment, of the financial condition of the corporation. The dollar amounts assigned to various assets are referred to as the "book value" of these assets. The "book value" of an asset is determined by accounting rules and may or may not bear any relation to the current fair market value of the asset.[3] Since a corporation's assets rarely are equal to its liabilities because of the history of corporate transactions, a balance sheet will also show the corporation's "net worth" (alternatively called "net assets," "shareholder's equity" or "capital") which may be generally defined as the difference between its assets and liabilities (See Section 2(i), MBCA). If the assets exceed the liabilities, then net worth is a positive number; if the liabilities exceed the as-

---

2. Chapter One discusses generally the concept of limited liability of shareholders and contrasts it to the personal liability of a proprietor and partners.

3. Generally speaking, the "book value" is the historical cost to a corporation of an asset. Inflation, obsolescence, scarcity, depreciation, wear and tear and many other factors can make the historical book value substantially different from the current fair market value. For example, a building built fifty years ago may be worth more now than when it was built; yet it may be fully depreciated to zero on the balance sheet.

sets, net worth is a negative number. A balance sheet must always "balance" because the assets of a corporation must always equal its liabilities and net worth.[4]

Before proceeding further, it would be helpful to set forth a hypothetical balance sheet of X Corporation:

## X CORPORATION

### Balance Sheet as of June 30, 1977

| Assets | | Liabilities | |
|---|---|---|---|
| Cash | $ 30,000 | Accounts Payable | $ 50,000 |
| | | **Net Worth** | |
| Accounts Receivable | 50,000 | Common Stock (1,000 shares, $10 par value, author- | |
| Inventory | 20,000 | ized, 100 shares issued and out- | |
| Equipment | 21,000 | standing) | 1,000 |
| | | Capital surplus | 9,000 |
| Real Estate | 25,000 | | |
| | | 7% Preferred | |
| Investment in Y Corporation (100 shares at $40 per share) | 4,000 | Stock (100 shares, $100 par value, authorized and outstanding) | 10,000 |
| | | Earned Surplus | 80,000 |
| Total Assets | $150,000 | Total Liabilities and Net Worth | $150,000 |

Perhaps the most revealing characteristic of the balance sheet is the references under the heading "Net Worth" to outstanding shares of common stock, preferred stock, capital surplus and earned surplus. The reasons for the references and their significance is found in the state corporate laws. Different state laws may have somewhat different definitions, but the MBCA is a common type of definitional pattern.

Section 2(j), MBCA, defines "stated capital" in part as the sum of:

"(1) the par value of all shares of the corporation having a par value that have been issued, (2) the amount of the consideration

---

**4.** In essence, the net worth, whether positive or negative, is the balancing figure between assets and liabilities.

received by the corporation for all shares of the corporation without par value that have been issued . . .."

On the balance sheet of X Corporation, the stated capital is $11,000, representing the aggregate par value of all shares of common stock and preferred stock outstanding.

## QUESTION

**If X Corporation had stock with no par value, what would have been the stated capital under the MBCA definition if $20,000 had been received in payment therefor? [5]**

The balance sheet also shows earned surplus of $80,000. Section 2(1), MBCA, defines earned surplus as follows:

> " 'Earned surplus' means the portion of the surplus of a corporation equal to the balance of its net profits, income, gains and losses from the date of incorporation, or from the latest date when a deficit was eliminated by an application of its capital surplus or stated capital or otherwise, after deducting subsequent distributions to shareholders and transfers to stated capital and capital surplus to the extent such distributions and transfers are made out of earned surplus."

If X Corporation was incorporated on July 1, 1976 and had never made a distribution to shareholders or made a transfer from earned surplus to stated capital and capital surplus, the $80,000 of earned surplus would mean that X Corporation had net profits of $80,000 during the period from July 1, 1976 to June 30, 1977.

## QUESTION

**If the $9,000 of capital surplus represented a transfer from earned surplus to capital surplus (as a stock dividend or otherwise) prior to June 30, 1977, how much money did X Corporation earn during the fiscal year?**

Additional relevant definitions from the MBCA follow:

1.  " 'Surplus' means the excess of the net assets of a corporation over its stated capital."
Section 2(k), MBCA.

2.  " 'Capital Surplus' means the entire surplus of a corporation other than its earned surplus."
Section 2(m), MBCA.

3.  " 'Insolvent' means inability of a corporation to pay its debts as they become due in the usual course of its business."
Section 2(n), MBCA.

---

5.  See Section II.C of Chapter Four for a discussion of par and no par value stock.

On the balance sheet of X Corporation, the surplus is $89,000, consisting of $80,000 of earned surplus and $9,000 of capital surplus. The capital surplus may have arisen because X Corporation sold 100 shares of common stock, with a par value of $10 per share, for $100 per share. The MBCA states the following:

> "In case of the issuance by a corporation of shares having a par value, the consideration received therefor shall constitute stated capital to the extent of the par value of such shares, and the excess, if any, of such consideration shall constitute capital surplus." Section 21, MBCA.

## QUESTION

What would have been the capital surplus under the MBCA definition if X Corporation sold 1000 shares of common stock, par value $10 per share, for $85 per share?

The significance of these terms will become clearer as we explore different types of corporate distributions. At the outset, however, it must be emphasized that "earned surplus" is not an asset, and, therefore, it is not on the asset side of the balance sheet. Nor is it something "extra" as the term "surplus" may imply; it is merely a legal term of art for the cumulation of profits and losses of the corporation (less distributions to shareholders) since its inception.

## PROBLEM

What is the "book value per share of common stock" for a corporation with the following shareholders' equity:

| | |
|---|---|
| Stated Capital | $1,200,000 |
| (1,000,000 shares of Common Stock, par value $1 per share, outstanding and 200,000 shares of Preferred Stock, par value $1 per share, outstanding) | |
| Capital Surplus | 2,800,000 |
| Earned Surplus | 4,000,000 |
| | $8,000,000 |

The liquidation price for the Preferred Stock is $10.00 per share.

## III.  CASH AND PROPERTY DIVIDENDS

### A.  DEFINITION

A dividend may be generally defined as a distribution by a corporation to shareholders with respect to its stock. A dividend is paid to shareholders in direct proportion to their shareholdings. Although dividends may be paid on one or more separate classes or series of stock, all holders of any series or class of stock must be treated equally and receive dividends in direct proportion to the number of shares of the class or series owned by them.

## B. RIGHT TO DIVIDENDS

Chapter Eight contains a description of the rights that holders of common stock and preferred stock have to receive dividends.

### QUESTION

**Does any shareholder have an absolute right to receive dividends?**

## C. PAYMENT OF DIVIDENDS

### 1. Restrictions

Because the common shareholders are the residual owners of the corporation, i. e., they are entitled to anything left after all creditors and preferred stockholders have been fully paid off, corporate statutes ordinarily place a limit on the amount that can be distributed to shareholders. The idea is to require some permanent commitment by shareholders to the corporation as some assurance that creditors will be paid. Section 45 of the MBCA is a typical type of restriction that permits the payment of dividends in cash or property only under the condition that a corporation is not rendered insolvent and has adequate earned surplus. Under certain restricted circumstances, some corporate statutes permit distributions to shareholders out of capital surplus as well.[6]

The amount of earned surplus is the amount of the maximum dividend that a corporation may legally pay. However, it is not a fund of money or an asset of any kind.

The balance sheet of X Corporation would appear to indicate that a maximum dividend of $80,000 could be declared and paid, since this is the amount of earned surplus. While legally this may be so, as a practical matter there are two reasons why an $80,000 dividend is unlikely:

(a) X Corporation has only $30,000 in cash, some of which is obviously needed to continue the ordinary business operations.[7] It, therefore, does not have sufficient cash to pay an $80,000 dividend. If the dividend were paid in the form of inventory, equipment or real property, the business may need still more cash to replenish these items.

---

6. See Section 46 of the MBCA.

7. Funds required for ordinary business operations are often referred to as "working capital."

(b) The board of directors must leave X Corporation with sufficient "liquid assets" (i. e., cash and other assets which may be quickly reduced to cash, such as accounts receivable) to pay the liabilities of $50,000 when payment is due and to allow for future growth and/or future losses. Otherwise, the corporation may be insolvent and unable to meet its debts as they become due in the usual course of business.

## 2. Procedure for Payment

### (a) *Board of Directors' Action*

Dividends can only be declared by action of the Board of Directors. The shareholders cannot declare dividends.

### QUESTION

**Why should shareholders not be entitled to be the body to declare dividends?**

Sample resolutions for the payment of dividends by X Corporation on the outstanding Common and Preferred Stock, including the establishment of both a record date and a payment date, are as follows:

## Common Stock:

"RESOLVED, that there shall be distributed on August 31, 19___, to holders of Common Stock of the Corporation of record on August 15, 19___, a cash dividend of $500 on the basis of $5.00 per share for each issued and outstanding share of Common Stock.

"RESOLVED, that any officer of the Corporation be and each of them hereby is authorized and directed to take such action as any one of them may deem necessary or proper to effect the foregoing dividend.

"RESOLVED, that the Treasurer of the Corporation be and hereby is authorized and directed to charge the earned surplus account with $500 and to make such other entries in the books of account of the Corporation as are necessary or proper to reflect the foregoing distribution."

## Preferred Stock:

"RESOLVED, that there shall be distributed on August 31, 19___, to holders of 7% Preferred Stock of the Corporation of record on August 15, 19___, the regular quarterly cash dividend of $175, on the basis of $1.75 per share for each issued and outstanding share of 7% Preferred Stock.

"RESOLVED, that any officer of the Corporation be and each of them hereby is authorized and directed to take such action as any one of them may deem necessary or proper to effect the foregoing dividend.

"RESOLVED, that the Treasurer of the Corporation be and hereby is authorized and directed to charge the earned surplus account with $175 and to make such other entries in the books of account of the Corporation as are necessary or proper to reflect the foregoing distribution."

Note that the resolutions effect the declaration of a dividend which differs from the actual payment of the dividend. The paralegal will ordinarily have the duty of drafting resolutions declaring the dividend.

### (b) *Payment of Dividends*

Pursuant to the authorization in the above resolutions, the shareholders of record of X Corporation on August 15, 19__ would receive on August 31, 19__ an aggregate of $500 in cash, as the dividend on the Common Stock, and an aggregate of $175 in cash, as the dividend on the Preferred Stock.

### (c) *Adjustment of Capital Accounts*

On August 31, 19__, the balance sheet of X Corporation would reflect the payment of the cash dividend by a reduction in cash of $675 (the total amount of the dividends) and a reduction in earned surplus of $675.

### QUESTION

**If X Corporation had paid a dividend aggregating $1000 on the common stock and $175 on the preferred stock, how would the entries on the balance sheet be reflected?**

## D.    TAX TREATMENT OF DIVIDENDS

## 1.   Introduction

The definition of the term "dividend" under state corporate law and the definition under Federal income tax law are not synonymous. For Federal income tax purposes, for it to be taxable, a dividend must be paid out of the corporation's "earnings and profits". The term "earnings and profits" for tax purposes is not synonymous with the term "earned surplus" for corporate purposes. For example, a transfer from earned surplus to stated capital in connection with an increase in the par value of outstanding stock serves to reduce "earned surplus" for purposes of state law but does not reduce "earnings and profits" for purposes of the Federal tax law. A simplistic definition of earnings and profits would be the cumulation of all profits of the corporation during its existence reduced by distribution to shareholders. Dividends (as defined under Federal income tax law) constitute ordinary income to the recipient shareholders, and are subject to tax at the shareholders' normal Federal income tax rates.

## 2. Double Taxation

All of a corporation's income is taxed at the corporate level. Dividends cannot be deducted from a corporation's profits in computing federal income taxes. When the shareholders receive a dividend, they, too, pay a personal income tax on such distributions. For example, the X Corporation must earn $962 of pre-tax income, assuming the pre-tax income is taxed at the maximum 48 percent corporate rate, in order to have enough income to pay a dividend of $500 to common stockholders. The distribution of $500 by X Corporation to A and B is taxed to them at their normal individual rates. If A and B are each in the 50 percent marginal tax bracket, they will each net $125 after payment of Federal income taxes.

There are many small corporations which do not look upon dividends with favor. The payment of dividends is not a deductible expense to the corporation; moreover, it results in taxable income to the recipient shareholder. If the shareholders are also employees of the corporation, an increase in salary or a bonus may possibly be given rather than a declaration of dividends. Additional salaries or bonuses will qualify as deductible expense to the corporation, if they are reasonable, and will satisfy the shareholder-employee's desire for additional income.

Consider that combined corporate and shareholder taxes on the $962 of pre-tax income of X Corporation were $712. X Corporation paid taxes of $462 and distributed the remainder as a dividend to A and B, who collectively paid taxes of $250. If A and B were to each receive salary increases of $481, in lieu of dividends of $250 each, the combined taxes to X Corporation and to A and B would be $481 (50% of the aggregate salary increase of $962). The salary would be a deductible expense to X Corporation and thus no taxes would be paid by it with respect to the $962 amount. By increasing salaries instead of paying dividends, A and B would each net, after taxes, $240.50 instead of the $125 from dividend payments and the cash flowing out of the corporation would remain the same as if the dividend had been paid.

Many large corporations will issue debt securities rather than a preferred stock because the interest on the debt is deductible while the preferred stock dividend is not. With interest, therefore, no double tax exists. However, against this advantage must be weighed the disadvantage that interest is a legal obligation that must be paid while dividends are paid if and only if the board of directors determine, in its discretion, to declare them.[8] It should be noted that efforts have repeatedly been made in the United States Congress to eliminate the so-called "double taxation" of dividends.

---

8. See Section II.H.1 of Chapter Eight for a discussion of dividends on preferred stock.

## E. PROPERTY DIVIDENDS

### 1. State Corporate Law

As can be seen in Section 45 of the MBCA, state laws typically treat property dividends in the identical manner as cash dividends.[9] When property of the corporation is distributed as a dividend, the value of the property, as shown on the corporation's balance sheet (the "book value"), will be removed from the "asset" side of the balance sheet and earned surplus will be reduced by the same amount.

### 2. Federal Tax Laws

For Federal income tax purposes, when property is distributed as a dividend, the "earnings and profits" of the corporation are reduced by the book value of the property so distributed. On the other hand, the shareholders of the corporation who receive property as a dividend must report as income the fair market value of the property received.

### QUESTION

Can the book value be greatly different from the fair market value?

If X Corporation distributes a dividend of 10 shares of Y stock which it owns, having a fair market value of $100 per share, but which originally cost X only $40 per share, X charges $400 to earned surplus and reduces its tax "earnings and profits" by the same $400. A and B, however, each recognize ordinary income of $500.

### PROBLEM

Using the format of resolutions contained in III.C above, draft resolutions declaring a dividend of X Corporation of $100 book value in inventory on each share of common stock outstanding.

## IV. STOCK DIVIDENDS, STOCK SPLITS AND REVERSE STOCK SPLITS

### A. GENERAL

This Section covers certain corporate actions which result in reducing or increasing the number of shares of outstanding stock of a particular class without the receipt by the corporation of any assets. In each of these corporate actions, the relative stock ownership of the shareholders of a corporation never changes. Each shareholder ends up with the same percentage ownership in the corporation as that held prior to the action. Only the number of shares held by the

---

9. QUESTIONS: What kinds of property can a corporation distribute to its shareholders? As a practical matter, are all types of property distributable?

shareholder changes, and each shareholder's holdings will change in the same proportion.

## B.   STOCK DIVIDENDS

### 1.   Definition

A stock dividend is a distribution by a corporation of shares of one or more of its classes of stock to the holders of that class or of a different class of stock.   No change in the par value or stated capital of any class of stock occurs in a stock dividend.   Unlike a cash dividend, a stock dividend in shares similar to those already held is really not a distribution at all.   A stock dividend merely serves to dilute each previously outstanding share and increase the number of units into which the evidence of a shareholders' ownership is divided.   Example: If a corporation with 1000 outstanding shares declares a 10% stock dividend, there will be 1100 shares outstanding after the dividend.   The assets of the corporation are unchanged, and each share is reduced in value by 10%.

### QUESTIONS

If the above corporation declared a 25% stock dividend after the 10% dividend, how many shares would then be outstanding? Would the shareholders or corporation have experienced any change in real assets by the dividend?

The corporation often issues a stock dividend rather than a cash or property dividend because it does not desire a distribution of assets.   However, the stock dividend increases the number of shares in the market.   The corporation may desire to do this.   Why?   Furthermore, even though nothing has really been given to the shareholders, a small stock dividend, such as 5%—five shares for each 100 owned —may tend to benefit the shareholders.   Investors in the stock market are accustomed to seeing a stock at a certain level, and the stock may tend to return to that level.   For example, a stock that sells at $100 per share would decline to $95 when a 5% stock dividend is declared if all other factors remain equal.   However, the stock may tend to return to its customary level of $100 after the dividend.   In such cases, the shareholders have benefited by holding 5% more stock with no offsetting decline in price.

### QUESTIONS

How much should the market price of a $100 stock decline if a 10% stock dividend is declared?   A 200% stock dividend?

### 2.   Restrictions

Section 45 of the MBCA is a usual type of provision, which authorizes stock dividends, but only under limited circumstances.

When the board of directors of a corporation considers the possibility of a stock dividend, it must first determine if the corporation has sufficient treasury shares or sufficient authorized but unissued stock with which to pay the dividend.

## QUESTION

**What is the difference between treasury stock and authorized but unissued stock?**

If the amount of authorized but unissued stock is insufficient, the corporation's articles of incorporation must be amended to increase the authorized number of shares of stock.[10]

If there is sufficient authorized stock, the board of directors must next determine if there is adequate surplus, which must be at least equal to the aggregate par value, or aggregate stated capital, if the shares are without par value, of the shares to be issued in the stock dividend. In the X Corporation example, $89,000 of surplus is available.

Finally, if the board of directors intends to pay a dividend in one class of stock to the holders of another class of stock, the articles of incorporation must be reviewed to determine if such a distribution is permitted. If the articles are silent, then shareholder approval under a provision such as Section 45(e), MBCA, is required. If the articles prohibit such a dividend, then they must be amended before a stock dividend may be paid. We shall assume for the purposes of this Chapter that the stock dividend will be in common stock and payable to holders of common stock. Any other type of stock dividend is very rare.

## 3. Tax Treatment of Stock Dividends

The general rule is that dividends of common stock to holders of common stock are not taxable as income to the recipient shareholders. Early in the history of the Federal income tax law, the Supreme Court of the United States held that it was unconstitutional to tax as income to the shareholders a distribution of common stock on common stock because a stock dividend takes nothing from the property of the corporation and adds nothing to that of its shareholders.

## 4. Payment of Stock Dividends

### (a) Board Authorization

The first step in the payment of a stock dividend is for the board of directors to adopt resolutions specifying the amount of the dividend and the record and payment dates:

> "RESOLVED, that a dividend payable in Common Stock of the Corporation, $10.00 par value, shall be paid on August 31, 19___, to

---

10. See Chapter Four for a discussion of the amendment of a corporation's articles of incorporation.

holders of Common Stock of record on August 15, 19__, at the rate of one-tenth of a share for each share of outstanding Common Stock.

"RESOLVED, that the Treasurer of the Corporation be and hereby is authorized and directed to charge the earned surplus account of the Corporation with the aggregate par value of the shares to be issued in the foregoing stock dividend and to credit the stated capital of the Corporation with such amount.

"RESOLVED, that no fractional shares of Common Stock shall be issuable pursuant to the foregoing stock dividend and that this Corporation shall pay in lieu of any fractional share an amount in cash which bears the same proportion to the closing price of the Common Stock on the American Stock Exchange on the date of the dividend as the fractional share bears to a whole share."

"RESOLVED, that any officer of the Corporation be and each of them hereby is authorized and directed to take all steps and prepare and sign all such documents as any one of them may deem necessary or proper to carry out the foregoing resolutions."

Fractional shares may be avoided by paying cash or rounding off the fraction.

### QUESTION

Why would a corporation desire to avoid issuing fractional shares?

### PROBLEM

Draft resolutions authorizing a 200% stock dividend in common stock payable on November 15 to holders of record on November 1. Include a resolution authorizing rounding off of a fractional share to the nearest whole share.

### (b) Issuance of Shares

On the payment date for the stock dividend, the officers of the corporation must execute certificates representing the shares of common stock of the corporation being issued in the stock dividend and deliver them to the shareholders of record as of the record date in accordance with the terms of the stock dividend resolution.

### 5. Accounting for Stock Dividends

The accounting adjustments to reflect the issuance of a stock dividend take place solely in the capital and surplus accounts, inasmuch as no cash or other property is being distributed. Section 45 of the MBCA requires that the par value of the shares issued in the stock dividend must be added to the corporation's stated capital and the same amount must be removed from the corporation's earned surplus. Using the foregoing resolutions of X Corporation as an example, the capital account of X Corporation on the payment date of the stock dividend would be revised as follows:

(a) The common stock account would be increased by $100:

Common Stock (1,000 shares, $10 par value, authorized, 110 shares issued and out-standing)        $1,100

(b) The earned surplus account would be reduced by $100:

Earned Surplus        $79,900

## C. STOCK SPLITS

### 1. Definition

A stock split is a division of the issued shares of any class of a corporation into a greater number of shares. Typically, the par value or stated value per share will be reduced by an amendment to the articles of incorporation in a stock split so that the aggregate stated capital of the corporation will be unaffected by the stock split.

### QUESTIONS

How does this procedure differ from a stock dividend? Does a stock dividend require an amendment to the articles?

The aggregate stated capital of a corporation does not have to remain constant in a stock split, however, and it may increase or de-crease, depending upon the terms of the stock split and (in the case of an increase) the availability of capital surplus or earned surplus to increase the stated capital of the corporation.

### 2. Mechanics of a Stock Split

If the MBCA is the governing law (recognizing that other states may differ widely), a stock split of a class of stock (whether with or without par value) is accomplished by an amendment of the articles of incorporation. Section 58(i), MBCA, permits a corporation to amend its articles of incorporation so as

"To change the shares of any class, whether issued or unissued, and whether with or without par value, into a different number of shares of the same class or into the same or a different number of shares, either with or without par value, of other classes."

If the corporation has an insufficient number of authorized shares to accomplish the stock split, the articles of incorporation must also be amended to increase the authorized number of shares. If, in the case of par value stock, the par value per share is to be reduced in connection with the stock split, the articles of incor-poration must also be amended to reflect the lower par value per share in effect after the stock split. If, in the case of no par value stock, the stated capital per share is to be reduced, it is appropriate to reflect such adjustment in the articles of amendment.[11]

The only unique element in an amendment in connection with a stock split is that Section 61(f) of the MBCA, requires the articles of amendment to set forth the mechanics of the stock split.

Once the appropriate action has been taken by the shareholders and directors of a corporation, the stock split is effected by the filing of articles of amendment. Typically, the corporation will deliver certificates to existing shareholders to represent only the additional shares of stock which are outstanding as a result of the stock split to avoid the difficulty of calling back the outstanding certificates.

### 3. Tax Treatment

Stock splits are not taxable income to the recipient shareholders since no distribution of the assets of the corporation has occurred.

### 4. Accounting for Stock Splits

Typically, there will be no changes in the dollar amounts of stated capital or any other capital account of the corporation as a result of a stock split. The only change will be in the number of shares issued. For example, if a corporation with 100 shares of Common Stock, par value $1.00 per share, authorized and outstanding, had a 2-for-1 stock split, the changes would be reflected as follows:

(a) *Before Stock Split*

|  |  |
|---|---|
| Common Stock (100 shares, $1.00 par value, authorized, 100 shares issued and outstanding) | $100 |

(b) *After Stock Split*

|  |  |
|---|---|
| Common Stock (200 shares, $.50 par value, authorized, 200 shares issued and outstanding) | $100 |

### QUESTION

How does this contrast to the accounting for a stock dividend? [12]

## D. REVERSE STOCK SPLIT

A reverse stock split is a combination of the issued shares of any class of a corporation so that there are a fewer number of shares is-

---

11. Chapter Four specifies the procedures for an amendment to the articles of incorporation.

12. See Section IV.B.5 of this Chapter for the discussion of accounting for stock dividends.

sued after the reverse stock split than before it.  As with a stock split, the relative interests of shareholders in a corporation does not change as a result of a reverse stock split.  It is a very unusual occurrence, as shareholders do not like having the number of shares held reduced even if their proportionate interest in the corporation is unchanged.

A reverse stock split can only be effected under Section 60 of the MBCA through an amendment of the articles of incorporation which reduces the authorized stock.  In addition to proposing an amendment of the articles, the board of directors must provide a procedure by which holders of certificates representing the issued shares prior to the reverse stock split turn in their old certificates.  This procedure can be difficult, if not impossible, to carry out in practice where there are many shareholders, some of whom may be difficult to locate or reluctant to send in their shares.

A reverse stock split may or may not increase the par value or stated capital of the shares of issued stock.  For example, if a corporation had 100,000 shares of Common Stock, par value $1.00 per share, outstanding prior to a reverse stock split, and a 1-for-5 reverse stock split occurred, the corporation would have 20,000 shares of Common Stock outstanding after the split.  The par value per share, however, could be $1.00 per share or $5.00 per share.  The amendment to the articles would indicate the change, if any, in the par value.

## E.  REDUCTION OF STATED CAPITAL

A corporation may decide, independently of any stock split, to reduce the stated capital per share of its outstanding stock.  The purpose of such an action would be to eliminate a negative earned surplus account or to increase capital surplus.  Why would a corporation do this? [13]  In either case, the objective would be to permit the corporation to be free to make distributions (or larger distributions) to shareholders.

In the case of par value stock, a reduction in stated capital means a reduction in the par value of outstanding shares.  Section 58(e) of the MBCA gives a corporation authority to decrease the par value of issued shares.

In the case of no par value stock, most corporate laws have a specific procedure for reducing stated capital such as Section 69 of MBCA.

As set forth in Section 68, resolutions of both the directors and shareholders are required to reduce stated capital.  A statement of

---

13.  See Section III.C of this Chapter.

reduction of stated capital must also be filed with the state. The MBCA model form of statement follows:

**EXAMPLE—Statement of Reduction of Stated Capital (MBCA)**

Filing fee: $_____

STATEMENT OF

REDUCTION OF STATED CAPITAL

OF

_____

To the Secretary of State
   of the State of _____:

Pursuant to the provisions of Section 69 of the _____ Business Corporation Act, the undersigned corporation submits the following statement of reduction of stated capital of the corporation not accompanied by any action requiring an amendment of its Articles of Incorporation or by a cancellation of shares:

FIRST: The name of the corporation is _____

_____.

SECOND: The following resolution approving a reduction of stated capital was adopted by the shareholders of the corporation on _____, 19__, in the manner prescribed by the _____ Business Corporation Act:

[*Insert copy of Resolution*]

THIRD: The number of shares of the corporation outstanding at the time of the adoption of such resolution was _____; and the number of shares entitled to vote thereon was _____.

FOURTH: The number of shares voted for such reduction in stated capital was _____; and the number of shares voted against such reduction was _____.

FIFTH: The manner in which such reduction in stated capital is effected, and the amount of stated capital of the corporation after giving effect to such reduction, are as follows:

_____

_____

_____.

Dated _____, 19__.

_____ (Note 1)

By _____

     Its _____ President

and _____   (Note 2)

     Its _____ Secretary

(Add Verification Form A)

Notes: 1. Exact corporate name of corporation making the statement.

2. Signatures and titles of officers signing for the corporation.

No tax consequences occur upon a reduction in stated capital and no other reports are required to be filed.

## V. PURCHASE BY CORPORATION OF ITS OWN SHARES

### A. AUTHORIZATION BY BOARD OF DIRECTORS

State corporate statutes generally permit the board of directors of a corporation to authorize the corporation to purchase its own shares,[14] but only to the extent of (i) the corporation's unreserved and unrestricted earned surplus,[15] and (ii) if the articles of incorporation permit *or* with the affirmative vote of the holders of a majority of all shares entitled to vote on the question, to the extent of unreserved and unrestricted capital surplus (see, e. g., Section 6, MBCA).

If one refers to the balance sheet of X Corporation, it can be seen that the corporation could purchase its own shares up to a maximum consideration of $80,000 or, under a statute with an MBCA-type approach, if shareholder approval is obtained, up to a maximum of $89,000.

### B. SAMPLE RESOLUTION

A sample resolution authorizing the officers of a corporation to purchase its own shares follows:

"RESOLVED, that the President, any Vice President, the Secretary or the Treasurer of this Corporation be and each of them hereby is authorized and empowered to purchase on behalf of the Corporation 25 shares of its Common Stock for cash in the amount of $25,000.

### C. PURCHASED SHARES HELD AS TREASURY SHARES

If the common stock of X Corporation is not redeemable, the purchase of shares will not constitute a cancellation of those shares. Instead, the shares will remain "issued" but not "outstanding", and will be referred to as "treasury shares" (Section 2(h), MBCA).

14. Why do the shareholders not vote on the question of a corporation's repurchase of its own stock?

15. Note that the purchase of treasury shares is restricted in a manner similar to that of cash and property dividends. This is because a purchase of treasury shares is another way of distributing property to shareholders.

## QUESTION

### Is common stock ordinarily redeemable?

Section 6, MBCA, provides that the corporation's earned surplus is "restricted" when it purchases shares which become treasury shares:

> "To the extent that earned surplus or capital is used as the measure of the corporation's right to purchase its own shares, such surplus shall be restricted so long as such shares are held as treasury shares, and upon the disposition or cancellation of any such shares the restriction shall be removed pro tanto."

Since further purchases of stock or dividends can only be made out of *unrestricted* and unreserved earned surplus, as long as the restriction exists, that portion of earned surplus may not be used in calculating the amount available.

From an accounting standpoint, the capital of X Corporation would appear as follows after the purchase of 25 shares for $25,000:

| | |
|---|---:|
| Common Stock (1000 shares, $10 par value, authorized, 100 shares issued) | $ 1,000 |
| 7% Preferred Stock (100 shares, $100 par value, authorized and issued) | 10,000 |
| Capital Surplus | 9,000 |
| Earned Surplus | 80,000 |
| Less: 25 shares of Common Stock, as Treasury Stock, at cost | ( 25,000) |
| | $75,000 |

## QUESTIONS

### Is the treasury stock "issued" ?  Is it "outstanding" ?

If X Corporation sold the 25 shares of Common Stock for less than $25,000, the loss would be charged against earned surplus. Any gain from the sale of treasury shares would be credited to capital surplus and the restriction would be removed.

## D.  CANCELLATION OF PURCHASED SHARES

Section 68 of the MBCA sets forth a procedure (which may differ from state to state) for the cancellation of non-redeemable shares acquired by the corporation.

A sample resolution of the board of directors effecting the cancellation under the MBCA provision follows:

"RESOLVED, that the 25 shares of Common Stock, par value $10 per share, heretofore purchased by the Corporation shall be cancelled; that any officer of the Corporation be and each of them hereby is authorized and directed to execute and file with the appropriate state official a statement of cancellation, as required by law, and to take such other action as any one of them may deem necessary or proper to effect said cancellation; and that, upon said cancellation, the stated capital of the Corporation shall be reduced by $250, the earned surplus of the Corporation by $22,500 and the capital surplus of the Corporation by $2,250."

After the statement of cancellation is filed, the Capital of X Corporation would appear as follows on its balance sheet:

| | |
|---|---:|
| Common Stock (1000 shares, $10 par value, authorized, 75 shares issued) | $    750 |
| 7% Preferred Stock (100 shares, $100 par value, authorized and issued) | 10,000 |
| Capital Surplus | 6,750 |
| Earned Surplus | 57,500 |
| | $75,000 |

The MBCA form of statement of cancellation to be filed with the state of incorporation is as follows:

**EXAMPLE—Statement of Cancellation of Reacquired Shares (MBCA)**

Filing fee: $_____

STATEMENT OF

CANCELLATION OF REACQUIRED SHARES

OF

_____

To the Secretary of State
of the State of _____:

Pursuant to the provisions of Section 68 of the _____ Business Corporation Act, the undersigned corporation submits the following statement of cancellation by resolution of its board of directors of shares of the corporation reacquired by it, other than redeemable shares redeemed or purchased:

FIRST: The name of the corporation is _____

_____.

SECOND: The number of reacquired shares of the corporation cancelled by resolution duly adopted by the board of directors of the corporation on _____, 19__, is _____, itemized as follows:

**Class**                **Series**                **Number of Shares**

THIRD: The aggregate number of issued shares of the corporation after giving effect to such cancellation is _____, itemized as follows:

**Class**                **Series**                **Number of Shares**

FOURTH: The amount of the stated capital of the corporation, after giving effect to such cancellation is $_____.

Dated _____, 19__.

(Note 1)

By _____ ⎫
    Its _____ President   ⎬ (Note 2)
and _____ ⎪
    Its _____ Secretary ⎭

(Add Verification Form A)

Notes: 1.  Exact corporate name of corporation making the statement.

2.  Signatures and titles of officers signing for the corporation.

### E.   TAX TREATMENT OF PURCHASE OF SHARES

A corporation does not realize a gain or loss for tax purposes upon the purchase of its stock. On the other hand, the selling shareholder will generally realize a gain or loss when selling stock to the issuing corporation. If A paid $2,500 for 25 shares of X stock which was later sold back to X for $25,000, A would recognize a gain of $22,500.

## F.  REPORTING OF STOCK PURCHASED TO INTERNAL REVENUE SERVICE

Within 30 days after the adoption of the resolution to purchase shares of its stock, a corporation should file Form 966 with the Internal Revenue Service because such a purchase constitutes a partial liquidation for tax purposes.  A sample Form 966 follows:

**EXAMPLE:**

| Form **966** (Rev. Nov. 1973) Department of the Treasury Internal Revenue Service | **Corporate Dissolution or Liquidation** (Required under Section 6043(a) of the Internal Revenue Code) | | |
|---|---|---|---|

Please type or print

| Name of corporation | Employer identification number | | |
|---|---|---|---|
| Address (Number and street) | **Check type of return** □ 1120   □ 1120DISC   □ 1120L | | |
| City or town, State and ZIP code | □ 1120M   □ 1120S | | |

| 1 Date incorporated | 2 Place incorporated | 3 Type of liquidation □ Complete   □ Partial |
|---|---|---|

**4** Internal Revenue Service Center where last income tax return was filed and taxable year covered thereby

Service Center ▶                                   Taxable year ▶

| 5 Date of adoption of resolution or plan of dissolution, or complete or partial liquidation | 6 Taxable year of final return | 7 Total number of shares outstanding at time of adoption of plan or liquidation |
|---|---|---|
| | | Common          Preferred |

| 8 Dates of any amendments to plan of dissolution | 9 Section of the Code under which the corporation is to be dissolved or liquidated | 10 If this return is in respect of an amendment of or supplement to a resolution or plan previously adopted and return has previously been filed in respect of such resolution or plan, give the date such return was filed |
|---|---|---|

**11. Liquidation Within One Calendar Month.**—If the corporation is a domestic corporation, and the plan of liquidation provides for a distribution in complete cancellation or redemption of all the capital stock of the corporation and for the transfer of all the property of the corporation under the liquidation entirely within one calendar month pursuant to section 333, and any shareholder claims the benefit of such section, then the corporation must also submit:
(a) A description of the voting power of each class of stock;
(b) A list of all the shareholders owning stock at the time of the adoption of the plan of liquidation, together with the number of shares of each class of stock owned by each shareholder, the certificate numbers thereof, and the total number of votes to which entitled on the adoption of the plan of liquidation;

(c) A list of all corporate shareholders as of January 1, 1954, together with the number of shares of each class of stock owned by each such shareholder, the certificate numbers thereof, the total number of votes to which entitled on the adoption of the plan of liquidation, and a statement of all changes in ownership of stock by corporate shareholders between January 1, 1954, and the date of the adoption of the plan of liquidation, both dates inclusive; and
(d) A computation as described in section 1.6043–2(b) (following the format in Revenue Procedure 65–10, C.B. 1965–1,738 and Revenue Procedure 67–12, C.B. 1967, 589) of accumulated earnings and profits including all items of income and expense accrued up to the date on which the transfer of all property is completed.

**Attach a certified copy of the resolution or plan, together with all amendments or supplements not previously filed.**

Under penalties of perjury, I declare that I have examined this return, including accompanying schedules and statements, and to the best of my knowledge and belief it is true, correct, and complete.

| The Internal Revenue Service does not require a seal on this form, but if one is used, please place it here. | Date | Signature of officer | Title |
|---|---|---|---|

### Instructions

**1. Who must file.**—This form must be filed by every corporation that is to be dissolved or whose stock is to be liquidated in whole or in part.
Shareholders electing to be covered under section 333 of the Code must also file Form 964 within 30 days after the date of adoption of the plan of liquidation.

**2. When to file.**—This form must be filed within 30 days after the adoption of the resolution or plan for or in respect of the dissolution of a corporation or the liquidation in whole or in part of its capital stock. If after the filing of a Form 966 there is an amendment or supplement to the resolution or plan, an additional Form 966 based on the resolution or plan as amended or supplemented must be filed within 30 days after the adoption of such amendment or supplement. A return in respect of an amendment

or supplement will be deemed sufficient if it gives the date the prior return was filed and contains a certified copy of such amendment or supplement and all other information required by this form which was not given in such prior return.

**3. Where to file.**—This form must be filed with the Internal Revenue Service Center with which the corporation is required to file its income tax return.

**4. Signature.**—The return must be signed either by the president, vice president, treasurer, assistant treasurer or chief accounting officer, or by any other corporate officer (such as tax officer) who is authorized to sign. A receiver, trustee, or assignee must sign any return which he is required to file on behalf of a corporation.

## VI. LIQUIDATIONS AND DISSOLUTIONS

### A. PRIOR TO COMMENCEMENT OF BUSINESS

Most state laws permit the incorporators, prior to the commencement of business and the issuance of shares, to elect to dissolve voluntarily, such as the MBCA provision at Section 82.

The form of Articles of Dissolution of Incorporators to be filed with the state of incorporation in such a case, as recommended by the MBCA follows:

**EXAMPLE—Articles of Dissolution by Incorporators (MBCA)**

Filing fee: $_____

ARTICLES OF DISSOLUTION
BY INCORPORATORS
OF

_____

Pursuant to the provisions of Section 82 of the _____ Business Corporation Act, the undersigned of the corporation hereinafter named, adopt the following Articles of Dissolution:

FIRST: The name of the corporation is _____

_____.

SECOND: The date of issuance of its certificate of incorporation was _____.

THIRD: None of its shares has been issued.

FOURTH: The corporation has not commenced business.

FIFTH: The amount, if any, actually paid in on subscriptions for its shares, less any part thereof disposed of for necessary expenses, has been returned to those entitled thereto.

SIXTH: No debts of the corporation remain unpaid.

SEVENTH: The sole incorporator or a majority of the incorporators elects that the corporation be dissolved.

Dated _____, 19__.

_____

_____

_____

Incorporators (Note 1)

(Add Verification Form B)

Note: 1. The sole incorporator or, if more than one, a majority, must execute and verify these Articles.

## B. DISSOLUTION AFTER COMMENCEMENT OF BUSINESS

State law establishes very specific procedures which must be followed in order for an active corporation to terminate its existence. Each state's law has a different procedure, which must be carefully carried out. The step-by-step requirements of the MBCA follow.

### 1. Initial Action by Shareholders and Directors

A state adopting a procedure such as the MBCA law requires that either

(a) the shareholders, by unanimous written consent, express their intention to dissolve or

(b) the board of directors adopt resolutions recommending dissolution and directing the matter to shareholders who, at a meeting of shareholders, approve the dissolution by majority vote.[17]

Many times a dissolution will be structured so as to take advantage of certain provisions of the Internal Revenue Code. In such a case, a Plan of Complete Liquidation complying with the specific statutory provision must be adopted by the board of directors and shareholders and filed with the Internal Revenue Service with Form 966.[18]

One type of Plan of Complete Liquidation is included below:

### EXAMPLE—Board of Directors' Resolutions Adopting a Plan of Complete Liquidation

WHEREAS, in the judgment of the Board of Directors of this Company, it is deemed advisable and for the benefit of this Company and its shareholders that it should be dissolved, it is:

RESOLVED, that, subject to the approval of the shareholders of this Company and effective with the date of such approval, a plan of complete liquidation be, and it hereby is, adopted to effect such liquidation and dissolution of this Company in accordance with the resolutions set forth below:

RESOLVED, that the directors, officers and counsel for the Company are authorized and directed to take the following steps to effect the complete liquidation and dissolution of the Company prior to August 1, 19___, which shall be liquidated under the provisions of Section 331(a) and Section 337 of the Internal Revenue Code of 1954:

1. Promptly after the date of the meeting at which the shareholders adopt the plan of liquidation, any officer of

---

17. Refer to Sections 83 and 84 of the MBCA.

**QUESTION: Could the shareholders vote by a unanimous consent in writing in lieu of a meeting under a Section 84 dissolution?**

18. See Section V.F of this Chapter for an example of Form 966.

this Company be and each of them hereby is authorized and directed to file a Certificate of Election to Dissolve in accordance with the laws of the Commonwealth of Pennsylvania.

2. Within thirty (30) days after the date of the meeting at which the shareholders adopt the plan of liquidation, counsel for this Company shall file Form 966 with the District Director of Internal Revenue, Philadelphia, Pennsylvania, together with a certified copy of this resolution.

3. Promptly after adoption of the plan of liquidation, the President of this Company be and hereby is authorized and directed to sell all of the assets of this Company, subject to all of its liabilities, for cash in an amount not less than $400,000.

4. The officers of this Company be and each of them hereby is authorized and directed to satisfy such advertising and notice requirements as may be required by applicable law in connection with this Plan of Complete Liquidation.

5. After the necessary notice has been given and advertising has appeared and after the sale of assets has occurred, the duly authorized officers and directors shall distribute the net proceeds of said sale, after the payment of all liabilities and obligations of this Company, first to the holders of Preferred Stock of this Company in the amount of $110 per share, being the liquidation price for said shares, plus any accrued and unpaid dividends thereon to the date of distribution, and no more, and the remaining assets of the corporation shall be distributed to the holders of the Common Stock of this Company in proportion to the number of shares of Common Stock held by each of them.

6. The complete liquidation of this Company shall be effected within 12 months from the time of the adoption by the shareholders of this Company of this plan of liquidation.

7. The proper officers of this Company shall file Articles of Dissolution pursuant to the laws of the Commonwealth of Pennsylvania upon the completion of the distribution to the shareholders as provided above.

8. The proper officers and Company counsel shall file all other forms and documents required by the Commonwealth of Pennsylvania and the Federal Government, including tax returns in connection with the liquidation and dissolution of this Company.

9. Specific authorization is given to counsel for this Company to prepare, sign and forward to the Commissioner of Internal Revenue, after the final tax return has been filed

for this Company, a request for prompt assessment of all federal taxes due from this Company.

10. The officers and directors of this Company are empowered, authorized and directed to carry out the provisions of this resolution, and to adopt any further resolutions that may be necessary in liquidating and dissolving this Company in accordance with the expressed intent of the shareholders under the plan adopted.

RESOLVED, that a special meeting of the shareholders of this Company be called for August 25, 19__, for the purpose of voting upon the resolution to liquidate and dissolve this Company, and for discussion and voting upon any other matters that may properly come before the meeting with respect to the means of carrying out the plan of liquidation and dissolution of this Company.

## 2. Filing Statement of Intent to Dissolve

After the shareholders have approved the dissolution, the MBCA requires that a Statement of Intent to Dissolve must be filed with the Secretary of State. One form of the statement suggested by the MBCA follows: [19]

**EXAMPLE:**

Filing fee: $_____

STATEMENT OF INTENT TO DISSOLVE

_____

BY ACT OF THE CORPORATION

To the Secretary of State
  of the State of _____:

Pursuant to the provisions of Section 84 of the _____ Business Corporation Act, the undersigned corporation submits the following statement of intent to dissolve the corporation by act of the corporation.

FIRST: The name of the corporation is _____

_____.

SECOND: The names and respective addresses of its officers are:

| Name | Office | Address |
| --- | --- | --- |
| _____ | _____ | _____ |
| _____ | _____ | _____ |
| _____ | _____ | _____ |
| _____ | _____ | _____ |

_____

19. See Section 84(d) of the MBCA.

THIRD: The names and respective addresses of its directors are:

| Name | Address |
| --- | --- |
| _____ | _____ |
| _____ | _____ |
| _____ | _____ |

FOURTH: The following resolution to dissolve the corporation was adopted by the shareholders of the corporation on _____, 19__:

*[Insert copy of Resolution]*

FIFTH: The number of shares of the corporation outstanding at the time of such adoption was _____; and the number of shares entitled to vote thereon was:

| Class | Number of Shares |
| --- | --- |

SIXTH: The number of shares voted for such resolution was _____; and the number of shares voted against such resolution was _____.

Dated _____, 19__.

                    _____

By _____

        Its _____ Secretary

## 3. Effect of Filing Statement of Intent to Dissolve

Section 86 of the MBCA requires the corporation to cease all business activity, except insofar as it may be necessary to wind-up the business of the corporation upon the filing of the Statement of Intent to Dissolve.

## 4. Advertisement and Notice

After the statement of Intent to Dissolve has been filed with the state, some states require that the corporation give notice of its winding-up to all creditors. Under the laws of some states, this is done by an advertisement. In many states, a "proof of advertisement", i. e., a certificate from the newspaper attesting to publication, must be filed with the state.[20]

## 5. Corporate Clearance Certificate

Many states require that, prior to dissolution, a corporation acquire certificates from the appropriate state taxing bureaus that all

---

20. See an example of a proof of publication in Section II.C of Chapter Two.

taxes to the state have been paid. Other states, such as Delaware, permit dissolution to precede tax clearances. Such clearances may take months or even more than a year to obtain.

### 6. Articles of Dissolution

After all debts and obligations have been paid or discharged, or adequate provision has been made for their payment, the corporation must file Articles of Dissolution with the state. After this filing, and upon the issuance of a certificate of dissolution, the corporate existence will expire.[21] A sample form of Articles of Dissolution suggested by the MBCA is included below:

**EXAMPLE—Articles of Dissolution (MBCA)**

Filing fee: $_____

ARTICLES OF DISSOLUTION
PURSUANT TO SECTION 92 OF THE
_____ BUSINESS CORPORATION ACT
OF

Pursuant to the provisions of Section 92 of the _____ Business Corporation Act, the undersigned corporation adopts the following Articles of Dissolution for the purpose of dissolving the corporation:

FIRST: The name of the corporation is _____.

SECOND: A statement of intent to dissolve the corporation was filed by the Secretary of State of _____ on _____, 19\_\_, pursuant to the provisions of Section 85 of the _____ Business Corporation Act.

THIRD: All debts, obligations and liabilities of the corporation have been paid and discharged, or adequate provision has been made therefor.

FOURTH: All remaining property and assets of the corporation have been distributed among its shareholders, in accordance with their respective rights and interests.

FIFTH: There are no suits pending against the corporation in any court in respect of which adequate provi-

---

21. See Sections 92 and 93 of the MBCA.

sion has not been made for the satisfaction of any judgment, order or decree which may be entered against it.

Dated _____, 19__

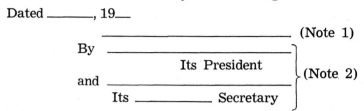

(Add Verification Form A)

Notes:   1.   Exact corporate name of corporation making the statement.

         2.   Signatures and titles of officers signing for the corporation.

# GLOSSARY

**Accounts Payable**—An obligation to pay an amount to a creditor.

**Accounts Receivable**—Amounts owed to the corporation on open account usually from customers in the ordinary course of business.

**Acknowledgment**—The act of signing a paper under oath before a public official such as a notary public; also known as notarization.

**Administrator**—The personal representative of a decedent who dies without a will.

**Affidavit**—A formal legal document signed with an acknowledgment.

**Affidavit of Mailing**—A statement under oath made by a person as to the time of depositing an item in the mails.

**Agreed Valuation**—A method for establishment of price, found in some shareholders' agreements, which fixes a specified dollar purchase price based on the parties' agreement.

**Allocation Formula**—A specified method for dividing up a sum among different parties or things.

**American Arbitration Association**—A private organization which makes available individuals who agree to serve on a panel to decide a disagreement arising under a contract. The arbitration is a private way of resolving disputes outside of the judicial system for expediting resolution of the conflict.

**Annual Meeting**—The regular meeting of the shareholders of the corporation required by statute which is held each year for election of directors.

**Anti-Dilution Provision**—A provision in options or agreements for sale of stock designed to prevent the purchaser from having a proportionate stock interest reduced by stock dividends, stock splits, other sales of stock, etc.

**Arbitration**—A method of settling controversies through a private forum rather than litigation in court.

**Articles of Amendment**—The formal document which modifies the articles of incorporation when properly filed with the state.

**Articles of Incorporation**—The formal document which creates a corporation when properly filed in accordance with the laws of a state; also known as corporate charter.

**Asset**—Something of value.

**Assigns**—Persons to whom rights or title to assets have been transferred.

**Attestation**—The act of formally witnessing the execution of a document by another.

**Attorney-in-Fact**—A person who has been granted a power of attorney by another person to act on a matter for the first person as fully as the first person could act directly.

**Authorized Capital**—The total number of shares of all classes of stock of a corporation authorized for issuance in its articles of incorporation.

**Authorized Stock**—The total number of shares of stock authorized by a corporation in its articles of incorporation (see authorized capital).

**Balance Sheet**—A financial statement setting forth, in dollar terms, the assets and liabilities of a person or entity as of a given point in time.

**Ballot**—A writing which exercises the right to vote on a matter.

**Bank Resolutions**—The resolutions adopted by the board of directors of a corporation authorizing a bank account and establishing which persons will have authority to sign for the corporation with respect to the account.

**Bankruptcy**—A formal judicial proceeding in which a person whose debts exceed assets can restructure his or her debts or be discharged from debts by a pro rata distribution of assets to creditors.

**Bearer**—One in possession of an instrument.

**Blue Sky Laws**—State securities laws.

**Board of Directors**—The group of individuals which collectively has the legal responsibility of exercising control over and managing the affairs of a corporation.

**"Boilerplate" Provisions**—Standard provisions repeatedly appearing in agreements or other documents.

**Bona Fide Offer**—An offer in writing by a person who is ready, willing and able to buy and who has no external constraint to buy.

**Bonds**—Secured indebtedness evidenced in writing.

**Book Value**—The historical cost to a corporation of an asset.

**Book Value Per Share**—An amount equal to the net assets (gross assets less liabilities) of the corporation divided by the number of outstanding shares of stock of the corporation.

**Business Corporations**—Corporations which operate for a profit.

**Bylaws**—The standards and procedures for the legal organization of a corporation adopted by the corporation in compliance with corporate statutes and the articles of incorporation.

**Capital Stock or Franchise Taxes**—The special tax levied on corporations by a state. These taxes are frequently based on the number of shares which a corporation is authorized to issue, the authorized capital of these shares, or some similar factors, and may be a one-time tax payable upon incorporation or an annual franchise tax or both.

**Capital Surplus**—The entire surplus of a corporation other than its earned surplus; also known as paid-in surplus.

**Cause of Action**—A set of facts which is asserted by a plaintiff and which, if proven, are sufficient to support a valid claim in a lawsuit.

**Certificate of Authority or Qualification**—The document issued by a state which acknowledges that a foreign corporation is entitled to transact business within the state.

**Certificate of Incorporation**—A formal document issued by the state acknowledging incorporation and stating the date of incorporation.

**Certificate of Withdrawal**—A formal document issued by a state acknowledging termination of a certificate of authority of a foreign corporation.

**Certificates**—Pieces of paper evidencing shares in a corporation.

**Certified or Audited Statements**—Financial statements which have been reviewed by an accountant that has performed such independent tests as are appropriate to verify the accuracy of the corporation's books and records.

**Classes of Stock**—The designation of different categories of shares, such as common stock and preferred stock.

**Classification of Directors**—A method whereby some corporations provide for election of only a portion of the board of directors each year.

**Clearance Certificate**—A formal acknowledgment from the various state taxing departments that all fees and franchise taxes have been paid.

**"Close" Corporation**—A corporation with few shareholders formed under special state provisions allowing greater managerial flexibility by shareholders.

**Closely-Held Corporation**—A corporation which has only a few shareholders.

**Closing the Transfer Books**—A procedure whereby a corporation freezes the list of shareholders entitled to vote at a meeting or receive dividends by suspending the ability to transfer stock on the corporate books.

**Collateral**—Asset which secures a debt so that if a debtor defaults, the creditor may obtain the asset.

**Common Stock**—A class of shares which is created when the articles of incorporation provide for a class without any special features which represents the residual equity of a corporation.

**Confession of Judgment**—A procedure now often disfavored by courts pursuant to which the holder of an obligation, without obtaining the obligor's consent or approval, may obtain an immediate judgment from a court against the obligor and enforce the judgment by levy and execution on the obligor's property in accordance with state law.

**Consideration**—Value received for a promise to perform an act.

**Consolidated Financial Statements**—A combination of the financial statements of the company and its subsidiaries.

**Consolidation**—The combination of two or more corporations to create an entirely new corporation which is different from any of the absorbed corporations.

**Contempt**—Willful disobedience of a direct court order.

**Conversion**—The process of exchanging one class of securities for another class of the same corporation.

**Conversion Rate**—The formula which determines the amount of one class of securities that can be exchanged for another class of the same corporation.

**Corporate Kit**—The corporate seal, minute book and stock certificate book of the corporation.

**Corporate Marriage**—A slang term for a merger or consolidation or other combination of several corporations.

**Corporate Seal**—The official imprint to be affixed to documents by a corporation.

**Corporation**—A legal entity which is a creature of the state of incorporation separate and apart from its owners.

**Creditor**—A person who is owed money by another person.

**Cumulative Dividends**—Dividends on preferred stock which have accrued over time but have not been paid and must be paid before any dividends can be paid on common stock.

**Cumulative Voting**—The right of a shareholder, voting in the election of directors, to multiply the number of votes to which the shareholder is entitled by the number of directors to be elected and to cast the whole number of such votes for one candidate or to distribute them among any two or more candidates.

**Damages**—A court award of money compensation to a litigant.

**Debentures**—Unsecured debt evidenced by a formal written document.

**Debt Security**—A formal written document evidencing a corporation's obligation.

**Debtor**—A person who owes money to another.

**Default**—An act of a borrower which violates the terms of a loan agreement.

**Defendant**—A person against whom a court action is commenced.

**Demand Note**—A written promise to pay money entitling the holder to require the payment of the principal at any time upon making demand to the obligor for payment.

**DGCL**—Delaware General Corporation Law.

**Dissolution**—The formal termination of corporate existence pursuant to statutory procedures of the state of incorporation.

**Distribution of Assets**—The transfer of cash or property by a corporation to its creditors or shareholders.

**Dividend**—A pro rata distribution of profits by a corporation of cash, stock or property to shareholders with respect to its shares.

**Dividend Arrearage**—A distribution on a cumulative preferred stock which has been scheduled to be paid to shareholders but has not been timely paid.

**Dividend Rights**—The specific terms setting forth circumstances under which a class of stock shall receive a distribution from the corporation.

**Division**—A part of the corporation's operations which is segregated for corporate and financial purposes by product, location, function or some other logical basis of differentiation.

**Document of Public Record**—A document which may be inspected by any person at the official office where the document is filed.

**"Doing Business"**—The acts of a foreign corporation in a specific state sufficient to require it to obtain a certificate of authority in that state.

**Domestic Corporation**—A corporation that is incorporated in a specific state is a domestic corporation with respect to that state.

**Double Taxation**—The concept that a corporation's income is taxed at the corporate level and again at the shareholders' level when it is received as dividends.

**Draw**—A payment of money as an advance against future commissions earned by an employee.

**Earned Surplus**—The sum total of a corporation's net profits, gains or losses from the date of incorporation, less distributions to shareholders and transfers to stated capital and capital surplus; also known as retained earnings.

**Earnings and Profits**—The income tax calculation of the accumulation of all profits of the corporation during its existence reduced by losses and distributions to shareholders; different from earned surplus.

**Earnings Multiples**—A formula used to fix the purchase price of stock which provides that the value of the corporation for purposes of determining the purchase price is the product obtained by multiplying the net income of the corporation by an arbitrary fixed number, such as 3 times earnings or 10 times earnings.

**Employment Agreement**—A formal written agreement between a corporation and an employee setting forth the terms and conditions of the employment relationship.

**Equity "Kicker"**—An agreement with a lender to permit it to acquire an interest in the stock of the corporation. It is designed to make the loan more attractive to the lender.

**Equity Securities**—Generally, the classes of stock of a corporation.

**ERISA**—Employee Retirement Income Security Act of 1974.

**Execution**—The act of formally signing a document.

**Executor**—The personal representative of a decedent named in the will.

**Fair Market Value**—The price which would be paid by a willing buyer to a willing seller.

**Family Transferees**—Members of the family of a shareholder to whom the shareholder may transfer stock pursuant to a shareholders' agreement.

**Fictitious Name**—Any assumed name, style or designation other than the proper corporate name of the corporation using such name.

**Fiduciary**—A person in a position of trust with respect to another person such as the relationship of a director or officer to the corporation. The law imposes certain obligations on the fiduciary.

**Financing Statements**—Documents which are filed to evidence a security interest of a creditor in personal property of the debtor.

**Fiscal Year**—The twelve consecutive calendar months which a corporation elects as its accounting and financial reporting year.

**Fringe Benefits**—Compensation to an employee of an indirect nature rather than wages or salary, such as health insurance, pension plans, life insurance, etc.

**Fully Paid and Nonassessable**—Stock on which the corporation can demand no further money because the original purchaser paid in the agreed amount.

**Good-Faith Purchaser for Value**—A person who bought stock (or other assets) in an arms'-length transaction without any knowledge or reason to know of any problem of the seller with respect to the title to the stock or asset.

**Group Life Insurance**—A life insurance program which covers all employees or all employees of a specific class; a type of fringe benefit.

**Incentive Compensation**—A method of determining employee compensation that ties the amount earned to the productivity of the employee in the employment.

**Incorporation**—The procedures to be followed in forming the corporation.

**Incorporator**—The person or entity who forms the corporation and signs the articles of incorporation which are filed with the state.

**Indemnification of Officers and Directors**—Payment by a corporation for losses incurred by a director or officer for actions on behalf of the corporation.

**Informal Shareholder Action With Less Than Unanimous Consent**— A procedure permitted by some corporate statutes pursuant to which written consent of less than all shareholders is adequate for effective action.

**Injunction**—A direct court order to a person to refrain from an action or risk jail for contempt of court.

**Insolvency**—The inability of a person or corporation to pay debts as they become due in the usual course of its business or the existence of more debts than assets.

**Interest**—Charge assessed by a creditor for the use of money in a loan transaction.

**Inter vivos**—Between or among living persons.

**Inventory**—Collectively, the raw materials, work in process and finished goods of a business which are manufactured and sold to customers in the ordinary course of business.

**I.R.C.**—The United States Internal Revenue Code of 1954, as amended.

**Issued Shares**—Shares that have been sold by proper corporate action to a shareholder for value.

**Joinder of Spouses**—The uniting of a husband or wife to an agreement to insure that he or she will be bound thereby even though otherwise not directly a party to the subject matter of the agreement.

**Joint Tenancy**—A method of ownership by two or more persons, where, when one owner dies, the survivor(s) get the decedent's share directly rather than having the property pass through the estate of the decedent.

**Judges of Election**—Persons selected at a shareholders meeting to tally the voting on an impartial basis.

**Key-Person Life Insurance**—A policy specifically on the life of a valuable individual employee to provide funds to the corporation in the event of the employee's death.

**Legend**—A statement on the face of a stock certificate indicating the existence of special rights or limitations.

**Liability**—An obligation to pay money.

**License Fee**—A special tax to which a corporation may be subject, especially as a foreign corporation.

**Limited Liability**—The limitation of the obligation of a shareholder of a corporation to the amount invested or agreed to be invested in the corporation.

**Liquid Assets**—Property of the corporation which is cash or which is easily convertible into cash such as government bonds.

**Liquidation**—The paying off of the debts of the corporation, winding up of its affairs and distributing the remaining assets among the shareholders of the corporation.

**Liquidation Rights**—The respective claims related to a corporation in the event of its liquidation.

**Litigant**—A party to a lawsuit.

**Mandatory Purchase**—The right of one person to compel another to purchase an asset owned by the first person; also known as a "put".

**Mandatory Sale**—The right of one person to compel another to sell an asset to the first person; also known as a "call".

**Matching Offers**—A requirement that a person with a right of first refusal pay the amount offered by a third party.

**M.B.C.A.**—The Model Business Corporation Act.

**Merger**—A formal combination of two or more corporations where one corporation is absorbed by another, the latter of which is called the surviving corporation.

**Minute Book**—A book containing the written legal history of a corporation and the written notes of proceedings at corporate shareholder and director meetings and official corporate documents.

**Minutes**—A summary of the proceedings of a corporate meeting including formal resolutions.

**Mortgage**—A written grant by a debtor to a creditor of a collateral interest in real estate owned by the debtor.

**Mortgagee**—The creditor in a mortgage relationship.

**Mortgagor**—The debtor in a mortgage relationship.

**Name Holding Corporation**—A corporation created in a state whose only purpose is to protect the availability of a name for future use.

**Net Assets**—The difference between assets and liabilities of a corporation.

**Net Worth**—The balancing figure between assets and liabilities; also known as "net assets", "shareholders equity" or "capital".

**Nominal Directors**—Persons who are designated directors only for the purpose of forming a corporation as required by some state laws and who will immediately resign in favor of the directors who will make business decisions.

**Nonassessable Stock**—Stock which has been issued for not less than par value, if any, or for the agreed consideration if of no par value, on which the owner cannot be charged for any further amount.

**Non-Cumulative Preferred Stock**—Preferred stock, the shareholders of which are not entitled to receive at a future time, any dividends which were not previously paid at the scheduled time.

**Notary Public**—A public officer authorized to administer oaths, witness documents, and take acknowledgments.

**Note**—The simplest form of written promise to pay money.

**Notice**—The providing of advance information of a future event such as a corporate meeting.

**Obligor**—A debtor.

**Ordinary and Necessary Expenses**—Generally, those costs which are deductible from revenues in computing taxable income because such expenses are those usually incurred by a business of that type.

**Organization Meeting**—The first meeting of the board of directors after incorporation at which initial actions are taken.

**Outstanding Shares**—Shares of stock which have been issued and are in the hands of shareholders other than the corporation itself; also, issued shares less treasury shares.

**Par Value**—The minimum amount that may legally be paid in for stock upon issuance to render it fully paid and nonassessable.

**Parent**—A corporation which owns all or a primary portion of the shares of another corporation.

**Parliamentary Procedure**—The formal rules of order used at a corporate meeting.

**Partnership**—An arrangement between two or more persons to carry on a business together and to share profits and losses therefrom where the individuals have personal liability.

**Payment Date**—The day on which a dividend which has been declared on stock is actually distributed to shareholders.

**P.B.C.L.**—Pennsylvania Business Corporation Law.

**Perfection of the Security Interest**—The filing of a financing statement or taking possession of the collateral.

**Perpetual Existence**—The designation of an unlimited life of a corporation in its articles of incorporation.

**Personal Liability**—The availability of the personal assets of an individual to business creditors for satisfaction of the obligations of the business.

**Personal Property**—All non-real estate assets, whether tangible or intangible.

**Personal Representative**—The individual who administers the estate of a decedent who dies without a will or who carries out the will of the decedent.

**Plaintiff**—A person who commences a court action against another.

**Pledge**—The granting of a security interest in personal property by delivering physical possession of the collateral to the creditor.

**Power of Attorney**—A writing which authorizes a person to act for and on behalf of the person signing the writing as described in the writing (see attorney-in-fact).

**Preemptive Rights**—The right of a shareholder to purchase a pro rata share of a new issue of common stock or security convertible into common stock which the corporation proposes to issue before any non-shareholder may be offered such security by the corporation.

**Preferred Stock**—A class of stock entitled to prior rights over another class of stock of the corporation with respect to dividends or the distribution of assets in the event of liquidation; also known as preference stock.

**Pre-Incorporation Subscription**—An agreement by a person before a corporation has been formed to buy stock of a corporation upon its incorporation.

**Prime Rate**—The rate of interest charged by a bank to its most credit-worthy borrowers for short-term unsecured debts.

**Proof of Publication**—A certificate of a newspaper that a legal notice has been published on a specific date.

**Prothonotary**—The head clerk of county courts in some states.

**Proxy**—A written authorization by a shareholder of record to another person to vote shares at a shareholders' meeting with the same effect as if the holder of the shares were present in person at the meeting.

**Proxy Statement**—A document that public companies mail with a request for a proxy to their shareholders which describes the actions to be taken at the meeting.

**Public Market**—Generally, the ability of the stock of a publicly-held corporation to be bought and sold by the public at large through stockbrokers.

**Public Offering**—A sale of securities, such as stock or bonds, to the general public in accordance with applicable federal and state laws.

**Publicly-Held Corporation**—Corporations, the stock of which is owned by a large number of persons, such as Xerox, General Motors, and IBM.

**Qualification**—The acquisition by a foreign corporation of a certificate of authority.

**Quorum**—The minimum number of people prescribed by statute or bylaws that must be present at a meeting in order to transact business.

**Ratification**—The process of confirming and adopting an act already performed on behalf of a corporation.

**Record Date**—A day set by the board of directors as the time for determination of those shareholders of record entitled to notice, dividends or other shareholder rights.

**Record Shareholders**—The owners of stock of a corporation as reflected in its stock transfer books.

**Registered Office**—The location of a corporation designated in its articles of incorporation or certificate of authority where legal documents may be served.

**Registry Statement**—A document filed with the articles of incorporation containing information about the officers and other corporate matters which is used by the corporate taxing bureau for its purposes.

**Regular Meeting**—A periodically scheduled shareholders' or directors' meeting at which any corporate business may be conducted.

**Resolution**—A formal written statement of the shareholders or directors of a corporation designating (i) an action that the corporation may take and (ii) those persons who may effectuate the action on its behalf.

**Restated Articles of Incorporation**—An amendment to the articles of incorporation which consolidates into one document all previous amendments of the articles.

**Restrictive Covenant**—A clause in an agreement which restricts the future employment or engagement in a business by a person.

**Reverse Stock Split**—A combination of the issued shares of any class of stock of a corporation so that there are a fewer number of shares issued after the reverse stock split than before it; opposite of stock split.

**Right of First Refusal**—The option of a person to decide whether to buy or refuse to buy an asset before the asset can be sold by another to anyone else.

**Right of Redemption**—The right of a corporation to require the holders of a class of securities to sell all or a part of their securities to the corporation at a specified price.

**/S/**—The symbol which conforms a copy of a manually executed document to indicate that it is a true and correct copy of the executed document.

**Sealed Instrument**—An agreement which, in many states, is enforceable even without consideration to the person against whom it is enforceable.

**Section 1244 Stock**—Stock issued by a corporation in compliance with Section 1244 of the I.R.C. which may confer tax benefits on purchasers of stock in the event of a loss on the disposition of the stock.

**Secured Debt**—An obligation for which the holder has a specific claim against designated collateral of a debtor in the event of failure to repay the debt at maturity.

**Secured Party**—A creditor that has obtained collateral for repayment of the debt.

**Security Agreement**—A contract between a debtor and a creditor which designates collateral to assure payment of the debt and the respective rights of the parties with respect to the collateral.

**Security Interest**—A collateral interest in real or personal property (such as a mortgage) which secures the payment of an obligation.

**Series Preferred Stock**—Preferred stock which may be authorized for issuance from time to time by the board of directors where state law permits and the articles of incorporation authorize the class of preferred stock.

**Severability Clause**—A boilerplate provision in an agreement stating that if a court finds another provision invalid or unenforceable, the remainder of the agreement shall be interpreted as if the invalid provision was not in the agreement.

**Shareholder**—One who is a holder of one or more shares of stock of a corporation; also known as stockholder.

**Shareholders' Agreement**—A written agreement entered into among two or more shareholders of a corporation with a small number of shareholders restricting transfers of stock by the parties to the agreement.

**Shareholders List**—A list of all shareholders of a corporation at a specific date.

**Shares**—The units into which the proprietary interests in a corporation are divided.

**Sinking Fund**—A required periodic payment for the purpose of (i) the redemption of a specified number of shares of preferred stock (or reduction of an indebtedness) each year or (ii) the future retirement of the preferred stock (or debt) at a specified date.

**Sole Proprietorship**—A form of business which is conducted by one person who has personal liability for the business debts.

**Special Meetings**—A meeting of shareholders or directors called for a specific purpose.

**Specific Performance**—A direct court order to a person to do a specific act or risk jail for contempt of court.

**Stated Capital**—The sum of the par value of all shares having a par value and the consideration received by a corporation for shares without par value.

**Statement of Cancellation**—A document required to be filed with some states when a corporation formally cancels treasury stock.

**Stock**—Shares of a corporation.

**Stock Dividend**—A distribution of additional shares of stock to stockholders by a corporation rather than money.

**Stock Option**—The right to purchase stock at some future date at a price which is specified at the time of creation of the option.

**Stock Split**—An increase in outstanding shares of stock of a corporation by dividing the existing shares into a greater number of shares, usually by an amendment to the articles, resulting in the owning of more shares by each shareholder but with a proportionately reduced value per share.

**Subchapter S Corporation**—A corporation which meets certain requirements permitting it to be taxed in a manner similar to a partnership, thereby avoiding double taxation.

**Subordinated Debt**—A class of securities which is junior in right of repayment to another class of debt securities of a corporation.

**Subscriber**—One who agrees to acquire shares in a corporation before or after incorporation.

**Subscription Rights**—Rights granted to existing shareholders to purchase additional shares of the corporation's stock at a specified price for a specified period of time.

**Subsidiary**—A corporation the shares of which are primarily or entirely owned by another corporation which is called the parent.

**Surplus**—The excess of the net assets of a corporation over its stated capital.

**Tenancy by the Entireties**—A type of ownership which is a joint tenancy where the two owners are husband and wife.

**Tenancy in Common**—A type of ownership of property by more than one person where each person has a transferable undivided interest in the property which will pass at death through the estate of the decedent; contrasted with joint tenancy.

**Trade Secret**—A plan or process, mechanism or compound known only to its owner and those of its employees to whom it is necessary to disclose it.

**Transfer Agent and Registrar**—Persons or entities appointed for the purpose of recording stock transfers for a corporation.

**Treasury Shares**—Shares of stock that have been repurchased by the corporation which had previously issued them; also known as issued but not outstanding stock.

**Trustee**—A fiduciary charged with the obligation to control properly assets or powers placed in his or her hands for the benefit of another.

**Trustee in Bankruptcy**—A fiduciary appointed to preserve and control the assets of a person in bankruptcy.

**Trust Indenture**—A formal agreement governing the rights and obligations of a creditor and debtor.

**Uniform Commercial Code**—A statute which has been adopted in every state but Louisiana in generally similar form providing for the governing of business and commercial transactions including security interests in personal property.

**Unissued Shares**—Authorized capital which has never been sold by a corporation.

**Unrestricted and Unreserved Earned Surplus**—The portion of earned surplus which is the legal maximum of dividends that may be distributed to shareholders.

**Unsecured Debt**—Debt in which the creditor only has a claim against the general assets of the corporation and has no special rights to any particular asset of the corporation.

**Voting Rights**—The ability of shareholders to make decisions on certain corporate matters based on the number and class of shares owned.

**Voting Trusts**—The deposit of shares by several shareholders in trust in the name of one or more persons who are the voting trustees for the purpose of voting the shares as a block to control the business of the corporation.

**Waiver of Notice**—A document signed by a shareholder or director before or after a meeting relinquishing the right to have advance information about the meeting.

**Working Capital**—Cash and other liquid assets required for ordinary business operations.

*

# APPENDIX I

## MODEL BUSINESS CORPORATION ACT

---

### TABLE OF SECTIONS

# APPENDIX I

# APPENDIX I

............... * BUSINESS

CORPORATION ACT

### § 1. Short Title

This Act shall be known and may be cited as the "...... *
Business Corporation Act."

### § 2. Definitions

As used in this Act, unless the context otherwise requires, the
term:

(a) "Corporation" or "domestic corporation" means a corporation for profit subject to the provisions of this Act, except a
foreign corporation.

(b) "Foreign corporation" means a corporation for profit organized under laws other than the laws of this State for a purpose or purposes for which a corporation may be organized under this Act.

(c) "Articles of incorporation" means the original or restated
articles of incorporation or articles of consolidation and all
amendments thereto including articles of merger.

(d) "Shares" means the units into which the proprietary interests in a corporation are divided.

(e) "Subscriber" means one who subscribes for shares in a
corporation, whether before or after incorporation.

(f) "Shareholder" means one who is a holder of record of
shares in a corporation.

(g) "Authorized shares" means the shares of all classes which
the corporation is authorized to issue.

* Supply name of State.

(h) "Treasury shares" means shares of a corporation which have been issued, have been subsequently acquired by and belong to the corporation, and have not, either by reason of the acquisition or thereafter, been cancelled or restored to the status of authorized but unissued shares. Treasury shares shall be deemed to be "issued" shares, but not "outstanding" shares.

(i) "Net assets" means the amount by which the total assets of a corporation exceed the total debts of the corporation.

(j) "Stated capital" means, at any particular time, the sum of (1) the par value of all shares of the corporation having a par value that have been issued, (2) the amount of the consideration received by the corporation for all shares of the corporation without par value that have been issued, except such part of the consideration therefor as may have been allocated to capital surplus in a manner permitted by law, and (3) such amounts not included in clauses (1) and (2) of this paragraph as have been transferred to stated capital of the corporation, whether upon the issue of shares as a share dividend or otherwise, minus all reductions from such sum as have been effected in a manner permitted by law. Irrespective of the manner of designation thereof by the laws under which a foreign corporation is organized, the stated capital of a foreign corporation shall be determined on the same basis and in the same manner as the stated capital of a domestic corporation, for the purpose of computing fees, franchise taxes and other charges imposed by this Act.

(k) "Surplus" means the excess of the net assets of a corporation over its stated capital.

(l) "Earned surplus" means the portion of the surplus of a corporation equal to the balance of its net profits, income, gains and losses from the date of incorporation, or from the latest date when a deficit was eliminated by an application of its capital surplus or stated capital or otherwise, after deducting subsequent distributions to shareholders and transfers to stated capital and capital surplus to the extent such distributions and transfers are made out of earned surplus. Earned surplus shall include also any portion of surplus allocated to earned surplus in mergers, consolidations or acquisitions of all or substantially all of the outstanding shares or of the property and assets of another corporation, domestic or foreign.

(m) "Capital surplus" means the entire surplus of a corporation other than its earned surplus.

(n) "Insolvent" means inability of a corporation to pay its debts as they become due in the usual course of its business.

(o) "Employee" includes officers but not directors. A director may accept duties which make him also an employee.

### § 3. Purposes

Corporations may be organized under this Act for any lawful purpose or purposes, except for the purpose of banking or insurance.

### § 4. General Powers

Each corporation shall have power:

(a) To have perpetual succession by its corporate name unless a limited period of duration is stated in its articles of incorporation.

(b) To sue and be sued, complain and defend, in its corporate name.

(c) To have a corporate seal which may be altered at pleasure, and to use the same by causing it, or a facsimile thereof, to be impressed or affixed or in any other manner reproduced.

(d) To purchase, take, receive, lease, or otherwise acquire, own, hold, improve, use and otherwise deal in and with, real or personal property, or any interest therein, wherever situated.

(e) To sell, convey, mortgage, pledge, lease, exchange, transfer and otherwise dispose of all or any part of its property and assets.

(f) To lend money and use its credit to assist its employees.

(g) To purchase, take, receive, subscribe for, or otherwise acquire, own, hold, vote, use, employ, sell, mortgage, lend, pledge, or otherwise dispose of, and otherwise use and deal in and with, shares or other interests in, or obligations of, other domestic or foreign corporations, associations, partnerships or individuals, or direct or indirect obligations of the United States or of any other government, state, territory, governmental district or municipality or of any instrumentality thereof.

(h) To make contracts and guarantees and incur liabilities, borrow money at such rates of interest as the corporation may determine, issue its notes, bonds, and other obligations, and secure any of its obligations by mortgage or pledge of all or any of its property, franchises and income.

(i) To lend money for its corporate purposes, invest and reinvest its funds, and take and hold real and personal property as security for the payment of funds so loaned or invested.

(j) To conduct its business, carry on its operations and have offices and exercise the powers granted by this Act, within or without this State.

(k) To elect or appoint officers and agents of the corporation, and define their duties and fix their compensation.

(*l*) To make and alter by-laws, not inconsistent with its articles of incorporation or with the laws of this State, for the administration and regulation of the affairs of the corporation.

(m) To make donations for the public welfare or for charitable, scientific or educational purposes.

(n) To transact any lawful business which the board of directors shall find will be in aid of governmental policy.

(*o*) To pay pensions and establish pension plans, pension trusts, profit sharing plans, stock bonus plans, stock option plans and other incentive plans for any or all of its directors, officers and employees.

(p) To be a promoter, partner, member, associate, or manager of any partnership, joint venture, trust or other enterprise.

(q) To have and exercise all powers necessary or convenient to effect its purposes.

## § 5. Indemnification of Officers, Directors, Employees and Agents

(a) A corporation shall have power to indemnify any person who was or is a party or is threatened to be made a party to any threatened, pending or completed action, suit or proceeding, whether civil, criminal, administrative or investigative (other than an action by or in the right of the corporation) by reason of the fact that he is or was a director, officer, employee or agent of the corporation, or is or was serving at the request of the corporation as a director, officer, employee or agent of another corporation, partnership, joint venture, trust or other enterprise, against expenses (including attorneys' fees), judgments, fines and amounts paid in settlement actually and reasonably incurred by him in connection with such action, suit or proceeding if he acted in good faith and in a manner he reasonably believed to be in or not opposed to the best interests of the corporation, and, with respect to any criminal action or proceeding, had no reasonable cause to believe his conduct was unlawful. The termination of any action, suit or proceeding by judgment, order, settlement, conviction, or upon a plea of nolo contendere or its equivalent, shall not, of itself, create a presumption that the person did not act in good faith and in a manner which he reasonably believed to be in or not opposed to the best interests of the corporation, and, with respect to any criminal action or proceeding, had reasonable cause to believe that his conduct was unlawful.

(b) A corporation shall have power to indemnify any person who was or is a party or is threatened to be made a party to any threatened, pending or completed action or suit by or in the right of the corporation to procure a judgment in its favor by reason of the fact that he is or was a director, officer, employee or agent of the corporation, or is or was serving at the request of the corporation as a director, officer, employee or agent of another corporation, partnership, joint venture, trust or other enterprise against expenses (including attorneys' fees) actually and reasonably incurred by him in connection with the defense or settlement of such action or suit if he acted in good faith and in a manner he reasonably believed to be in or not opposed to the best interests of the corporation and except that no indemnification shall be made in respect of any claim, issue or matter as to which such person shall have been adjudged to be liable for negligence or misconduct in the performance of his duty to the corporation unless and only to the extent that the court in which such action or suit was brought shall determine upon application that, despite the adjudication of liability but in view of all circumstances of the case, such person is fairly and reasonably entitled to indemnity for such expenses which such court shall deem proper.

(c) To the extent that a director, officer, employee or agent of a corporation has been successful on the merits or otherwise in defense of any action, suit or proceeding referred to in subsections (a) or (b), or in defense of any claim, issue or matter therein, he shall be indemnified against expenses (including attorneys' fees) actually and reasonably incurred by him in connection therewith.

(d) Any indemnification under subsections (a) or (b) (unless ordered by a court) shall be made by the corporation only as authorized in the specific case upon a determination that indemnification of the director, officer, employee or agent is proper in the circumstances because he has met the applicable standard of conduct set forth in subsections (a) or (b). Such determination shall be made (1) by the board of directors by a majority vote of a quorum consisting of directors who were not parties to such action, suit or proceeding, or (2) if such a quorum is not obtainable, or, even if obtainable a quorum of disinterested directors so directs, by independent legal counsel in a written opinion, or (3) by the shareholders.

(e) Expenses (including attorneys' fees) incurred in defending a civil or criminal action, suit or proceeding may be paid by the corporation in advance of the final disposition of such action, suit or proceeding as authorized in the manner provided in subsection (d) upon receipt of an undertaking by or on behalf of the director, officer, employee or agent to repay such amount unless it shall ultimately be determined that he is entitled to be indemnified by the corporation as authorized in this section.

(f) The indemnification provided by this section shall not be deemed exclusive of any other rights to which those indemnified may be entitled under any by-law, agreement, vote of shareholders or disinterested directors or otherwise, both as to action in his official capacity and as to action in another capacity while holding such office, and shall continue as to a person who has ceased to be a director, officer, employee or agent and shall inure to the benefit of the heirs, executors and administrators of such a person.

(g) A corporation shall have power to purchase and maintain insurance on behalf of any person who is or was a director, officer, employee or agent of the corporation, or is or was serving at the request of the corporation as a director, officer, employee or agent of another corporation, partnership, joint venture, trust or other enterprise against any liability asserted against him and incurred by him in any such capacity or arising out of his status as such, whether or not the corporation would have the power to indemnify him against such liability under the provisions of this section.

## § 6. Right of Corporation to Acquire and Dispose of Its Own Shares

A corporation shall have the right to purchase, take, receive or otherwise acquire, hold, own, pledge, transfer or otherwise dispose of its own shares, but purchases of its own shares, whether direct or indirect, shall be made only to the extent of unreserved and unrestricted earned surplus available therefor, and, if the articles of incorporation so permit or with the affirmative vote of the holders of a majority of all shares entitled to vote thereon, to the extent of unreserved and unrestricted capital surplus available therefor.

To the extent that earned surplus or capital surplus is used as the measure of the corporation's right to purchase its own shares, such surplus shall be restricted so long as such shares are held as treasury shares, and upon the disposition or cancellation of any such shares the restriction shall be removed pro tanto.

Notwithstanding the foregoing limitation, a corporation may purchase or otherwise acquire its own shares for the purpose of:

(a) Eliminating fractional shares.

(b) Collecting or compromising indebtedness to the corporation.

(c) Paying dissenting shareholders entitled to payment for their shares under the provisions of this Act.

(d) Effecting, subject to the other provisions of this Act, the retirement of its redeemable shares by redemption or by purchase at not to exceed the redemption price.

No purchase of or payment for its own shares shall be made at a time when the corporation is insolvent or when such purchase or payment would make it insolvent.

### § 7.  Defense of Ultra Vires

No act of a corporation and no conveyance or transfer of real or personal property to or by a corporation shall be invalid by reason of the fact that the corporation was without capacity or power to do such act or to make or receive such conveyance or transfer, but such lack of capacity or power may be asserted:

(a) In a proceeding by a shareholder against the corporation to enjoin the doing of any act or the transfer of real or personal property by or to the corporation.  If the unauthorized act or transfer sought to be enjoined is being, or is to be, performed or made pursuant to a contract to which the corporation is a party, the court may, if all of the parties to the contract are parties to the proceeding and if it deems the same to be equitable, set aside and enjoin the performance of such contract, and in so doing may allow to the corporation or to the other parties to the contract, as the case may be, compensation for the loss or damage sustained by either of them which may result from the action of the court in setting aside and enjoining the performance of such contract, but anticipated profits to be derived from the performance of the contract shall not be awarded by the court as a loss or damage sustained.

(b) In a proceeding by the corporation, whether acting directly or through a receiver, trustee, or other legal representative, or through shareholders in a representative suit, against the incumbent or former officers or directors of the corporation.

(c) In a proceeding by the Attorney General, as provided in this Act, to dissolve the corporation, or in a proceeding by the Attorney General to enjoin the corporation from the transaction of unauthorized business.

### § 8.  Corporate Name

The corporate name:

(a) Shall contain the word "corporation," "company," "incorporated" or "limited," or shall contain an abbreviation of one of such words.

(b) Shall not contain any word or phrase which indicates or implies that it is organized for any purpose other than one or more of the purposes contained in its articles of incorporation.

(c) Shall not be the same as, or deceptively similar to, the name of any domestic corporation existing under the laws of this State or any foreign corporation authorized to transact business in this State, or a name the exclusive right to which is, at the time, reserved in the manner provided in this Act, or the name of a corporation which has in effect a registration of its corporate name as provided in this Act, except that this provision shall not apply if the applicant files with the Secretary of State either of the following: (1) the written consent of such other corporation or holder of a reserved or registered name to use the same or deceptively similar name and one or more words are added to make such name distinguishable from such other name, or (2) a certified copy of a final decree of a court of competent jurisdiction establishing the prior right of the applicant to the use of such name in this State.

A corporation with which another corporation, domestic or foreign, is merged, or which is formed by the reorganization or consolidation of one or more domestic or foreign corporations or upon a sale, lease or other disposition to or exchange with, a domestic corporation of all or substantially all the assets of another corporation, domestic or foreign, including its name, may have the same name as that used in this State by any of such corporations if such other corporation was organized under the laws of, or is authorized to transact business in, this State.

## § 9. Reserved Name

The exclusive right to the use of a corporate name may be reserved by:

(a) Any person intending to organize a corporation under this Act.

(b) Any domestic corporation intending to change its name.

(c) Any foreign corporation intending to make application for a certificate of authority to transact business in this State.

(d) Any foreign corporation authorized to transact business in this State and intending to change its name.

(e) Any person intending to organize a foreign corporation and intending to have such corporation make application for a certificate of authority to transact business in this State.

The reservation shall be made by filing with the Secretary of State an application to reserve a specified corporate name, executed by the applicant. If the Secretary of State finds that the name is available for corporate use, he shall reserve the same for the exclusive use of the applicant for a period of one hundred and twenty days.

The right to the exclusive use of a specified corporate name so reserved may be transferred to any other person or corporation by filing in the office of the Secretary of State a notice of such transfer, executed by the applicant for whom the name was reserved, and specifying the name and address of the transferee.

## § 10. Registered Name

Any corporation organized and existing under the laws of any state or territory of the United States may register its corporate name under this Act, provided its corporate name is not the same as, or deceptively similar to, the name of any domestic corporation existing under the laws of this State, or the name of any foreign corporation authorized to transact business in this State, or any corporate name reserved or registered under this Act.

Such registration shall be made by:

(a) Filing with the Secretary of State (1) an application for registration executed by the corporation by an officer thereof, setting forth the name of the corporation, the state or territory under the laws of which it is incorporated, the date of its incorporation, a statement that it is carrying on or doing business, and a brief statement of the business in which it is engaged, and (2) a certificate setting forth that such corporation is in good standing under the laws of the state or territory wherein it is organized, executed by the Secretary of State of such state or territory or by such other official as may have custody of the records pertaining to corporations, and

(b) Paying to the Secretary of State a registration fee in the amount of . . . . . . . . . . . . . for each month, or fraction thereof, between the date of filing such application and December 31st of the calendar year in which such application is filed.

Such registration shall be effective until the close of the calendar year in which the application for registration is filed.

## § 11.   Renewal of Registered Name

A corporation which has in effect a registration of its corporate name, may renew such registration from year to year by annually filing an application for renewal setting forth the facts required to be set forth in an original application for registration and a certificate of good standing as required for the original registration and by paying a fee of . . . . . . . . . . . . . . . . . . . . .
A renewal application may be filed between the first day of Oc-

tober and the thirty-first day of December in each year, and shall extend the registration for the following calendar year.

## § 12.  Registered Office and Registered Agent

Each corporation shall have and continuously maintain in this State:

(a) A registered office which may be, but need not be, the same as its place of business.

(b) A registered agent, which agent may be either an individual resident in this State whose business office is identical with such registered office, or a domestic corporation, or a foreign corporation authorized to transact business in this State, having a business office identical with such registered office.

## § 13.  Change of Registered Office or Registered Agent

A corporation may change its registered office or change its registered agent, or both, upon filing in the office of the Secretary of State a statement setting forth:

(a) The name of the corporation.

(b) The address of its then registered office.

(c) If the address of its registered office is to be changed, the address to which the registered office is to be changed.

(d) The name of its then registered agent.

(e) If its registered agent is to be changed, the name of its successor registered agent.

(f) That the address of its registered office and the address of the business office of its registered agent, as changed, will be identical.

(g) That such change was authorized by resolution duly adopted by its board of directors.

Such statement shall be executed by the corporation by its president, or a vice president, and verified by him, and delivered to the Secretary of State.  If the Secretary of State finds that such statement conforms to the provisions of this Act, he shall file such statement in his office, and upon such filing the change of address of the registered office, or the appointment of a new registered agent, or both, as the case may be, shall become effective.

Any registered agent of a corporation may resign as such agent upon filing a written notice thereof, executed in duplicate, with the Secretary of State, who shall forthwith mail a copy thereof to the corporation at its registered office.  The appointment of such agent shall terminate upon the expiration of thirty days after receipt of such notice by the Secretary of State.

If a registered agent changes his or its business address to another place within the same ................*, he or it may change such address and the address of the registered office of any corporation of which he or it is registered agent by filing a statement as required above except that it need be signed only by the registered agent and need not be responsive to (e) or (g) and must recite that a copy of the statement has been mailed to the corporation.

### § 14. Service of Process on Corporation

The registered agent so appointed by a corporation shall be an agent of such corporation upon whom any process, notice or demand required or permitted by law to be served upon the corporation may be served.

Whenever a corporation shall fail to appoint or maintain a registered agent in this State, or whenever its registered agent cannot with reasonable diligence be found at the registered office, then the Secretary of State shall be an agent of such corporation upon whom any such process, notice, or demand may be served. Service on the Secretary of State of any such process, notice, or demand shall be made by delivering to and leaving with him, or with any clerk having charge of the corporation department of his office, duplicate copies of such process, notice or demand. In the event any such process, notice or demand is served on the Secretary of State, he shall immediately cause one of the copies thereof to be forwarded by registered mail, addressed to the corporation at its registered office. Any service so had on the Secretary of State shall be returnable in not less than thirty days.

The Secretary of State shall keep a record of all processes, notices and demands served upon him under this section, and shall record therein the time of such service and his action with reference thereto.

Nothing herein contained shall limit or affect the right to serve any process, notice or demand required or permitted by law to be served upon a corporation in any other manner now or hereafter permitted by law.

### § 15. Authorized Shares

Each corporation shall have power to create and issue the number of shares stated in its articles of incorporation. Such shares may be divided into one or more classes, any or all of which classes may consist of shares with par value or shares without par value, with such designations, preferences, limita-

---

* Supply designation of jurisdiction, such as county, etc., in accordance with local practice.

tions, and relative rights as shall be stated in the articles of incorporation. The articles of incorporation may limit or deny the voting rights of or provide special voting rights for the shares of any class to the extent not inconsistent with the provisions of this Act.

Without limiting the authority herein contained, a corporation, when so provided in its articles of incorporation, may issue shares of preferred or special classes:

(a) Subject to the right of the corporation to redeem any of such shares at the price fixed by the articles of incorporation for the redemption thereof.

(b) Entitling the holders thereof to cumulative, noncumulative or partially cumulative dividends.

(c) Having preference over any other class or classes of shares as to the payment of dividends.

(d) Having preference in the assets of the corporation over any other class or classes of shares upon the voluntary or involuntary liquidation of the corporation.

(e) Convertible into shares of any other class or into shares of any series of the same or any other class, except a class having prior or superior rights and preferences as to dividends or distribution of assets upon liquidation, but shares without par value shall not be converted into shares with par value unless that part of the stated capital of the corporation represented by such shares without par value is, at the time of conversion, at least equal to the aggregate par value of the shares into which the shares without par value are to be converted or the amount of any such deficiency is transferred from surplus to stated capital.

## § 16. Issuance of Shares of Preferred or Special Classes in Series

If the articles of incorporation so provide, the shares of any preferred or special class may be divided into and issued in series. If the shares of any such class are to be issued in series, then each series shall be so designated as to distinguish the shares thereof from the shares of all other series and classes. Any or all of the series of any such class and the variations in the relative rights and preferences as between different series may be fixed and determined by the articles of incorporation, but all shares of the same class shall be identical except as to the following relative rights and preferences, as to which there may be variations between different series:

(A) The rate of dividend.

(B) Whether shares may be redeemed and, if so, the redemption price and the terms and conditions of redemption.

(C) The amount payable upon shares in event of voluntary and involuntary liquidation.

(D) Sinking fund provisions, if any, for the redemption or purchase of shares.

(E) The terms and conditions, if any, on which shares may be converted.

(F) Voting rights, if any.

If the articles of incorporation shall expressly vest authority in the board of directors, then, to the extent that the articles of incorporation shall not have established series and fixed and determined the variations in the relative rights and preferences as between series, the board of directors shall have authority to divide any or all of such classes into series and, within the limitations set forth in this section and in the articles of incorporation, fix and determine the relative rights and preferences of the shares of any series so established.

In order for the board of directors to establish a series, where authority so to do is contained in the articles of incorporation, the board of directors shall adopt a resolution setting forth the designation of the series and fixing and determining the relative rights and preferences thereof, or so much thereof as shall not be fixed and determined by the articles of incorporation.

Prior to the issue of any shares of a series established by resolution adopted by the board of directors, the corporation shall file in the office of the Secretary of State a statement setting forth:

(a) The name of the corporation.

(b) A copy of the resolution establishing and designating the series, and fixing and determining the relative rights and preferences thereof.

(c) The date of adoption of such resolution.

(d) That such resolution was duly adopted by the board of directors.

Such statement shall be executed in duplicate by the corporation by its president or a vice president and by its secretary or an assistant secretary, and verified by one of the officers signing such statement, and shall be delivered to the Secretary of State. If the Secretary of State finds that such statement conforms to law, he shall, when all franchise taxes and fees have been paid as in this Act prescribed:

(1) Endorse on each of such duplicate originals the word "Filed," and the month, day, and year of the filing thereof.

(2) File one of such duplicate originals in his office.

(3) Return the other duplicate original to the corporation or its representative.

Upon the filing of such statement by the Secretary of State, the resolution establishing and designating the series and fixing and determining the relative rights and preferences thereof shall become effective and shall constitute an amendment of the articles of incorporation.

## § 17. Subscriptions for Shares

A subscription for shares of a corporation to be organized shall be irrevocable for a period of six months, unless otherwise provided by the terms of the subscription agreement or unless all of the subscribers consent to the revocation of such subscription.

Unless otherwise provided in the subscription agreement, subscriptions for shares, whether made before or after the organization of a corporation, shall be paid in full at such time, or in such installments and at such times, as shall be determined by the board of directors. Any call made by the board of directors for payment on subscriptions shall be uniform as to all shares of the same class or as to all shares of the same series, as the case may be. In case of default in the payment of any installment or call when such payment is due, the corporation may proceed to collect the amount due in the same manner as any debt due the corporation. The by-laws may prescribe other penalities for failure to pay installments or calls that may become due, but no penalty working a forfeiture of a subscription, or of the amounts paid thereon, shall be declared as against any subscriber unless the amount due thereon shall remain unpaid for a period of twenty days after written demand has been made therefor. If mailed, such written demand shall be deemed to be made when deposited in the United States mail in a sealed envelope addressed to the subscriber at his last post-office address known to the corporation, with postage thereon prepaid. In the event of the sale of any shares by reason of any forfeiture, the excess of proceeds realized over the amount due and unpaid on such shares shall be paid to the delinquent subscriber or to his legal representative.

## § 18. Consideration for Shares

Shares having a par value may be issued for such consideration expressed in dollars, not less than the par value thereof, as shall be fixed from time to time by the board of directors.

Shares without par value may be issued for such consideration expressed in dollars as may be fixed from time to time by the board of directors unless the articles of incorporation reserve to the shareholders the right to fix the consideration. In the event that such right be reserved as to any shares, the shareholders shall, prior to the issuance of such shares, fix the consideration to be received for such shares, by a vote of the holders of a majority of all shares entitled to vote thereon.

Treasury shares may be disposed of by the corporation for such consideration expressed in dollars as may be fixed from time to time by the board of directors.

That part of the surplus of a corporation which is transferred to stated capital upon the issuance of shares as a share dividend shall be deemed to be the consideration for the issuance of such shares.

In the event of the issuance of shares upon the conversion or exchange of indebtedness or shares, the consideration for the shares so issued shall be (1) the principal sum of, and accrued interest on, the indebtedness so exchanged or converted, or the stated capital then represented by the shares so exchanged or converted, and (2) that part of surplus, if any, transferred to stated capital upon the issuance of shares for the shares so exchanged or converted, and (3) any additional consideration paid to the corporation upon the issuance of shares for the indebtedness or shares so exchanged or converted.

## § 19. Payment for Shares

The consideration for the issuance of shares may be paid, in whole or in part, in money, in other property, tangible or intangible, or in labor or services actually performed for the corporation. When payment of the consideration for which shares are to be issued shall have been received by the corporation, such shares shall be deemed to be fully paid and nonassessable.

Neither promissory notes nor future services shall constitute payment or part payment for the issuance of shares of a corporation.

In the absence of fraud in the transaction, the judgment of the board of directors or the shareholders, as the case may be, as to the value of the consideration received for shares shall be conclusive.

## § 20. Stock Rights and Options

Subject to any provisions in respect thereof set forth in its articles of incorporation, a corporation may create and issue, whether or not in connection with the issuance and sale of any of its shares or other securities, rights or options entitling the holders thereof to purchase from the corporation shares of any class or classes. Such rights or options shall be evidenced in such manner as the board of directors shall approve and, subject to the provisions of the articles of incorporation, shall set forth the terms upon which, the time or times within which and the price or prices at which such shares may be purchased from the corporation upon the exercise of any such right or option. If such rights or options are to be issued to directors, officers or employees as such of the corporation or of any subsidiary thereof, and not to the shareholders generally, their issuance shall be approved by the affirmative vote of the holders of a majority of the shares entitled to vote thereon or shall be authorized by and consistent with a plan approved or ratified by such a vote of shareholders. In the absence of fraud in the transaction, the judgment of the board of directors as to the adequacy of the consideration received for such rights or options shall be conclusive. The price or prices to be received for any shares having a par value, other than treasury shares to be issued upon the exercise of such rights or options, shall not be less than the par value thereof.

## § 21. Determination of Amount of Stated Capital

In case of the issuance by a corporation of shares having a par value, the consideration received therefor shall constitute stated capital to the extent of the par value of such shares, and the excess, if any, of such consideration shall constitute capital surplus.

In case of the issuance by a corporation of shares without par value, the entire consideration received therefor shall constitute stated capital unless the corporation shall determine as provided in this section that only a part thereof shall be stated capital. Within a period of sixty days after the issuance of any shares without par value, the board of directors may allocate to capital surplus any portion of the consideration received for the issuance of such shares. No such allocation shall be made of any portion of the consideration received for shares without par value having a preference in the assets of the corporation in the event of involuntary liquidation except the amount, if any, of such consideration in excess of such preference.

If shares have been or shall be issued by a corporation in merger or consolidation or in acquisition of all or substantially all of the outstanding shares or of the property and assets of another corporation, whether domestic or foreign, any amount that would otherwise constitute capital surplus under the foregoing provisions of this section may instead be allocated to earned surplus by the board of directors of the issuing corporation except that its aggregate earned surplus shall not exceed the sum of the earned surpluses as defined in this Act of the issuing corporation and of all other corporations, domestic or foreign, that were merged or consolidated or of which the shares or assets were acquired.

The stated capital of a corporation may be increased from time to time by resolution of the board of directors directing that all or a part of the surplus of the corporation be transferred to stated capital. The board of directors may direct that the amount of the surplus so transferred shall be deemed to be stated capital in respect of any designated class of shares.

### § 22. Expenses of Organization, Reorganization and Financing

The reasonable charges and expenses of organization or reorganization of a corporation, and the reasonable expenses of and compensation for the sale or underwriting of its shares, may be paid or allowed by such corporation out of the consideration received by it in payment for its shares without thereby rendering such shares not fully paid or assessable.

### § 23. Certificates Representing Shares

The shares of a corporation shall be represented by certificates signed by the president or a vice president and the secretary or an assistant secretary of the corporation, and may be sealed with the seal of the corporation or a facsimile thereof. The signatures of the president or vice president and the secretary or assistant secretary upon a certificate may be facsimiles if the certificate is manually signed on behalf of a transfer agent or a registrar, other than the corporation itself or an employee of the corporation. In case any officer who has signed or whose facsimile signature has been placed upon such certificate shall have ceased to be such officer before such certificate is issued, it may be issued by the corporation with the same effect as if he were such officer at the date of its issue.

Every certificate representing shares issued by a corporation which is authorized to issue shares of more than one class shall set forth upon the face or back of the certificate, or shall state that the corporation will furnish to any shareholder upon request and without charge, a full statement of the designations, preferences, limitations, and relative rights of the shares of each class authorized to be issued, and if the corporation is authorized to issue any preferred or special class in series, the variations in the relative rights and preferences between the shares of each such series so far as the same have been fixed and deter-

413

mined and the authority of the board of directors to fix and determine the relative rights and preferences of subsequent series.

Each certificate representing shares shall state upon the face thereof:

(a) That the corporation is organized under the laws of this State.

(b) The name of the person to whom issued.

(c) The number and class of shares, and the designation of the series, if any, which such certificate represents.

(d) The par value of each share represented by such certificate, or a statement that the shares are without par value.

No certificate shall be issued for any share until such share is fully paid.

## § 24.  Fractional Shares

A corporation may (1) issue fractions of a share, (2) arrange for the disposition of fractional interests by those entitled thereto, (3) pay in cash the fair value of fractions of a share as of the time when those entitled to receive such fractions are determined, or (4) issue scrip in registered or bearer form which shall entitle the holder to receive a certificate for a full share upon the surrender of such scrip aggregating a full share.  A certificate for a fractional share shall, but scrip shall not unless otherwise provided therein, entitle the holder to exercise voting rights, to receive dividends thereon, and to participate in any of the assets of the corporation in the event of liquidation.  The board of directors may cause scrip to be issued subject to the condition that it shall become void if not exchanged for certificates representing full shares before a specified date, or subject to the condition that the shares for which scrip is exchangeable may be sold by the corporation and the proceeds thereof distributed to the holders of scrip, or subject to any other conditions which the board of directors may deem advisable.

## § 25.  Liability of Subscribers and Shareholders

A holder of or subscriber to shares of a corporation shall be under no obligation to the corporation or its creditors with respect to such shares other than the obligation to pay to the corporation the full consideration for which such shares were issued or to be issued.

Any person becoming an assignee or transferee of shares or of a subscription for shares in good faith and without knowledge or notice that the full consideration therefor has not been paid shall not be personally liable to the corporation or its creditors for any unpaid portion of such consideration.

An executor, administrator, conservator, guardian, trustee, assignee for the benefit of creditors, or receiver shall not be personally liable to the corporation as a holder of or subscriber to shares of a corporation but the estate and funds in his hands shall be so liable.

No pledgee or other holder of shares as collateral security shall be personally liable as a shareholder.

### § 26. Shareholders' Preemptive Rights

The shareholders of a corporation shall have no preemptive right to acquire unissued or treasury shares of the corporation, or securities of the corporation convertible into or carrying a right to subscribe to or acquire shares, except to the extent, if any, that such right is provided in the articles of incorporation.

### § 26A. Shareholders' Preemptive Rights [Alternative]

Except to the extent limited or denied by this section or by the articles of incorporation, shareholders shall have a preemptive right to acquire unissued or treasury shares or securities convertible into such shares or carrying a right to subscribe to or acquire shares.

Unless otherwise provided in the articles of incorporation,

(a) No preemptive right shall exist

(1) to acquire any shares issued to directors, officers or employees pursuant to approval by the affirmative vote of the holders of a majority of the shares entitled to vote thereon or when authorized by and consistent with a plan theretofore approved by such a vote of shareholders; or

(2) to acquire any shares sold otherwise than for cash.

(b) Holders of shares of any class that is preferred or limited as to dividends or assets shall not be entitled to any preemptive right.

(c) Holders of shares of common stock shall not be entitled to any preemptive right to shares of any class that is preferred or limited as to dividends or assets or to any obligations, unless convertible into shares of common stock or carrying a right to subscribe to or acquire shares of common stock.

(d) Holders of common stock without voting power shall have no preemptive right to shares of common stock with voting power.

(e) The preemptive right shall be only an opportunity to acquire shares or other securities under such terms and conditions as the board of directors may fix for the purpose of providing a fair and reasonable opportunity for the exercise of such right.

## § 27.  By-Laws

The initial by-laws of a corporation shall be adopted by its board of directors.  The power to alter, amend or repeal the by-laws or adopt new by-laws, subject to repeal or change by action of the shareholders, shall be vested in the board of directors unless reserved to the shareholders by the articles of incorporation. The by-laws may contain any provisions for the regulation and management of the affairs of the corporation not inconsistent with law or the articles of incorporation.

## § 27A.  By-Laws and Other Powers in Emergency [Optional]

The board of directors of any corporation may adopt emergency by-laws, subject to repeal or change by action of the shareholders, which shall, notwithstanding any different provision elsewhere in this Act or in the articles of incorporation or by-laws, be operative during any emergency in the conduct of the business of the corporation resulting from an attack on the United States or any nuclear or atomic disaster.  The emergency by-laws may make any provision that may be practical and necessary for the circumstances of the emergency, including provisions that:

(a) A meeting of the board of directors may be called by any officer or director in such manner and under such conditions as shall be prescribed in the emergency by-laws;

(b) The director or directors in attendance at the meeting, or any greater number fixed by the emergency by-laws, shall constitute a quorum; and

(c) The officers or other persons designated on a list approved by the board of directors before the emergency, all in such order of priority and subject to such conditions, and for such period of time (not longer than reasonably necessary after the termination of the emergency) as may be provided in the emergency by-laws or in the resolution approving the list shall, to the extent required to provide a quorum at any meeting of the board of directors, be deemed directors for such meeting.

The board of directors, either before or during any such emergency, may provide, and from time to time modify, lines of succession in the event that during such an emergency any or all officers or agents of the corporation shall for any reason be rendered incapable of discharging their duties.

The board of directors, either before or during any such emergency, may, effective in the emergency, change the head office or designate several alternative head offices or regional offices, or authorize the officers so to do.

To the extent not inconsistent with any emergency by-laws so adopted, the by-laws of the corporation shall remain in effect during any such emergency and upon its termination the emergency by-laws shall cease to be operative.

Unless otherwise provided in emergency by-laws, notice of any meeting of the board of directors during any such emergency may be given only to such of the directors as it may be feasible to reach at the time and by such means as may be feasible at the time, including publication or radio.

To the extent required to constitute a quorum at any meeting of the board of directors during any such emergency, the officers of the corporation who are present shall, unless otherwise provided in emergency by-laws, be deemed, in order of rank and within the same rank in order of seniority, directors for such meeting.

No officer, director or employee acting in accordance with any emergency by-laws shall be liable except for willful misconduct. No officer, director or employee shall be liable for any action taken by him in good faith in such an emergency in furtherance of the ordinary business affairs of the corporation even though not authorized by the by-laws then in effect.

## § 28. Meetings of Shareholders

Meetings of shareholders may be held at such place within or without this State as may be stated in or fixed in accordance with the by-laws. If no other place is stated or so fixed, meetings shall be held at the registered office of the corporation.

An annual meeting of the shareholders shall be held at such time as may be stated in or fixed in accordance with the by-laws. If the annual meeting is not held within any thirteen-month period the Court of ............. may, on the application of any shareholder, summarily order a meeting to be held.

Special meetings of the shareholders may be called by the board of directors, the holders of not less than one-tenth of all the shares entitled to vote at the meeting, or such other persons as may be authorized in the articles of incorporation or the by-laws.

## § 29. Notice of Shareholders' Meetings

Written notice stating the place, day and hour of the meeting and, in case of a special meeting, the purpose or purposes for which the meeting is called, shall be delivered not less than ten nor more than fifty days before the date of the meeting, either personally or by mail, by or at the direction of the president, the secretary, or the officer or persons calling the meeting, to each shareholder of record entitled to vote at such meeting. If mailed, such notice shall be deemed to be delivered when deposited in the United States mail addressed to the shareholder at his address as it appears on the stock transfer books of the corporation, with postage thereon prepaid.

### § 30. Closing of Transfer Books and Fixing Record Date

For the purpose of determining shareholders entitled to notice of or to vote at any meeting of shareholders or any adjournment thereof, or entitled to receive payment of any dividend, or in order to make a determination of shareholders for any other proper purpose, the board of directors of a corporation may provide that the stock transfer books shall be closed for a stated period but not to exceed, in any case, fifty days. If the stock transfer books shall be closed for the purpose of determining shareholders entitled to notice of or to vote at a meeting of shareholders, such books shall be closed for at least ten days immediately preceding such meeting. In lieu of closing the stock transfer books, the by-laws, or in the absence of an applicable by-law the board of directors, may fix in advance a date as the record date for any such determination of shareholders, such date in any case to be not more than fifty days and, in case of a meeting of shareholders, not less than ten days prior to the date on which the particular action, requiring such determination of shareholders, is to be taken. If the stock transfer books are not closed and no record date is fixed for the determination of shareholders entitled to notice of or to vote at a meeting of shareholders, or shareholders entitled to receive payment of a dividend, the date on which notice of the meeting is mailed or the date on which the resolution of the board of directors declaring such dividend is adopted, as the case may be, shall be the record date for such determination of shareholders. When a determination of shareholders entitled to vote at any meeting of shareholders has been made as provided in this section, such determination shall apply to any adjournment thereof.

### § 31. Voting Record

The officer or agent having charge of the stock transfer books for shares of a corporation shall make a complete record of the shareholders entitled to vote at such meeting or any adjournment thereof, arranged in alphabetical order, with the address of and the number of shares held by each. Such record shall be produced and kept open at the time and place of the meeting and shall be subject to the inspection of any shareholder during the whole time of the meeting for the purposes thereof.

Failure to comply with the requirements of this section shall not affect the validity of any action taken at such meeting.

An officer or agent having charge of the stock transfer books who shall fail to prepare the record of shareholders, or produce and keep it open for inspection at the meeting, as provided in this section, shall be liable to any shareholder suffering damage on account of such failure, to the extent of such damage.

### § 32. Quorum of Shareholders

Unless otherwise provided in the articles of incorporation, a majority of the shares entitled to vote, represented in person or by proxy, shall constitute a quorum at a meeting of shareholders, but in no event shall a quorum consist of less than one-third of the shares entitled to vote at the meeting. If a quorum is present, the affirmative vote of the majority of the shares represented at the meeting and entitled to vote on the subject matter shall be the act of the shareholders, unless the vote of a greater number or voting by classes is required by this Act or the articles of incorporation or by-laws.

### § 33. Voting of Shares

Each outstanding share, regardless of class, shall be entitled to one vote on each matter submitted to a vote at a meeting of shareholders, except as may be otherwise provided in the articles of incorporation. If the articles of incorporation provide for more or less than one vote for any share, on any matter, every reference in this Act to a majority or other proportion of shares shall refer to such a majority or other proportion of votes entitled to be cast.

Neither treasury shares, nor shares held by another corporation if a majority of the shares entitled to vote for the election of directors of such other corporation is held by the corporation, shall be voted at any meeting or counted in determining the total number of outstanding shares at any given time.

A shareholder may vote either in person or by proxy executed in writing by the shareholder or by his duly authorized attorney-in-fact. No proxy shall be valid after eleven months from the date of its execution, unless otherwise provided in the proxy.

[Either of the following prefatory phrases may be inserted here: "The articles of incorporation may provide that" or "Unless the articles of incorporation otherwise provide"] . . . at each election for directors every shareholder entitled to vote at such election shall have the right to vote, in person or by proxy, the number of shares owned by him for as many persons as there are directors to be elected and for whose election he has a right to vote, or to cumulate his votes by giving one candidate as many votes as the number of such directors multiplied by the number of his shares shall equal, or by distributing such votes on the same principle among any number of such candidates.

Shares standing in the name of another corporation, domestic or foreign, may be voted by such officer, agent or proxy as the by-laws of such other corporation may prescribe, or, in the absence of such provision, as the board of directors of such other corporation may determine.

Shares held by an administrator, executor, guardian or conservator may be voted by him, either in person or by proxy, without a transfer of such shares into his name. Shares standing in the name of a trustee may be voted by him, either in person or by proxy, but no trustee shall be entitled to vote shares held by him without a transfer of such shares into his name.

Shares standing in the name of a receiver may be voted by such receiver, and shares held by or under the control of a receiver may be voted by such receiver without the transfer thereof into his name if authority so to do be contained in an appropriate order of the court by which such receiver was appointed.

A shareholder whose shares are pledged shall be entitled to vote such shares until the shares have been transferred into the name of the pledgee, and thereafter the pledgee shall be entitled to vote the shares so transferred.

On and after the date on which written notice of redemption of redeemable shares has been mailed to the holders thereof and a sum sufficient to redeem such shares has been deposited with a bank or trust company with irrevocable instruction and authority to pay the redemption price to the holders thereof upon surrender of certificates therefor, such shares shall not be entitled to vote on any matter and shall not be deemed to be outstanding shares.

## § 34. Voting Trusts and Agreements Among Shareholders

Any number of shareholders of a corporation may create a voting trust for the purpose of conferring upon a trustee or trustees the right to vote or otherwise represent their shares, for a period of not to exceed ten years, by entering into a written voting trust agreement specifying the terms and conditions of the voting trust, by depositing a counterpart of the agreement with the corporation at its registered office, and by transferring their shares to such trustee or trustees for the purposes of the agreement. Such trustee or trustees shall keep a record of the holders of voting trust certificates evidencing a beneficial interest in the voting trust, giving the names and addresses of all such holders and the number and class of the shares in respect of which the voting trust certificates held by each are issued, and shall deposit a copy of such record with the corporation at its registered office. The counterpart of the voting trust agreement and the copy of such record so deposited with the corporation shall be subject to the same right of examination by a shareholder of the corporation, in person or by agent or attorney, as are the books and records of the corporation, and such counterpart and such copy of such record shall be subject to examination by any holder of record of voting trust certificates, either in person or by agent or attorney, at any reasonable time for any proper purpose.

Agreements among shareholders regarding the voting of their shares shall be valid and enforceable in accordance with their terms. Such agreements shall not be subject to the provisions of this section regarding voting trusts.

### § 35. Board of Directors

The business and affairs of a corporation shall be managed by a board of directors except as may be otherwise provided in the articles of incorporation. If any such provision is made in the articles of incorporation, the powers and duties conferred or imposed upon the board of directors by this Act shall be exercised or performed to such extent and by such person or persons as shall be provided in the articles of incorporation. Directors need not be residents of this State or shareholders of the corporation unless the articles of incorporation or by-laws so require. The articles of incorporation or by-laws may prescribe other qualifications for directors. The board of directors shall have authority to fix the compensation of directors unless otherwise provided in the articles of incorporation.

### § 36. Number and Election of Directors

The board of directors of a corporation shall consist of one or more members. The number of directors shall be fixed by, or in the manner provided in, the articles of incorporation or the by-laws, except as to the number constituting the initial board of directors, which number shall be fixed by the articles of incorporation. The number of directors may be increased or decreased from time to time by amendment to, or in the manner provided in, the articles of incorporation or the by-laws, but no decrease shall have the effect of shortening the term of any incumbent director. In the absence of a by-law providing for the number of directors, the number shall be the same as that provided for in the articles of incorporation. The names and addresses of the members of the first board of directors shall be stated in the articles of incorporation. Such persons shall hold office until the first annual meeting of shareholders, and until their successors shall have been elected and qualified. At the first annual meeting of shareholders and at each annual meeting thereafter the shareholders shall elect directors to hold office until the next succeeding annual meeting, except in case of the classification of directors as permitted by this Act. Each director shall hold office for the term for which he is elected and until his successor shall have been elected and qualified.

### § 37. Classification of Directors

When the board of directors shall consist of nine or more members, in lieu of electing the whole number of directors annually, the articles of incorporation may provide that the directors be divided into either two or three classes, each class to be as nearly equal in number as possible, the term of office of directors of the first class to expire at the first annual meeting of shareholders after their election, that of the second class to expire at the second annual meeting after their election, and that of the third class, if any, to expire at the third annual meeting after their election. At each annual meeting after such classification the number of directors equal to the number of the class whose term expires at the time of such meeting shall be elected to hold office until the second succeeding annual meeting, if there be two classes, or until the third succeeding annual meeting, if there be three classes. No classification of directors shall be effective prior to the first annual meeting of shareholders.

### § 38. Vacancies

Any vacancy occurring in the board of directors may be filled by the affirmative vote of a majority of the remaining directors though less than a quorum of the board of directors. A director elected to fill a vacancy shall be elected for the unexpired term of his predecessor in office. Any directorship to be filled by reason of an increase in the number of directors may be filled by the board of directors for a term of office continuing only until the next election of directors by the shareholders.

### § 39. Removal of Directors

At a meeting of shareholders called expressly for that purpose, directors may be removed in the manner provided in this section. Any director or the entire board of directors may be removed, with or without cause, by a vote of the holders of a majority of the shares then entitled to vote at an election of directors.

In the case of a corporation having cumulative voting, if less than the entire board is to be removed, no one of the directors may be removed if the votes cast against his removal would be sufficient to elect him if then cumulatively voted at an election of the entire board of directors, or, if there be classes of directors, at an election of the class of directors of which he is a part.

Whenever the holders of the shares of any class are entitled to elect one or more directors by the provisions of the articles of incorporation, the provisions of this section shall apply, in respect to the removal of a director or directors so elected, to the vote of the holders of the outstanding shares of that class and not to the vote of the outstanding shares as a whole.

## § 40.  Quorum of Directors

A majority of the number of directors fixed by or in the manner provided in the by-laws or in the absence of a by-law fixing or providing for the number of directors, then of the number stated in the articles of incorporation, shall constitute a quorum for the transaction of business unless a greater number is required by the articles of incorporation or the by-laws.  The act of the majority of the directors present at a meeting at which a quorum is present shall be the act of the board of directors, unless the act of a greater number is required by the articles of incorporation or the by-laws.

## § 41.  Director Conflicts of Interest

No contract or other transaction between a corporation and one or more of its directors or any other corporation, firm, association or entity in which one or more of its directors are directors or officers or are financially interested, shall be either void or voidable because of such relationship or interest or because such director or directors are present at the meeting of the board of directors or a committee thereof which authorizes, approves or ratifies such contract or transaction or because his or their votes are counted for such purpose, if:

(a) the fact of such relationship or interest is disclosed or known to the board of directors or committee which authorizes, approves or ratifies the contract or transaction by a vote or consent sufficient for the purpose without counting the votes or consents of such interested directors; or

(b) the fact of such relationship or interest is disclosed or known to the shareholders entitled to vote and they authorize, approve or ratify such contract or transaction by vote or written consent; or

(c) the contract or transaction is fair and reasonable to the corporation.

Common or interested directors may be counted in determining the presence of a quorum at a meeting of the board of directors or a committee thereof which authorizes, approves or ratifies such contract or transaction.

## § 42. Executive and Other Committees

If the articles of incorporation or the by-laws so provide, the board of directors, by resolution adopted by a majority of the full board of directors, may designate from among its members an executive committee and one or more other committees each of which, to the extent provided in such resolution or in the articles of incorporation or the by-laws of the corporation, shall have and may exercise all the authority of the board of directors, but no such committee shall have the authority of the board of directors in reference to amending the articles of incorporation, adopting a plan of merger or consolidation, recommending to the shareholders the sale, lease, exchange or other disposition of all or substantially all the property and assets of the corporation otherwise than in the usual and regular course of its business, recommending to the shareholders a voluntary dissolution of the corporation or a revocation thereof, or amending the by-laws of the corporation. The designation of any such committee and the delegation thereto of authority shall not operate to relieve the board of directors, or any member thereof, of any responsibility imposed by law.

## § 43. Place and Notice of Directors' Meetings

Meetings of the board of directors, regular or special, may be held either within or without this State.

Regular meetings of the board of directors may be held with or without notice as prescribed in the by-laws. Special meetings of the board of directors shall be held upon such notice as is prescribed in the by-laws. Attendance of a director at a meeting shall constitute a waiver of notice of such meeting, except where a director attends a meeting for the express purpose of objecting to the transaction of any business because the meeting is not lawfully called or convened. Neither the business to be transacted at, nor the purpose of, any regular or special meeting of the board of directors need be specified in the notice or waiver of notice of such meeting unless required by the by-laws.

## § 44. Action by Directors Without a Meeting

Unless otherwise provided by the articles of incorporation or by-laws, any action required by this Act to be taken at a meeting of the directors of a corporation, or any action which may be taken at a meeting of the directors or of a committee, may be taken without a meeting if a consent in writing, setting forth the action so taken, shall be signed by all of the directors, or all of the members of the committee, as the case may be. Such consent shall have the same effect as a unanimous vote.

### § 45. Dividends

The board of directors of a corporation may, from time to time, declare and the corporation may pay dividends in cash, property, or its own shares, except when the corporation is insolvent or when the payment thereof would render the corporation insolvent or when the declaration or payment thereof would be contrary to any restriction contained in the articles of incorporation, subject to the following provisions:

(a) Dividends may be declared and paid in cash or property only out of the unreserved and unrestricted earned surplus of the corporation, except as otherwise provided in this section.

[Alternative] (a) Dividends may be declared and paid in cash or property only out of the unreserved and unrestricted earned surplus of the corporation, or out of the unreserved and unrestricted net earnings of the current fiscal year and the next preceding fiscal year taken as a single period, except as otherwise provided in this section.

(b) If the articles of incorporation of a corporation engaged in the business of exploiting natural resources so provide, dividends may be declared and paid in cash out of the depletion reserves, but each such dividend shall be identified as a distribution of such reserves and the amount per share paid from such reserves shall be disclosed to the shareholders receiving the same concurrently with the distribution thereof.

(c) Dividends may be declared and paid in its own treasury shares.

(d) Dividends may be declared and paid in its own authorized but unissued shares out of any unreserved and unrestricted surplus of the corporation upon the following conditions:

(1) If a dividend is payable in its own shares having a par value, such shares shall be issued at not less than the par value thereof and there shall be transferred to stated capital at the time such dividend is paid an amount of surplus equal to the aggregate par value of the shares to be issued as a dividend.

(2) If a dividend is payable in its own shares without par value, such shares shall be issued at such stated value as shall be fixed by the board of directors by resolution adopted at the time

such dividend is declared, and there shall be transferred to stated capital at the time such dividend is paid an amount of surplus equal to the aggregate stated value so fixed in respect of such shares; and the amount per share so transferred to stated capital shall be disclosed to the shareholders receiving such dividend concurrently with the payment thereof.

(e) No dividend payable in shares of any class shall be paid to the holders of shares of any other class unless the articles of incorporation so provide or such payment is authorized by the affirmative vote or the written consent of the holders of at least a majority of the outstanding shares of the class in which the payment is to be made.

A split-up or division of the issued shares of any class into a greater number of shares of the same class without increasing the stated capital of the corporation shall not be construed to be a share dividend within the meaning of this section.

## § 46. Distributions from Capital Surplus

The board of directors of a corporation may, from time to time, distribute to its shareholders out of capital surplus of the corporation a portion of its assets, in cash or property, subject to the following provisions:

(a) No such distribution shall be made at a time when the corporation is insolvent or when such distribution would render the corporation insolvent.

(b) No such distribution shall be made unless the articles of incorporation so provide or such distribution is authorized by the affirmative vote of the holders of a majority of the outstanding shares of each class whether or not entitled to vote thereon by the provisions of the articles of incorporation of the corporation.

(c) No such distribution shall be made to the holders of any class of shares unless all cumulative dividends accrued on all preferred or special classes of shares entitled to preferential dividends shall have been fully paid.

(d) No such distribution shall be made to the holders of any class of shares which would reduce the remaining net assets of the corporation below the aggregate preferential amount payable in event of involuntary liquidation to the holders of shares having preferential rights to the assets of the corporation in the event of liquidation.

(e) Each such distribution, when made, shall be identified as a distribution from capital surplus and the amount per share disclosed to the shareholders receiving the same concurrently with the distribution thereof.

The board of directors of a corporation may also, from time to time, distribute to the holders of its outstanding shares having a cumulative preferential right to receive dividends, in discharge of their cumulative dividend rights, dividends payable in cash out of the capital surplus of the corporation, if at the time the corporation has no earned surplus and is not insolvent and would not thereby be rendered insolvent. Each such distribution when made, shall be identified as a payment of cumulative dividends out of capital surplus.

### § 47. Loans to Employees and Directors

A corporation shall not lend money to or use its credit to assist its directors without authorization in the particular case by its shareholders, but may lend money to and use its credit to assist any employee of the corporation or of a subsidiary, including any such employee who is a director of the corporation, if the board of directors decides that such loan or assistance may benefit the corporation.

### § 48. Liability of Directors in Certain Cases

In addition to any other liabilities imposed by law upon directors of a corporation:

(a) Directors of a corporation who vote for or assent to the declaration of any dividend or other distribution of the assets of a corporation to its shareholders contrary to the provisions of this Act or contrary to any restrictions contained in the articles of incorporation, shall be jointly and severally liable to the corporation for the amount of such dividend which is paid or the value of such assets which are distributed in excess of the amount of such dividend or distribution which could have been paid or distributed without a violation of the provisions of this Act or the restrictions in the articles of incorporation.

(b) Directors of a corporation who vote for or assent to the purchase of its own shares contrary to the provisions of this Act shall be jointly and severally liable to the corporation for the amount of consideration paid for such shares which is in excess of the maximum amount which could have been paid therefor without a violation of the provisions of this Act.

(c) The directors of a corporation who vote for or assent to any distribution of assets of a corporation to its shareholders during the liquidation of the corporation without the payment and discharge of, or making adequate provision for, all known debts, obligations, and liabilities of the corporation shall be jointly and severally liable to the corporation for the value of such assets which are distributed, to the extent that such debts, obligations and liabilities of the corporation are not thereafter paid and discharged.

A director of a corporation who is present at a meeting of its board of directors at which action on any corporate matter is taken shall be presumed to have assented to the action taken unless his dissent shall be entered in the minutes of the meeting or unless he shall file his written dissent to such action with the secretary of the meeting before the adjournment thereof or shall forward such dissent by registered mail to the secretary of the corporation immediately after the adjournment of the meeting. Such right to dissent shall not apply to a director who voted in favor of such action.

A director shall not be liable under (a), (b) or (c) of this section if he relied and acted in good faith upon financial statements of the corporation represented to him to be correct by the president or the officer of such corporation having charge of its books of account, or stated in a written report by an independent public or certified public accountant or firm of such accountants fairly to reflect the financial condition of such corporation, nor shall he be so liable if in good faith in determining the amount available for any such dividend or distribution he considered the assets to be of their book value.

Any director against whom a claim shall be asserted under or pursuant to this section for the payment of a dividend or other distribution of assets of a corporation and who shall be held liable thereon, shall be entitled to contribution from the shareholders who accepted or received any such dividend or assets, knowing such dividend or distribution to have been made in violation of this Act, in proportion to the amounts received by them.

Any director against whom a claim shall be asserted under or pursuant to this section shall be entitled to contribution from the other directors who voted for or assented to the action upon which the claim is asserted.

## § 49. Provisions Relating to Actions by Shareholders

No action shall be brought in this State by a shareholder in the right of a domestic or foreign corporation unless the plaintiff was a holder of record of shares or of voting trust certificates therefor at the time of the transaction of which he complains, or his shares or voting trust certificates thereafter devolved upon him by operation of law from a person who was a holder of record at such time.

In any action hereafter instituted in the right of any domestic or foreign corporation by the holder or holders of record of shares of such corporation or of voting trust certificates therefor, the court having jurisdiction, upon final judgment and a finding that the action was brought without reasonable cause, may require the plaintiff or plaintiffs to pay to the parties named as defendant the reasonable expenses, including fees of attorneys, incurred by them in the defense of such action.

In any action now pending or hereafter instituted or maintained in the right of any domestic or foreign corporation by the holder or holders of record of less than five per cent of the outstanding shares of any class of such corporation or of voting trust certificates therefor, unless the shares or voting trust certificates so held have a market value in excess of twenty-five thousand dollars, the corporation in whose right such action is brought shall be entitled at any time before final judgment to require the plaintiff or plaintiffs to give security for the reasonable expenses, including fees of attorneys, that may be incurred by it in connection with such action or may be incurred by other parties named as defendant for which it may become legally liable. Market value shall be determined as of the date that the plaintiff institutes the action or, in the case of an intervenor, as of the date that he becomes a party to the action. The amount of such security may from time to time be increased or decreased, in the discretion of the court, upon showing that the security provided has or may become inadequate or is excessive. The corporation shall have recourse to such security in such amount as the court having jurisdiction shall determine upon the termination of such action, whether or not the court finds the action was brought without reasonable cause.

## § 50. Officers

The officers of a corporation shall consist of a president, one or more vice presidents as may be prescribed by the by-laws, a secretary, and a treasurer, each of whom shall be elected by the board of directors at such time and in such manner as may be prescribed by the by-laws. Such other officers and assistant officers and agents as may be deemed necessary may be elected or appointed by the board of directors or chosen in such other manner as may be prescribed by the by-laws. Any two or more offices may be held by the same person, except the offices of president and secretary.

All officers and agents of the corporation, as between themselves and the corporation, shall have such authority and perform such duties in the management of the corporation as may be provided in the by-laws, or as may be determined by resolution of the board of directors not inconsistent with the by-laws.

### § 51. Removal of Officers

Any officer or agent may be removed by the board of directors whenever in its judgment the best interests of the corporation will be served thereby, but such removal shall be without prejudice to the contract rights, if any, of the person so removed. Election or appointment of an officer or agent shall not of itself create contract rights.

### § 52. Books and Records

Each corporation shall keep correct and complete books and records of account and shall keep minutes of the proceedings of its shareholders and board of directors and shall keep at its registered office or principal place of business, or at the office of its transfer agent or registrar, a record of its shareholders, giving the names and addresses of all shareholders and the number and class of the shares held by each. Any books, records and minutes may be in written form or in any other form capable of being converted into written form within a reasonable time.

Any person who shall have been a holder of record of shares or of voting trust certificates therefor at least six months immediately preceding his demand or shall be the holder of record of, or the holder of record of voting trust certificates for, at least five per cent of all the outstanding shares of the corporation, upon written demand stating the purpose thereof, shall have the right to examine, in person, or by agent or attorney, at any reasonable time or times, for any proper purpose its relevant books and records of account, minutes, and record of shareholders and to make extracts therefrom.

Any officer or agent who, or a corporation which, shall refuse to allow any such shareholder or holder of voting trust certificates, or his agent or attorney, so to examine and make extracts from its books and records of account, minutes, and record of shareholders, for any proper purpose, shall be liable to such shareholder or holder of voting trust certificates in a penalty of ten per cent of the value of the shares owned by such shareholder, or in respect of which such voting trust certificates are issued, in addition to any other damages or remedy afforded him by law. It shall be a defense to any action for penalties under this section that the person suing therefor has within two years sold or offered for sale any list of shareholders or of holders of voting trust certificates for shares of such corporation or any other corporation or has aided or abetted any person in procuring any list of shareholders or of holders of voting trust certificates for any such purpose, or has improperly used any information secured through any prior examination of the books and records of account, or minutes, or record of shareholders or of holders of voting trust certificates for shares of such corporation or any other corporation, or was not acting in good faith or for a proper purpose in making his demand.

Nothing herein contained shall impair the power of any court of competent jurisdiction, upon proof by a shareholder or holder of voting trust certificates of proper purpose, irrespective of the period of time during which such shareholder or holder of voting trust certificates shall have been a shareholder of record or a holder of record of voting trust certificates, and irrespective of the number of shares held by him or represented by voting trust certificates held by him, to compel the production for examination by such shareholder or holder of voting trust certificates of the books and records of account, minutes and record of shareholders of a corporation.

Upon the written request of any shareholder or holder of voting trust certificates for shares of a corporation, the corporation shall mail to such shareholder or holder of voting trust certificates its most recent financial statements showing in reasonable detail its assets and liabilities and the results of its operations.

### § 53.  Incorporators

One or more persons, or a domestic or foreign corporation, may act as incorporator or incorporators of a corporation by signing and delivering in duplicate to the Secretary of State articles of incorporation for such corporation.

### § 54.  Articles of Incorporation

The articles of incorporation shall set forth:

(a) The name of the corporation.

(b) The period of duration, which may be perpetual.

(c) The purpose or purposes for which the corporation is organized which may be stated to be, or to include, the transaction of any or all lawful business for which corporations may be incorporated under this Act.

(d) The aggregate number of shares which the corporation shall have authority to issue; if such shares are to consist of one class only, the par value of each of such shares, or a statement that all of such shares are without par value; or, if such shares are to be divided into classes, the number of shares of each class, and a statement of the par value of the shares of each such class or that such shares are to be without par value.

(e) If the shares are to be divided into classes, the designation of each class and a statement of the preferences, limitations and relative rights in respect of the shares of each class.

(f) If the corporation is to issue the shares of any preferred or special class in series, then the designation of each series and a statement of the variations in the relative rights and preferences as between series insofar as the same are to be fixed in the articles of incorporation, and a statement of any authority to be vested in the board of directors to establish series and fix and determine the variations in the relative rights and preferences as between series.

(g) If any preemptive right is to be granted to shareholders, the provisions therefor.

(h) Any provision, not inconsistent with law, which the incorporators elect to set forth in the articles of incorporation for the regulation of the internal affairs of the corporation, including any provision restricting the transfer of shares and any provision which under this Act is required or permitted to be set forth in the by-laws.

(i) The address of its initial registered office, and the name of its initial registered agent at such address.

(j) The number of directors constituting the initial board of directors and the names and addresses of the persons who are to serve as directors until the first annual meeting of shareholders or until their successors be elected and qualify.

(k) The name and address of each incorporator.

It shall not be necessary to set forth in the articles of incorporation any of the corporate powers enumerated in this Act.

## § 55.　Filing of Articles of Incorporation

Duplicate originals of the articles of incorporation shall be delivered to the Secretary of State. If the Secretary of State finds that the articles of incorporation conform to law, he shall, when all fees have been paid as in this Act prescribed:

(a) Endorse on each of such duplicate originals the word "Filed," and the month, day and year of the filing thereof.

(b) File one of such duplicate originals in his office.

(c) Issue a certificate of incorporation to which he shall affix the other duplicate original.

The certificate of incorporation, together with the duplicate original of the articles of incorporation affixed thereto by the Secretary of State, shall be returned to the incorporators or their representative.

## § 56.　Effect of Issuance of Certificate of Incorporation

Upon the issuance of the certificate of incorporation, the corporate existence shall begin, and such certificate of incorporation shall be conclusive evidence that all conditions precedent required to be performed by the incorporators have been complied with and that the corporation has been incorporated under this Act, except as against this State in a proceeding to cancel or revoke the certificate of incorporation or for involuntary dissolution of the corporation.

### § 57.   Organization Meeting of Directors

After the issuance of the certificate of incorporation an organization meeting of the board of directors named in the articles of incorporation shall be held, either within or without this State, at the call of a majority of the directors named in the articles of incorporation, for the purpose of adopting by-laws, electing officers and transacting such other business as may come before the meeting.   The directors calling the meeting shall give at least three days' notice thereof by mail to each director so named, stating the time and place of the meeting.

### § 58.   Right to Amend Articles of Incorporation

A corporation may amend its articles of incorporation, from time to time, in any and as many respects as may be desired, so long as its articles of incorporation as amended contain only such provisions as might be lawfully contained in original articles of incorporation at the time of making such amendment, and, if a change in shares or the rights of shareholders, or an exchange, reclassification or cancellation of shares or rights of shareholders is to be made, such provisions as may be necessary to effect such change, exchange, reclassification or cancellation.

In particular, and without limitation upon such general power of amendment, a corporation may amend its articles of incorporation, from time to time, so as:

(a)  To change its corporate name.

(b)  To change its period of duration.

(c)  To change, enlarge or diminish its corporate purposes.

(d)  To increase or decrease the aggregate number of shares, or shares of any class, which the corporation has authority to issue.

(e)  To increase or decrease the par value of the authorized shares of any class having a par value, whether issued or unissued.

(f)  To exchange, classify, reclassify or cancel all or any part of its shares, whether issued or unissued.

(g)  To change the designation of all or any part of its shares, whether issued or unissued, and to change the preferences, limitations, and the relative rights in respect of all or any part of its shares, whether issued or unissued.

(h) To change shares having the par value, whether issued or unissued, into the same or a different number of shares without par value, and to change shares without par value, whether issued or unissued, into the same or a different number of shares having a par value.

(i) To change the shares of any class, whether issued or unissued and whether with or without par value, into a different number of shares of the same class or into the same or a different number of shares, either with or without par value, of other classes.

(j) To create new classes of shares having rights and preferences either prior and superior or subordinate and inferior to the shares of any class then authorized, whether issued or unissued.

(k) To cancel or otherwise affect the right of the holders of the shares of any class to receive dividends which have accrued but have not been declared.

(*l*) To divide any preferred or special class of shares, whether issued or unissued, into series and fix and determine the designations of such series and the variations in the relative rights and preferences as between the shares of such series.

(m) To authorize the board of directors to establish, out of authorized but unissued shares, series of any preferred or special class of shares and fix and determine the relative rights and preferences of the shares of any series so established.

(n) To authorize the board of directors to fix and determine the relative rights and preferences of the authorized but unissued shares of series theretofore established in respect of which either the relative rights and preferences have not been fixed and determined or the relative rights and preferences theretofore fixed and determined are to be changed.

(o) To revoke, diminish, or enlarge the authority of the board of directors to establish series out of authorized but unissued shares of any preferred or special class and fix and determine the relative rights and preferences of the shares of any series so established.

(p) To limit, deny or grant to shareholders of any class the preemptive right to acquire additional or treasury shares of the corporation, whether then or thereafter authorized.

## § 59. Procedure to Amend Articles of Incorporation

Amendments to the articles of incorporation shall be made in the following manner:

(a) The board of directors shall adopt a resolution setting forth the proposed amendment and, if shares have been issued, directing that it be submitted to a vote at a meeting of shareholders, which may be either the annual or a special meeting. If no shares have been issued, the amendment shall be adopted by resolution of the board of directors and the provisions for adoption by shareholders shall not apply. The resolution may incorporate the proposed amendment in restated articles of incorporation which contain a statement that except for the designated amendment the restated articles of incorporation correctly set forth without change the corresponding provisions of the articles of incorporation as theretofore amended, and that the restated articles of incorporation together with the designated amendment supersede the original articles of incorporation and all amendments thereto.

(b) Written notice setting forth the proposed amendment or a summary of the changes to be effected thereby shall be given to each shareholder of record entitled to vote thereon within the time and in the manner provided in this Act for the giving of notice of meetings of shareholders. If the meeting be an annual meeting, the proposed amendment of such summary may be included in the notice of such annual meeting.

(c) At such meeting a vote of the shareholders entitled to vote thereon shall be taken on the proposed amendment. The proposed amendment shall be adopted upon receiving the affirmative vote of the holders of a majority of the shares entitled to vote thereon, unless any class of shares is entitled to vote thereon as a class, in which event the proposed amendment shall be adopted upon receiving the affirmative vote of the holders of a majority of the shares of each class of shares entitled to vote thereon as a class and of the total shares entitled to vote thereon.

Any number of amendments may be submitted to the shareholders, and voted upon by them, at one meeting.

### § 60. Class Voting on Amendments

The holders of the outstanding shares of a class shall be entitled to vote as a class upon a proposed amendment, whether or not entitled to vote thereon by the provisions of the articles of incorporation, if the amendment would:

(a) Increase or decrease the aggregate number of authorized shares of such class.

(b) Increase or decrease the par value of the shares of such class.

(c) Effect an exchange, reclassification or cancellation of all or part of the shares of such class.

(d) Effect an exchange, or create a right of exchange, of all or any part of the shares of another class into the shares of such class.

(e) Change the designations, preferences, limitations or relative rights of the shares of such class.

(f) Change the shares of such class, whether with or without par value, into the same or a different number of shares, either with or without par value, of the same class or another class or classes.

(g) Create a new class of shares having rights and preferences prior and superior to the shares of such class, or increase the rights and preferences or the number of authorized shares, of any class having rights and preferences prior or superior to the shares of such class.

(h) In the case of a preferred or special class of shares, divide the shares of such class into series and fix and determine the designation of such series and the variations in the relative rights and preferences between the shares of such series, or authorize the board of directors to do so.

(i) Limit or deny any existing preemptive rights of the shares of such class.

(j) Cancel or otherwise affect dividends on the shares of such class which have accrued but have not been declared.

## § 61. Articles of Amendment

The articles of amendment shall be executed in duplicate by the corporation by its president or a vice president and by its secretary or an assistant secretary, and verified by one of the officers signing such articles, and shall set forth:

(a) The name of the corporation.

(b) The amendments so adopted.

(c) The date of the adoption of the amendment by the shareholders, or by the board of directors where no shares have been issued.

(d) The number of shares outstanding, and the number of shares entitled to vote thereon, and if the shares of any class are entitled to vote thereon as a class, the designation and number of outstanding shares entitled to vote thereon of each such class.

(e) The number of shares voted for and against such amendment, respectively, and, if the shares of any class are entitled to vote thereon as a class, the number of shares of each such class voted for and against such amendment, respectively, or if no shares have been issued, a statement to that effect.

(f) If such amendment provides for an exchange, reclassification or cancellation of issued shares, and if the manner in which the same shall be effected is not set forth in the amendment, then a statement of the manner in which the same shall be effected.

(g) If such amendment effects a change in the amount of stated capital, then a statement of the manner in which the same is effected and a statement, expressed in dollars, of the amount of stated capital as changed by such amendment.

## § 62. Filing of Articles of Amendment

Duplicate originals of the articles of amendment shall be delivered to the Secretary of State. If the Secretary of State finds that the articles of amendment conform to law, he shall, when all fees and franchise taxes have been paid as in this Act prescribed:

(a) Endorse on each of such duplicate originals the word "Filed," and the month, day and year of the filing thereof.

(b) File one of such duplicate originals in his office.

(c) Issue a certificate of amendment to which he shall affix the other duplicate original.

The certificate of amendment, together with the duplicate original of the articles of amendment affixed thereto by the Secretary of State, shall be returned to the corporation or its representative.

## § 63. Effect of Certificate of Amendment

Upon the issuance of the certificate of amendment by the Secretary of State, the amendment shall become effective and the articles of incorporation shall be deemed to be amended accordingly.

No amendment shall affect any existing cause of action in favor of or against such corporation, or any pending suit to which such corporation shall be a party, or the existing rights of persons other than shareholders; and, in the event the corporate name shall be changed by amendment, no suit brought by or against such corporation under its former name shall abate for that reason.

## § 64. Restated Articles of Incorporation

A domestic corporation may at any time restate its articles of incorporation as theretofore amended, by a resolution adopted by the board of directors.

Upon the adoption of such resolution, restated articles of incorporation shall be executed in duplicate by the corporation by its president or a vice president and by its secretary or assistant secretary and verified by one of the officers signing such articles and shall set forth all of the operative provisions of the articles of incorporation as theretofore amended together with a statement that the restated articles of incorporation correctly set forth without change the corresponding provisions of the articles of incorporation as theretofore amended and that the restated articles of incorporation supersede the original articles of incorporation and all amendments thereto.

Duplicate originals of the restated articles of incorporation shall be delivered to the Secretary of State. If the Secretary of State finds that such restated articles of incorporation conform to law, he shall, when all fees and franchise taxes have been paid as in this Act prescribed:

(1) Endorse on each of such duplicate originals the word "Filed," and the month, day and year of the filing thereof.

(2) File one of such duplicate originals in his office.

(3) Issue a restated certificate of incorporation, to which he shall affix the other duplicate original.

The restated certificate of incorporation, together with the duplicate original of the restated articles of incorporation affixed thereto by the Secretary of State, shall be returned to the corporation or its representative.

Upon the issuance of the restated certificate of incorporation by the Secretary of State, the restated articles of incorporation shall become effective and shall supersede the original articles of incorporation and all amendments thereto.

## § 65. Amendment of Articles of Incorporation in Reorganization Proceedings

Whenever a plan of reorganization of a corporation has been confirmed by decree or order of a court of competent jurisdiction in proceedings for the reorganization of such corporation, pursuant to the provisions of any applicable statute of the United States relating to reorganizations of corporations, the articles of incorporation of the corporation may be amended, in the manner provided in this section, in as many respects as may be necessary to carry out the plan and put it into effect, so long as the articles of incorporation as amended contain only such provisions as might be lawfully contained in original articles of incorporation at the time of making such amendment.

In particular and without limitation upon such general power of amendment, the articles of incorporation may be amended for such purpose so as to:

(A) Change the corporate name, period of duration or corporate purposes of the corporation;

(B) Repeal, alter or amend the by-laws of the corporation;

(C) Change the aggregate number of shares or shares of any class, which the corporation has authority to issue;

(D) Change the preferences, limitations and relative rights in respect of all or any part of the shares of the corporation, and classify, reclassify or cancel all or any part thereof, whether issued or unissued;

(E) Authorize the issuance of bonds, debentures or other obligations of the corporation, whether or not convertible into shares of any class or bearing warrants or other evidences of optional rights to purchase or subscribe for shares of any class, and fix the terms and conditions thereof; and

(F) Constitute or reconstitute and classify or reclassify the board of directors of the corporation, and appoint directors and officers in place of or in addition to all or any of the directors or officers then in office.

Amendments to the articles of incorporation pursuant to this section shall be made in the following manner:

(a) Articles of amendment approved by decree or order of such court shall be executed and verified in duplicate by such person or persons as the court shall designate or appoint for the purpose, and shall set forth the name of the corporation, the amendments of the articles of incorporation approved by the court, the date of the decree or order approving the articles of amendment, the title of the proceedings in which the decree or order was entered, and a statement that such decree or order was entered by a court having jurisdiction of the proceedings for the reorganization of the corporation pursuant to the provisions of an applicable statute of the United States.

(b) Duplicate originals of the articles of amendment shall be delivered to the Secretary of State. If the Secretary of State finds that the articles of amendment conform to law, he shall, when all fees and franchise taxes have been paid as in this Act prescribed:

(1) Endorse on each of such duplicate originals the word "Filed," and the month, day and year of the filing thereof.

(2) File one of such duplicate originals in his office.

(3) Issue a certificate of amendment to which he shall affix the other duplicate original.

The certificate of amendment, together with the duplicate original of the articles of amendment affixed thereto by the Secretary of State, shall be returned to the corporation or its representative.

Upon the issuance of the certificate of amendment by the Secretary of State, the amendment shall become effective and the articles of incorporation shall be deemed to be amended accordingly, without any action thereon by the directors or shareholders of the corporation and with the same effect as if the amendments had been adopted by unanimous action of the directors and shareholders of the corporation.

## § 66. Restriction on Redemption or Purchase of Redeemable Shares

No redemption or purchase of redeemable shares shall be made by a corporation when it is insolvent or when such redemption or purchase would render it insolvent, or which would reduce the net assets below the aggregate amount payable to the holders of shares having prior or equal rights to the assets of the corporation upon involuntary dissolution.

## § 67. Cancellation of Redeemable Shares by Redemption or Purchase

When redeemable shares of a corporation are redeemed or purchased by the corporation, the redemption or purchase shall effect a cancellation of such shares, and a statement of cancellation shall be filed as provided in this section. Thereupon such shares shall be restored to the status of authorized but unissued shares, unless the articles of incorporation provide that such shares when redeemed or purchased shall not be reissued, in which case the filing of the statement of cancellation shall constitute an amendment to the articles of incorporation and shall reduce the number of shares of the class so cancelled which the corporation is authorized to issue by the number of shares so cancelled.

The statement of cancellation shall be executed in duplicate by the corporation by its president or a vice president and by its secretary or an assistant secretary, and verified by one of the officers signing such statement, and shall set forth:

(a) The name of the corporation.

(b) The number of redeemable shares cancelled through redemption or purchase, itemized by classes and series.

(c) The aggregate number of issued shares, itemized by classes and series, after giving effect to such cancellation.

(d) The amount, expressed in dollars, of the stated capital of the corporation after giving effect to such cancellation.

(e) If the articles of incorporation provide that the cancelled shares shall not be reissued, the number of shares which the corporation will have authority to issue itemized by classes and series, after giving effect to such cancellation.

Duplicate originals of such statement shall be delivered to the Secretary of State. If the Secretary of State finds that such statement conforms to law, he shall, when all fees and franchise taxes have been paid as in this Act prescribed:

(1) Endorse on each of such duplicate originals the word "Filed," and the month, day and year of the filing thereof.

(2) File one of such duplicate originals in his office.

(3) Return the other duplicate original to the corporation or its representative.

Upon the filing of such statement of cancellation, the stated capital of the corporation shall be deemed to be reduced by that part of the stated capital which was, at the time of such cancellation, represented by the shares so cancelled.

Nothing contained in this section shall be construed to forbid a cancellation of shares or a reduction of stated capital in any other manner permitted by this Act.

### § 68. Cancellation of Other Reacquired Shares

A corporation may at any time, by resolution of its board of directors, cancel all or any part of the shares of the corporation of any class reacquired by it, other than redeemable shares redeemed or purchased, and in such event a statement of cancellation shall be filed as provided in this section.

The statement of cancellation shall be executed in duplicate by the corporation by its president or a vice president and by its secretary or an assistant secretary, and verified by one of the officers signing such statement, and shall set forth:

(a) The name of the corporation.

(b) The number of reacquired shares cancelled by resolution duly adopted by the board of directors, itemized by classes and series, and the date of its adoption.

(c) The aggregate number of issued shares, itemized by classes and series, after giving effect to such cancellation.

(d) The amount, expressed in dollars, of the stated capital of the corporation after giving effect to such cancellation.

Duplicate originals of such statement shall be delivered to the Secretary of State. If the Secretary of State finds that such

441

statement conforms to law, he shall, when all fees and franchise taxes have been paid as in this Act prescribed:

(1) Endorse on each of such duplicate originals the word "Filed," and the month, day and year of the filing thereof.

(2) File one of such duplicate originals in his office.

(3) Return the other duplicate original to the corporation or its representative.

Upon the filing of such statement of cancellation, the stated capital of the corporation shall be deemed to be reduced by that part of the stated capital which was, at the time of such cancellation, represented by the shares so cancelled, and the shares so cancelled shall be restored to the status of authorized but unissued shares.

Nothing contained in this section shall be construed to forbid a cancellation of shares or a reduction of stated capital in any other manner permitted by this Act.

## § 69. Reduction of Stated Capital in Certain Cases

A reduction of the stated capital of a corporation, where such reduction is not accompanied by any action requiring an amendment of the articles of incorporation and not accompanied by a cancellation of shares, may be made in the following manner:

(A) The board of directors shall adopt a resolution setting forth the amount of the proposed reduction and the manner in which the reduction shall be effected, and directing that the question of such reduction be submitted to a vote at a meeting of shareholders, which may be either an annual or a special meeting.

(B) Written notice, stating that the purpose or one of the purposes of such meeting is to consider the question of reducing the stated capital of the corporation in the amount and manner proposed by the board of directors, shall be given to each shareholder of record entitled to vote thereon within the time and in the manner provided in this Act for the giving of notice of meetings of shareholders.

(C) At such meeting a vote of the shareholders entitled to vote thereon shall be taken on the question of approving the proposed reduction of stated capital, which shall require for its adoption the affirmative vote of the holders of a majority of the shares entitled to vote thereon.

When a reduction of the stated capital of a corporation has been approved as provided in this section, a statement shall be executed in duplicate by the corporation by its president or a vice president and by its secretary or an assistant secretary, and verified by one of the officers signing such statement, and shall set forth:

(a) The name of the corporation.

(b) A copy of the resolution of the shareholders approving such reduction, and the date of its adoption.

(c) The number of shares outstanding, and the number of shares entitled to vote thereon.

(d) The number of shares voted for and against such reduction, respectively.

(e) A statement of the manner in which such reduction is effected, and a statement, expressed in dollars, of the amount of stated capital of the corporation after giving effect to such reduction.

Duplicate originals of such statement shall be delivered to the Secretary of State. If the Secretary of State finds that such statement conforms to law, he shall, when all fees and franchise taxes have been paid as in this Act prescribed:

(1) Endorse on each of such duplicate originals the word "Filed," and the month, day and year of the filing thereof.

(2) File one of such duplicate originals in his office.

(3) Return the other duplicate original to the corporation or its representative.

Upon the filing of such statement, the stated capital of the corporation shall be reduced as therein set forth.

No reduction of stated capital shall be made under the provisions of this section which would reduce the amount of the aggregate stated capital of the corporation to an amount equal to or less than the aggregate preferential amounts payable upon all issued shares having a preferential right in the assets of the corporation in the event of involuntary liquidation, plus the aggregate par value of all issued shares having a par value but no preferential right in the assets of the corporation in the event of involuntary liquidation.

### § 70. Special Provisions Relating to Surplus and Reserves

The surplus, if any, created by or arising out of a reduction of the stated capital of a corporation shall be capital surplus.

The capital surplus of a corporation may be increased from time to time by resolution of the board of directors directing that all or a part of the earned surplus of the corporation be transferred to capital surplus.

A corporation may, by resolution of its board of directors, apply any part or all of its capital surplus to the reduction or elimination of any deficit arising from losses, however incurred, but only after first eliminating the earned surplus, if any, of the corporation by applying such losses against earned surplus and only to the extent that such losses exceed the earned surplus, if any. Each such application of capital surplus shall, to the extent thereof, effect a reduction of capital surplus.

A corporation may, by resolution of its board of directors, create a reserve or reserves out of its earned surplus for any proper purpose or purposes, and may abolish any such reserve in the same manner. Earned surplus of the corporation to the extent so reserved shall not be available for the payment of dividends or other distributions by the corporation except as expressly permitted by this Act.

### § 71.  Procedure for Merger

Any two or more domestic corporations may merge into one of such corporations pursuant to a plan of merger approved in the manner provided in this Act.

The board of directors of each corporation shall, by resolution adopted by each such board, approve a plan of merger setting forth:

(a) The names of the corporations proposing to merge, and the name of the corporation into which they propose to merge, which is hereinafter designated as the surviving corporation.

(b) The terms and conditions of the proposed merger.

(c) The manner and basis of converting the shares of each corporation into shares, obligations or other securities of the surviving corporation or of any other corporation or, in whole or in part, into cash or other property.

(d) A statement of any changes in the articles of incorporation of the surviving corporation to be effected by such merger.

(e) Such other provisions with respect to the proposed merger as are deemed necessary or desirable.

### § 72.  Procedure for Consolidation

Any two or more domestic corporations may consolidate into a new corporation pursuant to a plan of consolidation approved in the manner provided in this Act.

The board of directors of each corporation shall, by a resolution adopted by each such board, approve a plan of consolidation setting forth:

(a) The names of the corporations proposing to consolidate, and the name of the new corporation into which they propose to consolidate, which is hereinafter designated as the new corporation.

(b) The terms and conditions of the proposed consolidation.

(c) The manner and basis of converting the shares of each corporation into shares, obligations or other securities of the new corporation or of any other corporation or, in whole or in part, into cash or other property.

(d) With respect to the new corporation, all of the statements required to be set forth in articles of incorporation for corporations organized under this Act.

(e) Such other provisions with respect to the proposed consolidation as are deemed necessary or desirable.

### § 73. Approval by Shareholders

The board of directors of each corporation, upon approving such plan of merger or plan of consolidation, shall, by resolution, direct that the plan be submitted to a vote at a meeting of shareholders, which may be either an annual or a special meeting. Written notice shall be given to each shareholder of record, whether or not entitled to vote at such meeting, not less than twenty days before such meeting, in the manner provided in this Act for the giving of notice of meetings of shareholders, and, whether the meeting be an annual or a special meeting, shall state that the purpose or one of the purposes is to consider the proposed plan of merger or consolidation. A copy or a summary of the plan of merger or plan of consolidation, as the case may be, shall be included in or enclosed with such notice.

At each such meeting, a vote of the shareholders shall be taken on the proposed plan of merger or consolidation. The plan of merger or consolidation shall be approved upon receiving the affirmative vote of the holders of a majority of the shares entitled to vote thereon of each such corporation, unless any class of shares of any such corporation is entitled to vote thereon as a class, in which event, as to such corporation, the plan of merger, or consolidation shall be approved upon receiving the affirmative vote of the holders of a majority of the shares of each class of shares entitled to vote thereon as a class and of the total shares entitled to vote thereon. Any class of shares of any such corporation shall be entitled to vote as a class if the plan of merger or consolidation, as the case may be, contains any provision which, if contained in a proposed amendment to articles of incorporation, would entitle such class of shares to vote as a class.

After such approval by a vote of the shareholders of each corporation, and at any time prior to the filing of the articles of merger or consolidation, the merger or consolidation may be abandoned pursuant to provisions therefor, if any, set forth in the plan of merger or consolidation.

## § 74.  Articles of Merger or Consolidation

Upon such approval, articles of merger or articles of consolidation shall be executed in duplicate by each corporation by its president or a vice president and by its secretary or an assistant secretary, and verified by one of the officers of each corporation signing such articles, and shall set forth:

(a)  The plan of merger or the plan of consolidation.

(b)  As to each corporation, the number of shares outstanding, and, if the shares of any class are entitled to vote as a class, the designation and number of outstanding shares of each such class.

(c)  As to each corporation, the number of shares voted for and against such plan, respectively, and, if the shares of any class are entitled to vote as a class, the number of shares of each such class voted for and against such plan, respectively.

Duplicate originals of the articles of merger or articles of consolidation shall be delivered to the Secretary of State. If the Secretary of State finds that such articles conform to law, he shall, when all fees and franchise taxes have been paid as in this Act prescribed:

(1)  Endorse on each of such duplicate originals the word "Filed," and the month, day and year of the filing thereof.

(2)  File one of such duplicate originals in his office.

(3)  Issue a certificate of merger or a certificate of consolidation to which he shall affix the other duplicate original.

The certificate of merger or certificate of consolidation, together with the duplicate original of the articles of merger or articles of consolidation affixed thereto by the Secretary of State, shall be returned to the surviving or new corporation, as the case may be, or its representative.

## § 75.  Merger of Subsidiary Corporation

Any corporation owning at least ninety per cent of the outstanding shares of each class of another corporation may merge such other corporation into itself without approval by a vote of the shareholders of either corporation. Its board of directors shall, by resolution, approve a plan of merger setting forth:

(A)  The name of the subsidiary corporation and the name of the corporation owning at least ninety per cent of its shares, which is hereinafter designated as the surviving corporation.

(B) The manner and basis of converting the shares of the subsidiary corporation into shares, obligations or other securities of the surviving corporation or of any other corporation or, in whole or in part, into cash or other property.

A copy of such plan of merger shall be mailed to each shareholder of record of the subsidiary corporation.

Articles of merger shall be executed in duplicate by the surviving corporation by its president or a vice president and by its secretary or an assistant secretary, and verified by one of its officers signing such articles, and shall set forth:

(a) The plan of merger;

(b) The number of outstanding shares of each class of the subsidiary corporation and the number of such shares of each class owned by the surviving corporation; and

(c) The date of the mailing to shareholders of the subsidiary corporation of a copy of the plan of merger.

On and after the thirtieth day after the mailing of a copy of the plan of merger to shareholders of the subsidiary corporation or upon the waiver thereof by the holders of all outstanding shares duplicate originals of the articles of merger shall be delivered to the Secretary of State. If the Secretary of State finds that such articles conform to law, he shall, when all fees and franchise taxes have been paid as in this Act prescribed:

(1) Endorse on each of such duplicate originals the word "Filed," and the month, day and year of the filing thereof,

(2) File one of such duplicate originals in his office, and

(3) Issue a certificate of merger to which he shall affix the other duplicate original.

The certificate of merger, together with the duplicate original of the articles of merger affixed thereto by the Secretary of State, shall be returned to the surviving corporation or its representative.

### § 76. Effect of Merger or Consolidation

Upon the issuance of the certificate of merger or the certificate of consolidation by the Secretary of State, the merger or consolidation shall be effected.

When such merger or consolidation has been effected:

(a) The several corporations parties to the plan of merger or consolidation shall be a single corporation, which, in the case of a merger, shall be that corporation designated in the plan of merger as the surviving corporation, and, in the case of a consolidation, shall be the new corporation provided for in the plan of consolidation.

(b) The separate existence of all corporations parties to the plan of merger or consolidation, except the surviving or new corporation, shall cease.

(c) Such surviving or new corporation shall have all the rights, privileges, immunities and powers and shall be subject to all the duties and liabilities of a corporation organized under this Act.

(d) Such surviving or new corporation shall thereupon and thereafter possess all the rights, privileges, immunities, and franchises, of a public as well as of a private nature, of each of the merging or consolidating corporations; and all property, real, personal and mixed, and all debts due on whatever account, including subscriptions to shares, and all other choses in action, and all and every other interest of or belonging to or due to each of the corporations so merged or consolidated, shall be taken and deemed to be transferred to and vested in such single corporation without further act or deed; and the title to any real estate, or any interest therein, vested in any of such corporations shall not revert or be in any way impaired by reason of such merger or consolidation.

(e) Such surviving or new corporation shall thenceforth be responsible and liable for all the liabilities and obligations of each of the corporations so merged or consolidated; and any claim existing or action or proceeding pending by or against any of such corporations may be prosecuted as if such merger or consolidation had not taken place, or such surviving or new corporation may be substituted in its place. Neither the rights of creditors nor any liens upon the property of any such corporation shall be impaired by such merger or consolidation.

(f) In the case of a merger, the articles of incorporation of the surviving corporation shall be deemed to be amended to the extent, if any, that changes in its articles of incorporation are stated in the plan of merger; and, in the case of a consolidation, the statements set forth in the articles of consolidation and which are required or permitted to be set forth in the articles of incorporation of corporations organized under this Act shall be deemed to be the original articles of incorporation of the new corporation.

### § 77. Merger or Consolidation of Domestic and Foreign Corporations

One or more foreign corporations and one or more domestic corporations may be merged or consolidated in the following manner, if such merger or consolidation is permitted by the laws of the state under which each such foreign corporation is organized:

(a) Each domestic corporation shall comply with the provisions of this Act with respect to the merger or consolidation, as the case may be, of domestic corporations and each foreign corporation shall comply with the applicable provisions of the laws of the state under which it is organized.

(b) If the surviving or new corporation, as the case may be, is to be governed by the laws of any state other than this State, it shall comply with the provisions of this Act with respect to foreign corporations if it is to transact business in this State, and in every case it shall file with the Secretary of State of this State:

(1) An agreement that it may be served with process in this State in any proceeding for the enforcement of any obligation of any domestic corporation which is a party to such merger or consolidation and in any proceeding for the enforcement of the rights of a dissenting shareholder of any such domestic corporation against the surviving or new corporation;

(2) An irrevocable appointment of the Secretary of State of this State as its agent to accept service of process in any such proceeding; and

(3) An agreement that it will promptly pay to the dissenting shareholders of any such domestic corporation the amount, if any, to which they shall be entitled under the provisions of this Act with respect to the rights of dissenting shareholders.

The effect of such merger or consolidation shall be the same as in the case of the merger or consolidation of domestic corporations, if the surviving or new corporation is to be governed by the laws of this State. If the surviving or new corporation is to be governed by the laws of any state other than this State, the effect of such merger or consolidation shall be the same as in the case of the merger or consolidation of domestic corporations except insofar as the laws of such other state provide otherwise.

At any time prior to the filing of the articles of merger or consolidation, the merger or consolidation may be abandoned pursuant to provisions therefor, if any, set forth in the plan of merger or consolidation.

### § 78. Sale of Assets in Regular Course of Business and Mortgage or Pledge of Assets

The sale, lease, exchange, or other disposition of all, or substantially all, the property and assets of a corporation in the usual and regular course of its business and the mortgage or pledge of any or all property and assets of a corporation whether or not in the usual and regular course of business may be made upon such terms and conditions and for such consideration, which may consist in whole or in part of cash or other property, including shares, obligations or other securities of any other corporation, domestic or foreign, as shall be authorized by its board of directors; and in any such case no authorization or consent of the shareholders shall be required.

### § 79.  Sale of Assets Other Than in Regular Course of Business

A sale, lease, exchange, or other disposition of all, or substantially all, the property and assets, with or without the good will, of a corporation, if not in the usual and regular course of its business, may be made upon such terms and conditions and for such consideration, which may consist in whole or in part of cash or other property, including shares, obligations or other securities of any other corporation, domestic or foreign, as may be authorized in the following manner:

(a) The board of directors shall adopt a resolution recommending such sale, lease, exchange, or other disposition and directing the submission thereof to a vote at a meeting of shareholders, which may be either an annual or a special meeting.

(b) Written notice shall be given to each shareholder of record, whether or not entitled to vote at such meeting, not less than twenty days before such meeting, in the manner provided in this Act for the giving of notice of meetings of shareholders, and, whether the meeting be an annual or a special meeting, shall state that the purpose, or one of the purposes is to consider the proposed sale, lease, exchange, or other disposition.

(c) At such meeting the shareholders may authorize such sale, lease, exchange, or other disposition and may fix, or may authorize the board of directors to fix, any or all of the terms and conditions thereof and the consideration to be received by the corporation therefor.  Such authorization shall require the affirmative vote of the holders of a majority of the shares of the corporation entitled to vote thereon, unless any class of shares is entitled to vote thereon as a class, in which event such authorization shall require the affirmative vote of the holders of a majority of the shares of each class of shares entitled to vote as a class thereon and of the total shares entitled to vote thereon.

(d) After such authorization by a vote of shareholders, the board of directors nevertheless, in its discretion, may abandon such sale, lease, exchange, or other disposition of assets, subject to the rights of third parties under any contracts relating thereto, without further action or approval by shareholders.

## § 80.  Right of Shareholders to Dissent

Any shareholder of a corporation shall have the right to dissent from any of the following corporate actions:

(a) Any plan of merger or consolidation to which the corporation is a party;  or

(b) Any sale or exchange of all or substantially all of the property and assets of the corporation not made in the usual and regular course of its business, including a sale in dissolution, but not including a sale pursuant to an order of a court having jurisdiction in the premises or a sale for cash on terms requiring that all or substantially all of the net proceeds of sale be distributed to the shareholders in accordance with their respective interests within one year after the date of sale.

A shareholder may dissent as to less than all of the shares registered in his name.  In that event, his rights shall be determined as if the shares as to which he has dissented and his other shares were registered in the names of different shareholders.

This section shall not apply to the shareholders of the surviving corporation in a merger if a vote of the shareholders of such corporation is not necessary to authorize such merger.  Nor shall it apply to the holders of shares of any class or series if the shares of such class or series were registered on a national securities exchange on the date fixed to determine the shareholders entitled to vote at the meeting of shareholders at which a plan of merger or consolidation or a proposed sale or exchange of property and assets is to be acted upon unless the articles of incorporation of the corporation shall otherwise provide.

## § 81.  Rights of Dissenting Shareholders

Any shareholder electing to exercise such right of dissent shall file with the corporation, prior to or at the meeting of shareholders at which such proposed corporate action is submitted to a vote, a written objection to such proposed corporate action.  If such proposed corporate action be approved by the required vote and such shareholder shall not have voted in favor thereof, such shareholder may, within ten days after the date on which the vote was taken or if a corporation is to be merged without a vote of its shareholders into another corporation, any of its shareholders may, within fifteen days after the plan of such merger shall have been mailed to such shareholders, make written demand on the corporation, or, in the case of a merger or consolidation, on the surviving or new corporation, domestic or foreign, for payment of the fair value of such shareholder's shares, and, if such proposed corporate action is effected, such corporation shall pay to such shareholder, upon surrender of the certificate or certificates representing such shares, 'the fair value thereof as of the day prior to the date on which the vote was taken approving the proposed corporate action, excluding any appreciation or depreciation in anticipation of such corporate action. Any shareholder failing to make demand within the applicable ten-day or fifteen-day period shall be bound by the terms of the proposed corporate action. Any shareholder making such demand shall thereafter be entitled only to payment as in this section provided and shall not be entitled to vote or to exercise any other rights of a shareholder.

No such demand may be withdrawn unless the corporation shall consent thereto. If, however, such demand shall be withdrawn upon consent, or if the proposed corporate action shall be abandoned or rescinded or the shareholders shall revoke the authority to effect such action, or if, in the case of a merger, on the date of the filing of the articles of merger the surviving corporation is the owner of all the outstanding shares of the other corporations, domestic and foreign, that are parties to the merger, or if no demand or petition for the determination of fair value by a court shall have been made or filed within the time provided in this section, or if a court of competent jurisdiction shall determine that such shareholder is not entitled to the relief provided by this section, then the right of such shareholder to be paid the fair value of his shares shall cease and his status as a shareholder shall be restored, without prejudice to any corporate proceedings which may have been taken during the interim.

Within ten days after such corporate action is effected, the corporation, or, in the case of a merger or consolidation, the surviving or new corporation, domestic or foreign, shall give written notice thereof to each dissenting shareholder who has made demand as herein provided, and shall make a written offer to each such shareholder to pay for such shares at a specified price deemed by such corporation to be the fair value thereof. Such notice and offer shall be accompanied by a balance sheet of the corporation the shares of which the dissenting shareholder holds, as of the latest available date and not more than twelve months prior to the making of such offer, and a profit and loss statement of such corporation for the twelve months' period ended on the date of such balance sheet.

If within thirty days after the date on which such corporate action was effected the fair value of such shares is agreed upon between any such dissenting shareholder and the corporation, payment therefor shall be made within ninety days after the date on which such corporate action was effected, upon surrender of the certificate or certificates representing such shares.

Upon payment of the agreed value the dissenting shareholder shall cease to have any interest in such shares.

If within such period of thirty days a dissenting shareholder and the corporation do not so agree, then the corporation, within thirty days after receipt of written demand from any dissenting shareholder given within sixty days after the date on which such corporate action was effected, shall, or at its election at any time within such period of sixty days may, file a petition in any court of competent jurisdiction in the county in this State where the registered office of the corporation is located requesting that the fair value of such shares be found and determined. If, in the case of a merger or consolidation, the surviving or new corporation is a foreign corporation without a registered office in this State, such petition shall be filed in the county where the registered office of the domestic corporation was last located. If the corporation shall fail to institute the proceeding as herein provided, any dissenting shareholder may do so in the name of the corporation. All dissenting shareholders, wherever residing, shall be made parties to the proceeding as an action against their shares quasi in rem. A copy of the petition shall be served on each dissenting shareholder who is a resident of this State and shall be served by registered or certified mail on each dissenting shareholder who is a nonresident. Service on nonresidents shall also be made by publication as provided by law. The jurisdiction of the court shall be plenary and exclusive. All shareholders who are parties to the proceeding shall be entitled to judgment against the corporation for the amount of the fair value of their shares. The court may, if it so elects, appoint one or more persons as appraisers to receive evidence and recommend a decision on the question of fair value. The appraisers shall have such power and authority as shall be specified in the order of their appointment or an amendment thereof. The judgment shall be payable only upon and concurrently with the surrender to the corporation of the certificate or certificates representing such shares. Upon payment of the judgment, the dissenting shareholder shall cease to have any interest in such shares.

The judgment shall include an allowance for interest at such rate as the court may find to be fair and equitable in all the circumstances, from the date on which the vote was taken on the proposed corporate action to the date of payment.

The costs and expenses of any such proceeding shall be determined by the court and shall be assessed against the corporation, but all or any part of such costs and expenses may be apportioned and assessed as the court may deem equitable against any or all of the dissenting shareholders who are parties to the proceeding to whom the corporation shall have made an offer to pay for the shares if the court shall find that the action of such shareholders in failing to accept such offer was arbitrary or vexatious or not in good faith.  Such expenses shall include reasonable compensation for and reasonable expenses of the appraisers, but shall exclude the fees and expenses of counsel for and experts employed by any party; but if the fair value of the shares as determined materially exceeds the amount which the corporation offered to pay therefor, or if no offer was made, the court in its discretion may award to any shareholder who is a party to the proceeding such sum as the court may determine to be reasonable compensation to any expert or experts employed by the shareholder in the proceeding.

Within twenty days after demanding payment for his shares, each shareholder demanding payment shall submit the certificate or certificates representing his shares to the corporation for notation thereon that such demand has been made.  His failure to do so shall, at the option of the corporation, terminate his rights under this section unless a court of competent jurisdiction, for good and sufficient cause shown, shall otherwise direct. If shares represented by a certificate on which notation has been so made shall be transferred, each new certificate issued therefor shall bear similar notation, together with the name of the original dissenting holder of such shares, and a transferee of such shares shall acquire by such transfer no rights in the corporation other than those which the original dissenting shareholder had after making demand for payment of the fair value thereof.

Shares acquired by a corporation pursuant to payment of the agreed value therefor or to payment of the judgment entered therefor, as in this section provided, may be held and disposed of by such corporation as in the case of other treasury shares, except that, in the case of a merger or consolidation, they may be held and disposed of as the plan of merger or consolidation may otherwise provide.

### § 82.  Voluntary Dissolution by Incorporators

A corporation which has not commenced business and which has not issued any shares, may be voluntarily dissolved by its incorporators at any time in the following manner:

(a) Articles of dissolution shall be executed in duplicate by a majority of the incorporators, and verified by them, and shall set forth:

(1) The name of the corporation.

(2) The date of issuance of its certificate of incorporation.

(3) That none of its shares has been issued.

(4) That the corporation has not commenced business.

(5) That the amount, if any, actually paid in on subscriptions for its shares, less any part thereof disbursed for necessary expenses, has been returned to those entitled thereto.

(6) That no debts of the corporation remain unpaid.

(7) That a majority of the incorporators elect that the corporation be dissolved.

(b) Duplicate originals of the articles of dissolution shall be delivered to the Secretary of State. If the Secretary of State finds that the articles of dissolution conform to law, he shall, when all fees and franchise taxes have been paid as in this Act prescribed:

(1) Endorse on each of such duplicate originals the word "Filed," and the month, day and year of the filing thereof.

(2) File one of such duplicate originals in his office.

(3) Issue a certificate of dissolution to which he shall affix the other duplicate original.

The certificate of dissolution, together with the duplicate original of the articles of dissolution affixed thereto by the Secretary of State, shall be returned to the incorporators or their representative. Upon the issuance of such certificate of dissolution by the Secretary of State, the existence of the corporation shall cease.

### § 83. Voluntary Dissolution by Consent of Shareholders

A corporation may be voluntarily dissolved by the written consent of all of its shareholders.

Upon the execution of such written consent, a statement of intent to dissolve shall be executed in duplicate by the corporation by its president or a vice president and by its secretary or an assistant secretary, and verified by one of the officers signing such statement, which statement shall set forth:

(a) The name of the corporation.

(b) The names and respective addresses of its officers.

(c) The names and respective addresses of its directors.

(d) A copy of the written consent signed by all shareholders of the corporation.

(e) A statement that such written consent has been signed by all shareholders of the corporation or signed in their names by their attorneys thereunto duly authorized.

## § 84. Voluntary Dissolution by Act of Corporation

A corporation may be dissolved by the act of the corporation, when authorized in the following manner:

(a) The board of directors shall adopt a resolution recommending that the corporation be dissolved, and directing that the question of such dissolution be submitted to a vote at a meeting of shareholders, which may be either an annual or a special meeting.

(b) Written notice shall be given to each shareholder of record entitled to vote at such meeting within the time and in the manner provided in this Act for the giving of notice of meetings of shareholders, and, whether the meeting be an annual or special meeting, shall state that the purpose, or one of the purposes, of such meeting is to consider the advisability of dissolving the corporation.

(c) At such meeting a vote of shareholders entitled to vote thereat shall be taken on a resolution to dissolve the corporation. Such resolution shall be adopted upon receiving the affirmative vote of the holders of a majority of the shares of the corporation entitled to vote thereon, unless any class of shares is entitled to vote thereon as a class, in which event the resolution shall be adopted upon receiving the affirmative vote of the holders of a majority of the shares of each class of shares entitled to vote thereon as a class and of the total shares entitled to vote thereon.

(d) Upon the adoption of such resolution, a statement of intent to dissolve shall be executed in duplicate by the corporation by its president or a vice president and by its secretary or an assistant secretary, and verified by one of the officers signing such statement, which statement shall set forth:

(1) The name of the corporation.

(2) The names and respective addresses of its officers.

(3) The names and respective addresses of its directors.

(4) A copy of the resolution adopted by the shareholders authorizing the dissolution of the corporation.

(5) The number of shares outstanding, and, if the shares of any class are entitled to vote as a class, the designation and number of outstanding shares of each such class.

(6) The number of shares voted for and against the resolution, respectively, and, if the shares of any class are entitled to vote as a class, the number of shares of each such class voted for and against the resolution, respectively.

### § 85. Filing of Statement of Intent to Dissolve

Duplicate originals of the statement of intent to dissolve, whether by consent of shareholders or by act of the corporation, shall be delivered to the Secretary of State. If the Secretary of State finds that such statement conforms to law, he shall, when all fees and franchise taxes have been paid as in this Act prescribed:

(a) Endorse on each of such duplicate originals the word "Filed," and the month, day and year of the filing thereof.

(b) File one of such duplicate originals in his office.

(c) Return the other duplicate original to the corporation or its representative.

### § 86. Effect of Statement of Intent to Dissolve

Upon the filing by the Secretary of State of a statement of intent to dissolve, whether by consent of shareholders or by act of the corporation, the corporation shall cease to carry on its business, except insofar as may be necessary for the winding up thereof, but its corporate existence shall continue until a certificate of dissolution has been issued by the Secretary of State or until a decree dissolving the corporation has been entered by a court of competent jurisdiction as in this Act provided.

### § 87. Procedure after Filing of Statement of Intent to Dissolve

After the filing by the Secretary of State of a statement of intent to dissolve:

(a) The corporation shall immediately cause notice thereof to be mailed to each known creditor of the corporation.

(b) The corporation shall proceed to collect its assets, convey and dispose of such of its properties as are not to be distributed in kind to its shareholders, pay, satisfy and discharge its liabilities and obligations and do all other acts required to liquidate its business and affairs, and, after paying or adequately providing for the payment of all its obligations, distribute the remainder of its assets, either in cash or in kind, among its shareholders according to their respective rights and interests.

(c) The corporation, at any time during the liquidation of its business and affairs, may make application to a court of competent jurisdiction within the state and judicial subdivision in which the registered office or principal place of business of the corporation is situated, to have the liquidation continued under the supervision of the court as provided in this Act.

### § 88. Revocation of Voluntary Dissolution Proceedings by Consent of Shareholders

By the written consent of all of its shareholders, a corporation may, at any time prior to the issuance of a certificate of dissolution by the Secretary of State, revoke voluntary dissolution proceedings theretofore taken, in the following manner:

Upon the execution of such written consent, a statement of revocation of voluntary dissolution proceedings shall be executed in duplicate by the corporation by its president or a vice president and by its secretary or an assistant secretary, and verified by one of the officers signing such statement, which statement shall set forth:

(a) The name of the corporation.

(b) The names and respective addresses of its officers.

(c) The names and respective addresses of its directors.

(d) A copy of the written consent signed by all shareholders of the corporation revoking such voluntary dissolution proceedings.

(e) That such written consent has been signed by all shareholders of the corporation or signed in their names by their attorneys thereunto duly authorized.

### § 89. Revocation of Voluntary Dissolution Proceedings by Act of Corporation

By the act of the corporation, a corporation may, at any time prior to the issuance of a certificate of dissolution by the Secretary of State, revoke voluntary dissolution proceedings theretofore taken, in the following manner:

(a) The board of directors shall adopt a resolution recommending that the voluntary dissolution proceedings be revoked, and directing that the question of such revocation be submitted to a vote at a special meeting of shareholders.

(b) Written notice, stating that the purpose or one of the purposes of such meeting is to consider the advisability of revoking the voluntary dissolution proceedings, shall be given to each shareholder of record entitled to vote at such meeting within the time and in the manner provided in this Act for the giving of notice of special meetings of shareholders.

(c) At such meeting a vote of the shareholders entitled to vote thereat shall be taken on a resolution to revoke the voluntary dissolution proceedings, which shall require for its adoption the affirmative vote of the holders of a majority of the shares entitled to vote thereon.

(d) Upon the adoption of such resolution, a statement of revocation of voluntary dissolution proceedings shall be executed in duplicate by the corporation by its president or a vice president and by its secretary or an assistant secretary, and verified by one of the officers signing such statement, which statement shall set forth:

(1) The name of the corporation.

(2) The names and respective addresses of its officers.

(3) The names and respective addresses of its directors.

(4) A copy of the resolution adopted by the shareholders revoking the voluntary dissolution proceedings.

(5) The number of shares outstanding.

(6) The number of shares voted for and against the resolution, respectively.

### § 90. Filing of Statement of Revocation of Voluntary Dissolution Proceedings

Duplicate originals of the statement of revocation of voluntary dissolution proceedings, whether by consent of shareholders or by act of the corporation, shall be delivered to the Secretary of State. If the Secretary of State finds that such statement conforms to law, he shall, when all fees and franchise taxes have been paid as in this Act prescribed:

(a) Endorse on each of such duplicate originals the word "Filed," and the month, day and year of the filing thereof.

(b) File one of such duplicate originals in his office.

(c) Return the other duplicate original to the corporation or its representative.

### § 91. Effect of Statement of Revocation of Voluntary Dissolution Proceedings

Upon the filing by the Secretary of State of a statement of revocation of voluntary dissolution proceedings, whether by consent of shareholders or by act of the corporation, the revocation of the voluntary dissolution proceedings shall become effective and the corporation may again carry on its business.

### § 92. Articles of Dissolution

If voluntary dissolution proceedings have not been revoked, then when all debts, liabilities and obligations of the corporation have been paid and discharged, or adequate provision has been made therefor, and all of the remaining property and assets of the corporation have been distributed to its shareholders, articles of dissolution shall be executed in duplicate by the corporation by its president or a vice president and by its secretary or an assistant secretary, and verified by one of the officers signing such statement, which statement shall set forth:

(a) The name of the corporation.

(b) That the Secretary of State has theretofore filed a statement of intent to dissolve the corporation, and the date on which such statement was filed.

(c) That all debts, obligations and liabilities of the corporation have been paid and discharged or that adequate provision has been made therefor.

(d) That all the remaining property and assets of the corporation have been distributed among its shareholders in accordance with their respective rights and interests.

(e) That there are no suits pending against the corporation in any court, or that adequate provision has been made for the satisfaction of any judgment, order or decree which may be entered against it in any pending suit.

### § 93. Filing of Articles of Dissolution

Duplicate originals of such articles of dissolution shall be delivered to the Secretary of State. If the Secretary of State finds that such articles of dissolution conform to law, he shall, when all fees and franchise taxes have been paid as in this Act prescribed:

(a) Endorse on each of such duplicate originals the word "Filed," and the month, day and year of the filing thereof.

(b) File one of such duplicate originals in his office.

(c) Issue a certificate of dissolution to which he shall affix the other duplicate original.

The certificate of dissolution, together with the duplicate original of the articles of dissolution affixed thereto by the Secretary of State, shall be returned to the representative of the dissolved corporation. Upon the issuance of such certificate of dissolution the existence of the corporation shall cease, except for the purpose of suits, other proceedings and appropriate corporate action by shareholders, directors and officers as provided in this Act.

### § 94. Involuntary Dissolution

A corporation may be dissolved involuntarily by a decree of the ................ court in an action filed by the Attorney General when it is established that:

(a) The corporation has failed to file its annual report within the time required by this Act, or has failed to pay its franchise tax on or before the first day of August of the year in which such franchise tax becomes due and payable; or

(b) The corporation procured its articles of incorporation through fraud; or

(c) The corporation has continued to exceed or abuse the authority conferred upon it by law; or

(d) The corporation has failed for thirty days to appoint and maintain a registered agent in this State; or

(e) The corporation has failed for thirty days after change of its registered office or registered agent to file in the office of the Secretary of State a statement of such change.

### § 95. Notification to Attorney General

The Secretary of State, on or before the last day of December of each year, shall certify to the Attorney General the names of all corporations which have failed to file their annual reports or to pay franchise taxes in accordance with the provisions of this Act, together with the facts pertinent thereto. He shall also certify, from time to time, the names of all corporations which have given other cause for dissolution as provided in this Act, together with the facts pertinent thereto. Whenever the Secretary of State shall certify the name of a corporation to the Attorney General as having given any cause for dissolution, the Secretary of State shall concurrently mail to the corporation at its registered office a notice that such certification has been made. Upon the receipt of such certification, the Attorney General shall file an action in the name of the State against such corporation for its dissolution. Every such certificate from the Secretary of State to the Attorney General pertaining to the failure of a corporation to file an annual report or pay a franchise tax shall be taken and received in all courts as prima facie evidence of the facts therein stated. If, before action is filed, the corporation shall file its annual report or pay its franchise tax, together with all penalties thereon, or shall appoint or maintain a registered agent as provided in this Act, or shall file with the Secretary of State the required statement of change of registered office or registered agent, such fact shall be forthwith certified by the Secretary of State to the Attorney General and he shall not file an action against such corporation for such cause. If, after action is filed, the corporation shall file its annual report or pay its franchise tax, together with all penalties thereon, or shall appoint or maintain a registered agent as provided in this Act, or shall file with the Secretary of State the required statement of change of registered office or registered agent, and shall pay the costs of such action, the action for such cause shall abate.

## § 96.  Venue and Process

Every action for the involuntary dissolution of a corporation shall be commenced by the Attorney General either in the ........ court of the county in which the registered office of the corporation is situated, or in the .............. court of ........... county.  Summons shall issue and be served as in other civil actions.  If process is returned not found, the Attorney General shall cause publication to be made as in other civil cases in some newspaper published in the county where the registered office of the corporation is situated, containing a notice of the pendency of such action, the title of the court, the title of the action, and the date on or after which default may be entered.  The Attorney General may include in one notice the names of any number of corporations against which actions are then pending in the same court.  The Attorney General shall cause a copy of such notice to be mailed to the corporation at its registered office within ten days after the first publication thereof.  The certificate of the Attorney General of the mailing of such notice shall be prima facie evidence thereof.  Such notice shall be published at least once each week for two successive weeks, and the first publication thereof may begin at any time after the summons has been returned.  Unless a corporation shall have been served with summons, no default shall be taken against it earlier than thirty days after the first publication of such notice.

## § 97.  Jurisdiction of Court to Liquidate Assets and Business of Corporation

The ........ courts shall have full power to liquidate the assets and business of a corporation:

(a)  In an action by a shareholder when it is established:

(1)  That the directors are deadlocked in the management of the corporate affairs and the shareholders are unable to break the deadlock, and that irreparable injury to the corporation is being suffered or is threatened by reason thereof;  or

(2)  That the acts of the directors or those in control of the corporation are illegal, oppressive or fraudulent;  or

(3)  That the shareholders are deadlocked in voting power, and have failed, for a period which includes at least two consecutive annual meeting dates, to elect successors to directors whose terms have expired or would have expired upon the election of their successors;  or

(4)  That the corporate assets are being misapplied or wasted.

(b)  In an action by a creditor:

462

(1) When the claim of the creditor has been reduced to judgment and an execution thereon returned unsatisfied and it is established that the corporation is insolvent; or

(2) When the corporation has admitted in writing that the claim of the creditor is due and owing and it is established that the corporation is insolvent.

(c) Upon application by a corporation which has filed a statement of intent to dissolve, as provided in this Act, to have its liquidation continued under the supervision of the court.

(d) When an action has been filed by the Attorney General to dissolve a corporation and it is established that liquidation of its business and affairs should precede the entry of a decree of dissolution.

Proceedings under clause (a), (b) or (c) of this section shall be brought in the county in which the registered office or the principal office of the corporation is situated.

It shall not be necessary to make shareholders parties to any such action or proceeding unless relief is sought against them personally.

## § 98.    Procedure in Liquidation of Corporation by Court

In proceedings to liquidate the assets and business of a corporation the court shall have power to issue injunctions, to appoint a receiver or receivers pendente lite, with such powers and duties as the court, from time to time, may direct, and to take such other proceedings as may be requisite to preserve the corporate assets wherever situated, and carry on the business of the corporation until a full hearing can be had.

After a hearing had upon such notice as the court may direct to be given to all parties to the proceedings and to any other parties in interest designated by the court, the court may appoint a liquidating receiver or receivers with authority to collect the assets of the corporation, including all amounts owing to the corporation by subscribers on account of any unpaid portion of the consideration for the issuance of shares. Such liquidating receiver or receivers shall have authority, subject to the order of the court, to sell, convey and dispose of all or any part of the assets of the corporation wherever situated, either at public or private sale. The assets of the corporation or the proceeds resulting from a sale, conveyance or other disposition thereof shall be applied to the expenses of such liquidation and to the payment of the liabilities and obligations of the corporation, and any remaining assets or proceeds shall be distributed among its shareholders according to their respective rights and interests. The order appointing such liquidating receiver or receivers shall state their powers and duties. Such powers and duties may be increased or diminished at any time during the proceedings.

The court shall have power to allow from time to time as expenses of the liquidation compensation to the receiver or receivers and to attorneys in the proceeding, and to direct the payment thereof out of the assets of the corporation or the proceeds of any sale or disposition of such assets.

A receiver of a corporation appointed under the provisions of this section shall have authority to sue and defend in all courts in his own name as receiver of such corporation. The court appointing such receiver shall have exclusive jurisdiction of the corporation and its property, wherever situated.

### § 99. Qualifications of Receivers

A receiver shall in all cases be a natural person or a corporation authorized to act as receiver, which corporation may be a domestic corporation or a foreign corporation authorized to transact business in this State, and shall in all cases give such bond as the court may direct with such sureties as the court may require.

### § 100. Filing of Claims in Liquidation Proceedings

In proceedings to liquidate the assets and business of a corporation the court may require all creditors of the corporation to file with the clerk of the court or with the receiver, in such form as the court may prescribe, proofs under oath of their respective claims. If the court requires the filing of claims it shall fix a date, which shall be not less than four months from the date of the order, as the last day for the filing of claims, and shall prescribe the notice that shall be given to creditors and claimants of the date so fixed. Prior to the date so fixed, the court may extend the time for the filing of claims. Creditors and claimants failing to file proofs of claim on or before the date so fixed may be barred, by order of court, from participating in the distribution of the assets of the corporation.

### § 101. Discontinuance of Liquidation Proceedings

The liquidation of the assets and business of a corporation may be discontinued at any time during the liquidation proceedings when it is established that cause for liquidation no longer exists. In such event the court shall dismiss the proceedings and direct the receiver to redeliver to the corporation all its remaining property and assets.

## § 102. Decree of Involuntary Dissolution

In proceedings to liquidate the assets and business of a corporation, when the costs and expenses of such proceedings and all debts, obligations and liabilities of the corporation shall have been paid and discharged and all of its remaining property and assets distributed to its shareholders, or in case its property and assets are not sufficient to satisfy and discharge such costs, expenses, debts and obligations, all the property and assets have been applied so far as they will go to their payment, the court shall enter a decree dissolving the corporation, whereupon the existence of the corporation shall cease.

## § 103. Filing of Decree of Dissolution

In case the court shall enter a decree dissolving a corporation, it shall be the duty of the clerk of such court to cause a certified copy of the decree to be filed with the Secretary of State. No fee shall be charged by the Secretary of State for the filing thereof.

## § 104. Deposit with State Treasurer of Amount Due Certain Shareholders

Upon the voluntary or involuntary dissolution of a corporation, the portion of the assets distributable to a creditor or shareholder who is unknown or cannot be found, or who is under disability and there is no person legally competent to receive such distributive portion, shall be reduced to cash and deposited with the State Treasurer and shall be paid over to such creditor or shareholder or to his legal representative upon proof satisfactory to the State Treasurer of his right thereto.

## § 105. Survival of Remedy after Dissolution

The dissolution of a corporation either (1) by the issuance of a certificate of dissolution by the Secretary of State, or (2) by a decree of court when the court has not liquidated the assets and business of the corporation as provided in this Act, or (3) by expiration of its period of duration, shall not take away or impair any remedy available to or against such corporation, its directors, officers, or shareholders, for any right or claim existing, or any liability incurred, prior to such dissolution if action or other proceeding thereon is commenced within two years after the date of such dissolution. Any such action or proceeding by or against the corporation may be prosecuted or defended by the corporation in its corporate name. The shareholders, directors and officers shall have power to take such corporate or other action as shall be appropriate to protect such remedy, right or claim. If such corporation was dissolved by the expiration of its period of duration, such corporation may amend its articles of incorporation at any time during such period of two years so as to extend its period of duration.

## § 106.  Admission of Foreign Corporation

No foreign corporation shall have the right to transact business in this State until it shall have procured a certificate of authority so to do from the Secretary of State.  No foreign corporation shall be entitled to procure a certificate of authority under this Act to transact in this State any business which a corporation organized under this Act is not permitted to transact. A foreign corporation shall not be denied a certificate of authority by reason of the fact that the laws of the state or country under which such corporation is organized governing its organization and internal affairs differ from the laws of this State, and nothing in this Act contained shall be construed to authorize this State to regulate the organization or the internal affairs of such corporation.

Without excluding other activities which may not constitute transacting business in this State, a foreign corporation shall not be considered to be transacting business in this State, for the purposes of this Act, by reason of carrying on in this State any one or more of the following activities:

(a) Maintaining or defending any action or suit or any administrative or arbitration proceeding, or effecting the settlement thereof or the settlement of claims or disputes.

(b) Holding meetings of its directors or shareholders or carrying on other activities concerning its internal affairs.

(c) Maintaining bank accounts.

(d) Maintaining offices or agencies for the transfer, exchange and registration of its securities, or appointing and maintaining trustees or depositaries with relation to its securities.

(e) Effecting sales through independent contractors.

(f) Soliciting or procuring orders, whether by mail or through employees or agents or otherwise, where such orders require acceptance without this State before becoming binding contracts.

(g) Creating evidences of debt, mortgages or liens on real or personal property.

(h) Securing or collecting debts or enforcing any rights in property securing the same.

(i) Transacting any business in interstate commerce.

(j) Conducting an isolated transaction completed within a period of thirty days and not in the course of a number of repeated transactions of like nature.

### § 107. Powers of Foreign Corporation

A foreign corporation which shall have received a certificate of authority under this Act shall, until a certificate of revocation or of withdrawal shall have been issued as provided in this Act, enjoy the same, but no greater, rights and privileges as a domestic corporation organized for the purposes set forth in the application pursuant to which such certificate of authority is issued; and, except as in this Act otherwise provided, shall be subject to the same duties, restrictions, penalties and liabilities now or hereafter imposed upon a domestic corporation of like character.

### § 108. Corporate Name of Foreign Corporation

No certificate of authority shall be issued to a foreign corporation unless the corporate name of such corporation:

(a) Shall contain the word "corporation," "company," "incorporated," or "limited," or shall contain an abbreviation of one of such words, or such corporation shall, for use in this State, add at the end of its name one of such words or an abbreviation thereof.

(b) Shall not contain any word or phrase which indicates or implies that it is organized for any purpose other than one or more of the purposes contained in its articles of incorporation or that it is authorized or empowered to conduct the business of banking or insurance.

(c) Shall not be the same as, or deceptively similar to, the name of any domestic corporation existing under the laws of this State or any foreign corporation authorized to transact business in this State, or a name the exclusive right to which is, at the time, reserved in the manner provided in this Act, or the name of a corporation which has in effect a registration of its name as provided in this Act, except that this provision shall not apply if the foreign corporation applying for a certificate of authority files with the Secretary of State any one of the following:

(1) a resolution of its board of directors adopting a fictitious name for use in transacting business in this State which fictitious name is not deceptively similar to the name of any domestic corporation or of any foreign corporation authorized to transact business in this State or to any name reserved or registered as provided in this Act, or

(2) the written consent of such other corporation or holder of a reserved or registered name to use the same or deceptively similar name and one or more words are added to make such name distinguishable from such other name, or

(3) a certified copy of a final decree of a court of competent jurisdiction establishing the prior right of such foreign corporation to the use of such name in this State.

467

## § 109. Change of Name by Foreign Corporation

Whenever a foreign corporation which is authorized to transact business in this State shall change its name to one under which a certificate of authority would not be granted to it on application therefor, the certificate of authority of such corporation shall be suspended and it shall not thereafter transact any business in this State until it has changed its name to a name which is available to it under the laws of this State or has otherwise complied with the provisions of this Act.

## § 110. Application for Certificate of Authority

A foreign corporation, in order to procure a certificate of authority to transact business in this State, shall make application therefor to the Secretary of State, which application shall set forth:

(a) The name of the corporation and the state or country under the laws of which it is incorporated.

(b) If the name of the corporation does not contain the word "corporation," "company," "incorporated," or "limited," or does not contain an abbreviation of one of such words, then the name of the corporation with the word or abbreviation which it elects to add thereto for use in this State.

(c) The date of incorporation and the period of duration of the corporation.

(d) The address of the principal office of the corporation in the state or country under the laws of which it is incorporated.

(e) The address of the proposed registered office of the corporation in this State, and the name of its proposed registered agent in this State at such address.

(f) The purpose or purposes of the corporation which it proposes to pursue in the transaction of business in this State.

(g) The names and respective addresses of the directors and officers of the corporation.

(h) A statement of the aggregate number of shares which the corporation has authority to issue, itemized by classes, par value of shares, shares without par value, and series, if any, within a class.

(i) A statement of the aggregate number of issued shares itemized by classes, par value of shares, shares without par value, and series, if any, within a class.

(j) A statement, expressed in dollars, of the amount of stated capital of the corporation, as defined in this Act.

(k) An estimate, expressed in dollars, of the value of all property to be owned by the corporation for the following year, wherever located, and an estimate of the value of the property of the corporation to be located within this State during such year, and an estimate, expressed in dollars, of the gross amount of business which will be transacted by the corporation during such year, and an estimate of the gross amount thereof which will be transacted by the corporation at or from places of business in this State during such year.

(1) Such additional information as may be necessary or appropriate in order to enable the Secretary of State to determine whether such corporation is entitled to a certificate of authority to transact business in this State and to determine and assess the fees and franchise taxes payable as in this Act prescribed.

Such application shall be made on forms prescribed and furnished by the Secretary of State and shall be executed in duplicate by the corporation by its president or a vice president and by its secretary or an assistant secretary, and verified by one of the officers signing such application.

### § 111.   Filing of Application for Certificate of Authority

Duplicate originals of the application of the corporation for a certificate of authority shall be delivered to the Secretary of State, together with a copy of its articles of incorporation and all amendments thereto, duly authenticated by the proper officer of the state or country under the laws of which it is incorporated.

If the Secretary of State finds that such application conforms to law, he shall, when all fees and franchise taxes have been paid as in this Act prescribed:

(a) Endorse on each of such documents the word "Filed," and the month, day and year of the filing thereof.

(b) File in his office one of such duplicate originals of the application and the copy of the articles of incorporation and amendments thereto.

(c) Issue a certificate of authority to transact business in this State to which he shall affix the other duplicate original application.

The certificate of authority, together with the duplicate original of the application affixed thereto by the Secretary of State, shall be returned to the corporation or its representative.

### § 112.   Effect of Certificate of Authority

Upon the issuance of a certificate of authority by the Secretary of State, the corporation shall be authorized to transact business in this State for those purposes set forth in its application, subject, however, to the right of this State to suspend or to revoke such authority as provided in this Act.

### § 113. Registered Office and Registered Agent of Foreign Corporation

Each foreign corporation authorized to transact business in this State shall have and continuously maintain in this State:

(a) A registered office which may be, but need not be, the same as its place of business in this State.

(b) A registered agent, which agent may be either an individual resident in this State whose business office is identical with such registered office, or a domestic corporation, or a foreign corporation authorized to transact business in this State, having a business office identical with such registered office.

### § 114. Change of Registered Office or Registered Agent of Foreign Corporation

A foreign corporation authorized to transact business in this State may change its registered office or change its registered agent, or both, upon filing in the office of the Secretary of State a statement setting forth:

(a) The name of the corporation.

(b) The address of its then registered office.

(c) If the address of its registered office be changed, the address to which the registered office is to be changed.

(d) The name of its then registered agent.

(e) If its registered agent be changed, the name of its successor registered agent.

(f) That the address of its registered office and the address of the business office of its registered agent, as changed, will be identical.

(g) That such change was authorized by resolution duly adopted by its board of directors.

Such statement shall be executed by the corporation by its president or a vice president, and verified by him, and delivered to the Secretary of State. If the Secretary of State finds that such statement conforms to the provisions of this Act, he shall file such statement in his office, and upon such filing the change of address of the registered office, or the appointment of a new registered agent, or both, as the case may be, shall become effective.

Any registered agent of a foreign corporation may resign as such agent upon filing a written notice thereof, executed in duplicate, with the Secretary of State, who shall forthwith mail a copy thereof to the corporation at its principal office in the state or country under the laws of which it is incorporated. The appointment of such agent shall terminate upon the expiration of thirty days after receipt of such notice by the Secretary of State.

If a registered agent changes his or its business address to another place within the same .........................*, he or it may change such address and the address of the registered office of any corporation of which he or it is registered agent by filing a statement as required above except that it need be signed only by the registered agent and need not be responsive to (e) or (g) and must recite that a copy of the statement has been mailed to the corporation.

## § 115. Service of Process on Foreign Corporation

The registered agent so appointed by a foreign corporation authorized to transact business in this State shall be an agent of such corporation upon whom any process, notice or demand required or permitted by law to be served upon the corporation may be served.

Whenever a foreign corporation authorized to transact business in this State shall fail to appoint or maintain a registered agent in this State, or whenever any such registered agent cannot with reasonable diligence be found at the registered office, or whenever the certificate of authority of a foreign corporation shall be suspended or revoked, then the Secretary of State shall be an agent of such corporation upon whom any such process, notice, or demand may be served. Service on the Secretary of State of any such process, notice or demand shall be made by delivering to and leaving with him, or with any clerk having charge of the corporation department of his office, duplicate copies of such process, notice or demand. In the event any such process, notice or demand is served on the Secretary of State, he shall immediately cause one of such copies thereof to be forwarded by registered mail, addressed to the corporation at its principal office in the state or country under the laws of which it is incorporated. Any service so had on the Secretary of State shall be returnable in not less than thirty days.

The Secretary of State shall keep a record of all processes, notices and demands served upon him under this section, and shall record therein the time of such service and his action with reference thereto.

* Supply designation of jurisdiction, such as county, etc., in accordance with local practice.

Nothing herein contained shall limit or affect the right to serve any process, notice or demand, required or permitted by law to be served upon a foreign corporation in any other manner now or hereafter permitted by law.

## § 116. Amendment to Articles of Incorporation of Foreign Corporation

Whenever the articles of incorporation of a foreign corporation authorized to transact business in this State are amended, such foreign corporation shall, within thirty days after such amendment becomes effective, file in the office of the Secretary of State a copy of such amendment duly authenticated by the proper officer of the state or country under the laws of which it is incorporated; but the filing thereof shall not of itself enlarge or alter the purpose or purposes which such corporation is authorized to pursue in the transaction of business in this State, nor authorize such corporation to transact business in this State under any other name than the name set forth in its certificate of authority.

## § 117. Merger of Foreign Corporation Authorized to Transact Business in This State

Whenever a foreign corporation authorized to transact business in this State shall be a party to a statutory merger permitted by the laws of the state or country under the laws of which it is incorporated, and such corporation shall be the surviving corporation, it shall, within thirty days after such merger becomes effective, file with the Secretary of State a copy of the articles of merger duly authenticated by the proper officer of the state or country under the laws of which such statutory merger was effected; and it shall not be necessary for such corporation to procure either a new or amended certificate of authority to transact business in this State unless the name of such corporation be changed thereby or unless the corporation desires to pursue in this State other or additional purposes than those which it is then authorized to transact in this State.

## § 118. Amended Certificate of Authority

A foreign corporation authorized to transact business in this State shall procure an amended certificate of authority in the event it changes its corporate name, or desires to pursue in this State other or additional purposes than those set forth in its prior application for a certificate of authority, by making application therefor to the Secretary of State.

The requirements in respect to the form and contents of such application, the manner of its execution, the filing of duplicate originals thereof with the Secretary of State, the issuance of an amended certificate of authority and the effect thereof, shall be the same as in the case of an original application for a certificate of authority.

### § 119. Withdrawal of Foreign Corporation

A foreign corporation authorized to transact business in this State may withdraw from this State upon procuring from the Secretary of State a certificate of withdrawal. In order to procure such certificate of withdrawal, such foreign corporation shall deliver to the Secretary of State an application for withdrawal, which shall set forth:

(a) The name of the corporation and the state or country under the laws of which it is incorporated.

(b) That the corporation is not transacting business in this State.

(c) That the corporation surrenders its authority to transact business in this State.

(d) That the corporation revokes the authority of its registered agent in this State to accept service of process and consents that service of process in any action, suit or proceeding based upon any cause of action arising in this State during the time the corporation was authorized to transact business in this State may thereafter be made on such corporation by service thereof on the Secretary of State.

(e) A post-office address to which the Secretary of State may mail a copy of any process against the corporation that may be served on him.

(f) A statement of the aggregate number of shares which the corporation has authority to issue, itemized by classes, par value of shares, shares without par value, and series, if any, within a class, as of the date of such application.

(g) A statement of the aggregate number of issued shares, itemized by classes, par value of shares, shares without par value, and series, if any, within a class, as of the date of such application.

(h) A statement, expressed in dollars, of the amount of stated capital of the corporation, as of the date of such application.

(i) Such additional information as may be necessary or appropriate in order to enable the Secretary of State to determine and assess any unpaid fees or franchise taxes payable by such foreign corporation as in this Act prescribed.

The application for withdrawal shall be made on forms prescribed and furnished by the Secretary of State and shall be executed by the corporation by its president or a vice president and by its secretary or an assistant secretary, and verified by one of the officers signing the application, or, if the corporation is in the hands of a receiver or trustee, shall be executed on behalf of the corporation by such receiver or trustee and verified by him.

## § 120. Filing of Application for Withdrawal

Duplicate originals of such application for withdrawal shall be delivered to the Secretary of State. If the Secretary of State finds that such application conforms to the provisions of this Act, he shall, when all fees and franchise taxes have been paid as in this Act prescribed:

(a) Endorse on each of such duplicate originals the word "Filed," and the month, day and year of the filing thereof.

(b) File one of such duplicate originals in his office.

(c) Issue a certificate of withdrawal to which he shall affix the other duplicate original.

The certificate of withdrawal, together with the duplicate original of the application for withdrawal affixed thereto by the Secretary of State, shall be returned to the corporation or its representative. Upon the issuance of such certificate of withdrawal, the authority of the corporation to transact business in this State shall cease.

## § 121. Revocation of Certificate of Authority

The certificate of authority of a foreign corporation to transact business in this State may be revoked by the Secretary of State upon the conditions prescribed in this section when:

(a) The corporation has failed to file its annual report within the time required by this Act, or has failed to pay any fees, franchise taxes or penalties prescribed by this Act when they have become due and payable; or

(b) The corporation has failed to appoint and maintain a registered agent in this State as required by this Act; or

(c) The corporation has failed, after change of its registered office or registered agent, to file in the office of the Secretary of State a statement of such change as required by this Act; or

(d) The corporation has failed to file in the office of the Secretary of State any amendment to its articles of incorporation or any articles of merger within the time prescribed by this Act; or

(e) A misrepresentation has been made of any material matter in any application, report, affidavit, or other document submitted by such corporation pursuant to this Act.

No certificate of authority of a foreign corporation shall be revoked by the Secretary of State unless (1) he shall have given the corporation not less than sixty days' notice thereof by mail addressed to its registered office in this State, and (2) the corporation shall fail prior to revocation to file such annual report, or pay such fees, franchise taxes or penalties, or file the required statement of change of registered agent or registered office, or file such articles of amendment or articles of merger, or correct such misrepresentation.

### § 122.   Issuance of Certificate of Revocation

Upon revoking any such certificate of authority, the Secretary of State shall:

(a)  Issue a certificate of revocation in duplicate.

(b)  File one of such certificates in his office.

(c)  Mail to such corporation at its registered office in this State a notice of such revocation accompanied by one of such certificates.

Upon the issuance of such certificate of revocation, the authority of the corporation to transact business in this State shall cease.

### § 123.   Application to Corporations Heretofore Authorized to Transact Business in this State

Foreign corporations which are duly authorized to transact business in this State at the time this Act takes effect, for a purpose or purposes for which a corporation might secure such authority under this Act, shall, subject to the limitations set forth in their respective certificates of authority, be entitled to all the rights and privileges applicable to foreign corporations procuring certificates of authority to transact business in this State under this Act, and from the time this Act takes effect such corporations shall be subject to all the limitations, restrictions, liabilities, and duties prescribed herein for foreign corporations procuring certificates of authority to transact business in this State under this Act.

### § 124.   Transacting Business Without Certificate of Authority

No foreign corporation transacting business in this State without a certificate of authority shall be permitted to maintain any action, suit or proceeding in any court of this State, until such corporation shall have obtained a certificate of authority.  Nor shall any action, suit or proceeding be maintained in any court of this State by any successor or assignee of such corporation on any right, claim or demand arising out of the transaction of business by such corporation in this State, until a certificate of authority shall have been obtained by such corporation or by a corporation which has acquired all or substantially all of its assets.

The failure of a foreign corporation to obtain a certificate of authority to transact business in this State shall not impair the validity of any contract or act of such corporation, and shall not prevent such corporation from defending any action, suit or proceeding in any court of this State.

A foreign corporation which transacts business in this State without a certificate of authority shall be liable to this State, for the years or parts thereof during which it transacted business in this State without a certificate of authority, in an amount equal to all fees and franchise taxes which would have been imposed by this Act upon such corporation had it duly applied for and received a certificate of authority to transact business in this State as required by this Act and thereafter filed all reports required by this Act, plus all penalties imposed by this Act for failure to pay such fees and franchise taxes. The Attorney General shall bring proceedings to recover all amounts due this State under the provisions of this Section.

### § 125. Annual Report of Domestic and Foreign Corporations

Each domestic corporation, and each foreign corporation authorized to transact business in this State, shall file, within the time prescribed by this Act, an annual report setting forth:

(a) The name of the corporation and the state or country under the laws of which it is incorporated.

(b) The address of the registered office of the corporation in this State, and the name of its registered agent in this State at such address, and, in case of a foreign corporation, the address of its principal office in the state or country under the laws of which it is incorporated.

(c) A brief statement of the character of the business in which the corporation is actually engaged in this State.

(d) The names and respective addresses of the directors and officers of the corporation.

(e) A statement of the aggregate number of shares which the corporation has authority to issue, itemized by classes, par value of shares, shares without par value, and series, if any, within a class.

(f) A statement of the aggregate number of issued shares, itemized by classes, par value of shares, shares without par value, and series, if any, within a class.

(g) A statement, expressed in dollars, of the amount of stated capital of the corporation, as defined in this Act.

(h) A statement, expressed in dollars, of the value of all the property owned by the corporation, wherever located, and the value of the property of the corporation located within this State, and a statement, expressed in dollars, of the gross amount of business transacted by the corporation for the twelve months ended on the thirty-first day of December preceding the date herein provided for the filing of such report and the gross amount thereof transacted by the corporation at or from places of business in this State. If, on the thirty-first day of December preceding the time herein provided for the filing of such report, the corporation had not been in existence for a period of twelve months, or in the case of a foreign corporation had not been authorized to transact business in this State for a period of twelve months, the statement with respect to business transacted shall be furnished for the period between the date of incorporation or the date of its authorization to transact business in this State, as the case may be, and such thirty-first day of December. If all the property of the corporation is located in this State and all of its business is transacted at or from places of business in this State, or if the corporation elects to pay the annual franchise tax on the basis of its entire stated capital, then the information required by this subparagraph need not be set forth in such report.

(i) Such additional information as may be necessary or appropriate in order to enable the Secretary of State to determine and assess the proper amount of franchise taxes payable by such corporation.

Such annual report shall be made on forms prescribed and furnished by the Secretary of State, and the information therein contained shall be given as of the date of the execution of the report, except as to the information required by subparagraphs (g), (h) and (i) which shall be given as of the close of business on the thirty-first day of December next preceding the date herein provided for the filing of such report. It shall be executed by the corporation by its president, a vice president, secretary, an assistant secretary, or treasurer, and verified by the officer executing the report, or, if the corporation is in the hands of a receiver or trustee, it shall be executed on behalf of the corporation and verified by such receiver or trustee.

### § 126. Filing of Annual Report of Domestic and Foreign Corporations

Such annual report of a domestic or foreign corporation shall be delivered to the Secretary of State between the first day of

January and the first day of March of each year, except that the first annual report of a domestic or foreign corporation shall be filed between the first day of January and the first day of March of the year next succeeding the calendar year in which its certificate of incorporation or its certificate of authority, as the case may be, was issued by the Secretary of State. Proof to the satisfaction of the Secretary of State that prior to the first day of March such report was deposited in the United States mail in a sealed envelope, properly addressed, with postage prepaid, shall be deemed a compliance with this requirement. If the Secretary of State finds that such report conforms to the requirements of this Act, he shall file the same. If he finds that it does not so conform, he shall promptly return the same to the corporation for any necessary corrections, in which event the penalties hereinafter prescribed for failure to file such report within the time hereinabove provided shall not apply, if such report is corrected to conform to the requirements of this Act and returned to the Secretary of State within thirty days from the date on which it was mailed to the corporation by the Secretary of State.

### § 127. Fees, Franchise Taxes and Charges to be Collected by Secretary of State

The Secretary of State shall charge and collect in accordance with the provisions of this Act:

(a) Fees for filing documents and issuing certificates.

(b) Miscellaneous charges.

(c) License fees.

(d) Franchise taxes.

### § 128. Fees for Filing Documents and Issuing Certificates

The Secretary of State shall charge and collect for:

(a) Filing articles of incorporation and issuing a certificate of incorporation, ........ dollars.

(b) Filing articles of amendment and issuing a certificate of amendment, ........ dollars.

(c) Filing restated articles of incorporation, ........ dollars.

(d) Filing articles of merger or consolidation and issuing a certificate of merger or consolidation, ........ dollars.

(e) Filing an application to reserve a corporate name, ........ dollars.

(f) Filing a notice of transfer of a reserved corporate name, ........ dollars.

(g) Filing a statement of change of address of registered office or change of registered agent, or both, ........ dollars.

(h) Filing a statement of the establishment of a series of shares, ........ dollars.

(i) Filing a statement of cancellation of shares, ........ dollars.

(j) Filing a statement of reduction of stated capital, ........ dollars.

(k) Filing a statement of intent to dissolve, ........ dollars.

(*l*) Filing a statement of revocation of voluntary dissolution proceedings, ........ dollars.

(m) Filing articles of dissolution, ........ dollars.

(n) Filing an application of a foreign corporation for a certificate of authority to transact business in this State and issuing a certificate of authority, ........ dollars.

(*o*) Filing an application of a foreign corporation for an amended certificate of authority to transact business in this State and issuing an amended certificate of authority, ........ dollars.

(p) Filing a copy of an amendment to the articles of incorporation of a foreign corporation holding a certificate of authority to transact business in this State, ........ dollars.

(q) Filing a copy of articles of merger of a foreign corporation holding a certificate of authority to transact business in this State, ........ dollars.

(r) Filing an application for withdrawal of a foreign corporation and issuing a certificate of withdrawal, ........ dollars.

(s) Filing any other statement or report, except an annual report, of a domestic or foreign corporation, ........ dollars.

## § 129. Miscellaneous Charges

The Secretary of State shall charge and collect:

(a) For furnishing a certified copy of any document, instrument, or paper relating to a corporation, ........ cents per page and ........ dollars for the certificate and affixing the seal thereto.

(b) At the time of any service of process on him as resident agent of a corporation, ........ dollars, which amount may be recovered as taxable costs by the party to the suit or action causing such service to be made if such party prevails in the suit or action.

## § 130. License Fees Payable by Domestic Corporations

The Secretary of State shall charge and collect from each domestic corporation license fees, based upon the number of shares which it will have authority to issue or the increase in the number of shares which it will have authority to issue, at the time of:

(a) Filing articles of incorporation;

(b) Filing articles of amendment increasing the number of authorized shares; and

(c) Filing articles of merger or consolidation increasing the number of authorized shares which the surviving or new corporation, if a domestic corporation, will have the authority to issue above the aggregate number of shares which the constituent domestic corporations and constituent foreign corporations authorized to transact business in this State had authority to issue.

The license fees shall be at the rate of ........ cents per share up to and including the first 10,000 authorized shares, ........ cents per share for each authorized share in excess of 10,000 shares up to and including 100,000 shares, and ........ cents per share for each authorized share in excess of 100,000 shares, whether the shares are of par value or without par value.

The license fees payable on an increase in the number of authorized shares shall be imposed only on the increased number of shares, and the number of previously authorized shares shall be taken into account in determining the rate applicable to the increased number of authorized shares.

## § 131. License Fees Payable by Foreign Corporations

The Secretary of State shall charge and collect from each foreign corporation license fees, based upon the proportion represented in this State of the number of shares which it has authority to issue or the increase in the number of shares which it has authority to issue, at the time of:

(a) Filing an application for a certificate of authority to transact business in this State;

(b) Filing articles of amendment which increased the number of authorized shares; and

(c) Filing articles of merger or consolidation which increased the number of authorized shares which the surviving or new corporation, if a foreign corporation, has authority to issue above the aggregate number of shares which the constituent domestic corporations and constituent foreign corporations authorized to transact business in this State had authority to issue.

The license fees shall be at the rate of ....... cents per share up to and including the first 10,000 authorized shares represented in this State, ........ cents per share for each authorized share in excess of 10,000 shares up to and including 100,-000 shares represented in this State, and ........ cents per share for each authorized share in excess of 100,000 shares represented in this State, whether the shares are of par value or without par value.

The license fees payable on an increase in the number of authorized shares shall be imposed only on the increased number of such shares represented in this State, and the number of previously authorized shares represented in this State shall be taken into account in determining the rate applicable to the increased number of authorized shares.

The number of authorized shares represented in this State shall be that proportion of its total authorized shares which the sum of the value of its property located in this State and the gross amount of business transacted by it at or from places of business in this State bears to the sum of the value of all of its property, wherever located, and the gross amount of its business, wherever transacted. Such proportion shall be determined from information contained in the application for a certificate of authority to transact business in this State until the filing of an annual report and thereafter from information contained in the latest annual report filed by the corporation.

### § 132. Franchise Taxes Payable by Domestic Corporations

The Secretary of State shall charge and collect from each domestic corporation an initial franchise tax at the time of filing its articles of incorporation at the rate of one-twelfth of one-half of the license fee payable by such corporation under the provisions of this Act at the time of filing its articles of incorporation, for each calendar month, or fraction thereof, between the date of the issuance of the certificate of incorporation by the Secretary of State and the first day of July of the next succeeding calendar year.

The Secretary of State shall charge and collect from each domestic corporation an annual franchise tax, payable in advance for the period from July 1 in each year to July 1 in the succeeding year, beginning July 1 in the calendar year in which such corporation is required to file its first annual report under this Act, at the rate of ................ of ....... per cent of the amount represented in this State of the stated capital of the corporation, as disclosed by the latest report filed by the corporation with the Secretary of State.

The amount represented in this State of the stated capital of the corporation shall be that proportion of its stated capital which the sum of the value of its property located in this State and the gross amount of business transacted by it at or from places of business in this State bears to the sum of the value of all of its property, wherever located, and the gross amount of its business, wherever transacted, except as follows:

(a) If the corporation elects in its annual report in any year to pay its annual franchise tax on its entire stated capital, all franchise taxes accruing against the corporation after the filing of such annual report shall be assessed accordingly until the corporation elects otherwise in an annual report for a subsequent year.

(b) If the corporation fails to file its annual report in any year within the time prescribed by this Act, the proportion of its stated capital represented in this State shall be deemed to be its entire stated capital, unless its annual report is thereafter filed and its franchise tax thereafter adjusted by the Secretary of State in accordance with the provisions of this Act, in which case the proportion shall likewise be adjusted to the same proportion that would have prevailed if the corporation had filed its annual report within the time prescribed by this Act.

### § 133. Franchise Taxes Payable by Foreign Corporations

The Secretary of State shall charge and collect from each foreign corporation authorized to transact business in this State an initial franchise tax at the time of filing its application for a certificate of authority at the rate of one-twelfth of one-half of the license fee payable by such corporation under the provisions of this Act at the time of filing such application, for each month, or fraction thereof, between the date of the issuance of the certificate of authority by the Secretary of State and the first day of July of the next succeeding calendar year.

The Secretary of State shall charge and collect from each foreign corporation authorized to transact business in this State an annual franchise tax, payable in advance for the period from July 1 in each year to July 1 in the succeeding year, beginning July 1 in the calendar year in which such corporation is required to file its first annual report under this Act, at the rate of ............ per cent of the amount represented in this State of the stated capital of the corporation, as disclosed by the latest annual report filed by the corporation with the Secretary of State.

The amount represented in this State of the stated capital of the corporation shall be that proportion of its stated capital which the sum of the value of its property located in this State and the gross amount of business transacted by it at or from places of business in this State bears to the sum of the value of all of its property, wherever located, and the gross amount of its business, wherever transacted, except as follows:

(a) If the corporation elects in its annual report in any year to pay its annual franchise tax on its entire stated capital, all franchise taxes accruing against the corporation after the filing of such annual report shall be assessed accordingly until the corporation elects otherwise in an annual report for a subsequent year.

(b) If the corporation fails to file its annual report in any year within the time prescribed by this Act, the proportion of its stated capital represented in this State shall be deemed to be its entire stated capital, unless its annual report is thereafter filed and its franchise tax thereafter adjusted by the Secretary of State in accordance with the provisions of this Act, in which case the proportion shall likewise be adjusted to the same proportion that would have prevailed if the corporation had filed its annual report within the time prescribed by this Act.

### § 134. Assessment and Collection of Annual Franchise Taxes

It shall be the duty of the Secretary of State to collect all annual franchise taxes and penalties imposed by, or assessed in accordance with, this Act.

Between the first day of March and the first day of June of each year, the Secretary of State shall assess against each corporation, domestic and foreign, required to file an annual report in such year, the franchise tax payable by it for the period from July 1 of such year to July 1 of the succeeding year in accordance with the provisions of this Act, and, if it has failed to file its annual report within the time prescribed by this Act, the penalty imposed by this Act upon such corporation for its failure so to do; and shall mail a written notice to each corporation against which such tax is assessed, addressed to such corporation at its registered office in this State, notifying the corporation (1) of the amount of franchise tax assessed against it for the ensuing year and the amount of penalty, if any, assessed against it for failure to file its annual report; (2) that objections, if any, to such assessment will be heard by the officer making the assessment on or before the fifteenth day of June of such year, upon receipt of a request from the corporation; and (3) that such tax and penalty shall be payable to the Secretary of State on the first day of July next succeeding the date of the notice. Failure to receive such notice shall not relieve the corporation of its obligation to pay the tax and any penalty assessed, or invalidate the assessment thereof.

The Secretary of State shall have power to hear and determine objections to any assessment of franchise tax at any time after such assessment and, after hearing, to change or modify any such assessment. In the event of any adjustment of franchise tax with respect to which a penalty has been assessed for failure to file an annual report, the penalty shall be adjusted in accordance with the provisions of this Act imposing such penalty.

All annual franchise taxes and all penalties for failure to file annual reports shall be due and payable on the first day of July of each year. If the annual franchise tax assessed against any corporation subject to the provisions of this Act, together with all penalties assessed thereon, shall not be paid to the Secretary of State on or before the thirty-first day of July of the year in which such tax is due and payable, the Secretary of State shall certify such fact to the Attorney General on or before the fifteenth day of November of such year, whereupon the Attorney General may institute an action against such corporation in the name of this State, in any court of competent jurisdiction, for the recovery of the amount of such franchise tax and penalties, together with the cost of suit, and prosecute the same to final judgment.

For the purpose of enforcing collection, all annual franchise taxes assessed in accordance with this Act, and all penalties assessed thereon and all interest and costs that shall accrue in connection with the collection thereof, shall be a prior and first lien on the real and personal property of the corporation from and including the first day of July of the year when such franchise taxes become due and payable until such taxes, penalties, interest, and costs shall have been paid.

## § 135. Penalties Imposed upon Corporations

Each corporation, domestic or foreign, that fails or refuses to file its annual report for any year within the time prescribed by this Act shall be subject to a penalty of ten per cent of the amount of the franchise tax assessed against it for the period beginning July 1 of the year in which such report should have been filed. Such penalty shall be assessed by the Secretary of State at the time of the assessment of the franchise tax. If the amount of the franchise tax as originally assessed against such corporation be thereafter adjusted in accordance with the provisions of this Act, the amount of the penalty shall be likewise adjusted to ten per cent of the amount of the adjusted franchise tax. The amount of the franchise tax and the amount of the penalty shall be separately stated in any notice to the corporation with respect thereto.

If the franchise tax assessed in accordance with the provisions of this Act shall not be paid on or before the thirty-first day of July, it shall be deemed to be delinquent, and there shall be added a penalty of one per cent for each month or part of month that the same is delinquent, commencing with the month of August.

Each corporation, domestic or foreign, that fails or refuses to answer truthfully and fully within the time prescribed by this Act interrogatories propounded by the Secretary of State in accordance with the provisions of this Act, shall be deemed to be guilty of a misdemeanor and upon conviction thereof may be fined in any amount not exceeding five hundred dollars.

### § 136. Penalties Imposed upon Officers and Directors

Each officer and director of a corporation, domestic or foreign, who fails or refuses within the time prescribed by this Act to answer truthfully and fully interrogatories propounded to him by the Secretary of State in accordance with the provisions of this Act, or who signs any articles, statement, report, application or other document filed with the Secretary of State which is known to such officer or director to be false in any material respect, shall be deemed to be guilty of a misdemeanor, and upon conviction thereof may be fined in any amount not exceeding . . . . . . . . . . . . . . . dollars.

### § 137. Interrogatories by Secretary of State

The Secretary of State may propound to any corporation, domestic or foreign, subject to the provisions of this Act, and to any officer or director thereof, such interrogatories as may be reasonably necessary and proper to enable him to ascertain whether such corporation has complied with all the provisions of this Act applicable to such corporation. Such interrogatories shall be answered within thirty days after the mailing thereof, or within such additional time as shall be fixed by the Secretary of State, and the answers thereto shall be full and complete and shall be made in writing and under oath. If such interrogatories be directed to an individual they shall be answered by him, and if directed to a corporation they shall be answered by the president, vice president, secretary or assistant secretary thereof. The Secretary of State need not file any document to which such interrogatories relate until such interrogatories be answered as herein provided, and not then if the answers thereto disclose that such document is not in conformity with the provisions of this Act. The Secretary of State shall certify to the Attorney General, for such action as the Attorney General may deem appropriate, all interrogatories and answers thereto which disclose a violation of any of the provisions of this Act.

## § 138.   Information Disclosed by Interrogatories

Interrogatories propounded by the Secretary of State and the answers thereto shall not be open to public inspection nor shall the Secretary of State disclose any facts or information obtained therefrom except insofar as his official duty may require the same to be made public or in the event such interrogatories or the answers thereto are required for evidence in any criminal proceedings or in any other action by this State.

## § 139.   Powers of Secretary of State

The Secretary of State shall have the power and authority reasonably necessary to enable him to administer this Act efficiently and to perform the duties therein imposed upon him.

## § 140.   Appeal from Secretary of State

If the Secretary of State shall fail to approve any articles of incorporation, amendment, merger, consolidation or dissolution, or any other document required by this Act to be approved by the Secretary of State before the same shall be filed in his office, he shall, within ten days after the delivery thereof to him, give written notice of his disapproval to the person or corporation, domestic or foreign, delivering the same, specifying the reasons therefor. From such disapproval such person or corporation may appeal to the .......... court of the county in which the registered office of such corporation is, or is proposed to be, situated by filing with the clerk of such court a petition setting forth a copy of the articles or other document sought to be filed and a copy of the written disapproval thereof by the Secretary of State; whereupon the matter shall be tried de novo by the court, and the court shall either sustain the action of the Secretary of State or direct him to take such action as the court may deem proper.

If the Secretary of State shall revoke the certificate of authority to transact business in this State of any foreign corporation, pursuant to the provisions of this Act, such foreign corporation may likewise appeal to the .......... court of the county where the registered office of such corporation in this State is situated, by filing with the clerk of such court a petition setting forth a copy of its certificate of authority to transact business in this State and a copy of the notice of revocation given by the Secretary of State; whereupon the matter shall be tried de novo by the court, and the court shall either sustain the action of the Secretary of State or direct him to take such action as the court may deem proper.

Appeals from all final orders and judgments entered by the ......... court under this section in review of any ruling or decision of the Secretary of State may be taken as in other civil actions.

### § 141. Certificates and Certified Copies to be Received in Evidence

All certificates issued by the Secretary of State in accordance with the provisions of this Act, and all copies of documents filed in his office in accordance with the provisions of this Act when certified by him, shall be taken and received in all courts, public offices, and official bodies as prima facie evidence of the facts therein stated. A certificate by the Secretary of State under the great seal of this State, as to the existence or non-existence of the facts relating to corporations shall be taken and received in all courts, public offices, and official bodies as prima facie evidence of the existence or non-existence of the facts therein stated.

### § 142. Forms to be Furnished by Secretary of State

All reports required by this Act to be filed in the office of the Secretary of State shall be made on forms which shall be prescribed and furnished by the Secretary of State. Forms for all other documents to be filed in the office of the Secretary of State shall be furnished by the Secretary of State on request therefor, but the use thereof, unless otherwise specifically prescribed in this Act, shall not be mandatory.

### § 143. Greater Voting Requirements

Whenever, with respect to any action to be taken by the shareholders of a corporation, the articles of incorporation require the vote or concurrence of the holders of a greater proportion of the shares, or of any class or series thereof, than required by this Act with respect to such action, the provisions of the articles of incorporation shall control.

### § 144. Waiver of Notice

Whenever any notice is required to be given to any shareholder or director of a corporation under the provisions of this Act or under the provisions of the articles of incorporation or by-laws of the corporation, a waiver thereof in writing signed by the person or persons entitled to such notice, whether before or after the time stated therein, shall be equivalent to the giving of such notice.

## § 145. Action by Shareholders Without a Meeting

Any action required by this Act to be taken at a meeting of the shareholders of a corporation, or any action which may be taken at a meeting of the shareholders, may be taken without a meeting if a consent in writing, setting forth the action so taken, shall be signed by all of the shareholders entitled to vote with respect to the subject matter thereof.

Such consent shall have the same effect as a unanimous vote of shareholders, and may be stated as such in any articles or document filed with the Secretary of State under this Act.

## § 146. Unauthorized Assumption of Corporate Powers

All persons who assume to act as a corporation without authority so to do shall be jointly and severally liable for all debts and liabilities incurred or arising as a result thereof.

## § 147. Application to Existing Corporations

The provisions of this Act shall apply to all existing corporations organized under any general act of this State providing for the organization of corporations for a purpose or purposes for which a corporation might be organized under this Act, where the power has been reserved to amend, repeal or modify the act under which such corporation was organized and where such act is repealed by this Act.

## § 148. Application to Foreign and Interstate Commerce

The provisions of this Act shall apply to commerce with foreign nations and among the several states only insofar as the same may be permitted under the provisions of the Constitution of the United States.

## § 149. Reservation of Power

The ........* shall at all times have power to prescribe such regulations, provisions and limitations as it may deem advisable, which regulations, provisions and limitations shall be binding upon any and all corporations subject to the provisions of this Act, and the ........* shall have power to amend, repeal or modify this Act at pleasure.

* Insert name of legislative body.

## § 150. Effect of Repeal of Prior Acts

The repeal of a prior act by this Act shall not affect any right accrued or established, or any liability or penalty incurred, under the provisions of such act, prior to the repeal thereof.

## § 151. Effect of Invalidity of Part of this Act

If a court of competent jurisdiction shall adjudge to be invalid or unconstitutional any clause, sentence, paragraph, section or part of this Act, such judgment or decree shall not affect, impair, invalidate or nullify the remainder of this Act, but the effect thereof shall be confined to the clause, sentence, paragraph, section or part of this Act so adjudged to be invalid or unconstitutional.

## § 152. Repeal of Prior Acts

(Insert appropriate provisions)  . . . . . . . .

\*

# INDEX

### References are to Pages